Great Conversations
2

SELECTED AND EDITED BY
Daniel Born
Donald H. Whitfield
Mike Levine

CONTRIBUTORS
Bryan Gaul
Judith McCue
Gary Schoepfel
Donald C. Smith

Great Conversations

2

THE GREAT BOOKS FOUNDATION
A nonprofit educational organization

The Great Conversations series receives generous support from
Harrison Middleton University, a Great Books distance-learning college.

Published and distributed by

THE GREAT BOOKS FOUNDATION
A nonprofit educational organization

35 E. Wacker Drive, Suite 2300
Chicago, IL 60601-2205
www.greatbooks.org

With generous support from
Harrison Middleton University,
a Great Books distance-learning college
www.chumsci.edu
Shared Inquiry™ is a trademark of the Great Books Foundation. The contents of this publication
include proprietary trademarks and copyrighted materials, and may be used or quoted only with
permission and appropriate credit to the Foundation.

First printing
9 8 7 6 5 4 3 2 1

Library of Congress Cataloging-in-Publication Data
Great conversations 2 / selected and edited by Daniel Born, Donald H. Whitfield, & Mike Levine.
p. cm.
Contents: The story of Samson, Judges 13-16, New Revised Standard Version / anonymous—
Selected poems / John Donne—Meditations on first philosophy / René Descartes—The nose /
Nikolai Gogol—The brothers Karamazov / Fyodor Dostoevsky—The fall of the house of Usher /
Edgar Allan Poe—Bartleby the scrivener / Herman Melville—Goblin market / Christina Rossetti—
Physics and world philosophy / Max Planck—The playboy of the western world / John M. Synge—
The road to serfdom / Friedrich Hayek—Collected papers / John Rawls—Guests of the nation /
Frank O'Connor—Which new era would that be? / Nadine Gordimer—What we talk about when
we talk about love / Raymond Carver.
     ISBN   (paperback)
1.   Literature—Collections. I. Born, Daniel. II. Whitfield, Donald H. III. Levine, Mike.

PN6012.G75 2006
808.8--dc22

Book cover and interior design:
Judy Sickle, Forward Design
Chicago, Illinois

CONTENTS

This anthology is the second in our *Great Conversations* series designed for book groups and college courses in the humanities. It begins with the biblical narrative of Samson, written probably in the sixth century BCE, and ends with Raymond Carver's short story, "What We Talk About When We Talk About Love," first published in 1980. In between, there are more stories, a play, poems, and essays in science, economics, and philosophy, works written at various times and in different places, but all united by the bold claims they make on the human imagination. The selections come from across the disciplines and have earned their reputation as classics because they address concerns of perennial importance. The subject matter taken up in these selections is eclectic: the understanding of the self and self-awareness; the dynamics of power and authority; the relationship between love and sex; the psychology and ethics of warfare; the interplay between economics and justice; the effects of racial thinking; and our efforts to explain the physical world. The interpretive work these selections call for has challenged generations of readers.

Great Conversations 2 resembles its predecessor in format: fifteen selections overall, plus discussion guides to two longer works, the contents of which are not included in the anthology itself. Also appended at the back of this book is a table of connecting themes intended for instructors or book groups who don't necessarily want to read through the anthology in a linear way or who think that a cluster of readings on a similar theme or topic makes pedagogical sense. Moreover, these thematic clusters can provide readers with a sense that the selections don't exist in isolation from one another but are, in fact, continually in dialogue with one another and with us.

Each selection in the book is followed by questions that are set out to facilitate Shared Inquiry,™ the Great Books Foundation's method of text-based Socratic dialogue that can help make these texts accessible to nonspecialists.

The first section of questions following each selection is *interpretive* and calls for the task of close reading. What is the specific language of the writing meant to convey? Is there one or several interpretations, and can we justify our interpretation by appealing to the text itself? What key passages in the text help unlock its meaning? What are the most confusing passages that seem to defy understanding? In successful learning communities, close reading should evolve into a rich give-and-take between participants who are able to summon specific passages in order to make a point. Thus the text does not get lost in the conversation between speakers but is viewed as the principal voice in the dialogue itself.

The second set of questions ("For Further Reflection") is *evaluative*. These questions are an invitation to pull back and weigh the significance or validity of the work in a larger context. Thus evaluative questions call upon wider observation, experience, and reading. In the best discussions, evaluative questions can lead to the kind of extended dialogue or, for students in the classroom, written essays that help develop thoughtful persuasive arguments and articulation of ideas and beliefs.

But a note of caution is worth sounding here: *close reading and engagement with the text itself is essential for successful evaluative work and should usually precede the evaluative phase.* When personal experience, allusions to other reading, or insider knowledge about an author's life are deployed in a book discussion, what usually suffers is direct interpretation of the text. Several scenarios can develop. On the one hand, the so-called expert in the group may hijack the dialogue and resort to scholarly monologue. On the other hand, a group committed to shared conversation but not anchored in the close reading experience may well drift into personal anecdote or testimonials that have little to do with what the author has written. Both dynamics, while they may have their day and proper place, generally come at the expense of a genuine textual encounter. Evaluative questions, which provide important opportunities for personal reflection or experience, are best taken up after the direct interpretive task of reading and discussing the text has been given its due.

Great Conversations 2 should prove conducive to your reading pleasure and, ultimately, to the kind of participatory talk that develops the intellect and emboldens the imagination.

The book of Judges has inspired painters, writers, and critics for centuries, with its garish and sometimes spectacularly violent accounts of conflict between ancient Hebrew tribes and their Canaanite neighbors. The stories concern the time following Joshua's death and preceding the monarchy of Saul: by one reckoning a period of 480 years, although scholars place the events in Judges mostly in the twelfth and eleventh centuries BCE.

It should be made clear that "Judges" is something of a misnomer, for the leaders of ancient Israel and Judah in this period functioned more like warlords or even gangsters, less interested in adjudicating justice than in defending tribal affiliations in a land dotted with what one commentator describes as "minimonarchies." The book of Judges opens with an account of Judah and Simeon's pursuit and capture of the Perizzite king Adoni-bezek. They cut off his thumbs and big toes before transporting him to Jerusalem, where he dies. According to Hebrew linguists, perhaps the oldest written portion of the Bible is the Song of Deborah, recorded in Judges chapter 5, a poem probably written around 1125 BCE. There a powerful female leader celebrates the exploits of another woman warrior: we learn how Jael lured the enemy commander Sisera into her tent, fed him, tucked him into bed, and then took a hammer and coolly drove a tent peg through his skull.

But the story of Samson remains the most familiar, and famous, of all the narratives in Judges. In *Samson Agonistes*, Milton wrote about him as a tragic and thoughtful figure (unlike the stock Conan-style barbarian that he resembles in many contemporary children's storybooks), a man whose flaws led to humiliating blindness and captivity before he could destroy the temple of Dagon, killing himself but thousands of Philistines, as well, in the process. And it is because of the Samson story that the name "Delilah" has entered our lexicon, carrying—rightfully or not—a mantle of moral disapprobation usually reserved for the likes of Jezebel or Salome.

Like most ancient stories repeated generation after generation, the retellings of the Samson story in popular culture—including opera, Bible storybooks, cartoons, and Hollywood films—usually contain insight as well as distortion of the original. Samson's story involves complicated liaisons with a series of women, a puzzling relationship to his own parents and members of his Hebrew community, and cryptic riddles that mystify us even after they are explicated in the story. The narrator is minimal in his art. The Samson story shows us a hero in his prime who is able to slay, almost as an afterthought, 1,000 enemies with the jawbone of a donkey, but the narrative curve accelerates quickly toward the game-playing with Delilah and then to a man reduced by torture, blindness, and captivity. Mature readers understand that this is much more than a yarn about a big guy whose strength came from his hair, though readers of the Bible familiar with the story of David's son Absalom will understand that the power of hair, symbolic and literal, should never be underestimated.

Finally, like all great narratives, the story of Samson will be apprehended by each new generation carrying its particular, topical interests, and these will invariably shape interpretation. Though timeless, the story of Samson is also timely. About a year after the 2001 destruction of the World Trade Center, a British professor suggested that Samson was, "in effect, a suicide bomber," because he had pulled down the columns in the Philistine temple of Dagon, thereby killing not just himself but thousands more. The professor indicated that Milton's sympathetic account of that episode was "an incitement to terrorism" and therefore might be "withdrawn from schools and colleges and, indeed, banned more generally." When experts call for censorship, thoughtful readers ought to reach instinctively for the forbidden text and interpret it for themselves.

The text reprinted here is from the New Revised Standard Version of the Bible, which, according to most biblical scholars and linguists, is the best English translation of the ancient Hebrew. Readers who like their Bible to sound more like Shakespeare may still champion the 1611 King James Version, although the early modern English lexicon and syntax of the KJV frequently pose a stumbling block to younger readers.

The Story of Samson

13 The Israelites again did what was evil in the sight of the LORD, and the LORD gave them into the hand of the Philistines forty years.

2 There was a certain man of Zorah, of the tribe of the Danites, whose name was Manoah. His wife was barren, having borne no children. 3 And the angel of the LORD appeared to the woman and said to her, "Although you are barren, having borne no children, you shall conceive and bear a son. 4 Now be careful not to drink wine or strong drink, or to eat anything unclean, 5 for you shall conceive and bear a son. No razor is to come on his head, for the boy shall be a nazirite to God from birth. It is he who shall begin to deliver Israel from the hand of the Philistines." 6 Then the woman came and told her husband, "A man of God came to me, and his appearance was like that of an angel of God, most awe-inspiring; I did not ask him where he came from, and he did not tell me his name; 7 but he said to me, 'You shall conceive and bear a son. So then drink no wine or strong drink, and eat nothing unclean, for the boy shall be a nazirite to God from birth to the day of his death.'"

8 Then Manoah entreated the LORD, and said, "O, LORD, I pray, let the man of God whom you sent come to us again and teach us what we are to do concerning the boy who will be born." 9 God listened to Manoah, and the angel of God came again to the woman as she sat in the field; but her husband Manoah was not with her. 10 So the woman ran quickly and told her husband, "The man who came to me the other day has appeared to me." 11 Manoah got up and followed his wife, and came to the man and said to him, "Are you the man who spoke to this woman?" And he said, "I am." 12 Then Manoah said, "Now when your words come true, what is to be the boy's rule of life; what is he to do?" 13 The angel of the LORD said to Manoah, "Let the woman give heed to all that I said to her. 14 She may not eat of anything that comes from the vine. She is not to drink wine or strong drink, or eat any unclean thing. She is to observe everything that I commanded her."

15 Manoah said to the angel of the LORD, "Allow us to detain you, and prepare a kid for you." 16 The angel of the LORD said to Manoah, "If you detain me, I will not eat your food; but

if you want to prepare a burnt offering, then offer it to the LORD." (For Manoah did not know that he was the angel of the LORD.) 17 Then Manoah said to the angel of the LORD, "What is your name, so that we may honor you when your words come true?" 18 But the angel of the LORD said to him, "Why do you ask my name? It is too wonderful."

19 So Manoah took the kid with the grain offering, and offered it on the rock to the LORD, to him who works wonders. 20 When the flame went up toward heaven from the altar, the angel of the LORD ascended in the flame of the altar while Manoah and his wife looked on; and they fell on their faces to the ground. 21 The angel of the LORD did not appear again to Manoah and his wife. Then Manoah realized that it was the angel of the LORD. 22 And Manoah said to his wife, "We shall surely die, for we have seen God." 23 But his wife said to him, "If the LORD had meant to kill us, he would not have accepted a burnt offering and a grain offering at our hands, or shown us all these things, or now announced to us such things as these."

24 The woman bore a son, and named him Samson. The boy grew, and the LORD blessed him. 25 The spirit of the LORD began to stir him in Mahaneh-dan, between Zorah and Eshtaol.

14 Once Samson went down to Timnah, and at Timnah he saw a Philistine woman. 2 Then he came up, and told his father and mother, "I saw a Philistine woman at Timnah; now get her for me as my wife." 3 But his father and mother said to him, "Is there not a woman among your kin, or among all our people, that you must go to take a wife from the uncircumcised Philistines?" But Samson said to his father, "Get her for me, because she pleases me." 4 His father and mother did not know that this was from the LORD; for he was seeking a pretext to act against the Philistines. At that time the Philistines had dominion over Israel.

5 Then Samson went down with his father and mother to Timnah. When he came to the vineyards of Timnah, suddenly a young lion roared at him. 6 The spirit of the LORD rushed on him, and he tore the lion apart barehanded as one might tear apart a kid. But he did not tell his father or his mother what he had done. 7 Then he went down and talked with the woman, and she pleased Samson. 8 After a while he returned to marry her, and he turned aside to see the carcass of the lion, and there was a swarm of bees in the body of the lion, and honey. 9 He scraped it out into his hands, and went on, eating as he went. When he came to his father and mother, he gave some to them, and they ate it. But he did not tell them that he had taken the honey from the carcass of the lion.

10 His father went down to the woman, and Samson made a feast there as the young men were accustomed to do. 11 When the people saw him, they brought thirty companions to be with him. 12 Samson said to them, "Let me now put a riddle to you. If you can explain it to me within the seven days of the feast, and find it out, then I will give you thirty linen garments and thirty festal garments. 13 But if you cannot explain it to me, then you

shall give me thirty linen garments and thirty festal garments." So they said to him, "Ask your riddle; let us hear it." 14 He said to them,

> "Out of the eater came something to eat.
>
> Out of the strong came something sweet."

But for three days they could not explain the riddle.

15 On the fourth day they said to Samson's wife, "Coax your husband to explain the riddle to us or we will burn you and your father's house with fire. Have you invited us here to impoverish us?" 16 So Samson's wife wept before him, saying, "You hate me; you do not really love me. You have asked a riddle of my people; but you have not explained it to me." He said to her, "Look, I have not told my father or my mother. Why should I tell you?" 17 She wept before him the seven days that their feast lasted; and because she nagged him, on the seventh day he told her. Then she explained the riddle to her people. 18 The men of the town said to him on the seventh day before the sun went down,

> "What is sweeter than honey?
> What is stronger than a lion?"

And he said to them,

> "If you had not plowed with my heifer,
> you would not have found out my riddle."

19 Then the spirit of the LORD rushed on him, and he went down to Ashkelon. He killed thirty men of the town, took their spoil, and gave the festal garments to those who had explained the riddle. In hot anger he went back to his father's house. 20 And Samson's wife was given to his companion, who had been his best man.

15 After a while, at the time of the wheat harvest, Samson went to visit his wife, bringing along a kid. He said, "I want to go into my wife's room." But her father would not allow him to go in. 2 Her father said, "I was sure that you had rejected her; so I gave her to your companion. Is not her younger sister prettier than she? Why not take her instead?" 3 Samson said to them, "This time, when I do mischief to the Philistines, I will be without blame." 4 So Samson went and caught three hundred foxes, and took some torches; and he turned the foxes tail to tail, and put a torch between each pair of tails. 5 When he had set fire to the torches, he let the foxes go into the standing grain of the Philistines, and burned up the shocks and the standing grain, as well as the vineyards and olive groves. 6 Then the Philistines asked, "Who has done this?" And they said, "Samson, the son-in-law of the Timnite, because he has taken Samson's wife and given her to his companion." So the Philistines came up, and burned her and her father. 7 Samson said to them, "If this is what you do, I swear I will not stop until I have taken revenge on you." 8 He struck them down hip and thigh with great slaughter; and he went down and stayed in the cleft of the rock of Etam.

9 Then the Philistines came up and encamped in Judah, and made a raid on Lehi. 10 The men of Judah said, "Why have you come up against us?" They said, "We have come up to bind Samson, to do to him as he did to us."

11 Then three thousand men of Judah went down to the cleft of the rock of Etam, and they said to Samson, "Do you not know that the Philistines are rulers over us? What then have you done to us?" He replied, "As they did to me, so I have done to them." 12 They said to him, "We have come down to bind you, so that we may give you into the hands of the Philistines." Samson answered them, "Swear to me that you yourselves will not attack me." 13 They said to him, "No, we will only bind you and give you into their hands; we will not kill you." So they bound him with two new ropes, and brought him up from the rock.

14 When he came to Lehi, the Philistines came shouting to meet him; and the spirit of the LORD rushed on him, and the ropes that were on his arms became like flax that has caught fire, and his bonds melted off his hands. 15 Then he found a fresh jawbone of a donkey, reached down and took it, and with it he killed a thousand men. 16 And Samson said,

> "With the jawbone of a donkey,
> heaps upon heaps,
> with the jawbone of a donkey
> I have slain a thousand men."

17 When he had finished speaking, he threw away the jawbone; and that place was called Ramath-lehi.

18 By then he was very thirsty, and he called on the LORD, saying, "You have granted this great victory by the hand of your servant. Am I now to die of thirst, and fall into the hands of the uncircumcised?" 19 So God split open the hollow place that is at Lehi, and water came from it. When he drank, his spirit returned, and he revived. Therefore it was named En-hakkore, which is at Lehi to this day. 20 And he judged Israel in the days of the Philistines twenty years.

16 Once Samson went to Gaza, where he saw a prostitute and went in to her. 2 The Gazites were told, "Samson has come here." So they circled around and lay in wait for him all night at the city gate. They kept quiet all night, thinking, "Let us wait until the light of the morning; then we will kill him." 3 But Samson lay only until midnight. Then at midnight he rose up, took hold of the doors of the city gate and the two posts, pulled them up, bar and all, put them on his shoulders, and carried them to the top of the hill that is in front of Hebron.

4 After this he fell in love with a woman in the valley of Sorek, whose name was Delilah. 5 The lords of the Philistines came to her and said to her, "Coax him, and find out what makes his strength so great, and how we may overpower him, so that we may bind him in order to subdue him; and we will each give you eleven hundred pieces of silver." 6 So Delilah said to Samson, "Please tell me what makes your strength so great, and how you could be bound, so that one could subdue you." 7 Samson said to her, "If they bind me with seven fresh bowstrings that are not dried out, then I shall become weak, and be like anyone else." 8 Then the lords of the Philistines brought her seven fresh bowstrings that had not dried out, and she bound him with them. 9 While men were lying in wait in an inner chamber, she said to him, "The Philistines are upon you, Samson!" But he snapped the bowstrings, as a strand of fiber snaps when it touches

the fire. So the secret of his strength was not known.

10 Then Delilah said to Samson, "You have mocked me and told me lies; please tell me how you could be bound." 11 He said to her, "If they bind me with new ropes that have not been used, then I shall become weak, and be like anyone else." 12 So Delilah took new ropes and bound him with them, and said to him, "The Philistines are upon you, Samson!" (The men lying in wait were in an inner chamber.) But he snapped the ropes off his arms like a thread.

13 Then Delilah said to Samson, "Until now you have mocked me and told me lies; tell me how you could be bound." He said to her, "If you weave the seven locks of my head with the web and make it tight with the pin, then I shall become weak, and be like anyone else." 14 So while he slept, Delilah took the seven locks of his head and wove them into the web, and made them tight with the pin. Then she said to him, "The Philistines are upon you, Samson!" But he awoke from his sleep, and pulled away the pin, the loom, and the web.

15 Then she said to him, "How can you say, 'I love you,' when your heart is not with me? You have mocked me three times now and have not told me what makes your strength so great." 16 Finally, after she had nagged him with her words day after day, and pestered him, he was tired to death. 17 So he told her his whole secret, and said to her, "A razor has never come upon my head; for I have been a nazirite to God from my mother's womb. If my head were shaved, then my strength would leave me; I would become weak, and be like anyone else."

18 When Delilah realized that he had told her his whole secret, she sent and called the lords of the Philistines, saying, "This time come up, for he has told her his whole secret to me." Then the lords of the Philistines came up to her, and brought the money in their hands. 19 She let him fall asleep on her lap; and she called a man, and had him shave off the seven locks of his head. He began to weaken, and his strength left him. 20 Then she said, "The Philistines are upon you, Samson!" When he awoke from his sleep, he thought, "I will go out as at other times, and shake myself free." But he did not know that the LORD had left him. 21 So the Philistines seized him and gouged out his eyes. They brought him down to Gaza and bound him with bronze shackles; and he ground at the mill in the prison. 22 But the hair of his head began to grow again after it had been shaved.

23 Now the lords of the Philistines gathered to offer a great sacrifice to their god Dagon, and to rejoice; for they said, "Our god has given Samson our enemy into our hand." 24 When the people saw him, they praised their god; for they said, "Our god has given our enemy into our hand, the ravager of our country, who has killed many of us." 25 And when their hearts were merry, they said, "Call Samson, and let him entertain us." So they called Samson out of the prison, and he performed for them. They made him stand between the pillars; 26 and Samson said to the attendant who held him by the hand, "Let me feel the pillars on which the house rests, so that I may lean against them."

27 Now the house was full of men and women; all the lords of the Philistines were there, and on the roof there were about three thousand men and women, who looked on while Samson performed.

28 Then Samson called to the LORD and said, "Lord GOD, remember me and strengthen me only this once, O God, so that with this one act of revenge I may pay back the Philistines for my two eyes." 29 And Samson grasped the two middle pillars on which the house rested, and he leaned his weight against them, his right hand on the one and his left hand on the other. 30 Then Samson said, "Let me die with the Philistines." He strained with all his might; and the house fell on the lords and all the people who were in it. So those he killed at his death were more than those he had killed during his life. 31 Then his brothers and all his family came down and took him and brought him up and buried him between Zorah and Eshtaol in the tomb of his father Manoah. He had judged Israel twenty years.

QUESTIONS

1. Why does the angel say that the child Manoah's wife will bear shall only "begin to deliver Israel from the hand of the Philistines"? (13:5)

2. Why does Samson instruct his father to "get" the woman of Timnah for him? (14:3)

3. Why does Samson not tell his parents that he had killed a lion with his bare hands and then give them honey to eat from the carcass without revealing where it came from?

4. What is Samson's purpose in posing a riddle to the Philistines at his wedding?

5. When the Philistines threaten to burn the house of Samson's wife and father-in-law unless she "coaxes" the answer to the riddle from him, why doesn't she tell Samson of this threat? (14:15–17)

6. Why does Samson refer to his father and his mother when his wife asks why he hasn't told her the answer to his riddle?

7. If Samson suspects that the Philistines had "plowed" with his "heifer" in order to gain the answer to the riddle, why does he pay up? (14:18–19)

8. Even though Samson honored the wagering terms of the riddle, why was his wife given "to his companion, who had been his best man"? (14:19–20)

9. What is the primary obstacle to Samson consummating his marriage with the woman from Timnah?

10. If Samson suspects his wife of betraying him, then why does he visit her with a gift of a kid?

11. What does Samson mean when he says, "This time, when I do mischief to the Philistines, I will be without blame"? (15:3)

12. Why does Samson stay in the cleft of the rock at Etam until the men of Judah get him?

13. Why does Samson willingly allow himself to be bound by the men of Judah?

14. Why does Samson, speaking directly to the Lord, feel free to admonish God for allowing him to suffer thirst?

15. Why does the narrator include the story of the prostitute at Gaza?

16. Why does Samson tell Delilah the secret of his strength, especially since she never hides her political allegiances?

17. Why does the Lord abandon Samson after he falls in love with Delilah, but not earlier, even after he married a Philistine?

18. Are there any clues in this story that suggest what the attitude of the narrator is toward Samson?

FOR FURTHER REFLECTION

1. Does this narrative portray Samson as a heroic figure?

2. Why does this story focus so much attention on Samson's relationships with women? Do these relationships show Samson evolving in his maturity?

3. Does love weaken or strengthen us?

4. Does the narrator of this story share the same political philosophy as Samson? What political philosophy or philosophies are on display?

The wit, passion, and fierce intellect that animate John Donne's love poems pervade his religious writing as well, and this is surely one reason for his enduring allure. Donne rewards close reading—as much as any poet who has written in English—because, in a single poem, often with astonishing economy, he gives such subtle, original expression to the conflicts between thought and feeling that define so much of our experience. *Songs and Sonnets* may be, as Donne called them, "itchy outbreaks of far-fetched wit," but the best of them are love poems in the fullest sense of the word; rarely are the speaker's desires as clear as they first appear. Likewise, the *Holy Sonnets* are precisely about faith, which is to say that, though written by a man who would become a leading figure in the Church of England, they depict a struggle over what and how to believe.

John Donne (1572–1631) was born in London to Roman Catholic parents. He attended Oxford and Cambridge but did not receive a degree because doing so would have meant rejecting Catholicism. After studying law and serving as a volunteer on naval expeditions, Donne became a private secretary for Sir Thomas Egerton, Lord Keeper of the Great Seal. He aspired to public office, but his prospects were undermined by his decision in 1601 to secretly marry Anne More, Egerton's niece. Her father opposed the marriage, withholding his daughter's dowry and even sending Donne to prison briefly. These years were very difficult for Donne, prompting him to write *Biathanatos* (published in 1646), his defense of suicide. Donne and his family relied on patronage to survive. His wife died giving birth to a stillborn child, their twelfth, in 1617.

Donne had probably declared himself an Anglican by 1598, but it was not until 1615, after years of encouragement from various quarters and, finally, from King James, that Donne was ordained. In 1621, he was made dean of St. Paul's Cathedral. He devoted himself completely to the duties of his office, and his writing during this period primarily consists of sermons.

Except for his divine poems, Donne wrote nearly all of his poetry before 1601, but very little of it was published during his lifetime. A volume of collected poems came out in 1633, two years after his death. Donne's reputation declined in the eighteenth century, when Samuel Johnson introduced the term *metaphysical poets* to refer to Donne and several others who share aspects of his style, including Andrew Marvell and George Herbert. In the nineteenth century, a revival began, solidified by T. S. Eliot's essay "The Metaphysical Poets" in 1921. The subjects and conceits found in Donne's poems are often not unique to him; they appear in the work of his contemporaries, and Petrarch is an obvious model for the love poems. Like any great poet, his work absorbed that of certain predecessors, as well as the circumstances of the age in which he lived, but his voice remains inimitable.

The Flea

Mark but this flea, and mark in this,
How little that which thou deny'st me is;
Me it sucked first, and now sucks thee,
And in this flea, our two bloods mingled be;
Confess it, this cannot be said
A sin, or shame, or loss of maidenhead,
　　Yet this enjoys before it woo,
　　And pampered swells with one blood made of two,
　　And this, alas, is more then we would do.

Oh stay, three lives in one flea spare,
Where we almost, nay more than married are.
This flea is you and I, and this
Our marriage bed, and marriage temple is;
Though parents grudge, and you, we'are met,
And cloistered in these living walls of jet.
　　Though use make you apt to kill me,
　　Let not to this, self murder added be,
　　And sacrilege, three sins in killing three.

Cruel and sudden, hast thou since
Purpled thy nail, in blood of innocence?
In what could this flea guilty be,
Except in that drop which it sucked from thee?
Yet thou triumph'st, and say'st that thou
Find'st not thyself, nor me the weaker now;
　　'Tis true, then learn how false, fears be;
　　Just so much honour, when thou yield'st to me,
　　Will waste, as this flea's death took life from thee.

The Relic

When my grave is broke up again
Some second guest to entertain,
(For graves have learned that woman-head
To be to more then one a bed)
        And he that digs it, spies
A bracelet of bright hair about the bone,
        Will he not let us alone,
And think that there a loving couple lies,
Who thought that this device might be some way
To make their souls, at the last busy day,
Meet at this grave, and make a little stay?

        If this fall in a time, or land,
        Where mis-devotion doth command,
        Then, he that digs us up, will bring
        Us, to the Bishop, and the King,
        To make us relics; then
Thou shalt be a Mary Magdalen, and I
        A something else thereby;
All women shall adore us, and some men;
And since at such time, miracles are sought,
I would have that age by this paper taught
What miracles we harmless lovers wrought.

        First, we loved well and faithfully,
        Yet knew not what we loved, nor why,
        Difference of sex no more we knew,
        Than our guardian angels do;
        Coming and going, we
Perchance might kiss, but not between those meals;
        Our hands ne'er touched the seals,
Which nature, injured by late law, sets free:
These miracles we did; but now alas,
All measure, and all language, I should pass,
Should I tell what a miracle she was.

A Valediction: forbidding Mourning

As virtuous men pass mildly away,
  And whisper to their souls, to go,
Whilst some of their sad friends do say,
  The breath goes now, and some say, no:

So let us melt, and make no noise,
  No tear-floods, nor sigh-tempests move,
'Twere profanation of our joys
  To tell the laity our love.

Moving of th' earth brings harms and fears,
  Men reckon what it did and meant,
But trepidation of the spheres,   ·
  Though greater far, is innocent.

Dull sublunary lovers' love
  (Whose soul is sense) cannot admit
Absence, because it doth remove
  Those things which elemented it.

But we by a love, so much refined,
  That our selves know not what it is,
Inter-assured of the mind,
  Care less, eyes, lips, and hands to miss.

Our two souls therefore, which are one,
  Though I must go, endure not yet
A breach, but an expansion,
  Like gold to aery thinness beat.

If they be two, they are two so
  As stiff twin compasses are two,
Thy soul the fixed foot, makes no show
  To move, but doth, if th'other do.

And though it in the centre sit,
  Yet when the other far doth roam,
It leans, and hearkens after it,
  And grows erect, as that comes home.

Such wilt thou be to me, who must
  Like th' other foot, obliquely run;
Thy firmness makes my circle just,
  And makes me end, where I begun.

A Valediction: of Weeping

Let me pour forth
My tears before thy face, whilst I stay here,
For thy face coins them, and thy stamp they bear,
And by this mintage they are something worth,
　　For thus they be
　　Pregnant of thee;
Fruits of much grief they are, emblems of more,
When a tear falls, that thou falls which it bore,
So thou and I are nothing then, when on a divers shore.

　　On a round ball
A workman that hath copies by, can lay
An Europe, Afric, and an Asia,
And quickly make that, which was nothing, all,
　　So doth each tear,
　　Which thee doth wear,
A globe, yea world by that impression grow,
Till thy tears mixed with mine do overflow
This world, by waters sent from thee, my heaven dissolved so.

　　O more than moon,
Draw not up seas to drown me in thy sphere,
Weep me not dead, in thine arms, but forbear
To teach the sea, what it may do too soon;
　　Let not the wind
　　Example find,
To do me more harm, than it purposeth;
Since thou and I sigh one another's breath,
Whoe'er sighs most, is cruellest, and hastes the other's death.

Divine Meditation XIII

What if this present were the world's last night?
Mark in my heart, O soul, where thou dost dwell,
The picture of Christ crucified, and tell
Whether that countenance can thee affright,
Tears in his eyes quench the amazing light,
Blood fills his frowns, which from his pierced head fell,
And can that tongue adjudge thee unto hell,
Which prayed forgiveness for his foes' fierce spite?
No, no; but as in my idolatry
I said to all my profane mistresses,
Beauty, of pity, foulness only is
A sign of rigour: so I say to thee,
To wicked spirits are horrid shapes assigned,
This beauteous form assures a piteous mind.

QUESTIONS

"THE FLEA"

1. Why does the speaker think his beloved should submit to his will?

2. Why does the speaker want his beloved to spare the flea's life?

3. What does the speaker mean when he says that, in the flea, he and his beloved "more than married are"? Why does he at first say they are "almost" married? (17)

4. In what way has the speaker's beloved triumphed by killing the flea?

5. How does the speaker's argument change from one stanza to the next?

"THE RELIC"

1. Why does the speaker describe the love between himself and his beloved in terms of what will happen when his grave is opened?

2. What does the speaker wish the person who discovers his grave to think upon seeing the "bracelet of bright hair" buried with him? (18)

3. Why does the speaker imagine that his remains and the "bracelet of bright hair" will be treated as relics when his grave is opened? (18)

4. Why does the speaker make an implicit comparison between his beloved and Mary Magdalen? What does he mean when he says he is "A something else thereby"? (18)

5. In what sense does the speaker believe his beloved was a "miracle"? (18)

"A VALEDICTION: FORBIDDING MOURNING"

1. Why does the speaker ask his beloved not to mourn their coming separation?

2. Is the speaker confident that their love will survive physical separation?

3. To illustrate the condition of their souls while they're apart, why does the speaker compare them to "gold to aery thinness beat"? (19)

4. After asserting that the souls of he and his beloved are one, why does the speaker then speculate in the next stanza that their souls are two?

5. Based on the poem's last two lines, does the future of the relationship between the speaker and his beloved seem certain or uncertain?

"A VALEDICTION: OF WEEPING"

1. What does the speaker hope to accomplish by asking his beloved's permission to weep before they are separated?

2. What does the speaker mean when he says of his tears that "thy face coins them"? (20)

3. When the speaker says his tears are "emblems of more," does he mean that they are emblems of more grief or emblems of something besides grief? (20)

4. In the last stanza, what is the speaker asking his beloved to do?

5. What is the emotional tone of the poem's last two lines?

"DIVINE MEDITATION XIII" (What if this present were the world's last night?)

1. What emotional state is suggested by the poem's first line?

2. Why does the speaker feel the need to address his soul?

3. After posing the question of whether his soul will be damned, does the speaker seem convinced by his answer, "No"? (21)

4. In trying to predict the fate of his soul, why does the speaker compare Christ to a mistress?

5. Why does the speaker believe a "beauteous form assures a piteous mind"? (21)

FOR FURTHER REFLECTION

1. Is love's capacity to endure physical separation a sign of its strength?

2. What are the advantages and disadvantages of using rational arguments to influence another person's emotional state?

3. Do religious faith and romantic love satisfy similar needs or bring about similar states of mind?

RENÉ DESCARTES

Often identified as "the father of modern philosophy," René Descartes (1596–1650) was born into a family of minor gentry in the French province of Touraine. His mother died a year after his birth; few other details of his childhood are known, but his natural curiosity was apparent enough that his father referred to him as "his little philosopher." At the age of eight, young Descartes went to the new Jesuit school at La Flèche, where he would spend approximately ten years. There he excelled in his studies, particularly in mathematics. But by the time he graduated, he was disillusioned with most of the curriculum, dissatisfied that so much of his learning—including philosophy, theology, and literature—resulted in more rather than less uncertainty about the world and his place in it.

After La Flèche and further studies in law, Descartes set out on a quest to study "the book of the world," alternating bouts of travel through Italy, Germany, and France, and serving for a time as a military officer in several different armies that took him to eastern Europe as well. The young man's restless quest for experience alternated with periods of solitude and meditation, and a small inheritance from his mother allowed him to lead a life of comfortable, if not luxurious, leisure, devoted to his studies. In 1628 he moved to Holland, and there he wrote most of his famous works during the next two decades. He died in 1650 in Stockholm, Sweden, where he had arrived several months earlier at the invitation of Queen Christina, to act as her personal philosophy tutor.

His place at the beginning of modern philosophy is a result of his willingness to ask questions. He scrutinized many of his era's prevailing beliefs about the world and, most important, he sought a unifying principle that would encompass and explain all the seemingly discrete phenomena of the universe. He seems to have remained a devout Catholic throughout his life, even though his evolving philosophy often put him at odds with the teachings of his church. His method of reasoning serves as a critical transition in the intellectual evolution of Western civilization. He attempted to create a bridge between the Christian concept of a world created and controlled by a personal deity and the incipient scientific knowledge of that world that began in the Renaissance. This bridge would continue to deepen during his own lifetime and beyond, through the scientific and philosophical work of such contemporaries as Galileo, and, later, through the work of men such as Newton and Voltaire.

The works excerpted here are from his first two *Meditations*, (out of a total of six). The *Meditations* articulate a disciplined approach (stated in less detail in his earlier work, *Discourse on Method*) to questioning everything one believes one knows, or seeks to know, while rejecting any premise that is not absolutely demonstrable through logic. And each meditation forms a link in Descartes's method of reasoning wherein neither Scripture, traditional erudition, nor the potential deceptions of observation of the world around us can lead to the discovery of abstract truth. He believed that only the operation of the human mind can achieve this, because only it can be used to prove irrefutably authentic existence. This accounts for his distinct separation between the functions of the mind and of the body; in *Meditation One*, he explains the reasons why we ought to doubt the most apparent truths of the physical world around us. *Meditation Two* explains the need to suppose the nonexistence of all things of whose existence there can be the least doubt. It also describes the basic method for breaking any intellectual problem into constituent parts, so that its truth or falsehood can be reliably determined by the use of reason. The subsequent meditations describe the rest of this theory and its implications.

In these selections, we can see how Descartes positions human curiosity to explain the world through purely theoretical reasoning, independent of conventional religious doctrine. This critical first attempt at abstract philosophical analysis also invites us to meditate upon existence as an end in itself and not as a reflection of the physical sciences.

Meditations One *and* Two

MEDITATION ONE:
Concerning Those Things That Can Be Called into Doubt

Several years have now passed since I first realized how numerous were the false opinions that in my youth I had taken to be true, and thus how doubtful were all those that I had subsequently built upon them. And thus I realized that once in my life I had to raze everything to the ground and begin again from the original foundations, if I wanted to establish anything firm and lasting in the sciences. But the task seemed enormous, and I was waiting until I reached a point in my life that was so timely that no more suitable time for undertaking these plans of action would come to pass. For this reason, I procrastinated for so long that I would henceforth be at fault, were I to waste the time that remains for carrying out the project by brooding over it. Accordingly, I have today suitably freed my mind of all cares, secured for myself a period of leisurely tranquillity, and am withdrawing into solitude. At last I will apply myself earnestly and unreservedly to this general demolition of my opinions.

Yet to bring this about I will not need to show that all my opinions are false, which is perhaps something I could never accomplish. But reason now persuades me that I should withhold my assent no less carefully from opinions that are not completely certain and indubitable than I would from those that are patently false. For this reason, it will suffice for the rejection of all of these opinions, if I find in each of them some reason for doubt. Nor therefore need I survey each opinion individually, a task that would be endless. Rather, because undermining the foundations will cause whatever has been built upon them to crumble of its own accord, I will attack straightaway those principles which supported everything I once believed.

Surely whatever I had admitted until now as most true I received either from the senses or through the senses. However, I have noticed that the senses are sometimes deceptive; and it is a mark of prudence never to place our complete trust in those who have deceived us even once.

But perhaps, even though the senses do sometimes deceive us when it is a question of very small and distant things, still there are many other matters concerning which one simply cannot doubt, even though they are derived from the very same senses: for example, that I am sitting here next to the fire, wearing my winter dressing gown, that I am holding this sheet of paper in my hands, and the like. But on what grounds could one deny that these hands and this entire body are mine? Unless perhaps I were to liken myself to the insane, whose brains are impaired by such an unrelenting vapor of black bile that they steadfastly insist that they are kings when they are utter paupers, or that they are arrayed in purple robes when they are naked, or that they have heads made of clay, or that they are gourds, or that they are made of glass. But such people are mad, and I would appear no less mad, were I to take their behavior as an example for myself.

This would all be well and good, were I not a man who is accustomed to sleeping at night, and to experiencing in my dreams the very same things, or now and then even less plausible ones, as these insane people do when they are awake. How often does my evening slumber persuade me of such ordinary things as these: that I am here, clothed in my dressing gown, seated next to the fireplace—when in fact I am lying undressed in bed! But right now my eyes are certainly wide-awake when I gaze upon this sheet of paper. This head which I am shaking is not heavy with sleep. I extend this hand consciously and deliberately, and I feel it. Such things would not be so distinct for someone who is asleep. As if I did not recall having been deceived on other occasions even by similar thoughts in my dreams! As I consider these matters more carefully, I see so plainly that there are no definitive signs by which to distinguish being awake from being asleep. As a result, I am becoming quite dizzy, and this dizziness nearly convinces me that I am asleep.

Let us assume then, for the sake of argument, that we are dreaming and that such particulars as these are not true: that we are opening our eyes, moving our head, and extending our hands. Perhaps we do not even have such hands, or any such body at all. Nevertheless, it surely must be admitted that the things seen during slumber are, as it were, like painted images, which could only have been produced in the likeness of true things, and that therefore at least these general things—eyes, head, hands, and the whole body—are not imaginary things, but are true and exist. For indeed when painters themselves wish to represent sirens and satyrs by means of especially bizarre forms, they surely cannot assign to them utterly new natures. Rather, they simply fuse together the members of various animals. Or if perhaps they concoct something so utterly novel that nothing like it has ever been seen before (and thus is something utterly fictitious and false), yet certainly at the very least the colors from which they fashion it ought to be true. And by the same token, although even these general things—eyes, head, hands, and the like—could be imaginary, still one has to admit that at least certain other things that are even more simple and universal are true. It is from these components, as if from true colors, that all those images of things that are in our thought are fashioned, be they true or false.

This class of things appears to include corporeal nature in general, together with its extension; the shape of extended things; their quantity, that is, their size and number; as well as the place where they exist; the time through which they endure, and the like.

Thus it is not improper to conclude from this that physics, astronomy, medicine, and all the other disciplines that are dependent upon the consideration of composite things are doubtful, and that, on the other hand, arithmetic, geometry, and other such disciplines, which treat of nothing but the simplest and most general things and which are indifferent as to whether these things do or do not in fact exist, contain something certain and indubitable. For whether I am awake or asleep, two plus three make five, and a square does not have more than four sides. It does not seem possible that such obvious truths should be subject to the suspicion of being false.

Be that as it may, there is fixed in my mind a certain opinion of long-standing, namely that there exists a God who is able to do anything and by whom I, such as I am, have been created. How do I know that he did not bring it about that there is no earth at all, no heavens, no extended thing, no shape, no size, no place, and yet bringing it about that all these things appear to me to exist precisely as they do now? Moreover, since I judge that others sometimes make mistakes in matters that they believe they know most perfectly, may I not, in like fashion, be deceived every time I add two and three or count the sides of a square, or perform an even simpler operation, if that can be imagined? But perhaps God has not willed that I be deceived in this way, for he is said to be supremely good. Nonetheless, if it were repugnant to his goodness to have created me such that I be deceived all the time, it would also seem foreign to that same goodness to permit me to be deceived even occasionally. But we cannot make this last assertion.

Perhaps there are some who would rather deny so powerful a God than believe that everything else is uncertain. Let us not oppose them; rather, let us grant that everything said here about God is fictitious. Now they suppose that I came to be what I am either by fate, or by chance, or by a connected chain of events, or by some other way. But because being deceived and being mistaken appear to be a certain imperfection, the less powerful they take the author of my origin to be, the more probable it will be that I am so imperfect that I am always deceived. I have nothing to say in response to these arguments. But eventually I am forced to admit that there is nothing among the things I once believed to be true which it is not permissible to doubt—and not out of frivolity or lack of forethought, but for valid and considered reasons. Thus I must be no less careful to withhold assent henceforth even from these beliefs than I would from those that are patently false, if I wish to find anything certain.

But it is not enough simply to have realized these things; I must take steps to keep myself mindful of them. For longstanding opinions keep returning, and, almost against my will, they take advantage of my credulity, as if it were bound over to them by long use and the claims of intimacy. Nor will I ever get out of the habit of assenting to them and believing in them, so long as I take them to be exactly what they are, namely, in some respects doubtful, as has just now been shown, but nevertheless highly probable, so that it is much more consonant with reason to believe them than to deny them. Hence, it seems to me I would do well to deceive myself by turning my will in completely the opposite direction and pretend for a time that these opinions are wholly false and imaginary, until finally, as if with prejudices weighing down each side equally, no bad habit should turn my judgment any further from the correct perception of things. For indeed I know that meanwhile there is no danger or error in following this procedure, and that it is impossible for me to indulge in too much distrust, since I am now concentrating only on knowledge, not on action.

Accordingly, I will suppose not a supremely good God, the source of truth, but rather an evil genius, supremely powerful and clever, who has directed his entire effort at deceiving me. I will regard the heavens, the air, the earth, colors, shapes, sounds, and all external things as nothing but the bedeviling hoaxes of my dreams, with which he lays snares for my credulity. I will regard myself as not having hands, or eyes, or flesh, or blood, or any senses, but as nevertheless falsely believing that I possess all these things. I will remain resolute and steadfast in this meditation, and even if it is not within my power to know anything true, it certainly is within my power to take care resolutely to withhold my assent to what is false, lest this deceiver, however powerful, however clever he may be, have any effect on me. But this undertaking is arduous, and a certain laziness brings me back to my customary way of living. I am not unlike a prisoner who enjoyed an imaginary freedom during his sleep, but, when he later begins to suspect that he is dreaming, fears being awakened and nonchalantly conspires with these pleasant illusions. In just the same way, I fall back of my own accord into my old opinions, and dread being awakened, lest the toilsome wakefulness which follows upon a peaceful rest must be spent thenceforward not in the light but among the inextricable shadows of the difficulties now brought forward.

MEDITATION TWO:
Concerning the Nature of the Human Mind: That It Is Better Known Than the Body

Yesterday's meditation has thrown me into such doubts that I can no longer ignore them, yet I fail to see how they are to be resolved. It is as if I had suddenly fallen into a deep whirlpool; I am so tossed about that I can neither touch bottom with my foot, nor swim up to the top. Nevertheless I will work my way up and will once again attempt the same path I entered upon yesterday. I will accomplish this by putting aside everything that admits of the least doubt, as if I had discovered it to be completely false. I will stay on this course until I know something certain, or, if nothing else, until I at least know for certain that nothing is certain. Archimedes sought but one firm and immovable point in order to move the entire earth from one place to another. Just so, great things are also to be hoped for if I succeed in finding just one thing, however slight, that is certain and unshaken.

Therefore I suppose that everything I see is false. I believe that none of what my deceitful memory represents ever existed. I have no senses whatever. Body, shape, extension, movement, and place are all chimeras. What then will be true? Perhaps just the single fact that nothing is certain.

But how do I know there is not something else, over and above all those things that I have just reviewed, concerning which there is not even the slightest occasion for doubt? Is there not some God, or by whatever name I might call him, who instills these very thoughts in me? But why would I think that, since I myself could perhaps be the author of these thoughts? Am I not then at least something? But I have already denied that I have any senses and any body. Still I hesitate; for what follows from this? Am I so tied to a body and to the senses that I cannot exist without them? But I have persuaded myself that there is absolutely nothing in the world: no sky, no earth, no minds, no bodies. Is it then the case that I too do not exist? But doubtless I did exist, if I persuaded myself of something. But there is some deceiver or other who is supremely powerful and supremely sly and who is always deliberately deceiving me. Then too there is no doubt that I exist, if he is deceiving me. And let him do his best at deception, he will never bring it about that I am nothing so long as I shall think that I am something. Thus, after everything has been most carefully weighed, it must finally be established that this pronouncement "I am, I exist" is necessarily true every time I utter it or conceive it in my mind.

But I do not yet understand sufficiently what I am—I, who now necessarily exist. And so from this point on, I must be careful lest I unwittingly mistake something else for myself, and thus err in that very item of knowledge that I claim to be the most certain and evident of all. Thus, I will meditate once more on what I once believed myself to be, prior to embarking upon these thoughts. For this reason, then, I will set aside whatever can be weakened even to the slightest degree by the arguments brought forward, so that eventually all that remains is precisely nothing but what is certain and unshaken.

What then did I use to think I was? A man, of course. But what is a man? Might I not say a "rational animal"? No, because then I would have to inquire what "animal" and "rational" mean. And thus from one question I would slide into many more difficult ones. Nor do I now have enough free time that I want to waste it on subtleties of this sort. Instead, permit me to focus here on what came spontaneously and naturally into my thinking whenever I pondered what I was. Now it occurred to me first that I had a face, hands, arms, and this entire mechanism of bodily members: the very same as are discerned in a corpse, and which I referred to by the name "body." It next occurred to me that I took in food, that I walked about, and that I sensed and thought various things; these actions I used to attribute to the soul. But as to what this soul might be, I either did not think about it or else I imagined it a rarified I-know-not-what, like a wind, or a fire, or ether, which had been infused into my coarser parts. But as to the body I was not in any doubt. On the contrary, I was under the impression that I knew its nature distinctly. Were I perhaps tempted to describe this nature such as I conceived it in my mind, I would have described it thus: by "body," I understand all that is capable of being bounded by some shape, of being enclosed in a place, and of filling up a space in such a way as to exclude any other body from it; of being perceived by touch, sight, hearing, taste, or smell; of being moved in several ways, not, of course, by itself, but by whatever else impinges upon it. For it was my view that the power of self-motion, and likewise of sensing or of thinking, in no way belonged to the nature of the body. Indeed I used rather to marvel that such faculties were to be found in certain bodies.

But now what am I, when I suppose that there is some supremely powerful and, if I may be permitted to say so, malicious deceiver who deliberately tries to fool me in anyway he can? Can I not affirm that I possess at least a small measure of all those things which I have already said belong to the nature of the body? I focus my attention on them, I think about them, I review them again, but nothing comes to mind. I am tired of repeating this to no purpose. But what about those things I ascribed to the soul? What about being nourished or moving about? Since I now do not have a body, these are surely nothing but fictions. What about sensing? Surely this too does not take place without a body; and I seemed to have sensed in my dreams many things that I later realized I did not sense. What about thinking? Here I make my discovery: thought exists; it alone cannot be separated from me. I am; I exist—this is certain. But for how long? For as long as I am thinking; for perhaps it could also come to pass that if I were to cease all thinking I would then utterly cease to exist. At this time I admit nothing that is not necessarily true. I am therefore precisely nothing but a thinking thing; that is, a mind, or intellect, or understanding, or reason—words of whose meanings I was previously ignorant. Yet I am a true thing and am truly existing; but what kind of thing? I have said it already: a thinking thing.

What else am I? I will set my imagination in motion. I am not that concatenation of members we call the human body. Neither am I even some subtle air infused into these members, nor a wind, nor a fire, nor a vapor, nor a breath, nor anything I devise for myself. For I have supposed these things to be nothing. The assumption still stands; yet nevertheless I am something. But is it perhaps the case that these very things which I take to be nothing, because they are unknown to me, nevertheless are in fact no different from that "me" that I know? This I do not know, and I will not quarrel about it now. I can make a judgment only about things that are known to me. I know that I exist; I ask now who is this "I" whom I know? Most certainly, in the strict sense the knowledge of this "I" does not depend upon things of whose existence I do not yet have knowledge. Therefore it is not dependent upon any of those things that I simulate in my imagination. But this word *simulate* warns me of my error. For I would indeed be simulating were I to "imagine" that I was something, because imagining is merely the contemplating of the shape or image of a corporeal thing. But I now know with certainty that I am and also that all these images—and, generally, everything belonging to the nature of the body—could turn out to be nothing but dreams. Once I have realized this, I would seem to be speaking no less foolishly were I to say: "I will use my imagination in order to recognize more distinctly who I am," than were I to say: "Now I surely am awake, and I see something true; but since I do not yet see it clearly enough, I will deliberately fall asleep so that my dreams might represent it to me more truly and more clearly." Thus I realize that none of what I can grasp by means of the imagination pertains to this knowledge that I have of myself. Moreover, I realize that I must be most diligent about withdrawing my mind from these things so that it can perceive its nature as distinctly as possible.

But what then am I? A thing that thinks. What is that? A thing that doubts, understands, affirms, denies, wills, refuses, and that also imagines and senses.

Indeed it is no small matter if all of these things belong to me. But why should they not belong to me? Is it not the very same "I" who now doubts almost everything, who nevertheless understands something, who affirms that this one thing is true, who denies other things, who desires to know more, who wishes not to be deceived, who imagines many things even against my will, who also notices many things which appear to come from the senses? What is there in all of this that is not every bit as true as the fact that I exist—even if I am always asleep or even if my creator makes every effort to mislead me? Which of these things is distinct from my thought? Which of them can be said to be separate from myself? For it is so obvious that it is I who doubt, I who understand, and I who will, that there is nothing by which it could be explained more clearly. But indeed it is also the same "I" who imagines; for although perhaps, as I supposed before, absolutely nothing that I imagined is true, still the very power of imagining really does exist, and constitutes a part of my thought. Finally, it is this same "I" who senses or who is cognizant of bodily things as if through the senses. For example, I now see a light, I hear a noise, I feel heat. These things are false, since I am asleep. Yet I certainly do seem to see, hear, and feel warmth. This cannot be false. Properly speaking, this is what in me is called "sensing." But this, precisely so taken, is nothing other than thinking.

From these considerations I am beginning to know a little better what I am. But it still seems (and I cannot resist believing) that corporeal things— whose images are formed by thought, and which the senses themselves examine—are much more distinctly known than this mysterious "I" which does not fall within the imagination. And yet it would be strange indeed were I to grasp the very things I consider to be doubtful, unknown, and foreign to me more distinctly than what is true, what is known—than, in short, myself. But I see what is happening: my mind loves to wander and does not yet permit itself to be restricted within the confines of truth. So be it then; let us just this once allow it completely free rein, so that, a little while later, when the time has come to pull in the reins, the mind may more readily permit itself to be controlled.

Let us consider those things which are commonly believed to be the most distinctly grasped of all: namely the bodies we touch and see. Not bodies in general, mind you, for these general perceptions are apt to be somewhat more confused, but one body in particular. Let us take, for instance, this piece of wax. It has been taken quite recently from the honeycomb; it has not yet lost all the honey flavor. It retains some of the scent of the flowers from which it was collected. Its color, shape, and size are manifest. It is hard and cold; it is easy to touch. If you rap on it with your knuckle it will emit a sound. In short, everything is present in it that appears needed to enable a body to be known as distinctly as possible. But notice that, as I am speaking, I am bringing it close to the fire. The remaining traces of the honey flavor are disappearing; the scent is vanishing; the color is changing; the original shape is disappearing. Its size is increasing; it is becoming liquid and hot; you can hardly touch it. And now, when you rap on it, it no longer emits any sound. Does the same wax still remain? I must confess that it does; no one denies it; no one thinks otherwise. So what was there in the wax that was so distinctly grasped? Certainly none of the aspects that I reached by means of the senses. For whatever came under the senses of taste, smell, sight, touch, or hearing has now changed; and yet the wax remains.

Perhaps the wax was what I now think it is: namely that the wax itself never really was the sweetness of the honey, nor the fragrance of the flowers, nor the whiteness, nor the shape, nor the sound, but instead was a body that a short time ago manifested itself to me in these ways, and now does so in other ways. But just what precisely is this thing that I thus imagine? Let us focus our attention on this and see what remains after we have removed everything that does not belong to the wax: only that it is something extended, flexible, and mutable. But what is it to be flexible and mutable? Is it what my imagination shows it to be: namely, that this piece of wax can change from a round to a square shape, or from the latter to a triangular shape? Not at all; for I grasp that the wax is capable of innumerable changes of this sort, even though I am incapable of running through these innumerable changes by using my imagination. Therefore this insight is not achieved by the faculty of imagination. What is it to be extended? Is this thing's extension also unknown? For it becomes greater in wax that is beginning to melt, greater in boiling wax, and greater still as the heat is increased. And I would not judge correctly what the wax is if I did not believe that it takes on an even greater variety of dimensions than I could ever grasp with the imagination. It remains then for me to concede that I do not grasp what this wax is through the imagination; rather, I perceive it through the mind alone. The point I am making refers to this particular piece of wax, for the case of wax in general is clearer still. But what is this piece of wax which is perceived only by the mind? Surely it is the same piece of wax that I see, touch, and imagine; in short it is the same piece of wax I took it to be from the very beginning. But I need to realize that the perception of the wax is neither a seeing, nor a touching, nor an imagining. Nor has it ever been, even though it previously seemed so; rather it is an inspection on the part of the mind alone. This inspection can be imperfect and confused, as it was before, or clear and distinct, as it is now, depending on how closely I pay attention to the things in which the piece of wax consists.

But meanwhile I marvel at how prone my mind is to errors. For although I am considering these things within myself silently and without words, nevertheless I seize upon words themselves and I am nearly deceived by the ways in which people commonly speak. For we say that we see the wax itself, if it is present, and not that we judge it to be present from its color or shape. Whence I might conclude straightaway that I know the wax through the vision had by the eye, and not through an inspection on the part of the mind alone. But then were I perchance to look out my window and observe men crossing the square, I would ordinarily say I see the men themselves just as I say I see the wax. But what do I see aside from hats and clothes, which could conceal automatons? Yet I judge them to be men. Thus what I thought I had seen with my eyes, I actually grasped solely with the faculty of judgment, which is in my mind.

But a person who seeks to know more than the common crowd ought to be ashamed of himself for looking for doubt in common ways of speaking. Let us then go forward and inquire when it was that I perceived more perfectly and evidently what the piece of wax was. Was it when I first saw it and believed I knew it by the external sense, or at least by the so-called common sense, that is, the power of imagination? Or do I have more perfect knowledge now, when I have diligently examined both what the wax is and how it is known? Surely it is absurd to be in doubt about this matter. For what was there in my initial perception that was distinct? What was there that any animal seemed incapable of possessing? But indeed when I distinguish the wax from its external forms, as if stripping it of its clothing, and look at the wax in its nakedness, then, even though there can be still an error in my judgment, nevertheless I cannot perceive it thus without a human mind.

But what am I to say about this mind, that is, about myself? For as yet I admit nothing else to be in me over and above the mind. What, I ask, am I who seem to perceive this wax so distinctly? Do I not know myself not only much more truly and with greater certainty, but also much more distinctly and evidently? For if I judge that the wax exists from the fact that I see it, certainly from this same fact that I see the wax it follows much more evidently that I myself exist. For it could happen that what I see is not truly wax. It could happen that I have no eyes with which to see anything. But it is utterly impossible that, while I see or think I see (I do not now distinguish these two), I who think am not something. Likewise, if I judge that the wax exists from the fact that I touch it, the same outcome will again obtain, namely that I exist. If I judge that the wax exists from the fact that I imagine it, or for any other reason, plainly the same thing follows. But what I note regarding the wax applies to everything else that is external to me. Furthermore, if my perception of the wax seemed more distinct after it became known to me not only on account of sight or touch, but on account of many reasons, one has to admit how much more distinctly I am now known to myself. For there is not a single consideration that can aid in my perception of the wax or of any other body that fails to make even more manifest the nature of my mind. But there are still so many other things in the mind itself on the basis of which my knowledge of it can be rendered more distinct that it hardly seems worth enumerating those things which emanate to it from the body.

But lo and behold, I have returned on my own to where I wanted to be. For since I now know that even bodies are not, properly speaking, perceived by the senses or by the faculty of imagination, but by the intellect alone, and that they are not perceived through their being touched or seen, but only through their being understood, I manifestly know that nothing can be perceived more easily and more evidently than my own mind. But since the tendency to hang on to long-held beliefs cannot be put aside so quickly, I want to stop here, so that by the length of my meditation this new knowledge may be more deeply impressed upon my memory.

QUESTIONS

MEDITATION ONE

1. Why does Descartes withdraw into solitude to examine his opinions?

2. What is so significant about beliefs based on sense impressions that makes Descartes begin with these in questioning the foundation of his opinions?

3. Why does Descartes suggest that abstract things—such as extension, shape, quantity, place, and time—are more certain than what we directly perceive with our senses?

4. If Descartes has the long-standing opinion that there is an omnipotent God, why does he seem to reject the idea that this God could exercise his power to deceive him?

5. Why does Descartes decide that he must withhold his assent from opinions whose truth seems highly probable?

6. What distinction is Descartes making when he says, "it is impossible for me to indulge in too much distrust, since I am now concentrating only on knowledge, not on action"? (30)

7. What strategy is Descartes using in personifying the source of false opinion as an "evil genius"? (30) Why does he find it necessary to make this being willfully evil?

8. Why isn't Descartes's own willpower enough to sustain him in withholding his assent from what is false?

MEDITATION TWO

1. What are the "great things" that Descartes hopes for in finding at least one certainty? (31)

2. What leads Descartes to assert that "this pronouncement 'I am, I exist' is necessarily true every time I utter it or conceive it in my mind"? (31)

3. Why does Descartes reject definitions such as man is a "rational animal"? (32) Why does he refer to this kind of consideration as wasteful subtleties?

4. How does the act of thinking elude the deliberations of Descartes's malicious deceiver?

5. Why does Descartes claim that the imagination has no place in gaining knowledge of the "I"? (33)

6. What is the "distinct" quality that Descartes says the mind must have in order to perceive its nature? (34)

7. After discarding the possibility that certain knowledge comes through the senses, what does Descartes mean in suggesting that "sensing" is "nothing other than thinking"? (34)

8. After such deliberate mental activity, why does Descartes think that letting his mind have free rein will make it more readily controlled later?

9. What is Descartes attempting to demonstrate in meditating on the piece of wax?

10. What distinction is Descartes making between "seeing" and "judging" when he says, "I seize upon words themselves and I am nearly deceived by the ways in which people commonly speak"? (35)

11. Why does Descartes say that he does "not now distinguish" thinking and seeing? (36)

12. At the end of *Meditation Two*, what does Descartes mean in saying, "I have returned on my own to where I wanted to be?" Why does he emphasize that he has done so "on his own"? (36)

FOR FURTHER REFLECTION

1. Why does Descartes refer to his activity as meditation rather than philosophizing?

2. In *Meditations One* and *Two*, why does Descartes at several points emphasize procrastination and laziness as impediments to the introspective task he has set for himself?

3. Does the kind of certainty Descartes is seeking have implications for how people should act or only for how they can know?

4. Is the kind of deep introspection in which Descartes engages more appropriate at some stages of life than others?

5. Under what conditions might it be better to rely solely on one's own intellectual resources in pondering fundamental questions than to seek out the carefully considered opinions of others?

6. What risks are there in questioning, as thoroughly as Descartes, the most basic assumptions underlying our opinions?

At the age of nineteen, Nikolai Gogol (1809–1852) wrote, "I am considered a riddle by everyone." Seen through the literature he would later write, he seems no less enigmatic. "The Nose" shows why it is so difficult to precisely identify the source of his work's power. The story's premise seems utterly fantastic—a civil servant's nose suddenly detaches itself from his face and moves about Petersburg with all the attributes of the story's other characters, speaking to them and wearing a state councilor's uniform. The portrayal of the civil servant's response to this predicament can suggest a realistic, often satirical treatment of Russian society. Indeed, Gogol has been seen as the father of Russian realism, with Dostoevsky, Tolstoy, and Chekhov his great heirs. Approaching Gogol from this perspective, however, does little to illuminate what seem to be the most puzzling features of "The Nose." As the quotidian detail accumulates, the story generates the expectation that some kind of explanation awaits, if not the revelation of deep meaning.

In his most famous stories, Gogol employs an often surreal sense of juxtaposition to depict the urban life of St. Petersburg, where he began his career as a writer, but the Ukrainian countryside where he grew up, especially its rich tradition of folklore, remained an influence on his work. He was born in 1809 in Sorochintsy into a family belonging to the petty gentry. In high school, he wrote prose and poetry and performed in theatrical productions. Gogol left for St. Petersburg in 1828 and took the first of several unsatisfying civil service jobs. He tried to begin his literary career by printing at his own expense an epic poem, but he quickly burned nearly every copy. After deciding to emigrate to the United States, he only got as far as Germany before running out of money and returning to St. Petersburg. He began writing stories for periodicals in 1830, eight of which were published in two volumes under the title *Evenings on a Farm near Dikanka* (1831–1832). The book made Gogol an instant literary sensation, winning the praise of Alexander Pushkin, who later characterized Gogol's work as provoking "laughter through tears of sorrow."

Gogol then left the civil service to teach, taking a position at a girls' boarding school before being appointed a professor of history at the University of St. Petersburg in 1834. He held this position for only a year, but his literary reputation grew with the publication of two more collections in 1835, *Mirgorod* and *Arabesques.* While the stories in the former evoke the peasant life and Cossack traditions of his native Ukraine, the stories in the latter, such as "Diary of a Madman" and "Nevsky Prospect," reveal a darker, more extravagant imagination. In 1836, the year in which "The Nose" was first published in Pushkin's magazine *The Contemporary, The Inspector General* had its first production. Vladimir Nabokov considered this play—a fierce satire of provincial bureaucrats—the greatest ever written in Russian. The disturbance it caused contributed to Gogol's decision to leave Russia. He soon settled in Rome, where he wrote most of *Dead Souls,* his classic novel about a swindler's attempt to make money by purchasing dead serfs not yet removed from the census records. The novel was published in 1842, along with the story "The Overcoat," perhaps Gogol's best-known work.

Both *Dead Souls* and "The Overcoat" were greeted as masterpieces, which had the effect of convincing Gogol that his role was that of a savior. He conceived of two more volumes of *Dead Souls,* the whole work to be roughly analogous to the three parts of Dante's *Divine Comedy.* His inability to finish the second part led him to believe he was unworthy of saving Russia through his writing. Adopting an increasingly ascetic life, Gogol moved to Moscow in 1848. In 1852, he burned the manuscript of the second part of *Dead Souls* (though fragments survived). He died days later, the result of severe fasting.

The Nose

1

An incredible thing happened in Petersburg on March 25th. Ivan Yakovlevich, the barber on Voznesensky Avenue (his last name has been lost and does not even figure on the signboard bearing a picture of a gentleman with a soapy cheek and the inscription WE ALSO LET BLOOD HERE), woke up rather early and detected a smell of newly baked bread. He raised himself a little and saw that his wife, a quite respectable woman and one extremely fond of coffee, was taking fresh rolls out of the oven.

"Praskovia Osipovna," he said to his wife, "no coffee for me this morning. I'll have a hot roll with onions instead."

Actually Ivan Yakovlevich would have liked both but he knew his wife frowned on such whims. And, sure enough, she thought:

"It's fine with me if the fool wants bread. That'll leave me another cup of coffee."

And she tossed a roll onto the table.

Mindful of his manners, Ivan Yakovlevich put his frock coat on over his nightshirt, seated himself at the table, poured some salt, got a couple of onions, took a knife, and, assuming a dignified expression, proceeded to cut the roll in two.

Suddenly he stopped, surprised. There was something whitish in the middle of the roll. He poked at it with his knife, then felt it with his finger.

"It's quite compact . . ." he muttered under his breath. "Whatever can it be? . . .

He thrust in two fingers this time and pulled it out. It was a nose.

He almost fell off his chair. Then he rubbed his eyes and felt the thing again. It was a nose all right, no doubt about it. And, what's more, a nose that had something familiar about it. His features expressed intense horror.

But the intensity of the barber's horror was nothing compared with the intensity of his wife's indignation.

"Where," she screamed, "did you lop off that nose, you beast? You crook," she shouted, "you drunkard! I'll report you to the police myself, you thug! Three customers have complained to me before this about the way you keep pulling their noses when you shave them, so that it's a wonder they manage to stay on at all."

But Ivan Yakovlevich, at that moment more dead than alive, was immune to her attack. He had remembered where he had seen the nose before and it was on none other than Collegiate Assessor Kovalev, whom he shaved regularly each Wednesday and Sunday.

"Wait, my dear, I'll wrap it in a rag and put it away somewhere in a corner. Let it stay there for a while, then I'll take it away."

"I won't even listen to you! Do you really imagine that I'll allow a cut-off nose to remain in my place, you old crumb! All you can do is strop your damn razor and when it comes to your duties, you're no good. You stupid, lousy, skirt-chasing scum! So you want me to get into trouble with the police for your sake? Is that it, you dirty mug? You're a stupid log, you know. Get it out of here. Do what you like with it, you hear me, but don't let me ever see it here again."

The barber stood there dumbfounded. He thought and thought but couldn't think of anything.

"I'll be damned if I know how it happened," he said in the end, scratching behind his ear. "Was I drunk last night when I came home? I'm not sure. Anyway, it all sounds quite mad: bread is a baked product while a nose is something else again. Makes no sense to me. . . ."

So he fell silent. The thought that the police would find the nose on him and accuse him drove him to despair. He could already see the beautiful silver-braided, scarlet collars of the police and started trembling all over.

Still, in the end he stirred and went to get his trousers and his boots. He pulled on these sorry garments, wrapped the nose in a rag, and left under Praskovia Osipovna's unendearing barrage of recriminations.

He wanted to get rid of the nose, to leave it under a seat, stick it in a doorway, or just drop it as if by accident and then rush down a side street. But he kept meeting acquaintances who immediately proceeded to inquire where he was going or whom he was planning to shave so early in the morning, and he missed every opportunity. At one point he actually dropped the nose, but a watchman pointed to it with his halberd and informed him that he'd lost something. And Ivan Yakovlevich had to pick up the nose and stuff it back into his pocket. Things began to look completely hopeless for him when the stores began opening and the streets became more and more crowded.

Then he decided to try throwing the nose into the Neva from the Isakievsky Bridge. . . .

But, at this point, we should say a few words about Ivan Yakovlevich, a man who had a number of good points.

Like every self-respecting Russian tradesman, Ivan Yakovlevich was a terrible drunkard. And although he shaved other people's chins every day, his own looked permanently unshaven. His frock coat (he never wore an ordinary coat) was piebald. That is to say, it had been black originally but now it was studded with yellowish brown and gray spots. His collar was shiny and three threads dangling from his coat indicated where the missing buttons should have been. Ivan Yakovlevich was a terrible cynic.

While being shaved the collegiate assessor often complained:

"Your hands always stink, Ivan Yakovlevich!"

He would answer: "How can they stink?"

"I don't know how, man, but they stink!" the other would say.

In answer Ivan Yakovlevich would take a pinch of snuff and proceed to soap Kovalev's cheeks and under his nose and behind his ears and under his chin, in fact, anywhere he felt like.

By and by, this worthy citizen reached the Isakievsky Bridge. He glanced around and then, leaning over the parapet, peered under the bridge as if to ascertain the whereabouts of some fish. But actually he discreetly dropped the rag containing the nose. He felt as if a three-hundred-pound weight had been taken off his back. He let out a little laugh and, instead of going back to shave the chins of government employees, he decided he had to recuperate. He was setting out for an establishment that operated under the sign MEALS AND TEA, to treat himself to a glass of punch, when all of a sudden he saw a police inspector of most imposing appearance—handlebar mustache, three-cornered hat, saber, and all. He froze in his tracks. The policeman beckoned to him and said:

"Just step over here, fellow!"

Having great respect for this particular uniform, Ivan Yakovlevich pulled off his cap while he was still a good distance away, trotted toward the policeman, and said:

"Good morning, officer."

"Instead of good morning, you'd better tell me what you were doing in the middle of the bridge over there."

"I was on my way to shave people, officer, and I wanted to see whether the current was fast—"

"You're lying, man. You won't get away with it. You'd better answer my question."

"Officer, I'll give you two . . . no, three free shaves every week . . . what do you say, officer?" said Ivan Yakovlevich.

"Not a chance. I have three barbers to shave me as it is. And they consider it a great honor, too. So you get on with it and explain what you were doing."

Ivan Yakovlevich turned ashen. . . . But here the incident becomes befogged and it is completely unknown what happened after this point.

2

That morning Collegiate Assessor Kovalev had awakened rather early. He went brrr...brrr with his lips as he always did upon waking, although he himself could not explain why. He stretched himself and asked his man for the small mirror that stood on his dressing table. He needed it to examine a pimple that had broken out on his nose the day before. But he was bewildered to find that instead of his nose there was nothing but a bare smooth surface. Horrified, he asked for water and rubbed his eyes with a towel. There was no doubt about it: his nose was not there. He felt himself all over to make sure he was not asleep. It seemed he wasn't. Collegiate Assessor Kovalev jumped up then and shook himself. Still no nose. He called for his clothes and rushed directly to the police inspector.

But, in the meantime, a few things should be said about Kovalev to show what sort of collegiate assessor he was. Collegiate assessors who reach their positions by obtaining academic degrees cannot be compared with the collegiate assessors that used to be appointed in the Caucasus. They are two completely unrelated species. The collegiate assessors equipped with learning...

But Russia is a strange place and if we say something about one collegiate assessor, all of them, from Riga to Kamchatka, will take it personally. The same is true of all vocations and ranks.

Kovalev was a Caucasus-made collegiate assessor. Moreover, he had been a collegiate assessor for only two years. In order to feel distinguished and important he never referred to himself as a collegiate assessor but employed the equivalent military rank of major.

"Look here, my good woman," he used to say when he met a woman selling shirt fronts in the street, "I want you to deliver them to my place. I live on Sadovaya Street. Just ask for Major Kovalev's, anybody'll show you."

And if he met someone pretty, he would whisper to her discreetly: "You just ask for Major Kovalev's apartment, deary."

As a rule, Major Kovalev went out for a daily walk along Nevsky Avenue. The collar of his shirt was always clean and well starched. He had whiskers such as are still to be found on provincial surveyors, and architects if they happen to be Russian, among persons performing various police functions, and, in general, on men who have full faces, ruddy cheeks, and play a strong hand at certain games of chance. Whiskers of this type flow straight across the middle of the cheek up to the very nostrils.

Major Kovalev always carried with him a great quantity of seals, both seals engraved with coats of arms and others on which were carved WEDNESDAY, THURSDAY, MONDAY, and that sort of thing. He had come to Petersburg on business, namely, to find a position commensurate with his rank. He hoped, if lucky, to get a vice governorship; otherwise, he would consider a post as executive in some administration. Nor was Major Kovalev averse to matrimony, as long as the bride happened to have a capital of about two hundred thousand rubles.

And now that all this has been said about the major, it can be imagined how he felt when, instead of a quite acceptable looking, medium-sized nose, he found an absurd, smooth flatness.

And, to make things worse, there was not a cab to be seen in the street and he was forced to walk all the way wrapped in his cloak, his face covered with a handkerchief, pretending he was bleeding, and repeating to himself:

"Maybe it's just imagination. How could I possibly have lost my nose so stupidly? . . ."

He entered a tearoom simply to have a look in a mirror. Fortunately the place was empty except for waiters sweeping the floor and moving chairs around and some others who, with sleepy eyes, were carrying trays with hot buns somewhere. Yesterday's newspapers spotted with coffee were strewn around on tables and chairs.

"Well, thank heaven there's no one here," he said. "I'll be able to have a look."

Gingerly he approached the mirror and looked.

"Filth," he said, spitting, "goddammit. If only there was something to take the nose's place! But it's completely blank!"

He bit his lip in anger and, leaving the tearoom, decided that, contrary to his usual custom, he wouldn't look at the people he met or smile at anyone. Suddenly he stopped dead near the entrance door of a house. An incredible sequence of events unrolled before his eyes. A carriage stopped at the house entrance. Its door opened. A uniformed gentleman appeared. Stooping, he jumped out of the carriage, ran up the steps, and entered the house. A combination of horror and amazement swept over Kovalev when he recognized the stranger as his own nose. At this eerie sight, everything swayed before his eyes. But although he could hardly stand on his feet, he felt compelled to wait until the nose returned to the carriage. He waited, shaking as though he had malaria.

After two minutes or so, the nose emerged from the house. He wore a gold-braided, brightly colored uniform, buckskin breeches, a three-cornered hat, and a saber. The plumes on his hat indicated the rank of state councilor. From everything else it could be inferred that he was setting off on some sort of official visit. He looked left, then right, called out to the coachman to bring the carriage up to the very door, got in, and was off.

This almost drove poor Kovalev insane. He could no longer think coherently about the whole affair. No, really, how was it possible that the nose, until yesterday on his face, utterly incapable of walking or driving around, should show up like this today and, what's more, wearing a uniform! And Kovalev ran after the carriage, which, luckily for him, did not have far to go. It stopped before Kazan Cathedral.

Kovalev reached the spot and, rushing after the nose, had to elbow his way through a throng of old beggar women who used to make him laugh because of the way they kept their faces completely wrapped in rags, leaving only slits for their eyes. He entered the cathedral. There were a few worshipers around, all standing near the entrance. Kovalev was in such a depressed state that he could not possibly muster the strength to pray and instead his eyes scrutinized every recess in search of the gentleman. Finally he discovered him standing in a corner. The nose's face was completely concealed by his high, stand-up collar, and he was praying with an expression of the utmost piety.

"How shall I address him?" Kovalev wondered. "From his uniform, his hat, everything, about him, he must be a state councilor. Damned if I know what to do. . . ."

He approached and cleared his throat. But the nose never even changed his pious posture and remained absorbed in his worship.

"Excuse me, sir . . ." Kovalev said, scraping up all his courage.

"Yes?" the nose said, turning around.

"I don't know how to put it, sir . . . I would say . . . it seems . . . it seems you ought to know where you belong, and where do I find you? Of all places, in church. You must surely agree—"

"Pardon me, but I can make neither head nor tail of what you're saying. Just what do you want?"

Kovalev tried to think how he could explain to the nose what he had in mind and, taking a deep breath, said:

"Of course, sir, for my part . . . but after all, I am a major, you know, and it's most improper, in my position, to walk around without a nose. Some old woman selling peeled oranges by the Voskresensky Bridge might be able to get along without a nose. But for someone who is almost certain of a high administrative appointment . . . you can judge for yourself, sir. I really fail to understand . . . " At this point Kovalev shrugged. "You'll excuse me, but if this affair were handled according to the code of honor and duty . . . You can see for yourself—"

"I don't see anything," the nose said. "Kindly come to the point."

"Sir," Kovalev said with dignity, "I don't know how to interpret your words. The matter is quite clear, I believe. Unless you are trying . . . Don't you realize that you are my nose?"

The nose looked at the major and frowned slightly.

"You're mistaken, sir. I'm all on my own. Moreover, there couldn't possibly have been close relations between us. Judging by your dress, you must be employed by the Senate, or possibly by the Ministry of Justice, whereas my field is science."

And having said this, the nose turned away and resumed his prayers.

Kovalev was now completely at a loss. Then he heard the pleasant rustle of a feminine dress. He saw a middle-aged lady covered with lace and, with her, a pretty, slender thing in a white dress that set off a very moving waist-line, and with a straw hat as light as whipped cream. Behind them walked a tall man with side whiskers and a very complicated collar.

Kovalev worked his way toward them, pulled up the spotless collar of his shirt front to make sure it showed, straightened the seals that hung on a golden chain, and concentrated his attention on the young lady who, like a spring blossom, raised her white hand with its half-transparent fingers to her forehead. And Kovalev's smile spread twice as wide when, under the hat, he made out a chin of a tender whiteness and a cheek touched by the early spring coloring of a rose. But then he jumped back as though burned. He had remembered that instead of a nose he had absolutely nothing, and the tears sprang to his eyes.

He turned to the gentleman dressed as a state councilor to tell him that he was nothing but a fraud and a crook, nothing but his, Kovalev's, personally owned nose.

But the nose was nowhere to be seen. He must have driven off on another official visit.

Kovalev was in despair. He retraced his steps, stopped for a while under the colonnade, and looked intently around him in the hope of catching sight of the nose. He remembered that the nose had had a plumed hat and a gold-braided uniform, but he hadn't noticed his greatcoat, or the color of his carriage, or his horses, or even whether he had had a footman up behind him and, if so, what livery he wore. And then there were so many carriages rushing back and forth, all going so fast that he would have had difficulty in picking one out and no way of stopping it anyway. It was a lovely sunny day. Nevsky Avenue was thronged with people; from the central police station to Anichkin Bridge, ladies poured over the sidewalks in a colorful cascade. There went an acquaintance of his, a court councilor, whom he addressed as lieutenant colonel, especially in the presence of outsiders. Then Kovalev saw Yaryzhkin, head clerk in the Senate, a good friend who always lost whenever they played cards together. And there was another major, another Caucasus-made collegiate assessor, beckoning . . .

"Goddammit," Kovalev said, "what the hell does he want from me, Cabbie! To the police commissioner's!"

He got into the cab and kept exhorting the cabbie again and again: "Come on, let's go! Quick! Now turn into Ivanovskaya Street."

"Is the commissioner in?" he called out, as soon as he entered the house.

"No, sir," the doorman answered. "He left only a minute ago."

"That's really too much. . . ."

"Yes, sir," the doorman said. "If you'd come a minute earlier, you'd have caught him."

Kovalev, still holding his handkerchief to his face, got back into the cab and shouted in a desperate voice:

"Get going."

"Where to?"

"Straight ahead."

"Straight ahead? But this is a dead end. Shall I go right or left?"

Kovalev was caught off balance and forced to give the matter some thought. In his position, he ought first to go to the National Security Administration, not because it was directly connected with the police, but because its orders would be acted on more rapidly than those of others.

Certainly it was no use taking his grievance to the scientific department where the nose claimed to have a post. At best, it would be unwise, since, judging by his statement that he had never seen Kovalev before, it was obvious that he held nothing sacred and he might lie whenever he found it convenient. So Kovalev was about to tell the cabman to drive him to the National Security Administration when it occurred to him that the crook and impostor, who had just behaved so unscrupulously toward him, might very well try to slip out of town, in which case finding him would be quite hopeless or would take, God forbid, a whole month perhaps. Finally, he had what seemed like a divine inspiration. He decided to go straight to the Press Building to have an advertisement put in the papers with a detailed description of the nose in all his aspects, so that anyone who met him could turn him over to Kovalev, or at least inform him of the nose's whereabouts. So, having decided this, he told the cabman to take him to the Press Building and, during the entire ride, he kept pommeling him on the back with his fist and shouting:

"Faster, damn you! Faster!"

"Really, sir!" the cabman said, shaking his head and flicking the reins at his horse, which had hair as long as a lap dog's.

At last the cab came to a stop, and Kovalev, panting, burst into the small outer office where a gray-haired, bespectacled employee in an ancient frock coat was seated at a table, his pen clenched between his teeth, counting out the change someone had paid in.

"Who handles advertisements here?" shouted Kovalev. "Ah," he said, "good morning!"

"Good morning, sir," the gray-haired employee said, raising his eyes for a moment and lowering them again to the little piles of coins before him.

"I want to insert—"

"Excuse me. Would you mind waiting just a moment, please," the employee said, writing down a figure with his right hand while his left hand moved two beads on his abacus.

A footman, whose gold-braided livery and whole appearance testified to his service in an aristocratic house, stood by the old employee holding a piece of paper in his hand and, to prove his worldliness, started chattering away:

"Believe me, I'm quite sure the mutt isn't worth eighty kopeks. In fact, I wouldn't give eight kopeks, if you ask me. But the countess loves that cur—she has to if she's willing to give a hundred rubles to the person who finds it. Since we are among people who understand, I'll tell you one thing: it's all a matter of taste. I can understand a dog lover. But then, go and get a deerhound or maybe a poodle. Then, if you want to spend five hundred or a thousand on it, it's only natural. But, in my opinion, when you pay you are entitled to a *real* dog. . . ."

The elderly employee was listening to this speech with an important expression and was counting the number of letters in the text of the advertisement the manservant had handed him. The room was full of old women, shopkeepers, and doormen, all holding pieces of paper on which advertisements had been written out. In one a coachman, sober and dependable, was for hire; another announced that a carriage with very little mileage, brought from Paris in 1814, was for sale; a nineteen-year-old girl, a washerwoman's assistant, but suitable for other work too, wanted employment; also for sale were an excellent hansom cab (one spring missing) and a young, seventeen-year-old, dappled-gray horse, as well as a consignment of turnip and radish seeds straight from London, a summer house with a two-carriage coach house, and a piece of land very suitable for planting a lovely birch wood. Another advertisement invited persons desirous of buying secondhand shoe soles to present themselves in a certain salesroom between 8 a.m. and 3 p.m.

The reception room in which all these people waited was quite small and the air was getting stuffy. But the smell didn't bother Collegiate Assessor Kovalev because he kept his face covered with a handkerchief and also because his nose happened to be God knew where.

"Excuse me, sir . . . I don't want to bother you, but this is an emergency," he said impatiently at last.

Wait, wait . . . two rubles, forty-three kopeks, please. One minute, please! . . . One ruble, sixty-four, over there . . . " the old employee said, shoving sheets of paper under the noses of porters and old women. "Now, what can I do for you?" he said finally, turning to Kovalev.

"I wanted," Kovalev said, "to ask you to . . . a fraud, or perhaps a theft, has been committed. I'm still not clear. I want you to run an advertisement simply saying that whoever delivers that robber to me will get a handsome reward."

"Your name, please."

"My name? What for? I can't tell you my name. I have too many acquaintances, such as Mrs. Chekhtareva, the wife of a civil servant, and Palageya Grigorievna Podtochina, who's married to Captain Podtochin, an officer on the army general staff. . . . Suppose they found out, God forbid. Write simply 'a collegiate assessor' or, better still, 'a major.'"

"And the runaway, was he a household serf?"

"A household serf. That wouldn't be half so vicious a crime. The runaway is my nose . . . yes, my own nose. . . ."

"Hm . . . odd name. And now may I inquire the sum, the amount, of which this Mr. Nose has defrauded you?"

"No, no, you don't understand. I said nose. My own nose, which has disappeared God knows where. I am the victim of some foul joke. . . ."

"But how could it disappear? I still don't understand, sir."

"Well, I can't explain how, but the main thing is that he mustn't go all over town impersonating a state councilor. That's why I want you to advertise that anyone who catches him should contact me as quickly as possible. Besides, imagine how I feel with such a conspicuous part of my body missing. It's not just a matter of, say, a toe. You could simply stick your foot into your shoe and no one would be the wiser. On Thursdays, I usually visit Mrs. Chekhtareva, the wife of a state councilor. . . . And Mrs. Podtochina, the wife of the staff officer, has an extremely pretty daughter. They are close friends of mine, you see, and now tell me, what am I to do? . . . How can I show myself to them?"

The employee was thinking hard, as could be seen from his tightly pressed lips.

"I am sorry, sir, but I cannot accept your advertisement," he said, after a long silence.

"What's that! Why?"

"I just can't. A newspaper could lose its good name if everybody started advertising vagrant noses. . . . No, sir, as it is, too many absurdities and unfounded rumors manage to slip into print."

"Why is it absurd? I don't see anything so unusual about it."

"It may look that way to you. But just let me tell you . . . Last week, for instance, a government employee came to see me just as you have now. I even remember that his advertisement came to two rubles, seventy-three kopeks. But what it all boiled down to was that a black poodle had run away. You'd think there was nothing to it, wouldn't you? But wait. Turned out to be deliberate libel because the poodle in question happened to be the treasurer of I can't recall exactly what."

"But listen, I'm not advertising about a poodle but about my own nose, which is the same as myself."

"Sorry, I can't accept the advertisement."

"But I have lost my nose!"

"If you have, it is a matter for a doctor. I've heard that there are specialists who can fit you with any sort of nose you want. But I'm beginning to think that you are one of these cheerful people who likes to have his little joke."

"But I swear to you by all that's holy! And if it comes to that, I'll show you."

"Why take the trouble," the employee said, taking a pinch of snuff. "But then, after all, if you really don't mind," he added, making a slight movement indicating curiosity, "why, I wouldn't mind having a look."

Kovalev removed the handkerchief from his face.

"My! It *is* strange!" the employee said. "Why, it's as flat as a fresh-cooked pancake, incredibly smooth!"

"Well, now you won't refuse to run my advertisement, will you? It simply must be published. I will be very much obliged to you, and I'm very happy that this accident has given me a chance to make your acquaintance. . . ."

The major, it can be seen, had decided that he'd better make up to him a bit.

"Certainly, running it is no great problem," the employee said, "but I don't see that it would do you any good. However, if you absolutely want to see it in print, why not entrust it to someone who can really write and ask him to present it as a rare natural phenomenon and have it published in the *Northern Bee*"—here he took another pinch of snuff—"for the edification of the young"—here he wiped his nose—"or just as a matter of general interest."

The collegiate assessor was taken aback. He lowered his eyes and his glance happened to fall on the theatrical announcements at the bottom of the page of a newspaper. His face was just about to break into a smile at the sight of the name of a very pretty actress and his hand had already plunged into his pocket to see whether he had a five ruble bill on him, since, in his opinion, an officer of his rank should sit in the stalls, when he remembered the nose and everything was ruined.

The employee, too, seemed touched by Kovalev's awkward position. To alleviate his distress, he thought it would be appropriate to express his sympathy in a few words:

"I'm very sorry that such a painful thing should have happened to you. Perhaps you'd feel better if you took a pinch of snuff. It eases people's headaches and cheers them up. It's even good for hemorrhoids."

As he said this, the employee offered Kovalev his snuffbox, rather deftly folding back the lid, which had a picture on it of some lady in a hat.

At this unintentional provocation, Kovalev's patience snapped.

"I simply don't understand how you can make a joke of it," he said angrily. "Can't you see that I am missing just what I would need to take a pinch of snuff with? You know what you can do with your snuff! I can't even look at it now, especially not at your cheap Berezinsky brand. You might at least have offered me something better . . ."

Incensed, he rushed out of the Press Building. He decided to take his case to the borough police commissioner.

At the moment when Kovalev entered the office of the commissioner, the latter had just finished stretching himself and reflecting:

"I might as well treat myself to a nap. A couple of hours or so."

Thus it would have been easy to predict that the major's visit was rather poorly timed. Incidentally, the commissioner, though a great lover of the arts and of commerce, still preferred a bill put in circulation by the Imperial Russian Bank over anything else. His opinion on the matter was as follows:

"It has everything: it doesn't have to be fed, it doesn't take up much room, and, in any case, can always be fitted into a pocket. If you drop it, it doesn't break."

The commissioner was rather cold with Kovalev. Right after a meal, he said, was not the proper time for investigations. Nature itself, he said, dictated rest when one's belly was full. From this, the collegiate assessor was able to gather that the commissioner was rather familiar with the maxims of the wise men of antiquity.

"Moreover," the commissioner said, "they don't tear noses off decent citizens' faces."

Bull's-eye! We must note here that Kovalev was quick to take offense. He could forgive anything that was said about himself personally, but he couldn't stand anything that he considered a slur on his rank and position. He even held the view that, in dramatic works, while a disparaging reference to subaltern ranks was permissible, it became intolerable when applied to officers above the rank of captain. He was so disconcerted by the reception given him by the commissioner that he shook his head slightly, shrugged, and, on his way out, said in a dignified tone:

"Well, I must say . . . after your offensive remarks I have nothing further to add."

He reached home hardly able to feel his feet beneath him. It was getting dark. After his futile search, his place looked sad and repulsive. As he walked in, he saw Ivan, his manservant, lying on his back on the old leather divan in the entrance hall spitting at the ceiling—very successfully it must be said. Ivan was hitting the same spot again and again. But such indifference enraged Kovalev. He hit him on the head with his hat and said bitterly:

"Swine! You think of nothing but trivialities."

Ivan jumped up and started anxiously to help Kovalev off with his coat.

The major went into his room and let himself fall into an armchair, sad and exhausted. He let out a few sighs, after which he said:

"Good heavens! Why is all this happening to *me*? What have *I* done wrong? It would have been better to have lost an arm or a leg. It would have been bad enough without ears, yet still bearable. But without a nose a man is not a man but God knows what—neither fish nor fowl. He can't even be a proper citizen anymore. If only I had had it lopped off during a war or in a duel or if *I* had been responsible for the loss. But I lost it for no reason and for nothing; I haven't even got a kopek out of it! No, it's impossible," he added after a pause, "it is impossible that the nose could have disappeared. Incredible! It is probably a dream or just a hallucination . . . maybe, by mistake, I drank a glassful of the vodka with which I rub my face after shaving? That fool Ivan must have forgotten to put it away and I must have swallowed it inadvertently."

To prove to himself that he was really drunk, the major pinched himself so hard that he let out a moan. The pain convinced him that he was quite sober. Then, slowly, as though stalking something, he approached the mirror, his eyes half-closed, in the vague hope that, who knows, perhaps the nose would be in its proper place. But immediately he jumped away.

"What a slanderous sight!"

It was really quite bewildering. Many things get lost: a button, a silver spoon, a watch, or some such object. But to disappear just like that. . . . And what's more, in his own apartment! Having weighed the matter, Major Kovalev came to what seemed to be the most likely explanation: the culprit behind it all was Mrs. Podtochina, who wanted him to marry her daughter. He rather enjoyed the girl's company himself but he was just not ready for a final decision. And when Mrs. Podtochina had told him plainly that she wanted him to marry her daughter, he had quietly beaten a polite retreat, saying that he was still very young and that he ought to devote another five years or so to his career, after which he would be at least forty-two. So, probably, that was when Mrs. Podtochina had decided to maim him and had hired witches or something for the purpose, because by no stretch of the imagination could it be assumed that the nose had been cut off; no one had entered his bedroom; Ivan Yakovlevich, the barber, hadn't shaved him since Wednesday and during the rest of that day and even on Thursday, his nose, all in one piece, had been on his face. He was absolutely certain of it. Moreover, had the nose been cut off he would have felt pain and the wound could never have healed so fast and become as smooth as a pancake. . . .

All sorts of plans clashed in his head: should he take the lady to court or would it be better to go directly to her and denounce her to her face? But his thoughts were interrupted by light seeping in through the cracks in the door, indicating that Ivan had lit a candle in the entrance hall. Soon Ivan appeared carrying the candle high above his head, lighting up the entire room. Kovalev's first thought was to grab the handkerchief and cover the place where, only yesterday, the nose had sat, so that this stupid man should not stand there gaping, noticing the peculiar state of his master's face.

But no sooner had Ivan left than he heard an unknown voice coming from the apartment door ask:

"Does Collegiate Assessor Kovalev live here?"

"Come in. Major Kovalev is in," Kovalev shouted, jumping up and rushing into the hall.

It was a police officer, a quite handsome man with whiskers neither too light nor too dark and with rather full cheeks. In fact it was the same one who, at the beginning of this story, had been standing by the Isakievsy Bridge.

"Did you happen to lose your nose, sir?"

"Yes, I did."

"It has been found."

"Is it possible?"

Joy paralyzed the major's tongue. He stared at the police officer standing in front of him, the reflection of the candlelight shining on his damp, full lips.

"How did it happen?" he managed to say at last.

"By sheer coincidence. Your nose was caught as he was getting on the stagecoach for Riga. He had a passport made out in the name of a government official and the strange thing is that, at first, I myself took him for a gentleman. But luckily I had my glasses with me, so I put them on and recognized immediately that he was a nose. The thing is, I am very shortsighted, sir, and with you standing right in front of me there, I can make out your face but I can't discern your beard, or your nose, or anything else. My mother-in-law, that's the mother of my wife, can't see a thing either."

Kovalev was beside himself with excitement.

"Where is he? Where? I'll run over there now. . . ."

"Don't trouble, sir. I thought you might need it so I brought it along. But you know, the funny part about it is that the main suspect in the affair is the barber from Voznesensky Avenue, a crook who's now being held at the police station. I've had my eye on him for some time because I suspected him of being a thief and a drunkard. As a matter of fact, he lifted a box of buttons in a store the other day. By the way, your nose is exactly as before, sir."

Saying this, the police officer put his hand in his pocket and extracted the nose wrapped in a piece of paper.

"That's it! That's it!" Kovalev shouted. "No doubt about it! Do come in and have some tea with me, won't you?"

"It would be a great honor, sir, but I am afraid I can't. I must stop over at the house of correction—prices are going up, sir. . . . My mother-in-law, I mean the wife's mother, is living with me . . . we have children too. The eldest son is particularly promising, a very clever boy, but we have no money for his education. . . ."

When the police officer had left, the collegiate assessor remained for some minutes in an indeterminate state, just barely able to see and feel. It was his immense joy that had plunged him into this half-consciousness. Very carefully he held his just-recovered nose in his cupped hands and once again looked it over.

"Yes, that's it, that's it all right. And here, on the left side, is the pimple that sprang up the other day."

The major almost shouted with pleasure.

But there is nothing long-lived in this world and one's joy in the minute that follows the first is no longer as vivid. It further weakens during the third and finally dissolves into one's everyday state just as the circles produced on the surface of a pond by the fall of a pebble dissolve into the smooth surface. Kovalev began to ponder and realized that his troubles were not quite over: the nose had been found. That was fine; but it still had to be put back, fixed in its old place.

"And what if it doesn't stick?"

As he asked himself this question, the major turned white.

With inexpressible anxiety he leapt toward his dressing table and pulled the mirror closer, fearing that he would stick the nose on crooked. His hands trembled. Finally, with infinite hesitations and precautions he pressed the nose into place. Oh, horror! It wouldn't stick! He brought it close to his mouth and warmed it slightly with his breath. Then he placed it again on top of the smooth area between his two cheeks. But the nose would not stay on.

"Come on! Come on now! Stick—you fool!" Kovalev told the nose again and again. But the nose felt as if it were made of wood and kept falling off. And as it hit the dressing table it produced a queer light sound, like a cork. The major's face twisted spasmodically. Panic pervaded him.

"Can it possibly *not* stick?"

He repeatedly pressed the nose against the approximate spot, but his efforts were futile. Then he decided to send Ivan to fetch the doctor who occupied the best apartment in the house where the major lived.

The doctor was a fine figure of a man. He had pitch-black whiskers and a quite fresh and healthy wife. Furthermore, he ate fresh apples in the morning and kept his mouth in a state of incredible cleanliness, rinsing it for about three-quarters of an hour at a time and then brushing his teeth with five different kinds of toothbrush.

The doctor arrived within the minute. Having asked the major how long ago the misfortune had struck, he grabbed him by the chin and tweaked him so hard on the former site of his nose that Kovalev recoiled violently and banged the back of his head against the wall. The doctor said that it was quite all right and, advising him to move a bit farther away from the wall, ordered him to bend his head to the right, felt the spot vacated by the nose with his fingers and said, "Hmmm. . . ." Then he asked him to bend his head to the left, touched the spot again and said, "Hmmm. . . ." Finally the doctor delivered another tweak with his thumb and forefinger, making Kovalev toss up his head like a horse whose teeth are being inspected.

Having thus completed his examination, the doctor shook his head and declared:

"No. Can't be done. You'd better stay as you are or your condition might deteriorate even further. Of course, it is possible to stick it on. I could have stuck it on now. But, take my advice, that would make it worse for you."

"That's fine! And how can I stay without a nose? And how could I be worse off than I am? It is absolutely disgusting! And where can I show myself in this obscene condition? I have an active social life. Why, even today I was invited to two important parties. And I have many connections . . . Mrs. Chekhtareva, the wife of a state councilor, Mrs. Podtochina, the wife of a senior army officer . . . although after this business I don't want to have anything to do with her, except through the police. . . ."

And Kovalev added imploringly:

"Do me a great favor, Doctor, can't you think of a way? Make it stick somehow. It doesn't matter if it doesn't hold too well—just as long as it stays on somehow. I could even support it with my hand in case of emergency. I don't even dance, you know, and so couldn't jeopardize it by some inadvertent jerk. As to my appreciation of your services, please rest assured that in the measure of my resources—"

"Believe it or not," the doctor said neither too loudly nor too softly but with persuasiveness and magnetic force, "I never dispense my services out of material considerations. It would be contrary to my principles and to professional ethics. True, I do charge for my visits but only in order not to offend people by refusing to accept a fee. Of course I could stick your nose back on, but I assure you, on my honor, if you won't take my simple word for it, that it will be much worse. You're better off letting things take their natural course. Wash often with cold water and I assure you that you'll feel just as healthy without a nose as you felt with one. As to the nose, you can put it in a jar of alcohol or, better still, add two soup spoonfuls of vodka and warmed-up vinegar to it. I'll bet you could make money out of it. In fact, I'd purchase it myself if it weren't too expensive."

"No, no! I'll never sell it," shouted the desolate major, "I'd rather it disappeared again!"

"Forgive me," the doctor said, "I was simply trying to help. Well, I can do no more. At least you see that I tried."

The doctor departed with dignity. Kovalev had not even looked at his face; dazed as he was, he was only aware of the spotless white cuffs sticking out of the black sleeves of the doctor's frock coat.

The next day Kovalev decided to write to Mrs. Podtochina asking her to restore to him voluntarily what was rightfully his and saying that otherwise he would be forced to lodge a complaint. The letter he composed read as follows:

Dear Madam,

I am at a loss to understand your strange action. Rest assured that you will achieve nothing by acting this way, and you certainly won't force me to marry your daughter. Please believe me, madam, that I am fully aware of exactly what happened to my nose as well as of the fact that you, and nobody else, are the prime instigator of this affair. Its sudden detachment from its assigned place, its desertion, and its masquerading first as a state councilor and then in its natural shape is nothing but the result of witchcraft practiced by you or by those specialized in such pursuits. For my part, I deem it my duty to warn you that if the above-mentioned nose is not back in its proper place this very day, I shall be forced to avail myself of my rights and ask for the protection of the law.

I remain,

Faithfully yours,

Platon Kovalev

To which the lady sent an immediate reply:

My dear Platon,

I was very surprised by your letter. To be perfectly frank, I never expected anything this kind from you, especially your unfair reproaches. For your information, I have never received the state councilor you mention at my house, either in disguise or in his natural shape. However, I did receive Philip Ivanovich, but, despite the fact that he asked me for my daughter's hand and was a man of irreproachable character, sober habits, and great learning, I never held out any hopes for him. You also mention your nose. If you mean it symbolically, that I wanted you to stop nosing around my daughter, i.e., that I had decided to refuse you her hand, I am surprised at your saying such things when you are fully aware of my feelings on the subject, namely that, if you asked for her hand formally tomorrow, I would be prepared to grant your request forthwith, since it has always been in agreement with my wishes and in hope of which,

I remain,

Always at your service,

Alexandra Podtochina

"She," Kovalev said, after he had read the letter, "is certainly not involved. Someone guilty of a crime couldn't write such a letter."

And the collegiate assessor knew what he was talking about because he had taken part in several judicial investigations back in the Caucasus.

"But then, how the devil did it happen, after all? How'll I ever get it straight?" he said, dropping his arms to his sides.

In the meantime, rumors about the extraordinary occurrence spread all over the capital and, as was to be expected, not without all sorts of embellishments. At that time people were prone to fall for supernatural things: only a short time before, experiments with magnetism had caused a sensation. Also, the story about the dancing chairs of Stables Street was still fresh, and people soon began to repeat that Collegiate Assessor Kovalev's nose was to be seen taking a daily walk on Nevsky Avenue at 3:00 p.m. sharp. And every day a multitude of the curious gathered there. Then someone said that the nose was in Junker's Department Store, and, as a result, such a melee developed there that the police had to interfere. A shady character with side whiskers, who nevertheless looked very respectable, and who sold all sorts of dry cakes at the entrance to the theater, got hold of some special wooden benches, perfectly safe to stand on, and invited the curious to do so for a fee of eighty kopeks per person. A highly respected colonel, who had left his home especially early for this purpose, managed to make his way through the dense throng with great difficulty only to see in the display window not a nose but an ordinary woolen sweater and a lithograph of a girl pulling up her stocking with a well-dressed gentleman wearing a waistcoat with lapels and a small beard, a lithograph that had rested there, in the identical spot, for more than ten years. As the colonel left, he declared:

"It shouldn't be allowed—befuddling people with such stupid and improbable rumors!"

Then a rumor spread that Major Kovalev's nose was taking promenades, not on Nevsky Avenue, but in the Tavrichesky Gardens, and that it had been doing so for some time now. In fact, even when Khosrov Mirza lived there he used to marvel at this freak of nature. Students from the School of Surgeons went there. One socially prominent lady wrote a special letter to the director of the park suggesting that he show this rare object to children, if possible with explanations and instructions that would edify the younger generation.

All this was quite welcome to those who never miss a party and like to display their wit before the ladies; without it topics of conversation would have been exhausted. But there was also a dissatisfied and displeased minority among respectable people. One gentleman said he could not understand how it was possible in our enlightened age for such preposterous lies to be believed and that he was flabbergasted at the passivity of the authorities. Apparently this gentleman was one of those who desire the government to interfere in everything, including his daily fights with his wife.

Following these events . . . but here again, things become beclouded and what followed these events has remained completely unknown.

3

The world is full of absolute nonsense. Sometimes it is really unbelievable. Suddenly, the very nose that used to go around as a state councilor and caused such a stir all over the city turned up, as though nothing had happened, in its proper place, namely between the cheeks of Major Kovalev. This happened on April 7. Waking up and chancing to glance in the mirror, what did he see but his nose! He grabbed it with his hand—no doubt about it—it was his nose, all right!

"Aha!" Kovalev said.

And in his infinite joy he would have performed a jig, barefoot as he was, had not Ivan come in at that moment. He ordered Ivan to bring him some water to wash with and, while washing, looked again into the mirror: he had his nose. Drying himself with his towel, he looked again—the nose was still there!

"Here, Ivan, look, I think I have a pimple on my nose," he said, all the while thinking anxiously: "Wouldn't it be terrible if Ivan came out with something like, 'No, sir, not only is there no pimple on your nose, there is no nose on your face.'"

But Ivan simply said:

"Nothing, sir, I see no pimple, the nose is clear."

"Feels good, dammit!" the major said to himself and snapped his fingers gaily.

At that moment, through the partly opened door, there appeared the head of Ivan Yakovlevich, the barber, wearing the expression of a cat that had just been smacked for the theft of a piece of suet.

"Your hands clean?" Kovalev shouted out to him.

"They're clean, sir."

"Liar!"

"I swear they're clean."

"You know, they'd better be."

Kovalev sat down. The barber wrapped a towel around his neck and in one instant transformed the major's whiskers and a part of his cheek into whipped cream of the kind that is likely to be served at a birthday party in the house of a rich merchant.

"Well, I'll be damned!" Ivan Yakovlevich muttered under his breath, looking at the nose. Then he turned the major's head and looked at the nose from the other side and muttered. "Well, well, well . . . who would have thought . . ." and he stared at the nose for a moment.

Then, with a daintiness that can only be imagined, he lifted two fingers to catch the nose by its tip. Such was Ivan Yakovlevich's shaving style.

"Look out, look out, careful!" Kovalev shouted and Ivan Yakovlevich dropped his hand and stood there frozen and embarrassed as never before.

Finally he snapped out of it and started carefully tickling the major under his chin with the razor. And although it felt quite awkward and unusual for him to shave someone without holding him by the olfactory organ of the human body, he managed, somehow, by resting his rough thumb on Kovalev's cheek, then on his lower gum, to overcome all the obstacles and complete the shaving operation.

When he was through being shaved, Kovalev hurried to get dressed, rushed out, took a cab, and drove to the tearoom. Before even sitting down, he shouted: "Waiter, a cup of chocolate!" then rushed over to the mirror: the nose was there. Happy, he glanced around the room and twisted his face into a sarcastic expression by slightly screwing up his eyes, when he saw two army officers, one of whom had a nose about the size of a waistcoat button. Then he left for the department through which he was trying to get the vice gubernatorial post or, failing that, a position in the administration. Walking through the reception room, he glanced in the mirror: the nose was in its place.

Then he drove to see another collegiate assessor, that is, a major like himself. This major was a biting wit, and, parrying his digs, Kovalev would often say to him:

"Oh, I see through you clearly, you needler!"

On his way there, Kovalev thought: "Now, if the major does not split his sides with laughter when he sees me, that will be a sure sign that whatever I may have is sitting in its proper place."

And when the other collegiate assessor showed no signs of hilarity, Kovalev thought:

"Fine! It feels good, it feels good, dammit!"

In the street he met Mrs. Podtochina and her daughter and was greeted with joyful exclamations, which went to show that they did not find he was missing anything. He had a very long talk with them and, on purpose, took out his snuffbox and filled his nose with great deliberation, through both orifices, muttering under his breath:

"Here, look and admire, you hens! But still, I won't marry the daughter, just paramour as they say, but nothing more. . . ."

And from then on, Major Kovalev could be seen on Nevsky Avenue, in theaters, everywhere. And the nose was there, sitting on his face, as though nothing had happened. And after that, Major Kovalev was always in good spirits, smiling, pursuing absolutely every pretty lady without exception and even stopping one day in front of a small shop and purchasing some sort of ribbon for his lapel, although his reason for doing so remained a mystery because he had never been made a knight of any order.

So that's what happened in the northern capital of our vast country. Only now, on further thought, do we see that there is much that is improbable in it. Without even mentioning the strangeness of such a supernatural severance of the nose and its appearance in various places in the form of a state councilor, how could Kovalev have failed to understand that he could not go and advertise about a nose in the press? I don't mean that I think that an advertisement would have cost too much, that would be nonsense and I'm not stingy; but it's not decent, it's not clever, and it's not proper! And then too, how could the nose have got into the roll of bread, and how could Ivan Yakovlevich himself? . . . Now, that I cannot understand. It's absolutely beyond me. But strangest of all, the most incomprehensible thing, is that there are authors who can choose such subjects to write about. This, I confess, is completely inexplicable, it's like . . . no, no, I can't understand it at all. In the first place, there is absolutely no advantage in it for our mother country. Secondly . . . well, what advantage is there in it at all? I simply cannot understand what it is. . . .

However, when all is said and done, and although, of course, we conceive the possibility, one and the other, and maybe even . . . Well, but then what exists without inconsistencies? And still, if you give it a thought, there *is* something to it. Whatever you may say, such things *do* happen—seldom, but they do.

QUESTIONS

1. Why does the story begin with Yakovlevich, Kovalev's barber, finding a nose in a loaf of bread?

2. Why is Ivan Yakovlevich described as "more dead than alive"? (44)

3. Why does getting rid of the nose that appeared in his bread prove so difficult for Yakovlevich?

4. Why do the first and second parts of the story end with the narrator declaring that "the incident becomes befogged" and that "things become beclouded"? (45,60)

5. Why is Kovalev's nose seen wearing a state councilor's uniform?

6. When Kovalev approaches the nose, why does he say to it, "you ought to know where you belong"? (48)

7. Why does Kovalev go to the police instead of a doctor when he realizes his nose is missing?

8. Why does Kovalev say that losing his nose is worse than losing other parts of his body because, without a nose, "a man is not a man but God knows what"? (54)

9. Why does Kovalev think that, because he has not agreed to marry her daughter, Podtochina may be to blame for the loss of his nose?

10. In his letter to Podtochina, why does Kovalev describe his nose as "masquerading first as a state councilor and then in its natural shape"? (59)

11. After Kovalev recovers his nose and the doctor advises against putting it back on his face, why does he wake up to find it suddenly back in place, "as though nothing had happened"? (62)

12. After his nose returns, why does Kovalev expect to be told at any moment that it is gone again?

13. Near the end of the story, the narrator says of its many implausible elements, "It's absolutely beyond me." (63) What is beyond him?

14. When the narrator says of his story, "there *is* something to it," is he trying to convince himself or us that this is the case? If he is right, what is there to his story? (63)

15. How are we to understand the narrator's assertion at the end of the story that "such things *do* happen"? (63)

FOR FURTHER REFLECTION

1. What part does your body play in your sense of who you are?

2. How much of your identity is dependent on how others think of you?

3. What most determines your status in society?

4. Why do we tend to assume there is an explanation for every phenomenon? What are the advantages and disadvantages of this tendency?

5. How does the reliability of a story's narrator affect your interpretation of the story?

FYODOR DOSTOEVSKY

The life and works of Fyodor Dostoevsky (1821–1881) reflect the unresolved turmoil and extremes of nineteenth-century Russian society. Dominated by his mercurial father, an ennobled but impoverished army surgeon, Dostoevsky trained as a military engineer. Only after his father's violent death did he openly reject military service and devote himself entirely to writing. Although celebrated throughout his literary career, he endured the hardships of financial insecurity, arrest in 1849 for political activities, a firing squad and last minute reprieve, and imprisonment in a Siberian labor camp. He was pardoned by Czar Alexander II after serving four years of hard labor and ultimately returned to St. Petersburg.

Despite the acclaim that greeted publication of his works, he was continuously hounded by personal crises. He was plagued by epilepsy, and a ruinous gambling addiction forced him and his young wife to flee Russia in the late 1860s to escape creditors. After they returned in 1871, his wife, Anna Grigorievna, whom he had originally hired as a stenographer, took over his business affairs. At last they began to enjoy some financial and domestic stability, but it was short-lived. Their son Alexei, born in 1875, died three years later. Dostoevsky began work on a serialized form of *The Brothers Karamazov* a month after Alexei's death and completed it in 1880, a year before his own death. The novel has been described as the "most intensely personal" of Dostoevsky's works.

The specific experience in Dostoevsky's life that laid the groundwork for the novel had taken place some twenty-five years earlier. While serving part of his sentence in Omsk prison, Dostoevsky had experienced a religious and spiritual awakening, which permanently shifted his earlier political stance of a young utopian radical to that of a "Slavophile" conservative. But Dostoevsky was no simple convert. In a letter to a friend he wrote, "I will tell you that . . . one thirsts like 'parched grass' for faith and finds it precisely because truth shines in misfortune. I will tell you regarding myself that I am a child of the age, a child of nonbelief and doubt up till now and even (I know it) until my coffin closes." Throughout *The Brothers Karamazov*, Dostoevsky confronts us with unceasing ambiguity. Characters articulating clear ideas and beliefs are set up, only to be challenged by juxtaposition with their opposites. In one of the most famous excerpts from *The Brothers Karamazov*, titled "The Grand Inquisitor," the tension between religious faith and unbelief is given one of its fullest expressions.

By the end of his life, Dosteovsky was being feted at court and had become a darling of St. Petersburg's aristocratic salons, yet his work reflects a profoundly modern consciousness. Although he died well before the end of the nineteenth century, he has been read as a precursor of both psychoanalysis and existentialism. His iconic status for the Russian people was expressed in a funeral of majestic proportions. According to one authority, "30,000 people accompanied his coffin, seventy delegations carried wreaths and fifteen choirs took part in the procession."

FYODOR DOSTOEVSKY

The Grand Inquisitor

But here, too, it's impossible to do without a preface, a literary preface, that is—pah!" Ivan laughed, "and what sort of writer am I! You see, my action takes place in the sixteenth century, and back then—by the way, you must have learned this in school—back then it was customary in poetic works to bring higher powers down to earth. I don't need to mention Dante. In France, court clerks, as well as monks in the monasteries, gave whole performances in which they brought the Madonna, angels, saints, Christ, and God himself on stage. At the time it was all done quite artlessly. In Victor Hugo's *Notre Dame de Paris*, in the Paris of Louis XI, to honor the birth of the French dauphin, an edifying performance is given free of charge for the people in the city hall, entitled *Le bon jugement de la très sainte et gracieuse Vierge Marie*, in which she herself appears in person and pronounces her *bon jugement*. With us in Moscow, in pre-Petrine antiquity, much the same kind of dramatic performances, especially from the Old Testament, were given from time to time; but, besides dramatic performances, there were many stories and 'verses' floating around the world in which saints, angels, and all the powers of heaven took part as needed. In our monasteries such poems were translated, recopied, even composed—and when?—under the Tartars. There is, for example, one little monastery poem (from the Greek, of course): *The Mother of God Visits the Torments*, with scenes of a boldness not inferior to Dante's. The Mother of God visits hell and the Archangel Michael guides her through 'the torments.' She sees sinners and their sufferings. Among them, by the way, there is a most amusing class of sinners in a burning lake: some of them sink so far down into the lake that they can no longer come up again, and 'these God forgets'—an expression of extraordinary depth and force. And so the Mother of God, shocked and weeping, falls before the throne of God and asks pardon for everyone in hell, everyone she has seen there, without distinction. Her conversation with God is immensely interesting. She pleads, she won't go away, and when God points out to her the nail-pierced hands and feet of her Son and asks: 'How can I forgive his tormentors?' she bids all the saints, all the martyrs, all the angels

69

and archangels to fall down together with her and plead for the pardon of all without discrimination. In the end she extorts from God a cessation of torments every year, from Holy Friday to Pentecost, and the sinners in hell at once thank the Lord and cry out to him: 'Just art thou, O Lord, who hast judged so.' Well, my little poem would have been of the same kind if it had appeared back then. He comes onstage in it; actually, he says nothing in the poem, he just appears and passes on. Fifteen centuries have gone by since he gave the promise to come in his Kingdom, fifteen centuries since his prophet wrote: 'Behold, I come quickly.' 'Of that day and that hour knoweth not even the Son, but only my heavenly Father,' as he himself declared while still on earth. But mankind awaits him with the same faith and the same tender emotion. Oh, even with greater faith, for fifteen centuries have gone by since men ceased to receive pledges from heaven:

> Believe what the heart tells you,
> For heaven offers no pledge.

Only faith in what the heart tells you! True, there were also many miracles then. There were saints who performed miraculous healings; to some righteous men, according to their biographies, the Queen of Heaven herself came down. But the devil never rests, and there had already arisen in mankind some doubt as to the authenticity of these miracles. Just then, in the north, in Germany, a horrible new heresy appeared. A great star, 'like a lamp' (that is, the church), 'fell upon the fountains of waters, and they were made bitter.' These heretics began blasphemously denying miracles. But those who still believed became all the more ardent in their belief. The tears of mankind rose up to him as before, they waited for him, loved him, hoped in him, yearned to suffer and die for him as before . . . And for so many centuries mankind had been pleading with faith and fire: 'God our Lord, reveal thyself to us,' for so many centuries they had been calling out to him, that he in his immeasurable compassion desired to descend to those who were pleading. He had descended even before then, he had visited some righteous men, martyrs, and holy hermits while they were still on earth, as is written in their 'lives.' Our own Tyutchev, who deeply believed in the truth of his words, proclaimed that:

> Bent under the burden of the Cross,
> The King of Heaven in the form of a slave
> Walked the length and breadth of you,
> Blessing you, my native land.

It must needs have been so, let me tell you. And so he desired to appear to people if only for a moment—to his tormented, suffering people, rank with sin but loving him like children. My action is set in Spain, in Seville, in the most horrible time of the Inquisition, when fires blazed every day to the glory of God, and

> In the splendid auto-da-fé
> Evil heretics were burnt.

Oh, of course, this was not that coming in which he will appear, according to his promise, at the end of time, in all his heavenly glory, and which will be as sudden 'as the lightning that shineth out of the east unto the west.' No, he desired to visit his children if only for a moment and precisely where the fires of the heretics had begun to crackle. In his infinite mercy he walked once again among men, in the same human image in which he had walked for three years among men fifteen centuries earlier. He came down to the 'scorched squares' of a southern town where just the day before, in a 'splendid auto-da-fé,' in the presence of the king, the court, knights, cardinals, and the loveliest court ladies, before the teeming populace of all Seville, the Cardinal Grand Inquisitor had burned almost a hundred heretics at once *ad majorem gloriam Dei*. He appeared quietly, inconspicuously, but, strange to say, everyone recognized him. This could be one of the best passages in the poem, I mean, why it is exactly that they recognize him. People are drawn to him by an invincible force, they flock to him, surround him, follow him. He passes silently among them with a quiet smile of infinite compassion. The sun of love shines in his heart, rays of light, enlightenment, and power stream from his eyes and, pouring over the people, shake their hearts with responding love. He stretches forth his hands to them, blesses them, and from the touch of him, even only of his garments, comes a healing power. Here an old man, blind from childhood, calls out from the crowd: 'Lord, heal me so that I, too, can see you,' and it is as if the scales fell from his eyes, and the blind man sees him. People weep and kiss the earth he walks upon. Children throw down flowers before him, sing, and cry 'Hosanna!' to him. 'It's he, it's really he,' everyone repeats, 'it must be he, it can be no one but he.' He stops at the porch of the Seville cathedral at the very moment when a child's little, open, white coffin is being brought in with weeping: in it lies a seven-year-old girl, the only daughter of a noble citizen. The dead child is covered with flowers. 'He will raise your child,' people in the crowd shout to the weeping mother. The cathedral padre, who has come out to meet the coffin, looks perplexed and frowns. Suddenly a wail comes from the dead child's mother. She throws herself down at his feet: 'If it is you, then raise my child!' she exclaims, stretching her hands out to him. The procession halts, the little coffin is lowered down onto the porch at his feet. He looks with compassion and his lips once again softly utter: '*Talitha cumi*'—'and the damsel arose.'[1] The girl rises in her coffin, sits up and, smiling, looks around her in wide-eyed astonishment. She is still holding the bunch of white roses with which she had been lying in the coffin. There is a commotion among the people, cries, weeping, and at this very moment the Cardinal Grand Inquisitor himself crosses the square in front of the cathedral. He is an old man, almost ninety, tall and straight, with a gaunt face and sunken eyes, from which a glitter still shines like a fiery spark. Oh, he is not wearing his magnificent cardinal's robes in which he had displayed himself to the people the day before, when the enemies of the Roman faith were burned—no, at this moment he is wearing only his old, coarse monastic cassock. He is followed at a certain distance by his grim assistants and slaves, and by the 'holy' guard. At the sight of the crowd he stops and watches from afar. He has seen everything, seen the coffin set down at his feet, seen the girl rise, and his face darkens. He scowls with his thick, gray eyebrows, and his eyes shine with a sinister fire. He stretches forth his finger and orders the guard to take him. And such is his power, so tamed, submissive, and tremblingly obedient to his will are the people, that the crowd immediately parts before the guard, and they, amidst the deathly silence that has suddenly fallen, lay their hands on him and lead him away. As one man the crowd immediately bows to the ground before the aged Inquisitor, who silently blesses the people and moves on. The guard lead their prisoner to the small, gloomy, vaulted prison in the old building of the holy court and lock him there. The day is over, the Seville night comes, dark, hot, and 'breathless.' The air is 'fragrant with laurel and lemon.' In the deep darkness, the iron door of the prison suddenly opens, and the old Grand Inquisitor himself slowly enters carrying a lamp. He is alone, the door is immediately locked behind him. He stands in the entrance and for a long time, for a minute or two, gazes into his face. At last he quietly approaches, sets the lamp on the table, and says to him: 'Is it you? You?' But receiving no answer, he quickly adds: 'Do not answer, be silent. After all, what could you say? I know too well what you would say. And you have no right to add anything to what you already said once. Why, then, have you come to interfere with us? For you have come to interfere with us and you know it yourself. But do you know what will happen tomorrow? I do not know who you are, and I do not want to know: whether it is you, or only his likeness; but tomorrow I shall condemn you and burn you at the stake as the most evil of heretics, and the very people who today kissed your feet, tomorrow, at a nod from me, will rush to heap the coals up around your stake, do you know that? Yes, perhaps you do know it,' he added, pondering deeply, never for a moment taking his eyes from his prisoner."

1.[*Talitha cumi*: "damsel arise" in Aramaic: Mark 5:40–42.—TRANS.]

"I don't quite understand what this is, Ivan," Alyosha, who all the while had been listening silently, smiled. "Is it boundless fantasy, or some mistake on the old man's part, some impossible quid pro quo?"[2]

"Assume it's the latter, if you like," Ivan laughed, "if you're so spoiled by modern realism and can't stand anything fantastic—if you want it to be quid pro quo, let it be. Of course," he laughed again, "the man is ninety years old and might have lost his mind long ago over his idea. He might have been struck by the prisoner's appearance. It might, finally, have been simple delirium, the vision of a ninety-year-old man nearing death, and who is excited, besides, by the auto-da-fé of a hundred burnt heretics the day before. But isn't it all the same to you and me whether it's quid pro quo or boundless fantasy? The only thing is that the old man needs to speak out, that finally after all his ninety years, he speaks out, and says aloud all that he has been silent about for ninety years."

"And the prisoner is silent, too? Just looks at him without saying a word?"

"But that must be so in any case," Ivan laughed again. "The old man himself points out to him that he has no right to add anything to what has already been said once. That, if you like, is the most basic feature of Roman Catholicism, in my opinion at least: 'Everything,' they say, 'has been handed over by you to the pope, therefore everything now belongs to the pope, and you may as well not come at all now, or at least don't interfere with us for the time being.' They not only speak this way, they also write this way, at least the Jesuits do. I've read it in their theologians myself. 'Have you the right to proclaim to us even one of the mysteries of that world from which you have come?' my old man asks him, and answers the question himself: 'No, you have not, so as not to add to what has already been said once, and so as not to deprive people of freedom, for which you stood so firmly when you were on earth. Anything you proclaim anew will encroach upon the freedom of men's faith, for it will come as a miracle, and the freedom of their faith was the dearest of all things to you, even then, one-and-a-half thousand years ago. Was it not you who so often said then: "I want to make you free"? But now you have seen these "free" men,' the old man suddenly adds with a pensive smile. 'Yes, this work has cost us dearly,' he goes on, looking sternly at him, 'but we have finally finished this work in your name. For fifteen hundred years we have been at pains over this freedom, but now it is finished, and well finished. You do not believe that it is well finished? You look at me meekly and do not deign even to be indignant with me. Know, then, that now, precisely now, these people are more certain than ever before that they are completely free, and at the same time they themselves have brought us their freedom and obediently laid it at our feet. It is our doing, but is it what you wanted? This sort of freedom?'"

2.[*quid pro quo*: Latin legal term: "one for another, " i.e., mistaken identity.—TRANS.]

"Again I don't understand," Alyosha interrupted. "Is he being ironic? Is he laughing?"

"Not in the least. He precisely lays it to his and his colleagues' credit that they have finally overcome freedom, and have done so in order to make people happy. 'For only now' (he is referring, of course, to the Inquisition) 'has it become possible to think for the first time about human happiness. Man was made a rebel; can rebels be happy? You were warned,' he says to him, 'you had no lack of warnings and indications, but you did not heed the warnings, you rejected the only way of arranging for human happiness, but fortunately, on your departure, you handed the work over to us. You promised, you established with your word, you gave us the right to bind and loose, and surely you cannot even think of taking this right away from us now. Why, then, have you come to interfere with us?'"

"What does it mean, that he had no lack of warnings and indications?" Alyosha asked.

"You see, that is the main thing that the old man needs to speak about.

"'The dread and intelligent spirit, the spirit of self-destruction and nonbeing,' the old man goes on, 'the great spirit spoke with you in the wilderness, and it has been passed on to us in books that he supposedly "tempted" you. Did he really? And was it possible to say anything more true than what he proclaimed to you in his three questions, which you rejected, and which the books refer to as "temptations"? And at the same time, if ever a real, thundering miracle was performed on earth, it was on that day, the day of those three temptations. The miracle lay precisely in the appearance of those three questions. If it were possible to imagine, just as a trial and an example, that those three questions of the dread spirit had been lost from the books without a trace, and it was necessary that they be restored, thought up and invented anew, to be put back into the books, and to that end all the wise men on earth—rulers, high priests, scholars, philosophers, poets—were brought together and given this task: to think up, to invent three questions such as would not only correspond to the scale of the event, but, moreover, would express in three words, in three human phrases only, the entire future history of the world and mankind—do you think that all the combined wisdom of the earth could think up anything faintly resembling in force and depth those three questions that were actually presented to you then by the powerful and intelligent spirit in the wilderness? By the questions alone, simply by the miracle of their appearance, one can see that one is dealing with a mind not human and transient but eternal and absolute. For in these three questions all of subsequent human history is as if brought together into a single whole and foretold; three images are revealed that will take in all the insoluble historical contradictions of human nature over all the earth. This could not have been seen so well at the time, for the future was unknown, but now that fifteen centuries have gone by, we can see that in these three questions everything was so precisely divined and foretold, and has proved so completely true, that to add to them or subtract anything from them is impossible.

"'Decide yourself who was right: you or the one who questioned you then? Recall the first question; its meaning, though not literally, was this: "You want to go into the world, and you are going empty-handed, with some promise of freedom, which they in their simplicity and innate lawlessness cannot even comprehend, which they dread and fear—for nothing has ever been more insufferable for man and for human society than freedom! But do you see these stones in this bare, scorching desert? Turn them into bread and mankind will run after you like sheep, grateful and obedient, though eternally trembling lest you withdraw your hand and your loaves cease for them." But you did not want to deprive man of freedom and rejected the offer, for what sort of freedom is it, you reasoned, if obedience is bought with loaves of bread? You objected that man does not live by bread alone, but do you know that in the name of this very earthly bread, the spirit of the earth will rise against you and fight with you and defeat you, and everyone will follow him exclaiming: "Who can compare to this beast, for he has given us fire from heaven!" Do you know that centuries will pass and mankind will proclaim with the mouth of its wisdom and science that there is no crime, and therefore no sin, but only hungry men? "Feed them first, then ask virtue of them!"—that is what they will write on the banner they raise against you, and by which your temple will be destroyed. In place of your temple a new edifice will be raised, the terrible Tower of Babel will be raised again, and though, like the former one, this one will not be completed either, still you could have avoided this new tower and shortened people's suffering by a thousand years—for it is to us they will come after suffering for a thousand years with their tower! They will seek us out again, underground, in catacombs, hiding (for again we shall be persecuted and tortured), they will find us and cry out: "Feed us, for those who promised us fire from heaven did not give it." And then we shall finish building their tower, for only he who feeds them will finish it, and only we shall feed them, in your name, for we shall lie that it is in your name. Oh, never, never will they feed themselves without us! No science will give them bread as long as they remain free, but in the end they will lay their freedom at our feet and say to us: "Better that you enslave us, but feed us." They will finally understand that freedom and earthly bread in plenty for everyone are inconceivable together, for never, never will they be able to share among themselves. They will also be convinced that they are forever incapable of being free, because they are feeble, depraved, nonentities, and rebels. You promised them heavenly bread, but, I repeat again, can it compare with earthly bread in the eyes of the weak, eternally depraved, and eternally ignoble human race? And if in the name of heavenly bread thousands and tens of thousands will follow you, what will become of the millions and tens of thousands of millions of creatures who will not be strong enough to forgo earthly bread for the sake of the heavenly? Is it that only the tens of thousands of the great and strong are dear to you, and the remaining millions, numerous as the sands of the sea, weak but loving you, should serve only as material for the great and the strong? No, the weak, too, are dear to us. They are depraved and rebels, but in the end it is they who will become obedient. They will marvel at us, and look upon us as gods, because we, standing at their head, have agreed to suffer freedom and to rule over them—so terrible will it become for them in the end to be free! But we shall say that we are obedient to you and rule in your name. We shall deceive them again, for this time we shall not allow you to come to us. This deceit will constitute our suffering, for we shall have to lie. This is what that first question in the wilderness meant, and this is what you rejected in the name of freedom, which you placed above everything. And yet this question contains the great mystery of this world. Had you accepted the "loaves," you would have answered the universal and everlasting anguish of man as an individual being, and of the whole of mankind together, namely: "before whom shall I bow down?" There is no more ceaseless or tormenting care for man, as long as he remains free, than to find someone to bow down to as soon as possible. But man seeks to bow down before that which is indisputable, so indisputable that all men at once would agree to the univesal worship of it. For the care of these pitiful creatures is not just to find something before which I or some other man can bow down, but to find something that everyone else will also believe in and bow down to, for it must needs be *all together*. And this need for *communality* of worship is the chief torment of each man individually, and of mankind as a whole, from the beginning of the ages. In the cause of universal worship, they have destroyed each other with the sword. They have made gods and called upon each other: "Abandon your gods and come and worship ours, otherwise death to you and your gods!" And so it will be until the end of the world, even when all gods have disappeared from the earth: they will still fall down before idols. You knew, you could not but know, this essential mystery of human nature, but you rejected the only absolute banner, which was offered to you to make all men bow down to you indisputably—the banner of earthly bread; and you rejected it in the name of freedom and heavenly bread. Now see what you did next. And all again in the name of freedom! I tell you that man has no more tormenting care than to find someone to whom he can hand over as quickly as possible that gift of freedom with which the miserable creature is born. But he alone can take over the freedom of men who appeases their conscience. With bread you were given an indisputable banner: give man bread and he will bow down to you, for there is nothing more indisputable than bread. But if at the same time someone else takes over his conscience—oh, then he will even throw down your bread and follow him who has seduced his conscience. In this you were right. For the mystery of man's being is not only in living, but in what one lives for. Without a firm idea of what he lives for, man will not consent to live and will sooner destroy himself than remain on earth, even if there is bread all around him. That is so, but what came of it? Instead of taking over men's freedom, you increased it still more for them! Did you forget that peace and even death are dearer to man than free choice in the knowledge of good and evil? There is nothing more seductive for man than the freedom of his conscience, but there is nothing more tormenting either. And so, instead of a firm foundation for appeasing human conscience once and for all, you chose everything that was unusual, enigmatic, and indefinite, you chose everything that was beyond men's strength, and thereby acted as if you did not love them at all—and who did this? He who came to give his life for them! Instead of taking over men's freedom, you increased it and forever burdened the kingdom of the human soul with its torments. You desired the free love of man, that he should follow you freely, seduced and captivated by you. Instead of the firm ancient law, man had henceforth to decide for himself, with a free heart, what is good and what is evil, having only your image before him as a guide—but did it not occur to you that he would eventually reject and dispute even your image and your truth if he was oppressed by so terrible a burden as freedom of choice? They will finally cry out that the truth is not in you, for it was impossible to leave them in greater confusion and torment than you did, abandoning them to so many cares and insoluble problems. Thus you yourself laid the foundation for the destruction of your own kingdom, and do not blame anyone else for it. Yet is this what was offered you? There are three powers, only three powers on earth, capable of conquering and holding captive forever the conscience of these feeble rebels, for their own happiness—these powers are miracle, mystery, and authority. You rejected the first, the second, and the third, and gave yourself as an example of that. When the dread and wise spirit set you on a pinnacle of the Temple and said to you: "If you would know whether or not you are the Son of God, cast yourself down; for it is written of him, that the angels will bear him up, and he will not fall or be hurt, and then you will know whether you are the Son of God, and will prove what faith you have in your Father." But you heard and rejected the offer and did not yield and did not throw yourself down. Oh, of course, in this you acted proudly and magnificently, like God, but mankind, that weak, rebellious tribe—are they gods? Oh, you knew then that if you made just one step, just one movement toward throwing yourself down, you would immediately have tempted the Lord and would have lost all faith in him and been dashed against the earth you came to save, and the intelligent spirit who was tempting you would rejoice. But, I repeat, are there many like you?

And, indeed, could you possibly have assumed, even for a moment, that mankind, too, would be strong enough for such a temptation? Is that how human nature was created—to reject the miracle, and in those terrible moments of life, the moments of the most terrible, essential, and torment-ing questions of the soul, to remain only with the free decision of the heart? Oh, you knew that your deed would be preserved in books, would reach the depths of the ages and the utmost limits of the earth, and you hoped that, following you, man, too, would remain with God, having no need of miracles. But you did not know that as soon as man rejects miracles, he will at once reject God as well, for man seeks not so much God as miracles. And since man cannot bear to be left without miracles, he will go and create new miracles for himself, his own miracles this time, and will bow down to the miracles of quacks, or women's magic, though he be rebellious, heretical, and godless a hundred times over. You did not come down from the cross when they shouted to you, mocking and reviling you: "Come down from the cross and we will believe that it is you." You did not come down because, again, you did not want to enslave man by a miracle and thirsted for faith that is free, not miraculous. You thirsted for love that is free, and not for the servile raptures of a slave before a power that has left him permanently terrified. But here, too, you overestimated mankind, for, of course, they are slaves, though they were created rebels. Behold and judge, now that fifteen centuries have passed, take a look at them: whom have you raised up to yourself? I swear, man is created weaker and baser than you thought him! How, how can he ever accomplish the same things as you? Respecting him so much, you behaved as if you had ceased to be compas-sionate, because you demanded too much of him—and who did this? He who loved him more than himself! Respecting him less, you would have demanded less of him, and that would be closer to love, for his burden would be lighter. He is weak and mean. What matter that he now rebels everywhere against our power, and takes pride in this rebellion? The pride of a child and a schoolboy! They are little children, who rebel in class and drive out the teacher. But there will also come an end to the children's delight, and it will cost them dearly. They will tear down the temples and drench the earth with blood. But finally the foolish children will understand that although they are rebels, they are feeble rebels, who cannot endure their own rebellion. Pouring out their foolish tears, they will finally acknowledge that he who created them rebels no doubt intended to laugh at them. They will say it in despair, and what they say will be a blasphemy that will make them even more unhappy, for human nature cannot bear blasphemy and in the end always takes revenge for it. And so, turmoil, confusion, and unhappiness—these are the present lot of mankind, after you suffered so much for their freedom! Your great prophet tells in a vision and an allegory that he saw all those who took part in the first resurrection and that they were twelve thousand from each tribe. But even if there were so many, they, too, were not like men, as it were, but gods. They endured your cross, they endured scores of years of hungry and naked wilderness, eating locusts and roots, and of course you can point with pride to these children of freedom, of free love, of free and magnificent sacrifice in your name. But remember that there were only several thousand of them, and they were gods. What of the rest? Is it the fault of the rest of feeble mankind that they could not endure what the mighty endured? Is it the fault of the weak soul that it is unable to contain such terrible gifts? Can it be that you indeed came only to the chosen ones and for the chosen ones? But if so, there is a mystery here, and we cannot understand it. And if it is a mystery, then we, too, had the right to preach mystery and to teach them that it is not the free choice of the heart that matters, and not love, but the mystery, which they must blindly obey, even setting aside their own conscience. And so we did. We corrected your deed and based it on *miracle*, *mystery*, and *authority*. And mankind rejoiced that they were once more led like sheep, and that at last such a terrible gift, which had brought them so much suffering, had been taken from their hearts. Tell me, were we right in teaching and doing so? Have we not, indeed, loved mankind, in so humbly recognizing their impotence, in so lovingly alleviating their burden and allowing their feeble nature even to sin, with our permission? Why have you come to interfere with us now? And why are you looking at me so silently and understandingly with your meek eyes? Be angry! I do not want your love, for I do not love you. And what can I hide from you? Do I not know with whom I am speaking? What I have to tell you is all known to you already, I can read it in your eyes. And is it for me to hide our secret from you? Perhaps you precisely want to hear it from my lips. Listen, then: we are not with you, but with *him*, that is our secret! For a long time now— eight centuries already—we have not been with you, but with *him*. Exactly eight centuries ago we took from him what you so indignantly rejected,[3] that last gift he offered you when he showed you all the kingdoms of the earth: we took Rome and the sword of Caesar from him, and proclaimed ourselves sole rulers of the earth, the only rulers, though we have not yet succeeded in bringing our cause to its full conclusion. But whose fault is that? Oh, this work is still in its very beginnings, but it has begun. There is still long to wait before its completion, and the earth still has much to suffer, but we shall accomplish it and we shall be caesars, and then we shall think about the universal happiness of mankind. And yet you could have taken the sword of Caesar even then. Why did you reject that last gift? Had

---

3.[*Exactly eight centuries ago . . .* : in 755 A.D., eight centuries before the Inquisitor's time (mid-sixteenth century), Pepin the Short, king of the Franks, took the Byzantine exarchate of Ravenna and the Pentapolis ("five cities": i.e., Rimini, Pesaro, Fano, Sinnigaglia, and Ancona) from the Lombards and turned the territories over to Pope Stephen II, thus initiating the secular power of the papacy. —TRANS.]

you accepted that third counsel of the mighty spirit, you would have furnished all that man seeks on earth, that is: someone to bow down to, someone to take over his conscience, and a means for uniting everyone at last into a common, concordant, and incontestable anthill—for the need for universal union is the third and last torment of men. Mankind in its entirety has always yearned to arrange things so that they must be universal. There have been many great nations with great histories, but the higher these nations stood, the unhappier they were, for they were more strongly aware than others of the need for a universal union of mankind. Great conquerors, Tamerlanes and Genghis Khans, swept over the earth like a whirlwind, yearning to conquer the cosmos, but they, too, expressed, albeit unconsciously, the same great need of mankind for universal and general union. Had you accepted the world and Caesar's purple, you would have founded a universal kingdom and granted universal peace. For who shall possess mankind if not those who possess their conscience and give them their bread! And so we took Caesar's sword, and in taking it, of course, we rejected you and followed *him*. Oh, there will be centuries more of the lawlessness of free reason, of their science and anthropophagy—for, having begun to build their Tower of Babel without us, they will end in anthropophagy. And it is then that the beast will come crawling to us and lick our feet and spatter them with tears of blood from its eyes. And we shall sit upon the beast and raise the cup, and on it will be written: "Mystery!" But then, and then only, will the kingdom of peace and happiness come for mankind. You are proud of your chosen ones, but you have only your chosen ones, while we will pacify all. And there is still more: how many among those chosen ones, the strong ones who might have become chosen ones, have finally grown tired of waiting for you, and have brought and will yet bring the powers of their spirit and the ardor of their hearts to another field, and will end by raising their *free* banner against you! But you raised that banner yourself. With us everyone will be happy, and they will no longer rebel or destroy each other, as in your freedom, everywhere. Oh, we shall convince them that they will only become free when they resign their freedom to us, and submit to us. Will we be right, do you think, or will we be lying? They themselves will be convinced that we are right, for they will remember to what horrors of slavery and confusion your freedom led them. Freedom, free reason, and science will lead them into such a maze, and confront them with such miracles and insoluble mysteries, that some of them, unruly and ferocious, will exterminate themselves; others, unruly but feeble, will exterminate each other; and the remaining third, feeble and wretched, will crawl to our feet and cry out to us: "Yes, you were right, you alone possess his mystery, and we are coming back to you—save us from ourselves." Receiving bread from us, they will see clearly, of course, that we take from them the bread they have procured with their own hands, in order to distribute it among them, without any miracle; they will see that we have not turned stones into bread; but, indeed, more than over the bread itself, they will rejoice over taking it from our hands! For they will remember only too well that before, without us, the very bread they procured for themselves turned to stones in their hands, and when they came back to us, the very stones in their hands turned to bread. Too well, far too well, will they appreciate what it means to submit once and for all! And until men understand this, they will be unhappy. Who contributed most of all to this lack of understanding, tell me? Who broke up the flock and scattered it upon paths unknown? But the flock will gather again, and again submit, and this time once and for all. Then we shall give them quiet, humble happiness, the happiness of feeble creatures, such as they were created. Oh, we shall finally convince them not to be proud, for you raised them up and thereby taught them pride; we shall prove to them that they are feeble, that they are only pitiful children, but that a child's happiness is sweeter than any other. They will become timid and look to us and cling to us in fear, like chicks to a hen. They will marvel and stand in awe of us and be proud that we are so powerful and so intelligent as to have been able to subdue a tempestuous flock of thousands of millions. They will tremble limply before our wrath, their minds will grow timid, their eyes will become as tearful as children's or women's, but just as readily at a gesture from us they will pass over to gaiety and laughter, to bright joy and happy children's song. Yes, we will make them work, but in the hours free from labor we will arrange their lives like a children's game, with children's songs, choruses, and innocent dancing. Oh, we will allow them to sin, too; they are weak and powerless, and they will love us like children for allowing them to sin. We will tell them that every sin will be redeemed if it is committed with our permission; and that we allow them to sin because we love them, and as for the punishment for these sins, very well, we take it upon ourselves. And we will take it upon ourselves, and they will adore us as benefactors, who have borne their sins before God. And they will have no secrets from us. We will allow or forbid them to live with their wives and mistresses, to have or not to have children—all depending on their obedience—and they will submit to us gladly and joyfully. The most tormenting secrets of their conscience— all, all they will bring to us, and we will decide all things, and they will joyfully believe our decision, because it will deliver them from their great care and their present terrible torments of personal and free decision. And everyone will be happy, all the millions of creatures, except for the hundred thousand of those who govern them. For only we, we who keep the mystery, only we shall be unhappy. There will be thousands of millions of happy babes, and a hundred thousand sufferers who have taken upon themselves the curse of the knowledge of good and evil. Peacefully they will die, peacefully they will expire in your name, and beyond the grave they will find only death. But we will keep the secret, and for their own happiness we will entice them with a heavenly and eternal reward. For even if there were anything in the next world, it would not, of course, be for such as they. It is said and prophesied that you will come and once more be victorious, you will come with your chosen ones, with your proud and mighty ones, but we will say that they saved only themselves, while we have saved everyone. It is said that the harlot who sits upon the beast and holds *mystery* in her hands will be disgraced, that the feeble will rebel again, that they will tear her purple and strip bare her "loathsome" body. But then I will stand up and point out to you the thousands of millions of happy babes who do not know sin. And we, who took their sins upon ourselves for their happiness, we will stand before you and say: "Judge us if you can and dare." Know that I am not afraid of you. Know that I, too, was in the wilderness, and I, too, ate locusts and roots; that I, too, blessed freedom, with which you have blessed mankind, and I, too, was preparing to enter the number of your chosen ones, the number of the strong and mighty, with a thirst "that the number be complete." But I awoke and did not want to serve madness. I returned and joined the host of those who have *corrected your deed*. I left the proud and returned to the humble, for the happiness of the humble. What I am telling you will come true, and our kingdom will be established. Tomorrow, I repeat, you will see this obedient flock, which at my first gesture will rush to heap hot coals around your stake, at which I shall burn you for having come to interfere with us. For if anyone has ever deserved our stake, it is you. Tomorrow I shall burn you. *Dixi.*'"[4]

Ivan stopped. He was flushed from speaking, and from speaking with such enthusiasm; but when he finished, he suddenly smiled.

Alyosha, who all the while had listened to him silently, though toward the end, in great agitation, he had started many times to interrupt his brother's speech but obviously restrained himself, suddenly spoke as if tearing himself loose.

"But . . . that's absurd!" he cried, blushing. "Your poem praises Jesus, it doesn't revile him . . . as you meant it to. And who will believe you about freedom? Is that, is that any way to understand it? It's a far cry from the Orthodox idea . . . It's Rome, and not even the whole of Rome, that isn't true—they're the worst of Catholicism, the Inquisitors, the Jesuits . . . ! But there could not even possibly be such a fantastic person as your Inquisitor. What sins do they take on themselves? Who are these bearers of the mystery who took some sort of curse upon themselves for men's happiness? Has anyone ever seen them? We know the Jesuits, bad things are said about them, but are they what you have there? They're not that, not that at all . . . They're simply a Roman army, for a future universal earthly kingdom, with the

---

4. [*Dixi*: "I have spoken."—TRANS.]

emperor—the pontiff of Rome—at their head . . . that's their ideal, but without any mysteries or lofty sadness . . . Simply the lust for power, for filthy earthly lucre, enslavement . . . a sort of future serfdom with them as the landowners . . . that's all they have. Maybe they don't even believe in God. Your suffering Inquisitor is only a fantasy . . ."

"But wait, wait," Ivan was laughing, "don't get so excited. A fantasy, you say? Let it be. Of course it's a fantasy. But still, let me ask: do you really think that this whole Catholic movement of the past few centuries is really nothing but the lust for power only for the sake of filthy lucre? Did Father Paissy teach you that?"

"No, no, on the contrary, Father Paissy once even said something like what you . . . but not like that, of course, not at all like that," Alyosha suddenly recollected himself.

"A precious bit of information, however, despite your 'not at all like that.' I ask you specifically: why should your Jesuits and Inquisitors have joined together only for material wicked lucre? Why can't there happen to be among them at least one sufferer who is tormented by great sadness and loves mankind? Look, suppose that one among all those who desire only material and filthy lucre, that one of them, at least, is like my old Inquisitor, who himself ate roots in the desert and raved, overcoming his flesh, in order to make himself free and perfect, but who still loved mankind all his life, and suddenly opened his eyes and saw that there is no great moral blessedness in achieving perfection of the will only to become convinced, at the same time, that millions of the rest of God's creatures have been set up only for mockery, that they will never be strong enough to manage their freedom, that from such pitiful rebels will never come giants to complete the tower, that it was not for such geese that the great idealist had his dream of harmony. Having understood all that, he returned and joined . . . the intelligent people. Couldn't this have happened?"

"Whom did he join? What intelligent people?" Alyosha exclaimed, almost passionately. "They are not so very intelligent, nor do they have any great mysteries and secrets . . . Except maybe for godlessness, that's their whole secret. Your Inquisitor doesn't believe in God, that's his whole secret!"

"What of it! At last you've understood. Yes, indeed, that alone is the whole secret, but is it not suffering, if only for such a man as he, who has wasted his whole life on a great deed in the wilderness and still has not been cured of his love for mankind? In his declining years he comes to the clear conviction that only the counsels of the great and dread spirit could at least somehow organize the feeble rebels, 'the unfinished, trial creatures created in mockery,' in a tolerable way. And so, convinced of that, he sees that one must follow the directives of the intelligent spirit, the dread spirit of death and destruction, and to that end accept lies and deceit, and lead people, consciously now, to death and destruction, deceiving them, moreover, all along the way, so that they somehow do not notice where they are being led, so that at least on the way these pitiful, blind men consider themselves happy. And deceive them, notice, in the name of him in whose ideal the old man believed so passionately all his life! Is that not a misfortune? And if even one such man, at least, finds himself at the head of that whole army 'lusting for power only for the sake of filthy lucre,' is one such man, at least, not enough to make a tragedy? Moreover, one such man standing at its head would be enough to bring out finally the real ruling idea of the whole Roman cause, with all its armies and Jesuits—the highest idea of this cause. I tell you outright that I firmly believe that this one man has never been lacking among those standing at the head of the movement. Who knows, perhaps such 'ones' have even been found among the Roman pontiffs. Who knows, maybe this accursed old man, who loves mankind so stubbornly in his own way, exists even now, in the form of a great host of such old men, and by no means accidentally, but in concert, as a secret union, organized long ago for the purpose of keeping the mystery, of keeping it from unhappy and feeble mankind with the aim of making them happy. It surely exists, and it should be so. I imagine that even the Masons have something like this mystery as their basis, and that Catholics hate the Masons so much because they see them as competitors, breaking up the unity of the idea, whereas there should be one flock and one shepherd . . . However, the way I'm defending my thought makes me seem like an author who did not stand up to your criticism. Enough of that."

"Maybe you're a Mason yourself!" suddenly escaped from Alyosha. "You don't believe in God," he added, this time with great sorrow. Besides, it seemed to him that his brother was looking at him mockingly. "And how does your poem end," he asked suddenly, staring at the ground, "or was that the end?"

"I was going to end it like this: when the Inquisitor fell silent, he waited some time for his prisoner to reply. His silence weighed on him. He had seen how the captive listened to him all the while intently and calmly, looking him straight in the eye, and apparently not wishing to contradict anything. The old man would have liked him to say something, even something bitter, terrible. But suddenly he approaches the old man in silence and gently kisses him on his bloodless, ninety-year-old lips. That is the whole answer. The old man shudders. Something stirs at the corners of his mouth; he walks to the door, opens it, and says to him: 'Go and do not come again . . . do not come at all . . . never, never!' And he lets him out into the 'dark squares of the city.' The prisoner goes away."

"And the old man?"

"The kiss burns in his heart, but the old man holds to his former idea."

"And you with him!" Alyosha exclaimed ruefully. Ivan laughed.

"But it's nonsense, Alyosha, it's just the muddled poem of a muddled student who never wrote two lines of verse. Why are you taking it so seriously?

You don't think I'll go straight to the Jesuits now, to join the host of those who are correcting his deed! Good lord, what do I care? As I told you: I just want to drag on until I'm thirty, and then—smash the cup on the floor!"

"And the sticky little leaves, and the precious graves, and the blue sky, and the woman you love! How will you live, what will you love them with?" Alyosha exclaimed ruefully. "Is it possible, with such hell in your heart and in your head? No, you're precisely going in order to join them . . . and if not, you'll kill yourself, you won't endure it!"

"There is a force that will endure everything," said Ivan, this time with a cold smirk.

"What force?"

"The Karamazov force . . . the force of the Karamazov baseness."

"To drown in depravity, to stifle your soul with corruption, is that it?"

"That, too, perhaps . . . only until my thirtieth year maybe I'll escape it, and then . . ."

"How will you escape it? By means of what? With your thoughts, it's impossible."

"Again, in Karamazov fashion."

"You mean 'everything is permitted'? Everything is permitted, is that right, is it?"

Ivan frowned, and suddenly turned somehow strangely pale.

"Ah, you caught that little remark yesterday, which offended Miusov so much . . . and that brother Dmitri so naively popped up and rephrased?" he grinned crookedly. "Yes, perhaps 'everything is permitted,' since the word has already been spoken. I do not renounce it. And Mitenka's version is not so bad."

Alyosha was looking at him silently.

"I thought, brother, that when I left here I'd have you, at least, in all the world," Ivan suddenly spoke with unexpected feeling, "but now I see that in your heart, too, there is no room for me, my dear hermit. The formula, 'everything is permitted,' I will not renounce, and what then? Will you renounce me for that? Will you?"

Alyosha stood up, went over to him in silence, and gently kissed him on the lips.

"Literary theft!" Ivan cried, suddenly going into some kind of rapture. "You stole that from my poem! Thank you, however. Get up, Alyosha, let's go, it's time we both did."

They went out, but stopped on the porch of the tavern.

"So, Alyosha," Ivan spoke in a firm voice, "if, indeed, I hold out for the sticky little leaves, I shall love them only remembering you. It's enough for me that you are here somewhere, and I shall not stop wanting to live. Is that enough for you? If you wish, you can take it as a declaration of love. And now you go right, I'll go left—and enough, you hear, enough. I mean, even if I don't go away tomorrow (but it seems I certainly shall), and we somehow meet again, not another word to me on any of these subjects. An urgent request. And with regard to brother Dmitri, too, I ask you particularly, do not ever even mention him to me again," he suddenly added irritably. "It's all exhausted, it's all talked out, isn't it? And in return for that, I will also make you a promise: when I'm thirty and want 'to smash the cup on the floor,' then, wherever you may be, I will still come to talk things over with you once more . . . even from America, I assure you. I will make a point of it. It will also be very interesting to have a look at you by then, to see what's become of you. Rather a solemn promise, you see. And indeed, perhaps we're saying goodbye for some seven or ten years. Well, go now to your Pater Seraphicus;[5] he's dying, and if he dies without you, you may be angry with me for having kept you. Goodbye, kiss me once more—so—and now go . . ."

Ivan turned suddenly and went his way without looking back. It was similar to the way his brother Dmitri had left Alyosha the day before, though the day before it was something quite different. This strange little observation flashed like an arrow through the sad mind of Alyosha, sad and sorrowful at that moment. He waited a little, looking after his brother. For some reason he suddenly noticed that his brother Ivan somehow swayed as he walked, and that his right shoulder, seen from behind, appeared lower than his left. He had never noticed it before. But suddenly he, too, turned and almost ran to the monastery. It was already getting quite dark, and he felt almost frightened; something new was growing in him, which he would have been unable to explain. The wind rose again as it had yesterday, and the centuries-old pine trees rustled gloomily around him as he entered the hermitage woods. He was almost running. "Pater Seraphicus—he got that name from somewhere—but where?" flashed through Alyosha's mind. "Ivan, poor Ivan, when shall I see you again . . . ? Lord, here's the hermitage! Yes, yes, that's him, Pater Seraphicus, he will save me . . . from him, and forever!"

Several times, later in his life, in great perplexity, he wondered how he could suddenly, after parting with his brother Ivan, so completely forget about his brother Dmitri, when he had resolved that morning, only a few hours earlier, that he must find him, and would not leave until he did, even if it meant not returning to the monastery that night.

5.[*Pater Seraphicus*: "Seraphic Father." An epithet applied to St Francis of Assisi.—Trans.]

QUESTIONS

1. In Ivan's poem, why does the prisoner remain silent throughout?

2. Why does the Grand Inquisitor arrest the man everyone recognizes?

3. According to the Grand Inquisitor, why is the prisoner the "most evil of heretics"? (72)

4. Why does the Grand Inquisitor say, "I do not know who you are, and I do not want to know"? (72)

5. According to Ivan, why does the Grand Inquisitor have a need to speak out in the presence of the prisoner?

6. What is meant by Ivan's claim that the old man and his colleagues have overcome freedom in order to make people happy?

7. What does the Grand Inquisitor mean by referring to the tempter's three questions as a "thundering miracle"? (74)

8. Why do the three questions reveal "a mind not human and transient but eternal and absolute"? (74)

9. What does the Grand Inquisitor understand by his claim that "freedom and earthly bread in plenty for everyone are inconceivable together"? (75)

10. According to the Grand Inquisitor, why should freedom result in "no crime, and therefore no sin, but only hungry men"? (75)

11. Why, according to the Grand Inquisitor, is the need for "communality of worship" one of man's chief torments? (76)

12. Why does the Grand Inquisitor accuse the prisoner of acting both "proudly and magnificently" when he rejected the devil's temptation to cast himself down from the temple? (77)

13. What, according to the Grand Inquisitor, makes miracle, mystery, and authority capable of conquering man's conscience?

14. What is the universal union man longs for, according to the Grand Inquisitor?

15. Why, according to the Grand Inquisitor, will man be unhappy until he appreciates what it means to submit?

16. Why does Ivan have the prisoner kiss the Grand Inquisitor? Why does the kiss burn in the Grand Inquisitor's heart?

17. Why does the Grand Inquisitor let the prisoner go free?

FOR FURTHER REFLECTION

1. Do humans long for "communality of worship"? If so, why?

2. Is the Grand Inquisitor correct in asserting that we have a need for a universal and general union of humanity?

3. Is happiness possible only as an illusion? Can we be truly happy living under an illusion?

4. Must humans sin in order to be happy?

5. In what sense can freedom be a source of unhappiness?

K nown today as one of the most celebrated writers of horror fiction in the nineteenth century, and generally credited with writing the first modern detective story, "The Murders in the Rue Morgue," Edgar Allan Poe (1809–1849) was most familiar to his contemporaries for "The Raven." This long poem made him instantly famous if not rich (he received $15 for the first printing) upon its publication in New York's *Evening Mirror* in 1845. During his career, Poe also worked as an editor for various literary magazines including the *Southern Literary Messenger, Burton's Gentleman's Magazine,* and *Graham's Magazine,* the last increasing its circulation from 5,000 to 37,000 under Poe's watch.

Poe was born in Boston, the child of two traveling stage actors. His father apparently abandoned the family early on, and his mother died when Edgar was not quite three years old. He was subsequently taken into the household of John and Frances Allan of Richmond, Virginia. The couple never legally adopted him, though they raised and educated him, first in Richmond, and then, between 1815 and 1820, at two boarding schools in London, England. Poe enrolled at the University of Virginia in Charlottesville in 1826, where he proceeded to rack up gambling debts of $2,000. The next year was momentous: he had a major falling out with John Allan, saw publication of his first book, *Tamerlane and Other Poems,* and enlisted in the U.S. Army under the name Edgar A. Perry. In 1830 Poe was accepted into West Point, where, because of his absenteeism from classes and church, he was court-martialed and dismissed. Poe returned to Richmond and in 1836 married his thirteen-year-old cousin Virginia, who would die from tuberculosis eleven years later in Fordham, New York.

Through the 1830s, Poe developed into an ambitious and industrious literary editor and continued to write steadily, publishing several collections of prose and poetry that established his reputation. By the 1840s he had achieved enough of an audience to initiate a series of public lectures on poetry. Poe's death in 1849 in Baltimore, while on a lecture tour to raise money for a proposed new magazine, *The Stylus*, occurred in a haze of strange, and still controversial, circumstances. By one physician's account, Poe was terminally inebriated; other testimony refuted that claim and contended that he was found badly beaten shortly before arriving at Washington College Hospital.

Poe is important to literary history as the first writer to offer a working theory of the short story genre itself. Reviewing Nathaniel Hawthorne's *Twice-Told Tales* in 1842, he asserted that the "short prose narrative" normally requires "from a half-hour to one or two hours in its perusal," or in other words, unlike a novel, it can be read "at one sitting." Poe argued that a successful short story must be organized around a unifying aesthetic; it should evoke "a certain unique or single effect" on the reader, and therefore all the "incidents" in the plot, in fact every word in the narrative, must contribute to "one preestablished design."

Written in 1839, "The Fall of the House of Usher" succeeds as one of the finest examples of Poe's theory that a story's parts must contribute to the unity of a single effect. Generations of Poe readers and scholars have appreciated the story for its rich imbroglio of esoterica, ranking it among this author's finest, and psychologically most disturbing, works.

EDGAR ALLAN POE

The Fall of the House of Usher

Son cœur est un luth suspendu;
Sitôt qu'on le touche il résonne.
—De Béranger

During the whole of a dull, dark, and soundless day in the autumn of the year, when the clouds hung oppressively low in the heavens, I had been passing alone, on horseback, through a singularly dreary tract of country; and at length found myself, as the shades of the evening drew on, within view of the melancholy House of Usher. I know not how it was—but, with the first glimpse of the building, a sense of insufferable gloom pervaded my spirit. I say insufferable; for the feeling was unrelieved by any of that half-pleasurable, because poetic, sentiment with which the mind usually receives even the sternest natural images of the desolate or terrible. I looked upon the scene before me—upon the mere house, and the simple landscape features of the domain—upon the bleak walls—upon the vacant eyelike windows—upon a few rank sedges—and upon a few white trunks of decayed trees—with an utter depression of soul which I can compare to no earthly sensation more properly than to the after-dream of the reveler upon opium—the bitter lapse into everyday life—the hideous dropping off of the veil. There was an iciness, a sinking, a sickening of the heart—an unredeemed dreariness of thought which no goading of the imagination could torture into aught of the sublime. What was it—I paused to think—what was it that so unnerved me in the contemplation of the House of Usher? It was a mystery all insoluble; nor could I grapple with the shadowy fancies that crowded upon me as I pondered. I was forced to fall back upon the unsatisfactory conclusion, that while, beyond doubt, there *are* combinations of very simple natural objects which have the power of thus affecting us, still the analysis of this power lies among considerations beyond our depth. It was possible, I reflected, that a mere different arrangement of the particulars of the scene, of the details of the picture, would be sufficient to modify, or perhaps to annihilate its capacity for sorrowful impression; and, acting upon this idea, I reined my horse to the precipitous brink of a black and lurid tarn that lay in unruffled luster by the dwelling, and gazed down—but with a shudder even more thrilling than before—upon the re-modeled and inverted images of the gray sedge, and the ghastly tree stems, and the vacant and eyelike windows.

Nevertheless, in this mansion of gloom I now proposed to myself a sojourn of some weeks. Its proprietor, Roderick Usher, had been one of my boon companions in boyhood; but many years had elapsed since our last meeting. A letter, however, had lately reached me in a distant part of the country—a letter from him—which, in its wildly importunate nature, had admitted of no other than a personal reply. The MS. gave evidence of nervous agitation. The writer spoke of acute bodily illness—of a mental disorder which oppressed him—and of an earnest desire to see me, as his best, and indeed his only personal friend, with a view of attempting, by the cheerfulness of my society, some alleviation of his malady. It was the manner in which all this, and much more, was said—it was the apparent *heart* that went with his request—which allowed me no room for hesitation; and I accordingly obeyed forthwith what I still considered a very singular summons.

Although, as boys, we had been even intimate associates, yet I really knew little of my friend. His reserve had been always excessive and habitual. I was aware, however, that his very ancient family had been noted, time out of mind, for a peculiar sensibility of temperament, displaying itself, through long ages, in many works of exalted art, and manifested, of late, in repeated deeds of munificent yet unobtrusive charity, as well as in a passionate devotion to the intricacies, perhaps even more than to the orthodox and easily recognizable beauties, of musical science. I had learned, too, the very remarkable fact, that the stem of the Usher race, all time-honored as it was, had put forth, at no period, any enduring branch; in other words, that the entire family lay in the direct line of descent, and had always, with very trifling and very temporary variation, so lain. It was this deficiency, I considered, while running over in thought the perfect keeping of the character of the premises with the accredited character of the people, and while speculating upon the possible influence which the one, in the long lapse of centuries, might have exercised upon the other—it was this deficiency, perhaps, of collateral issue, and the consequent undeviating transmission, from sire to son, of the patrimony with the name, which had, at length, so identified the two as to merge the original title of the estate in the quaint and equivocal appellation of the "House of Usher"—an appellation which seemed to include, in the minds of the peasantry who used it, both the family and the family mansion.

I have said that the sole effect of my somewhat childish experiment—that of looking down within the tarn—had been to deepen the first singular impression. There can be no doubt that the consciousness of the rapid increase of my superstition—for why should I not so term it?—served mainly to accelerate the increase itself. Such, I have long known, is the paradoxical law of all sentiments having terror as a basis. And it might have been for this reason only, that, when I again uplifted my eyes to the house itself, from its image in the pool, there grew in my mind a strange fancy—a fancy so ridiculous, indeed, that I but mention it to show the vivid force of the sensations which oppressed me. I had so worked upon my imagination as really to believe that about the whole mansion and domain there hung an atmosphere peculiar to themselves and their immediate vicinity—an atmosphere which had no affinity with the air of heaven, but which had reeked up from the decayed trees, and the gray wall, and the silent tarn—a pestilent and mystic vapor, dull, sluggish, faintly discernible, and leaden-hued.

Shaking off from my spirit what *must* have been a dream, I scanned more narrowly the real aspect of the building. Its principal feature seemed to be that of an excessive antiquity. The discoloration of ages had been great. Minute fungi overspread the whole exterior, hanging in a fine tangled web-work from the eaves. Yet all this was apart from any extraordinary dilapidation. No portion of the masonry had fallen; and there appeared to be a wild inconsistency between its still perfect adaptation of parts, and the crumbling condition of the individual stones. In this there was much that reminded me of the specious totality of old woodwork which has rotted for long years in some neglected vault, with no disturbance from the breath of the external air. Beyond this indication of extensive decay, however, the fabric gave little token of instability. Perhaps the eye of a scrutinizing observer might have discovered a barely perceptible fissure, which, extending from the roof of the building in front, made its way down the wall in a zigzag direction, until it became lost in the sullen waters of the tarn.

Noticing these things, I rode over a short causeway to the house. A servant in waiting took my horse, and I entered the Gothic archway of the hall. A valet, of stealthy step, thence conducted me, in silence, through many dark and intricate passages in my progress to the *studio* of his master. Much that I encountered on the way contributed, I know not how, to heighten the vague sentiments of which I have already spoken. While the objects around me—while the carvings of the ceilings, the somber tapestries of the walls, the ebon blackness of the floors, and the phantasmagoric armorial trophies which rattled as I strode, were but matters to which, or to such as which, I had been accustomed from my infancy—while I hesitated not to acknowledge how familiar was all this—I still wondered to find how unfamiliar were the fancies which ordinary images were stirring up. On one of the staircases, I met the physician of the family. His countenance, I thought, wore a mingled expression of low cunning and perplexity. He accosted me with trepidation and passed on. The valet now threw open a door and ushered me into the presence of his master.

The room in which I found myself was very large and lofty. The windows were long, narrow, and pointed, and at so vast a distance from the black oaken floor as to be altogether inaccessible from within. Feeble gleams of encrimsoned light made their way through the trellised panes, and served to render sufficiently distinct the more prominent objects around; the eye, however, struggled in vain to reach the remoter angles of the chamber, or the recesses of the vaulted and fretted ceiling. Dark draperies hung upon the walls. The general furniture was profuse, comfortless, antique, and tattered. Many books and musical instruments lay scattered about, but failed to give any vitality to the scene. I felt that I breathed an atmosphere of sorrow. An air of stern, deep, and irredeemable gloom hung over and pervaded all.

Upon my entrance, Usher arose from a sofa on which he had been lying at full length, and greeted me with a vivacious warmth which had much in it, I at first thought, of an overdone cordiality—of the constrained effort of the *ennuyé* man of the world. A glance, however, at his countenance, convinced me of his perfect sincerity. We sat down; and for some moments, while he spoke not, I gazed upon him with a feeling half of pity, half of awe. Surely, man had never before so terribly altered, in so brief a period, as had Roderick Usher! It was with difficulty that I could bring myself to admit the identity of the wan being before me with the companion of my early boyhood. Yet the character of his face had been at all times remarkable. A cadaverousness of complexion; an eye large, liquid, and luminous beyond comparison; lips somewhat thin and very pallid, but of a surpassingly beautiful curve; a nose of a delicate Hebrew model, but with a breadth of nostril unusual in similar formations; a finely molded chin, speaking, in its want of prominence, of a want of moral energy; hair of a more than weblike softness and tenuity; these features, with an inordinate expansion above the regions of the temple, made up altogether a countenance not easily to be forgotten. And now in the mere exaggeration of the prevailing character of these features, and of the expression they were wont to convey, lay so much of change that I doubted to whom I spoke. The now ghastly pallor of the skin, and the now miraculous luster of the eye, above all things startled and even awed me. The silken hair, too, had been suffered to grow all unheeded, and as, in its wild gossamer texture, it floated rather than fell about the face, I could not, even with effort, connect its arabesque expression with any idea of simple humanity.

In the manner of my friend I was at once struck with an incoherence— an inconsistency; and I soon found this to arise from a series of feeble and futile struggles to overcome a habitual trepidancy—an excessive nervous agitation. For something of this nature I had indeed been prepared, no less by his letter, than by reminiscences of certain boyish traits, and by conclusions deduced from his peculiar physical conformation and temperament.

His action was alternately vivacious and sullen. His voice varied rapidly from a tremulous indecision (when the animal spirits seemed utterly in abeyance) to that species of energetic concision—that abrupt, weighty, unhurried, and hollow-sounding enunciation—that leaden, self-balanced, and perfectly modulated guttural utterance, which may be observed in the lost drunkard, or the irreclaimable eater of opium, during the periods of his most intense excitement.

It was thus that he spoke of the object of my visit, of his earnest desire to see me, and of the solace he expected me to afford him. He entered, at some length, into what he conceived to be the nature of his malady. It was, he said, a constitutional and a family evil, and one for which he despaired to find a remedy—a mere nervous affection, he immediately added, which would undoubtedly soon pass off. It displayed itself in a host of unnatural sensations. Some of these, as he detailed them, interested and bewildered me; although, perhaps, the terms, and the general manner of the narration had their weight. He suffered much from a morbid acuteness of the senses; the most insipid food was alone endurable; he could wear only garments of certain texture; the odors of all flowers were oppressive; his eyes were tortured by even a faint light; and there were but peculiar sounds, and these from stringed instruments, which did not inspire him with horror.

To an anomalous species of terror I found him a bounden slave. "I shall perish," said he, "I *must* perish in this deplorable folly. Thus, thus, and not otherwise, shall I be lost. I dread the events of the future, not in themselves, but in their results. I shudder at the thought of any, even the most trivial, incident, which may operate upon this intolerable agitation of soul. I have, indeed, no abhorrence of danger, except in its absolute effect—in terror. In this unnerved—in this pitiable condition—I feel that the period will sooner or later arrive when I must abandon life and reason together, in some struggle with the grim phantasm, FEAR."

I learned, moreover, at intervals, and through broken and equivocal hints, another singular feature of his mental condition. He was enchained by certain superstitious impressions in regard to the dwelling which he tenanted, and whence, for many years, he had never ventured forth—in regard to an influence whose supposititious force was conveyed in terms too shadowy here to be restated—an influence which some peculiarities in the mere form and substance of his family mansion, had, by dint of long sufferance, he said, obtained over his spirit—an effect which the *physique* of the gray walls and turrets, and of the dim tarn into which they all looked down, had, at length, brought about upon the *morale* of his existence.

He admitted, however, although with hesitation, that much of the peculiar gloom which thus afflicted him could be traced to a more natural and far more palpable origin—to the severe and long-continued illness—indeed to the evidently approaching dissolution—of a tenderly beloved sister—his sole companion for long years—his last and only relative on earth. "Her decease," he said, with a bitterness which I can never forget, "would leave him (him the hopeless and the frail) the last of the ancient race of the Ushers." While he spoke, the lady Madeline (for so was she called) passed slowly through a remote portion of the apartment, and, without having noticed my presence, disappeared. I regarded her with an utter astonishment not unmingled with dread—and yet I found it impossible to account for such feelings. A sensation of stupor oppressed me, as my eyes followed her retreating steps. When a door, at length, closed upon her, my glance sought instinctively and eagerly the countenance of the brother—but he had buried his face in his hands, and I could only perceive that a far more than ordinary wanness had overspread the emaciated fingers through which trickled many passionate tears.

The disease of the lady Madeline had long baffled the skill of her physicians. A settled apathy, a gradual wasting away of the person, and frequent although transient affections of a partially cataleptical character, were the unusual diagnosis. Hitherto she had steadily borne up against the pressure of her malady, and had not betaken herself finally to bed; but, on the closing in of the evening of my arrival at the house, she succumbed (as her brother told me at night with inexpressible agitation) to the prostrating power of the destroyer; and learned that the glimpse I had obtained of her person would thus probably be the last I should obtain—that the lady, at least while living, would be seen by me no more.

For several days ensuing, her name was unmentioned by either Usher or myself: and during this period I was busied in earnest endeavors to alleviate the melancholy of my friend. We painted and read together; or I listened, as if in a dream, to the wild improvisations of his speaking guitar. And thus, as a closer and still closer intimacy admitted me more unreservedly into the recesses of his spirit, the more bitterly did I perceive the futility of all attempt at cheering a mind from which darkness, as if an inherent positive quality, poured forth upon all objects of the moral and physical universe, in one unceasing radiation of gloom.

I shall ever bear about me a memory of the many solemn hours I thus spent alone with the master of the House of Usher. Yet I should fail in any attempt to convey an idea of the exact character of the studies, or of the occupations, in which he involved me, or led me the way. An excited and highly distempered ideality threw a sulphureous luster over all. His long improvised dirges will ring forever in my ears. Among other things, I hold painfully in mind a certain singular perversion and amplification of the wild air of the last waltz of Von Weber. From the paintings over which his elaborate fancy brooded, and which grew, touch by touch, into vaguenesses at which I shuddered the more thrillingly, because I shuddered knowing not why—from these paintings (vivid as their images now are before me) I would in vain endeavor to educe more than a small portion which should lie within the compass of merely written words. By the utter simplicity, by the nakedness of his designs, he arrested and overawed attention. If ever mortal painted an idea, that mortal was Roderick Usher. For me at least—in the circumstances then surrounding me—there arose out of the pure abstractions which the hypochondriac contrived to throw upon his canvas, an intensity of intolerable awe, no shadow of which felt I ever yet in the contemplation of the certainly glowing yet too concrete reveries of Fuseli.

One of the phantasmagoric conceptions of my friend, partaking not so rigidly of the spirit of abstraction, may be shadowed forth, although feebly, in words. A small picture presented the interior of an immensely long and rectangular vault or tunnel, with low walls, smooth, white, and without interruption or device. Certain accessory points of the design served well to convey the idea that this excavation lay at an exceeding depth below the surface of the earth. No outlet was observed in any portion of its vast extent, and no torch, or other artificial source of light was discernible; yet a flood of intense rays rolled throughout, and bathed the whole in a ghastly and inappropriate splendor.

I have just spoken of that morbid condition of the auditory nerve which rendered all music intolerable to the sufferer, with the exception of certain effects of stringed instruments. It was, perhaps, the narrow limits to which he thus confined himself upon the guitar, which gave birth, in great measure, to the fantastic character of his performances. But the fervid *facility* of his *impromptus* could not be so accounted for. They must have been, and were, in the notes, as well as in the words of his wild fantasias (for he not unfrequently accompanied himself with rhymed verbal improvisations), the result of that intense mental collectedness and concentration to which I have previously alluded as observable only in particular moments of the highest artificial excitement. The words of one of these rhapsodies I have easily remembered. I was, perhaps, the more forcibly impressed with it, as he gave it, because, in the under or mystic current of its meaning, I fancied that I perceived, and for the first time, a full consciousness on the part of Usher, of the tottering of his lofty reason upon her throne. The verses, which were entitled "The Haunted Palace," ran very nearly, if not accurately, thus:

I

In the greenest of our valleys,
    By good angels tenanted,
Once a fair and stately palace—
    Radiant palace—reared its head.
In the monarch Thought's dominion—
    It stood there!
Never seraph spread a pinion
    Over fabric half so fair.

II

Banners yellow, glorious, golden,
     On its roof did float and flow;
(This—all this—was in the olden
     Time long ago)
And every gentle air that dallied,
     In that sweet day,
Along the ramparts plumed and pallid,
     A winged odor went away.

III

Wanderers in that happy valley
     Through two luminous windows saw
Spirits moving musically
     To a lute's well-tunèd law,
Round about a throne, where sitting
     (Porphyrogene!)
In state his glory well befitting,
     The ruler of the realm was seen.

IV

And all with pearl and ruby glowing
     Was the fair palace door,
Through which came flowing, flowing, flowing
     And sparkling evermore,
A troop of Echoes whose sweet duty
     Was but to sing,
In voices of surpassing beauty,
     The wit and wisdom of their king.

V

But evil things, in robes of sorrow,
     Assailed the monarch's high estate;
(Ah, let us mourn, for never morrow
     Shall dawn upon him, desolate!)
And, round about his home, the glory
     That blushed and bloomed
Is but a dim-remembered story
     Of the oldtime entombed.

VI

And travelers now within that valley,
  Through the red-litten windows, see
Vast forms that move fantastically
  To a discordant melody;
While, like a rapid ghastly river,
  Through the pale door,
A hideous throng rush out forever,
  And laugh—but smile no more.

I well remember that suggestions arising from this ballad led us into a train of thought wherein there became manifest an opinion of Usher's which I mention not so much on account of its novelty (for other men have thought thus), as on account of the pertinacity with which he maintained it. This opinion, in its general form, was that of the sentience of all vegetable things. But, in his disordered fancy, the idea had assumed a more daring character, and trespassed, under certain conditions, upon the kingdom of inorganization. I lack words to express the full extent, of the earnest *abandon* of his persuasion. The belief, however, was connected (as I have previously hinted) with the gray stones of the home of his forefathers. The conditions of the sentience had been here, he imagined, fulfilled in the method of collocation of these stones—in the order of their arrangement, as well as in that of the many *fungi* which overspread them, and of the decayed trees which stood around—above all, in the long undisturbed endurance of this arrangement, and in its reduplication in the still waters of the tarn. Its evidence—the evidence of the sentience—was to be seen, he said (and I here started as he spoke), in the gradual yet certain condensation of an atmosphere of their own about the waters and the walls. The result was discoverable, he added, in that silent, yet importunate and terrible influence which for centuries had molded the destinies of his family, and which made *him* what I now saw him—what he was. Such opinions need no comment, and I will make none.

Our books—the books which, for years, had formed no small portion of the mental existence of the invalid—were, as might be supposed, in strict keeping with this character of phantasm. We pored together over such works as the *Ververt et Chartreuse* of Gresset; the *Belphegor* of Machiavelli; the *Heaven and Hell* of Swedenborg; the *Subterranean Voyage of Nicholas Klimm* by Holberg; the *Chiromancy* of Robert Flud, of Jean D'Indaginé, and of De la Chambre; the *Journey into the Blue Distance* of Tieck; and the *City of the Sun* of Campanella. One favorite volume was a small octavo edition of the *Directorium Inquisitorum*, by the Dominican Eymeric de Gironne; and there were passages in Pomponius Mela, about the old African Satyrs and Aegipans, over which Usher would sit dreaming for hours. His chief delight, however, was found in the perusal of an exceedingly rare and curious book in quarto Gothic—the manual of a forgotten church—the *Vigiliae Mortuorum secundum Chorum Ecclesiae Maguntinae.*

I could not help thinking of the wild ritual of this work, and of its probable influence upon the hypochondriac, when, one evening, having informed me abruptly that the lady Madeline was no more, he stated his intention of preserving her corpse for a fortnight (previously to its final interment), in one of the numerous vaults within the main walls of the building. The worldly reason, however, assigned for this singular proceeding, was one which I did not feel at liberty to dispute. The brother had been led to his resolution (so he told me) by consideration of the unusual character of the malady of the deceased, of certain obtrusive and eager inquiries on the part of her medical men, and of the remote and exposed situation of the burial ground of the family. I will not deny that when I called to mind the sinister countenance of the person whom I met upon the staircase, on the day of my arrival at the house, I had no desire to oppose what I regarded as at best but a harmless, and by no means an unnatural, precaution.

At the request of Usher, I personally aided him in the arrangements for the temporary entombment. The body having been encoffined, we two alone bore it to its rest. The vault in which we placed it (and which had been so long unopened that our torches, half smothered in its oppressive atmosphere, gave us little opportunity for investigation) was small, damp, and entirely without means of admission for light; lying, at great depth, immediately beneath that portion of the building in which was my own sleeping apartment. It had been used, apparently, in remote feudal times, for the worst purposes of a donjon-keep, and, in later days, as a place of deposit for powder, or some other highly combustible substance, as a portion of its floor, and the whole interior of a long archway through which we reached it, were carefully sheathed with copper. The door, of massive iron, had been, also, similarly protected. Its immense weight caused an unusually sharp grating sound, as it moved upon its hinges.

Having deposited our mournful burden upon trestles within this region of horror, we partially turned aside the yet unscrewed lid of the coffin, and looked upon the face of the tenant. A striking similitude between the brother and sister now first arrested my attention; and Usher, divining, perhaps, my thoughts, murmured out some few words from which I learned that the deceased and himself had been twins, and that sympathies of a scarcely intelligible nature had always existed between them. Our glances, however, rested not long upon the dead—for we could not regard her unawed. The disease which had thus entombed the lady in the maturity of youth, had left, as usual in all maladies of a strictly cataleptic character, the mockery of a faint blush upon the bosom and the face, and that suspiciously lingering smile upon the lip which is so terrible in death. We replaced and screwed down the lid, and, having secured the door of iron, made our way, with toil, into the scarcely less gloomy apartments of the upper portion of the house.

And now, some days of bitter grief having elapsed, an observable change came over the features of the mental disorder of my friend. His ordinary manner had vanished. His ordinary occupations were neglected or forgotten. He roamed from chamber to chamber with hurried, unequal, and objectless step. The pallor of his countenance had assumed, if possible, a more ghastly hue—but the luminousness of his eye had utterly gone out. The once occasional huskiness of his tone was heard no more; and a tremulous quaver, as if of extreme terror, habitually characterized his utterance. There were times, indeed, when I thought his unceasingly agitated mind was laboring with some oppressive secret, to divulge which he struggled for the necessary courage. At times, again, I was obliged to resolve all into the mere inexplicable vagaries of madness, for I beheld him gazing upon vacancy for long hours, in an attitude of the profoundest attention, as if listening to some imaginary sound. It was no wonder that his condition terrified—that it infected me. I felt creeping upon me by slow yet certain degrees, the wild influences of his own fantastic yet impressive superstitions.

It was, especially, upon retiring to bed late in the night of the seventh or eighth day after the placing of the lady Madeline within the donjon, that I experienced the full power of such feelings. Sleep came not near my couch—while the hours waned and waned away. I struggled to reason off the nervousness which had dominion over me. I endeavored to believe that much, if not all of what I felt, was due to the bewildering influence of the gloomy furniture of the room—of the dark and tattered draperies, which, tortured into motion by the breath of a rising tempest, swayed fitfully to and fro upon the walls, and rustled uneasily about the decorations of the bed. But my efforts were fruitless. An irrepressible tremor gradually pervaded my frame; and, at length, there sat upon my very heart an incubus of utterly causeless alarm. Shaking this off with a gasp and a struggle, I uplifted myself upon the pillows, and, peering earnestly within the intense darkness of the chamber, hearkened—I know not why, except that an instinctive spirit prompted me—to certain low and indefinite sounds which came, through the pauses of the storm, at long intervals, I knew not whence. Overpowered by an intense sentiment of horror, unaccountable yet unendurable, I threw on my clothes with haste (for I felt that I should sleep no more during the night), and endeavored to arouse myself from the pitiable condition into which I had fallen, by pacing rapidly to and fro through the apartment.

I had taken but few turns in this manner, when a light step on an adjoining staircase arrested my attention. I presently recognized it as that of Usher. In an instant afterward he rapped, with a gentle touch, at my door, and entered, bearing a lamp. His countenance was, as usual, cadaverously wan—but, moreover, there was a species of mad hilarity in his eyes—an evidently restrained *hysteria* in his whole demeanor. His air appalled me—but anything was preferable to the solitude which I had so long endured, and I even welcomed his presence as a relief.

"And you have not seen it?" he said abruptly, after having stared about him for some moments in silence—"you have not then seen it?—but, stay! you shall." Thus speaking, and having carefully shaded his lamp, he hurried to one of the casements, and threw it freely open to the storm.

The impetuous fury of the entering gust nearly lifted us from our feet. It was, indeed, a tempestuous yet sternly beautiful night, and one wildly singular in its terror and its beauty. A whirlwind had apparently collected its force in our vicinity; for there were frequent and violent alterations in the direction of the wind; and the exceeding density of the clouds (which hung so low as to press upon the turrets of the house) did not prevent our perceiving the lifelike velocity with which they flew careering from all points against each other, without passing away into the distance. I say that even their exceeding density did not prevent our perceiving this—yet we had no glimpse of the moon or stars—nor was there any flashing forth of the lightning. But the under surfaces of the huge masses of agitated vapor, as well as all terrestrial objects immediately around us, were glowing in the unnatural light of a faintly luminous and distinctly visible gaseous exhalation which hung about and enshrouded the mansion.

"You must not—you shall not behold this!" said I, shudderingly, to Usher, as I led him, with a gentle violence, from the window to a seat. "These appearances, which bewilder you, are merely electrical phenomena not uncommon—or it may be that they have their ghastly origin in the rank miasma of the tarn. Let us close this casement—the air is chilling and dangerous to your frame. Here is one of your favorite romances. I will read, and you shall listen—and so we will pass away this terrible night together."

The antique volume which I had taken up was the "Mad Trist" of Sir Launcelot Canning; but I had called it a favorite of Usher's more in sad jest than in earnest; for, in truth, there is little in its uncouth and unimaginative prolixity which could have had interest for the lofty and spiritual ideality of my friend. It was, however, the only book immediately at hand; and I indulged a vague hope that the excitement which now agitated the hypochondriac, might find relief (for the history of mental disorder is full of similar anomalies) even in the extremeness of the folly which I should read. Could I have judged, indeed, by the wild overstrained air of vivacity with which he hearkened, or apparently hearkened, to the words of the tale, I might well have congratulated myself upon the success of my design.

I had arrived at that well-known portion of the story where Ethelred, the hero of the Trist, having sought in vain for peaceable admission into the dwelling of the hermit, proceeds to make good an entrance by force. Here, it will be remembered, the words of the narrative run thus:

"And Ethelred, who was by nature of a doughty heart, and who was now mighty withal, on account of the powerfulness of the wine which he had drunken, waited no longer to hold parley with the hermit, who, in sooth, was of an obstinate and maliceful turn, but, feeling the rain upon his shoulders, and fearing the rising of the tempest, uplifted his mace outright, and, with blows, made quickly room in the plankings of the door for his gauntleted hand; and now pulling therewith sturdily, he so cracked, and ripped, and tore all asunder, that the noise of the dry and hollow-sounding wood alarumed and reverberated throughout the forest."

At the termination of this sentence I started, and for a moment, paused; for it appeared to me (although I at once concluded that my excited fancy had deceived me)—it appeared to me that, from some very remote portion of the mansion, there came, indistinctly, to my ears, what might have been, in its exact similarity of character, the echo (but a stifled and dull one certainly) of the very cracking and ripping sound which Sir Launcelot had so particularly described. It was, beyond doubt, the coincidence alone which had arrested my attention; for, amid the rattling of the sashes of the casements, and the ordinary commingled noises of the still increasing storm, the sound, in itself, had nothing, surely which should have interested or disturbed me. I continued the story:

"But the good champion Ethelred, now entering within the door, was sore enraged and amazed to perceive no signal of the maliceful hermit; but, in the stead thereof, a dragon of a scaly and prodigious demeanor, and of a fiery tongue, which sate in guard before a palace of gold, with a floor of silver; and upon the wall there hung a shield of shining brass with this legend enwritten—

Who entereth herein, a conqueror hath bin;
Who slayeth the dragon, the shield he shall win.

And Ethelred uplifted his mace, and struck upon the head of the dragon, which fell before him, and gave up his pesty breath, with a shriek so horrid and harsh, and withal so piercing, that Ethelred had fain to close his ears with his hands against the dreadful noise of it, the like whereof was never before heard."

Here again I paused abruptly, and now with a feeling of wild amazement—for there could be no doubt whatever that, in this instance, I did actually hear (although from what direction it proceeded I found it impossible to say) a low and apparently distant, but harsh, protracted, and most unusual screaming or grating sound—the exact counterpart of what my fancy had already conjured up for the dragon's unnatural shriek, as described by the romancer.

Oppressed, as I certainly was, upon the occurrence of the second and most extraordinary coincidence, by a thousand conflicting sensations, in which wonder and extreme terror were predominant, I still retained sufficient presence of mind to avoid exciting, by any observation, the sensitive nervousness of my companion. I was by no means certain that he had noticed the sounds in question; although, assuredly, a strange alteration had, during the last few minutes, taken place in his demeanor. From a position fronting my own, he had gradually brought round his chair, so as to sit with his face to the door of the chamber; and thus I could but partially perceive his features, although I saw that his lips trembled as if he were murmuring inaudibly. His head had dropped upon his breast—yet I knew that he was not asleep, from the wide and rigid opening of the eye as I caught a glance of it in profile. The motion of his body, too, was at variance with this idea—for he rocked from side to side with a gentle yet constant and uniform sway. Having rapidly taken notice of all this, I resumed the narrative of Sir Launcelot, which thus proceeded:

"And now, the champion, having escaped from the terrible fury of the dragon, bethinking himself of the brazen shield and of the breaking up of the enchantment which was upon it, removed the carcass from out of the way before him, and approached valorously over the silver pavement of the castle to where the shield was upon the wall; which in sooth tarried not for his full coming, but fell down at his feet upon the silver floor, with a mighty great and terrible ringing sound."

No sooner had these syllables passed my lips, than—as if a shield of brass had indeed, at the moment, fallen heavily upon a floor of silver—I became aware of a distinct, hollow, metallic, and clangorous, yet apparently muffled reverberation. Completely unnerved, I leaped to my feet; but the measured rocking movement of Usher was undisturbed. I rushed to the chair in which he sat. His eyes were bent fixedly before him, and throughout his whole countenance there reigned a stony rigidity. But, as I placed my hand upon his shoulder, there came a strong shudder over his whole person; a sickly smile quivered about his lips; and I saw that he spoke in a low, hurried, and gibbering murmur, as if unconscious of my presence. Bending closely over him, I at length drank in the hideous import of his words.

"Not hear it?—yes, I hear it, and *have* heard it. Long—long—long— many minutes, many hours, many days, have I heard it—yet I dared not— oh, pity me, miserable wretch that I am!—I dared not—I *dared* not speak! *We have put her living in the tomb!* Said I not that my senses were acute? I *now* tell you that I heard her first feeble movements in the hollow coffin. I heard them—many, many days ago—yet I dared not—*I dared not speak!* And now—tonight—Ethelred—ha! ha!—the breaking of the hermit's door, and the death cry of the dragon, and the clangor of the shield!—say, rather, the rending of her coffin, and the grating of the iron hinges of her prison, and her struggles within the coppered archway of the vault! Oh whither shall I fly? Will she not be here anon? Is she not hurrying to upbraid me for my haste? Have I not heard her footstep on the stair? Do I not distinguish that heavy and horrible beating of her heart? MADMAN!" Here he sprang furiously to his feet, and shrieked out his syllables, as if in the effort he were giving up his soul—"MADMAN! I TELL YOU THAT SHE NOW STANDS WITHOUT THE DOOR!"

As if in the superhuman energy of his utterance there had been found the potency of a spell—the huge antique panels to which the speaker pointed, threw slowly back, upon the instant, their ponderous and ebony jaws. It was the work of the rushing gust—but then without those doors there DID did stand the lofty and enshrouded figure of the lady Madeline of Usher. There was blood upon her white robes, and the evidence of some bitter struggle upon every portion of her emaciated frame. For a moment she remained trembling and reeling to and fro upon the threshold, then, with a low moaning cry, fell heavily inward upon the person of her brother, and in her violent and now final death-agonies, bore him to the floor a corpse, and a victim to the terrors he had anticipated.

From that chamber, and from that mansion, I fled aghast. The storm was still abroad in all its wrath as I found myself crossing the old causeway. Suddenly there shot along the path a wild light, and I turned to see whence a gleam so unusual could have issued; for the vast house and its shadows were alone behind me. The radiance was that of the full, setting, and blood-red moon which now shone vividly through that once barely discernible fissure of which I have before spoken as extending from the roof of the building, in a zigzag direction, to the base. While I gazed, this fissure rapidly widened—there came a fierce breath of the whirlwind—the entire orb of the satellite burst at once upon my sight—my brain reeled as I saw the mighty walls rushing asunder—there was a long tumultuous shouting sound like the voice of a thousand waters—and the deep and dank tarn at my feet closed sullenly and silently over the fragments of the "HOUSE OF USHER."

QUESTIONS

1. Why does the narrator make the point that even the "sternest natural images of the desolate or terrible" can be pleasurable because they are "poetic"? (91)

2. Is the "mystery" the narrator speaks of, as to why the sight of the House of Usher so unnerves him, ever solved later in the story? (91)

3. If "there are combinations of very simple natural objects which have the power of thus affecting us," then why does the narrator say "the analysis of this power lies among considerations beyond our depth?" (91)

4. Why does the narrator describe, at such length, the tenuous perpetuation of the Usher family from generation to generation? Why does he see the lack of "collateral issue" as so significant? (92)

5. What roles do the valet and the physician play in this story?

6. What accounts for Roderick Usher's "malady"? (95)

7. Why does the narrator experience feelings of "utter astonishment not un-mingled with dread" at the sight of Madeline Usher? (96)

8. Is there an underlying significance to Roderick Usher's creative pursuits (reading esoteric books, painting, musical and poetical improvisation) beyond self-expression?

9. What is "the kingdom of inorganization," and how is it related to Usher's belief in "the sentience of all vegetable things"? (99)

10. Is it significant that the narrator mentions an event as important as the death of Madeline Usher in such a seemingly offhand way?

11. Since Roderick Usher is aware of Madeline's cataleptic symptoms, why might he take the "precaution" of sealing her in a coffin in a stifling chamber for two weeks? (100)

12. Is it significant that the story does not mention early on the fact that Roderick and Madeline Usher are twins and then does so only in passing?

13. What might the story of Sir Ethelred in the "Mad Trist," with its images of using force to reach a treasure within the hermit's dwelling, be meant to convey about the House of Usher? (102)

14. Why had Usher "dared not" speak of hearing Madeline moving within her coffin—that he in fact suspected his sister was buried alive—until it was too late? (104)

15. Who is the "Madman" whom Usher addresses when he screams that his sister is approaching? Why does he use this word? (105)

FOR FURTHER REFLECTION

1. How is it significant that even though they had been "intimate associates" in boyhood, the narrator admits that Usher's temperament prevented him from ever really coming to know him well?

2. Are we to trust the narrator's account of events? Why or why not?

3. Does one have to resort to supernatural explanations to comprehend this story?

4. Bearing in mind that, early in the story, it is noted that the term "House of Usher" refers to both the Usher family and their ancestral home, discuss the coincidence of the deaths of Madeline and Roderick with the (immediately following) collapse of the building itself.

5. How do we explain the pleasure that so many people experience when reading horror fiction?

erman Melville's "Bartleby the Scrivener: A Story of Wall Street" can seem almost too full of meaning. But in trying to take hold of what it offers, we may find ourselves in a situation resembling that of the narrator with respect to his new employee. In forming an interpretation, are we illuminating its depths, or are we merely staring into a mirror? The bleak circumstances into which the narrator invites the copyist—he sits reading and writing legal documents all day in a room with a view of a wall three feet from his window—suggest the tendency of American capitalism to sacrifice all that is most human to economic survival. This aspect of the story is particularly compelling in the context of its publication in *Putnam's Monthly Magazine* in 1853, two years after the critical and commercial failure of *Moby-Dick* (1851), Melville's great novel. In a letter to his friend Nathaniel Hawthorne, Melville wrote, "What I feel most moved to write, that is banned—it will not pay." But the story's implications reach beyond an economic system to the dynamics of human relations. From the moment of the narrator's first request of Bartleby, he exhibits an unrelenting passivity that, while it seems related to immense, unspeakable suffering, becomes a strangely powerful force.

Herman Melville (1819–1891) is now considered one of America's greatest writers, but his life contained only a few short years of literary fame and fortune, preceded and followed by struggle and despair. He was born in New York City to a family whose ancestors included Dutch and Scottish settlers of New York and leaders of the American Revolution. But the collapse of the family import business in 1830 and the death of Melville's father in 1832 left the family in financial ruin. Melville held various low-wage jobs before sailing on a whaler to the South Seas in 1841, a voyage that became the subject of his first novel, *Typee* (1846). With the exception of *Mardi* (1849), a more experimental work, Melville's next three novels—*Omoo* (1847), *Redburn* (1849), and *White-Jacket* (1850)—solidified his reputation as a bankable writer of entertaining sea adventures.

Melville married Elizabeth Shaw in 1847. In 1850, he met Nathaniel Hawthorne, who was then living near Pittsfield, Massachusetts. Melville bought a nearby farm, and Hawthorne became a close friend. Influenced by Hawthorne and by his intensive reading of Shakespeare, Melville wrote *Moby-Dick* in a blaze of creative energy, publishing it in late 1851. Wounded by its failure but undeterred, Melville immediately began writing *Pierre* (1852), a more personal and obscure novel whose reception was even more dismal. Though he continued to write and publish fiction for five more years, including his best short stories ("Bartleby the Scrivener" and "Benito Cereno") and *The Confidence-Man* (1857)—an intricate satire about commerce and corruption—his reputation diminished steadily until his work was revived by scholars in the 1920s.

He turned to writing verse in the late 1850s and, in 1866, privately published his first book of poems, *Battle-Pieces and Aspects of the War*, largely concerned with the Civil War. A few months later, he became a customs inspector on the docks of New York City, which gave him a measure of financial security for the next nineteen years. He continued to write, producing several more works, including two more volumes of poetry and *Billy Budd*, an unfinished novella posthumously published in 1924. He also endured immense family strife and tragedy, including the deaths of two sons. His death on September 28, 1891, prompted few obituaries and little public notice.

HERMAN MELVILLE

Bartleby the Scrivener:
A Story of Wall Street

I am a rather elderly man. The nature of my avocations for the last thirty years has brought me into more than ordinary contact with what would seem an interesting and somewhat singular set of men, of whom as yet nothing that I know of has ever been written—I mean the law copyists or scriveners. I have known very many of them, professionally and privately, and if I pleased, could relate divers histories, at which good-natured gentlemen might smile, and sentimental souls might weep. But I waive the biographies of all other scriveners for a few passages in the life of Bartleby, who was a scrivener the strangest I ever saw or heard of. While of other law copyists I might write the complete life, of Bartleby nothing of that sort can be done. I believe that no materials exist for a full and satisfactory biography of this man. It is an irreparable loss to literature. Bartleby was one of those beings of whom nothing is ascertainable, except from the original sources, and in his case those are very small. What my own astonished eyes saw of Bartleby, *that* is all I know of him, except, indeed, one vague report which will appear in the sequel.

Ere introducing the scrivener, as he first appeared to me, it is fit I make some mention of myself, my *employés*, my business, my chambers, and general surroundings; because some such description is indispensable to an adequate understanding of the chief character about to be presented.

Imprimis: I am a man who, from his youth upward, has been filled with a profound conviction that the easiest way of life is the best. Hence, though I belong to a profession proverbially energetic and nervous, even to turbulence, at times, yet nothing of that sort have I ever suffered to invade my peace. I am one of those unambitious lawyers who never addresses a jury, or in any way draws down public applause; but in the cool tranquillity of a snug retreat, do a snug business among rich men's bonds and mortgages and title-deeds. All who know me, consider me an eminently *safe* man. The late John Jacob Astor, a personage little given to poetic enthusiasm, had no hesitation in pronouncing my first grand point to be prudence; my next, method. I do not speak it in vanity, but simply record the fact, that I was not unemployed in my profession by the late John Jacob Astor; a name which, I admit, I love to repeat, for it hath a rounded and orbicular sound to it, and rings like unto bullion. I will freely add, that I was not insensible to the late John Jacob Astor's good opinion.

Some time prior to the period at which this little history begins, my avocations had been largely increased. The old office, now extinct in the state of New York, of a master in chancery, had been conferred upon me. It was not a very arduous office, but very pleasantly remunerative. I seldom lose my temper; much more seldom indulge in dangerous indignation at wrongs and outrages; but I must be permitted to be rash here and declare that I consider the sudden and violent abrogation of the office of master in chancery, by the new Constitution, as a —— premature act; inasmuch as I had counted upon a life-lease of the profits, whereas I only received those of a few short years. But this is by the way.

My chambers were upstairs at No. —— Wall Street. At one end they looked upon the white wall of the interior of a spacious skylight shaft, penetrating the building from top to bottom. This view might have been considered rather tame than otherwise, deficient in what landscape painters call "life." But if so, the view from the other end of my chambers offered, at least, a contrast, if nothing more. In that direction my windows commanded an unobstructed view of a lofty brick wall, black by age and everlasting shade; which wall required no spyglass to bring out its lurking beauties, but for the benefit of all nearsighted spectators, was pushed up to within ten feet of my windowpanes. Owing to the great height of the surrounding buildings, and my chambers being on the second floor, the interval between this wall and mine not a little resembled a huge square cistern.

At the period just preceding the advent of Bartleby, I had two persons as copyists in my employment, and a promising lad as an office boy. First, Turkey; second, Nippers; third, Ginger Nut. These may seem names, the like of which are not usually found in the directory. In truth they were nicknames, mutually conferred upon each other by my three clerks, and were deemed expressive of their respective persons or characters. Turkey was a short, pursy Englishman of about my own age, that is, somewhere not far from sixty. In the morning, one might say, his face was of a fine florid hue, but after twelve o'clock, meridian—his dinner hour—it blazed like a grate full of Christmas coals; and continued blazing—but, as it were, with a gradual wane—till six o'clock p.m. or thereabouts, after which I saw no more of the proprietor of the face, which, gaining its meridian with the sun, seemed to set with it, to rise, culminate, and decline the following day, with the like regularity and undiminished glory. There are many singular coincidences I have known in the course of my life, not the least among which was the fact, that exactly when Turkey displayed his fullest beams from his red and radiant countenance, just then, too, at that critical moment, began the daily period when I considered his business capacities as seriously disturbed for the remainder of the twenty-four hours. Not that he was absolutely idle, or averse to business then; far from it. The difficulty was, he was apt to be altogether too energetic. There was a strange, inflamed, flurried, flighty recklessness of activity about him. He would be incautious in dipping his pen into his inkstand. All his blots upon my documents were dropped there after twelve o'clock, meridian. Indeed, not only would he be reckless and sadly given to making blots in the afternoon, but some days he went further, and was rather noisy. At such times, too, his face flamed with augmented blazonry, as if cannel coal had been heaped on anthracite. He made an unpleasant racket with his chair; spilled his sand-box; in mending his pens, impatiently split them all to pieces and threw them on the floor in a sudden passion; stood up and leaned over his table, boxing his papers about in a most indecorous manner, very sad to behold in an elderly man like him. Nevertheless, as he was in many ways a most valuable person to me, and all the time before twelve o'clock, meridian, was the quickest, steadiest creature, too, accomplishing a great deal of work in a style not easy to be matched—for these reasons, I was willing to overlook his eccentricities, though, indeed, occasionally, I remonstrated with him. I did this very gently, however, because, though the civilest, nay, the blandest and most reverential of men in the morning, yet in the afternoon he was disposed, upon provocation, to be slightly rash with his tongue, in fact, insolent. Now, valuing his morning services as I did, and resolving not to lose them—yet, at the same time, made uncomfortable by his inflamed ways after twelve o'clock; and being a man of peace, unwilling by my admonitions to call forth unseemly retorts from him—I took upon me, one Saturday noon (he was always worse on Saturdays), to hint to him, very kindly, that perhaps now that he was growing old, it might be well to abridge his labors; in short, he need not come to my chambers after twelve o'clock, but, dinner over, had best go home to his lodgings and rest himself till teatime. But no; he insisted upon his afternoon devotions. His countenance became intolerably fervid, as he oratorically assured me—gesticulating, with a long ruler, at the other side of the room—that if his services in the morning were useful, how indispensable, then, in the afternoon?

"With submission, sir," said Turkey on this occasion, "I consider myself your righthand man. In the morning I but marshal and deploy my columns; but in the afternoon I put myself at their head and gallantly charge the foe, thus!"—and he made a violent thrust with the ruler.

"But the blots, Turkey," intimated I.

"True—but, with submission, sir, behold these hairs! I am getting old. Surely, sir, a blot or two of a warm afternoon is not to be severely urged against gray hairs. Old age—even if it blot the page—is honorable. With submission, sir, we *both* are getting old."

This appeal to my fellow feeling was hardly to be resisted. At all events, l saw that go he would not. So I made up my mind to let him stay, resolving, nevertheless, to see to it, that during the afternoon he had to do with my less important papers.

Nippers, the second on my list, was a whiskered, sallow, and, upon the whole, rather piratical-looking young man of about five and twenty. I always deemed him the victim of two evil powers—ambition and indigestion. The ambition was evinced by a certain impatience of the duties of a mere copyist—an unwarrantable usurpation of strictly professional affairs, such as the original drawing up of legal documents. The indigestion seemed betokened in an occasional nervous testiness and grinning irritability, causing the teeth to audibly grind together over mistakes committed in copying; unnecessary maledictions, hissed, rather than spoken, in the heat of business; and especially by a continual discontent with the height of the table where he worked. Though of a very ingenious mechanical turn, Nippers could never get this table to suit him. He put chips under it, blocks of various sorts, bits of pasteboard, and at last went so far as to attempt an exquisite adjustment by final pieces of folded blotting paper. But no invention would answer. If, for the sake of easing his back, he brought the table lid at a sharp angle well up toward his chin, and wrote there like a man using the steep roof of a Dutch house for his desk—then he declared that it stopped the circulation in his arms. If now he lowered the table to his waistbands, and stooped over it in writing, then there was a sore aching in his back. In short, the truth of the matter was, Nippers knew not what he wanted. Or, if he wanted anything, it was to be rid of a scrivener's table altogether. Among the manifestations of his diseased ambition was a fondness he had for receiving visits from certain ambiguous-looking fellows in seedy coats, whom he called his clients. Indeed I was aware that not only was he, at times, considerable of a ward politician, but he occasionally did a little business at the Justices' courts, and was not unknown on the steps of the Tombs. I have good reason to believe, however, that one individual who called upon him at my chambers, and who, with a grand air, he insisted was his client, was no other than a dun, and the alleged title-deed, a bill. But with all his failings, and the annoyances he caused me, Nippers, like his compatriot Turkey, was a very useful man to me; wrote a neat, swift hand; and, when he chose, was not deficient in a gentlemanly sort of deportment. Added to this, he always dressed in a gentlemanly sort of way; and so, incidentally, reflected credit upon my chambers. Whereas with respect to Turkey, I had much ado to keep him from being a reproach to me. His clothes were apt to look oily and smell of eating houses. He wore his pantaloons very loose and baggy in summer. His coats were execrable; his hat not to be handled.

But while the hat was a thing of indifference to me, inasmuch as his natural civility and deference, as a dependent Englishman, always led him to doff it the moment he entered the room, yet his coat was another matter. Concerning his coats, I reasoned with him; but with no effect. The truth was, I suppose, that a man with so small an income could not afford to sport such a lustrous face and a lustrous coat at one and the same time. As Nippers once observed, Turkey's money went chiefly for red ink. One winter day I presented Turkey with a highly respectable looking coat of my own, a padded gray coat, of a most comfortable warmth, and which buttoned straight up from the knee to the neck. I thought Turkey would appreciate the favor, and abate his rashness and obstreperousness of afternoons. But no. I verily believe that buttoning himself up in so downy and blanketlike a coat had a pernicious effect upon him; upon the same principle that too much oats are bad for horses. In fact, precisely as a rash, restive horse is said to feel his oats, so Turkey felt his coat. It made him insolent. He was a man whom prosperity harmed.

Though concerning the self-indulgent habits of Turkey I had my own private surmises, yet touching Nippers I was well persuaded that whatever might be his faults in other respects, he was, at least, a temperate young man. But, indeed, nature herself seemed to have been his vintner, and at his birth charged him so thoroughly with an irritable, brandylike disposition, that all subsequent potations were needless. When I consider how, amid the stillness of my chambers, Nippers would sometimes impatiently rise from his seat, and stooping over his table, spread his arms wide apart, seize the whole desk, and move it, and jerk it, with a grim, grinding motion on the floor, as if the table were a perverse voluntary agent, intent on thwarting and vexing him; I plainly perceive that for Nippers, brandy and water were altogether superfluous.

It was fortunate for me that, owing to its peculiar cause—indigestion—the irritability and consequent nervousness of Nippers were mainly observable in the morning, while, in the afternoon he was comparatively mild. So that Turkey's paroxysms only coming on about twelve o'clock, I never had to do with their eccentricities at one time. Their fits relieved each other like guards. When Nippers's was on, Turkey's was off; and vice versa. This was a good natural arrangement under the circumstances.

Ginger Nut, the third on my list, was a lad some twelve years old. His father was a carman, ambitious of seeing his son on the bench instead of a cart, before he died. So he sent him to my office as student at law, errand boy, and cleaner and sweeper, at the rate of one dollar a week. He had a little desk to himself, but he did not use it much. Upon inspection, the drawer exhibited a great array of the shells of various sorts of nuts. Indeed, to this quick-witted youth the whole noble science of the law was contained in a nutshell. Not the least among the employments of Ginger Nut, as well as one which he discharged with the most alacrity, was his duty as cake and apple purveyor for Turkey and Nippers. Copying law papers being proverbially a dry, husky sort of business, my two scriveners were fain to moisten their mouths very often with Spitzenbergs to be had at the numerous stalls nigh the custom house and post office. Also, they sent Ginger Nut very frequently for that peculiar cake—small, flat, round, and very spicy—after which he had been named by them. Of a cold morning, when business was but dull, Turkey would gobble up scores of these cakes, as if they were mere wafers—indeed they sell them at the rate of six or eight for a penny—the scrape of his pen blending with the crunching of the crisp particles in his mouth. Of all the fiery afternoon blunders and flurried rashness of Turkey, was his once moistening a ginger cake between his lips, and clapping it on to a mortgage for a seal. I came within an ace of dismissing him then. But he mollified me by making an oriental bow and saying—"With submission, sir, it was generous of me to find you in stationery on my own account."

Now my original business—that of a conveyancer and title hunter, and drawer-up of recondite documents of all sorts—was considerably increased by receiving the master's office. There was now great work for scriveners. Not only must I push the clerks already with me, but I must have additional help. In answer to my advertisement, a motionless young man one morning stood upon my office threshold, the door being open, for it was summer. I can see that figure now—pallidly neat, pitiably respectable, incurably forlorn! It was Bartleby.

After a few words touching his qualifications, I engaged him, glad to have among my corps of copyists a man of so singularly sedate an aspect, which I thought might operate beneficially upon the flighty temper of Turkey, and the fiery one of Nippers.

I should have stated before that ground-glass folding doors divided my premises into two parts, one of which was occupied by my scriveners, the other by myself. According to my humor I threw open these doors, or closed them. I resolved to assign Bartleby a corner by the folding doors, but on my side of them, so as to have this quiet man within easy call, in case any trifling thing was to be done. I placed his desk close up to a small side window in that part of the room, a window which originally had afforded a lateral view of certain grimy backyards and bricks, but which, owing to subsequent erections, commanded at present no view at all, though it gave some light. Within three feet of the panes was a wall, and the light came down from far above, between two lofty buildings, as from a very small opening in a dome. Still further to a satisfactory arrangement, I procured a high green folding screen, which might entirely isolate Bartleby from my sight, though not remove him from my voice. And thus, in a manner, privacy and society were conjoined.

At first Bartleby did an extraordinary quantity of writing. As if long famishing for something to copy, he seemed to gorge himself on my documents. There was no pause for digestion. He ran a day and night line, copying by sunlight and by candlelight. I should have been quite delighted with his application, had he been cheerfully industrious. But he wrote on silently, palely, mechanically.

It is, of course, an indispensable part of a scrivener's business to verify the accuracy of his copy, word by word. Where there are two or more scriveners in an office, they assist each other in this examination, one reading from the copy, the other holding the original. It is a very dull, wearisome, and lethargic affair. I can readily imagine that to some sanguine temperaments it would be altogether intolerable. For example, I cannot credit that the mettlesome poet Byron would have contentedly sat down with Bartleby to examine a law document of, say five hundred pages, closely written in a crimpy hand.

Now and then, in the haste of business, it had been my habit to assist in comparing some brief document myself, calling Turkey or Nippers for this purpose. One object I had in placing Bartleby so handy to me behind the screen was to avail myself of his services on such trivial occasions. It was on the third day, I think, of his being with me, and before any necessity had arisen for having his own writing examined, that, being much hurried to complete a small affair I had in hand, I abruptly called to Bartleby. In my haste and natural expectancy of instant compliance, I sat with my head bent over the original on my desk, and my right hand sideways, and somewhat nervously extended with the copy, so that immediately upon emerging from his retreat, Bartleby might snatch it and proceed to business without the least delay.

In this very attitude did I sit when I called to him, rapidly stating what it was I wanted him to do—namely, to examine a small paper with me. Imagine my surprise, nay, my consternation, when without moving from his privacy, Bartleby in a singularly mild, firm voice, replied, "I would prefer not to."

I sat awhile in perfect silence, rallying my stunned faculties. Immediately it occurred to me that my ears had deceived me, or Bartleby had entirely misunderstood my meaning. I repeated my request in the clearest tone I could assume. But in quite as clear a one came the previous reply, "I would prefer not to."

"Prefer not to," echoed I, rising in high excitement and crossing the room with a stride. "What do you mean? Are you moonstruck? I want you to help me compare this sheet here—take it," and I thrust it toward him.

"I would prefer not to," said he.

I looked at him steadfastly. His face was leanly composed; his gray eye dimly calm. Not a wrinkle of agitation rippled him. Had there been the least uneasiness, anger, impatience, or impertinence in his manner; in other words, had there been anything ordinarily human about him; doubtless I should have violently dismissed him from the premises. But as it was, I should have as soon thought of turning my pale plaster-of-Paris bust of Cicero out of doors. I stood gazing at him awhile, as he went on with his own writing, and then reseated myself at my desk. This is very strange, thought I. What had one best do? But my business hurried me. I concluded to forget the matter for the present, reserving it for my future leisure. So calling Nippers from the other room, the paper was speedily examined.

A few days after this, Bartleby concluded four lengthy documents, being quadruplicates of a week's testimony taken before me in my High Court of Chancery. It became necessary to examine them. It was an important suit, and great accuracy was imperative. Having all things arranged, I called Turkey, Nippers, and Ginger Nut from the next room, meaning to place the four copies in the hands of my four clerks, while I should read from the original. Accordingly Turkey, Nippers, and Ginger Nut had taken their seats in row, each with his document in hand, when I called to Bartleby to join this interesting group.

"Bartleby! quick, I am waiting."

I heard a slow scrape of his chair legs on the uncarpeted floor, and soon he appeared standing at the entrance of his hermitage.

"What is wanted?" said he mildly.

"The copies, the copies," said I hurriedly. "We are going to examine them. There"—and I held toward him the fourth quadruplicate.

"I would prefer not to," he said, and gently disappeared behind the screen.

For a few moments I was turned into a pillar of salt, standing at the head of my seated column of clerks. Recovering myself, I advanced toward the screen, and demanded the reason for such extraordinary conduct.

"*Why* do you refuse?"

"I would prefer not to."

With any other man I should have flown outright into a dreadful passion, scorned all further words, and thrust him ignominiously from my presence. But there was something about Bartleby that not only strangely disarmed me, but in a wonderful manner touched and disconcerted me. I began to reason with him.

"These are your own copies we are about to examine. It is labor saving to you, because one examination will answer for your four papers. It is common usage. Every copyist is bound to help examine his copy. Is it not so? Will you not speak? Answer!"

"I prefer not to," he replied in a flutelike tone. It seemed to me that while I had been addressing him, he carefully revolved every statement that I made; fully comprehended the meaning; could not gainsay the irresistible conclusion; but, at the same time, some paramount consideration prevailed with him to reply as he did.

"You are decided, then, not to comply with my request—a request made according to common usage and common sense?"

He briefly gave me to understand that on that point my judgment was sound. Yes: his decision was irreversible.

It is not seldom the case that when a man is browbeaten in some unprecedented and violently unreasonable way, he begins to stagger in his own plainest faith. He begins, as it were, vaguely to surmise that, wonderful as it may be, all the justice and all the reason are on the other side. Accordingly, if any disinterested persons are present, he turns to them for some reinforcement for his own faltering mind.

"Turkey," said I, "what do you think of this? Am I not right?"

"With submission, sir," said Turkey, with his blandest tone, "I think that you are."

"Nippers," said I, "what do *you* think of it?"

"I think I should kick him out of the office."

(The reader of nice perceptions will here perceive that, it being morning, Turkey's answer is couched in polite and tranquil terms but Nippers's reply in ill-tempered ones. Or to repeat a previous sentence, Nippers's ugly mood was on duty, and Turkey's off.)

"Ginger Nut," said I, willing to enlist the smallest suffrage in my behalf, "what do *you* think of it?"

"I think, sir, he's a little *luny*," replied Ginger Nut, with a grin.

"You hear what they say," said I, turning toward the screen, "come forth and do your duty."

But he vouchsafed no reply. I pondered a moment in sore perplexity. But once more business hurried me. I determined again to postpone the consideration of this dilemma to my future leisure. With a little trouble we made out to examine the papers without Bartleby, though at every page or two, Turkey deferentially dropped his opinion that this proceeding was quite out of the common; while Nippers, twitching in his chair with a dyspeptic nervousness, ground out between his set teeth occasional hissing maledictions against the stubborn oaf behind the screen. And for his (Nippers's) part, this was the first and the last time he would do another man's business without pay.

Meanwhile Bartleby sat in his hermitage, oblivious to everything but his own peculiar business there.

Some days passed, the scrivener being employed upon another lengthy work. His late remarkable conduct led me to regard his ways narrowly. I observed that he never went to dinner; indeed that he never went anywhere. As yet I had never of my personal knowledge known him to be outside of my office. He was a perpetual sentry in the corner. At about eleven o'clock though, in the morning, I noticed that Ginger Nut would advance toward the opening in Bartleby's screen, as if silently beckoned thither by a gesture invisible to me where I sat. The boy would then leave the office jingling a few pence, and reappear with a handful of ginger nuts which he delivered in the hermitage, receiving two of the cakes for his trouble.

He lives, then, on ginger nuts, thought I; never eats a dinner, properly speaking; he must be a vegetarian then; but no; he never eats even vegetables, he eats nothing but ginger nuts. My mind then ran on in reveries concerning the probable effects upon the human constitution of living entirely on ginger nuts. Ginger nuts are so called because they contain ginger as one of their peculiar constituents, and the final flavoring one. Now what was ginger? A hot, spicy thing. Was Bartleby hot and spicy? Not at all. Ginger, then, had no effect upon Bartleby. Probably he preferred it should have none.

Nothing so aggravates an earnest person as a passive resistance. If the individual so resisted be of a not inhumane temper, and the resisting one perfectly harmless in his passivity; then, in the better moods of the former, he will endeavor charitably to construe to his imagination what proves impossible to be solved by his judgment. Even so, for the most part, I regarded Bartleby and his ways. Poor fellow! thought I, he means no mischief; it is plain he intends no insolence; his aspect sufficiently evinces that his eccentricities are involuntary. He is useful to me. I can get along with him. If I turn him away, the chances are he will fall in with some less indulgent employer, and then he will be rudely treated, and perhaps driven forth mierably to starve. Yes. Here I can cheaply purchase a delicious self-approval. To befriend Bartleby; to humor him in his strange willfulness, will cost me little or nothing, while I lay up in my soul what will eventually prove a sweet morsel for my conscience. But this mood was not invariable with me. The passiveness of Bartleby sometimes irritated me. I felt strangely goaded on to encounter him in new opposition, to elicit some angry spark from him answerable to my own. But indeed I might as well have essayed to strike fire with my knuckles against a bit of Windsor soap. But one afternoon the evil impulse in me mastered me, and the following little scene ensued:

"Bartleby," said I, "when those papers are all copied, I will compare them with you."

"I would prefer not to."

"How? Surely you do not mean to persist in that mulish vagary?"

No answer.

I threw open the folding doors nearby, and turning upon Turkey and Nippers, exclaimed in an excited manner:

"He says, a second time, he won't examine his papers. What do you think of it, Turkey?"

It was afternoon, be it remembered. Turkey sat glowing like a brass boiler, his bald head steaming, his hands reeling among his blotted papers.

"Think of it?" roared Turkey; "I think I'll just step behind his screen and black his eyes for him!"

So saying, Turkey rose to his feet and threw his arms into a pugilistic position. He was hurrying away to make good his promise, when I detained him, alarmed at the effect of incautiously rousing Turkey's combativeness after dinner.

"Sit down, Turkey," said I, "and hear what Nippers has to say. What do you think of it, Nippers? Would I not be justified in immediately dismissing Bartleby?"

"Excuse me, that is for you to decide, sir. I think his conduct quite unusual, and indeed unjust, as regards Turkey and myself. But it may only be a passing whim."

"Ah," exclaimed I, "you have strangely changed your mind then—you speak very gently of him now."

"All beer," cried Turkey; "gentleness is effects of beer—Nippers and I dined together today. You see how gentle *I* am, sir. Shall I go and black his eyes?"

"You refer to Bartleby, I suppose. No, not today, Turkey," I replied; "pray, put up your fists."

I closed the doors, and again advanced toward Bartleby. I felt additional incentives tempting me to my fate. I burned to be rebelled against again. I remembered that Bartleby never left the office.

"Bartleby," said I, "Ginger Nut is away; just step round to the post office, won't you? (it was but a three minutes' walk), and see if there is anything for me."

"I would prefer not to."

"You *will* not?"

"I *prefer* not."

I staggered to my desk, and sat there in a deep study. My blind inveteracy returned. Was there any other thing in which I could procure myself to be ignominiously repulsed by this lean, penniless wight?—my hired clerk? What added thing is there, perfectly reasonable, that he will be sure to refuse to do?

"Bartleby!"

No answer.

"Bartleby," in a louder tone.

No answer.

"Bartleby," I roared.

Like a very ghost, agreeably to the laws of magical invocation, at the third summons, he appeared at the entrance of his hermitage.

"Go to the next room, and tell Nippers to come to me."

"I prefer not to," he respectfully and slowly said, and mildly disappeared.

"Very good, Bartleby," said I, in a quiet sort of serenely severe self-possessed tone, intimating the unalterable purpose of some terrible retribution very close at hand. At the moment I half intended something of the kind. But upon the whole, as it was drawing toward my dinner hour, I thought it best to put on my hat and walk home for the day, suffering much from perplexity and distress of mind.

Shall I acknowledge it? The conclusion of this whole business was, that it soon became a fixed fact of my chambers, that a pale young scrivener, by the name of Bartleby, had a desk there; that he copied for me at the usual rate of four cents a folio (one hundred words); but he was permanently exempt from examining the work done by him, that duty being transferred to Turkey and Nippers, out of compliment doubtless to their superior acuteness; moreover, said Bartleby was never on any account to be dispatched on the most trivial errand of any sort; and that even if entreated to take upon him such a matter, it was generally understood that he would prefer not to—in other words, that he would refuse point-blank.

As days passed on, I became considerably reconciled to Bartleby. His steadiness, his freedom from all dissipation, his incessant industry (except when he chose to throw himself into a standing reverie behind his screen), his great stillness, his unalterableness of demeanor under all circumstances, made him a valuable acquisition. One prime thing was this: *he was always there*—first in the morning, continually through the day, and the last at night. I had a singular confidence in his honesty. I felt my most precious papers perfectly safe in his hands. Sometimes to be sure I could not, for the very soul of me, avoid falling into sudden spasmodic passions with him. For it was exceeding difficult to bear in mind all the time those strange peculiarities, privileges, and unheard-of exemptions, forming the tacit stipulations on Bartleby's part under which he remained in my office. Now and then, in the eagerness of dispatching pressing business, I would inadvertently summon Bartleby, in a short, rapid tone, to put his finger, say, on the incipient tie of a bit of red tape with which I was about compressing some papers. Of course, from behind the screen the usual answer, "I prefer not to," was sure to come; and then, how could a human creature with the common infirmities of our nature, refrain from bitterly exclaiming upon such perverseness—such unreasonableness. However, every added repulse of this sort which I received only tended to lessen the probability of my repeating the inadvertence.

Here it must be said, that according to the custom of most legal gentlemen occupying chambers in densely populated law buildings, there were several keys to my door. One was kept by a woman residing in the attic, which person weekly scrubbed and daily swept and dusted my apartments. Another was kept by Turkey for convenience' sake. The third I sometimes carried in my own pocket. The fourth I knew not who had.

Now, one Sunday morning I happened to go to Trinity Church, to hear a celebrated preacher, and finding myself rather early on the ground, I thought I would walk round to my chambers for awhile. Luckily I had my key with me; but upon applying it to the lock, I found it resisted by something inserted from the inside. Quite surprised, I called out; when to my consternation a key was turned from within; and thrusting his lean visage at me, and holding the door ajar, the apparition of Bartleby appeared, in his shirt sleeves, and otherwise in a strangely tattered dishabille, saying quietly that he was sorry, but he was deeply engaged just then, and—preferred not admitting me at present. In a brief word or two, he moreover added, that perhaps I had better walk round the block two or three times, and by that time he would probably have concluded his affairs.

Now, the utterly unsurmised appearance of Bartleby, tenanting my law chambers of a Sunday morning, with his cadaverously gentlemanly nonchalance, yet withal firm and self-possessed, had such a strange effect upon me, that incontinently I slunk away from my own door, and did as desired. But not without sundry twinges of impotent rebellion against the mild effrontery of this unaccountable scrivener. Indeed, it was his wonderful mildness chiefly which not only disarmed me, but unmanned me, as it were. For I consider that one, for the time, is in a way unmanned when he tranquilly permits his hired clerk to dictate to him, and order him away from his own premises. Furthermore, I was full of uneasiness as to what Bartleby could be doing in my office in his shirt sleeves, and in an otherwise dismantled condition of a Sunday morning. Was anything amiss going on? Nay, that was out of the question. It was not to be thought of for a moment that Bartleby was an immoral person. But what could he be doing there—copying? Nay again, whatever might be his eccentricities, Bartleby was an eminently decorous person. He would be the last man to sit down to his desk in any state approaching to nudity. Besides, it was Sunday; and there was something about Bartleby that forbade the supposition that he would by any secular occupation violate the proprieties of the day.

Nevertheless, my mind was not pacified; and full of a restless curiosity, at last I returned to the door. Without hindrance I inserted my key, opened it, and entered. Bartleby was not to be seen. I looked round anxiously, peeped behind his screen; but it was very plain that he was gone. Upon more closely examining the place, I surmised that for an indefinite period Bartleby must have ate, dressed, and slept in my office, and that too without plate, mirror, or bed. The cushioned seat of a rickety old sofa in one corner bore the faint impress of a lean, reclining form. Rolled away under his desk, I found a blanket; under the empty grate, a blacking box and brush; on a chair, a tin basin, with soap and a ragged towel; in a newspaper a few crumbs of ginger nuts and a morsel of cheese. Yes, thought I, it is evident enough that Bartleby has been making his home here, keeping bachelor's hall all by himself. Immediately then the thought came sweeping across me, What miserable friendlessness and loneliness are here revealed! His poverty is great; but his solitude, how horrible! Think of it. Of a Sunday, Wall Street is deserted as Petra; and every night of every day it is an emptiness. This building too, which of weekdays hums with industry and life, at nightfall echoes with sheer vacancy and all through Sunday is forlorn. And here Bartleby makes his home; sole spectator of a solitude which he has seen all populous—a sort of innocent and transformed Marius brooding among the ruins of Carthage!

For the first time in my life a feeling of overpowering stinging melancholy seized me. Before, I had never experienced aught but a not-unpleasing sadness. The bond of a common humanity now drew me irresistibly to gloom. A fraternal melancholy! For both I and Bartleby were sons of Adam. I remembered the bright silks and sparkling faces I had seen that day, in gala trim, swanlike sailing down the Mississippi of Broadway; and I contrasted them with the pallid copyist, and thought to myself, Ah, happiness courts the light, so we deem the world is gay; but misery hides aloof, so we deem that misery there is none. These sad fancyings—chimeras, doubtless, of a sick and silly brain—led on to other and more special thoughts, concerning the eccentricities of Bartleby. Presentiments of strange discoveries hovered round me. The scrivener's pale form appeared to me laid out, among uncaring strangers, in its shivering winding sheet.

Suddenly I was attracted by Bartleby's closed desk, the key in open sight left in the lock.

I mean no mischief, seek the gratification of no heartless curiosity, thought I; besides, the desk is mine, and its contents, too, so I will make bold to look within. Everything was methodically arranged, the papers smoothly placed. The pigeon holes were deep, and, removing the files of documents, I groped into their recesses. Presently I felt something there, and dragged it out. It was an old bandanna handkerchief, heavy and knotted. I opened it, and saw it was a savings bank.

I now recalled all the quiet mysteries which I had noted in the man. I remembered that he never spoke but to answer; that though at intervals he had considerable time to himself, yet I had never seen him reading—no, not even a newspaper; that for long periods he would stand looking out, at his pale window behind the screen, upon the dead brick wall; I was quite sure he never visited any refectory or eating house; while his pale face clearly indicated that he never drank beer like Turkey, or tea and coffee even, like other men; that he never went anywhere in particular that I could learn; never went out for a walk, unless indeed that was the case at present; that he had declined telling who he was, or whence he came, or whether he had any relatives in the world; that though so thin and pale, he never complained of ill health. And more than all, I remembered a certain unconscious air of pallid—how shall I call it?—of pallid haughtiness, say, or rather an austere reserve about him, which had positively awed me into my tame compliance with his eccentricities, when I had feared to ask him to do the slightest incidental thing for me, even though I might know, from his long-continued motionlessness, that behind his screen he must be standing in one of those dead-wall reveries of his.

Revolving all these things, and coupling them with the recently discovered fact that he made my office his constant abiding place and home, and not forgetful of his morbid moodiness; revolving all these things, a prudential feeling began to steal over me. My first emotions had been those of pure melancholy and sincerest pity; but just in proportion as the forlornness of Bartleby grew and grew to my imagination, did that same melancholy merge into fear, that pity into repulsion. So true it is, and so terrible, too, that up to a certain point the thought or sight of misery enlists our best affections; but, in certain special cases, beyond that point it does not. They err who would assert that invariably this is owing to the inherent selfishness of the human heart. It rather proceeds from a certain hopelessness of remedying excessive and organic ill. To a sensitive being, pity is not seldom pain. And when at last it is perceived that such pity cannot lead to effectual succor, common sense bids the soul be rid of it. What I saw that morning persuaded me that the scrivener was the victim of innate and incurable disorder. I might give alms to his body; but his body did not pain him; it was his soul that suffered, and his soul I could not reach.

I did not accomplish the purpose of going to Trinity Church that morning. Somehow, the things I had seen disqualified me for the time from churchgoing. I walked homeward, thinking what I would do with Bartleby. Finally, I resolved upon this—I would put certain calm questions to him the next morning, touching his history, etc., and if he declined to answer them openly and unreservedly (and I supposed he would prefer not), then to give him a twenty dollar bill over and above whatever I might owe him, and tell him his services were no longer required; but that if in any other way I could assist him, I would be happy to do so, especially if he desired to return to his native place, wherever that might be, I would willingly help to defray the expenses. Moreover, if, after reaching home, he found himself at any time in want of aid, a letter from him would be sure of a reply.

The next morning came.

"Bartleby," said I, gently calling to him behind his screen.

No reply.

"Bartleby," said I, in a still gentler tone, "come here; I am not going to ask you to do anything you would prefer not to do—I simply wish to speak to you."

Upon this he noiselessly slid into view.

"Will you tell me, Bartleby, where you were born?"

"I would prefer not to."

"Will you tell me *anything* about yourself?"

"I would prefer not to."

"But what reasonable objection can you have to speak to me? I feel friendly toward you."

He did not look at me while I spoke, but kept his glance fixed upon my bust of Cicero, which, as I then sat, was directly behind me, some six inches above my head.

"What is your answer, Bartleby?" said I, after waiting a considerable time for a reply, during which his countenance remained immovable, only there was the faintest conceivable tremor of the white attenuated mouth.

"At present I prefer to give no answer," he said, and retired into his hermitage.

It was rather weak in me I confess, but his manner on this occasion nettled me. Not only did there seem to lurk in it a certain calm disdain, but his perverseness seemed ungrateful, considering the undeniable good usage and indulgence he had received from me.

Again I sat ruminating what I should do. Mortified as I was at his behavior, and resolved as I had been to dismiss him when I entered my office, nevertheless I strangely felt something superstitious knocking at my heart, and forbidding me to carry out my purpose, and denouncing me for a villain if I dared to breathe one bitter word against this forlornest of mankind. At last, familiarly drawing my chair behind his screen, I sat down and said: "Bartleby, never mind then about revealing your history; but let me entreat you, as a friend, to comply as far as may be with the usages of this office. Say now you will help to examine papers tomorrow or next day: in short, say now that in a day or two you will begin to be a little reasonable— say so, Bartleby."

"At present I would prefer not to be a little reasonable," was his mildly cadaverous reply.

Just then the folding doors opened, and Nippers approached. He seemed suffering from an unusually bad night's rest, induced by severer indigestion than common. He overheard those final words of Bartleby.

"*Prefer not*, eh?" gritted Nippers—"I'd *prefer* him, if I were you, sir," addressing me—"I'd *prefer* him; I'd give him preferences, the stubborn mule! What is it, sir, pray, that he *prefers* not to do now?"

Bartleby moved not a limb.

"Mr. Nippers," said I, "I'd prefer that you would withdraw for the present."

Somehow, of late I had got into the way of involuntarily using this word *prefer* upon all sorts of not exactly suitable occasions. And I trembled to think that my contact with the scrivener had already and seriously affected me in a mental way. And what further and deeper aberration might it not yet produce? This apprehension had not been without efficacy in determining me to summary means.

As Nippers, looking very sour and sulky, was departing, Turkey blandly and deferentially approached.

"With submission, sir," said he, "yesterday I was thinking about Bartleby here, and I think that if he would but prefer to take a quart of good ale every day, it would do much toward mending him, and enabling him to assist in examining his papers."

"So you have got the word, too," said I, slightly excited.

"With submission, what word, sir," asked Turkey, respectfully crowding himself into the contracted space behind the screen, and by so doing, making me jostle the scrivener. "What word, sir?"

"I would prefer to be left alone here," said Bartleby, as if offended at being mobbed in his privacy.

"*That's* the word, Turkey," said I—"*that's* it."

"Oh, *prefer*? oh, yes—queer word. I never use it myself. But, sir, as I was saying, if he would but prefer—"

"Turkey," interrupted I, "you will please withdraw."

"Oh certainly, sir, if you prefer that I should."

As he opened the folding door to retire, Nippers at his desk caught a glimpse of me, and asked whether I would prefer to have a certain paper copied on blue paper or white. He did not in the least roguishly accent the word *prefer*. It was plain that it involuntarily rolled from his tongue. I thought to myself, surely I must get rid of a demented man, who already has in some degree turned the tongues, if not the heads, of myself and clerks. But I thought it prudent not to break the dismission at once.

The next day I noticed that Bartleby did nothing but stand at his window in his dead-wall reverie. Upon asking him why he did not write, he said that he had decided upon doing no more writing.

"Why, how now? what next?" exclaimed I, "do no more writing?"

"No more."

"And what is the reason?"

"Do you not see the reason for yourself?" he indifferently replied.

I looked steadfastly at him, and perceived that his eyes looked dull and glazed. Instantly it occurred to me, that his unexampled diligence in copying by his dim window for the first few weeks of his stay with me might have temporarily impaired his vision.

I was touched. I said something in condolence with him. I hinted that, of course, he did wisely in abstaining from writing for a while, and urged him to embrace that opportunity of taking wholesome exercise in the open air. This, however, he did not do. A few days after this, my other clerks being absent, and being in a great hurry to dispatch certain letters by the mail, I thought that, having nothing else earthly to do, Bartleby would surely be less inflexible than usual, and carry these letters to the post office. But he blankly declined. So, much to my inconvenience, I went myself.

Still added days went by. Whether Bartleby's eyes improved or not, I could not say. To all appearance, I thought they did. But when I asked him if they did, he vouchsafed no answer. At all events, he would do no copying. At last, in reply to my urgings, he informed me that he had permanently given up copying.

"What!" exclaimed I; "suppose your eyes should get entirely well—better than ever before—would you not copy then?"

"I have given up copying," he answered and slid aside.

He remained, as ever, a fixture in my chamber. Nay—if that were possible —he became still more of a fixture than before. What was to be done? He would do nothing in the office: why should he stay there? In plain fact, he had now become a millstone to me, not only useless as a necklace, but afflictive to bear. Yet I was sorry for him. I speak less than truth when I say that, on his own account, he occasioned me uneasiness. If he would but have named a single relative or friend, I would instantly have written, and urged their taking the poor fellow away to some convenient retreat. But he seemed alone, absolutely alone in the universe. A bit of wreckage in the mid-Atlantic. At length, necessities connected with my business tyrannized over all other considerations. Decently as I could, I told Bartleby that in six days' time he must unconditionally leave the office. I warned him to take measures, in the interval, for procuring some other abode. I offered to assist him in this endeavor, if he himself would but take the first step toward a removal. "And when you finally quit me, Bartleby," added I, "I shall see that you go away not entirely unprovided. Six days from this hour, remember."

At the expiration of that period, I peeped behind the screen, and lo! Bartleby was there.

I buttoned up my coat, balanced myself; advanced slowly toward him, touched his shoulder, and said, "The time has come; you must quit this place; I am sorry for you; here is money; but you must go."

"I would prefer not," he replied, with his back still toward me.

"You *must*."

He remained silent.

Now I had an unbounded confidence in this man's common honesty. He had frequently restored to me sixpences and shillings carelessly dropped upon the floor, for I am apt to be very reckless in such shirt-button affairs. The proceeding then which followed will not be deemed extraordinary.

"Bartleby," said I, "I owe you twelve dollars on account; here are thirty-two; the odd twenty are yours.—Will you take it?" and I handed the bills toward him.

But he made no motion.

"I will leave them here then," putting them under a weight on the table.

Then taking my hat and cane and going to the door, I tranquilly turned and added—"After you have removed your things from these offices, Bartleby, you will of course lock the door—since every one is now gone for the day but you—and if you please, slip your key underneath the mat, so that I may have it in the morning. I shall not see you again; so goodbye to you. If hereafter in your new place of abode I can be of any service to you, do not fail to advise me by letter. Goodbye, Bartleby, and fare you well."

But he answered not a word; like the last column of some ruined temple, he remained standing mute and solitary in the middle of the otherwise deserted room.

As I walked home in a pensive mood, my vanity got the better of my pity. I could not but highly plume myself on my masterly management in getting rid of Bartleby. Masterly I call it, and such it must appear to any dispassionate thinker. The beauty of my procedure seemed to consist in its perfect quietness. There was no vulgar bullying, no bravado of any sort, no choleric hectoring, no striding to and fro across the apartment, jerking out vehement commands for Bartleby to bundle himself off with his beggarly traps. Nothing of the kind. Without loudly bidding Bartleby depart—as an inferior genius might have done—I *assumed* the ground that depart he must; and upon that assumption built all I had to say. The more I thought over my procedure, the more I was charmed with it. Nevertheless, next morning, upon awakening, I had my doubts,—I had somehow slept off the fumes of vanity. One of the coolest and wisest hours a man has, is just after he awakes in the morning. My procedure seemed as sagacious as ever,—but only in theory. How it would prove in practice—there was the rub. It was truly a beautiful thought to have assumed Bartleby's departure; but, after all, that assumption was simply my own, and none of Bartleby's. The great point was, not whether I had assumed that he would quit me, but whether he would prefer so to do. He was more a man of preferences than assumptions.

After breakfast, I walked downtown, arguing the probabilities pro and con. One moment I thought it would prove a miserable failure, and Bartleby would be found all alive at my office as usual; the next moment it seemed certain that I should see his chair empty. And so I kept veering about. At the corner of Broadway and Canal Street, I saw quite an excited group of people standing in earnest conversation.

"I'll take odds he doesn't," said a voice as I passed.

"Doesn't go?—done!" said I, "put up your money."

I was instinctively putting my hand in my pocket to produce my own, when I remembered that this was an election day. The words I had overheard bore no reference to Bartleby, but to the success or nonsuccess of some candidate for the mayoralty. In my intent frame of mind, I had, as it were, imagined that all Broadway shared in my excitement, and were debating the same question with me. I passed on, very thankful that the uproar of the street screened my momentary absent-mindedness.

As I had intended, I was earlier than usual at my office door. I stood listening for a moment. All was still. He must be gone. I tried the knob. The door was locked. Yes, my procedure had worked to a charm; he indeed must be vanished. Yet a certain melancholy mixed with this: I was almost sorry for my brilliant success. I was fumbling under the doormat for the key, which Bartleby was to have left there for me, when accidentally my knee knocked against a panel, producing a summoning sound, and in response a voice came to me from within—"Not yet; I am occupied."

It was Bartleby.

I was thunderstruck. For an instant I stood like the man who, pipe in mouth, was killed one cloudless afternoon long ago in Virginia, by summer lightning; at his own warm open window he was killed, and remained leaning out there upon the dreamy afternoon, till someone touched him, and he fell.

"Not gone!" I murmured at last. But again obeying that wondrous ascendency which the inscrutable scrivener had over me—and from which ascendency, for all my chafing, I could not completely escape—I slowly went downstairs and out into the street, and while walking round the block, considered what I should next do in this unheard-of perplexity. Turn the man out by an actual thrusting I could not; to drive him away by calling him hard names would not do; calling in the police was an unpleasant idea; and yet, permit him to enjoy his cadaverous triumph over me—this too I could not think of. What was to be done? or, if nothing could be done, was there anything further that I could *assume* in the matter? Yes, as before I had prospectively assumed that Bartleby would depart, so now I might retrospectively assume that departed he was. In the legitimate carrying out of this assumption, I might enter my office in a great hurry, and pretending not to see Bartleby at all, walk straight against him as if he were air. Such a proceeding would in a singular degree have the appearance of a home-thrust. It was hardly possible that Bartleby could withstand such an application of the doctrine of assumptions. But, upon second thought, the success of the plan seemed rather dubious. I resolved to argue the matter over with him again.

"Bartleby," said I, entering the office, with a quietly severe expression, "I am seriously displeased. I am pained, Bartleby. I had thought better of you. I had imagined you of such a gentlemanly organization, that in any delicate dilemma a slight hint would suffice—in short, an assumption; but it appears I am deceived. Why," I added, unaffectedly starting, "you have not even touched that money yet," pointing to it, just where I had left it the evening previous.

He answered nothing.

"Will you, or will you not, quit me?" I now demanded in a sudden passion, advancing close to him.

"I would prefer *not* to quit you," he replied, gently emphasizing the *not*.

"What earthly right have you to stay here? Do you pay any rent? Do you pay my taxes? Or is this property yours?"

He answered nothing.

"Are you ready to go on and write now? Are your eyes recovered? Could you copy a small paper for me this morning? or help examine a few lines? or step round to the post office? In a word, will you do anything at all, to give a coloring to your refusal to depart the premises?"

He silently retired into his hermitage.

I was now in such a state of nervous resentment that I thought it but prudent to check myself, at present, from further demonstrations. Bartleby and I were alone. I remembered the tragedy of the unfortunate Adams and the still more unfortunate Colt in the solitary office of the latter; and how poor Colt, being dreadfully incensed by Adams, and imprudently permitting himself to get wildly excited, was at unawares hurried into his fatal act—an act which certainly no man could possibly deplore more than the actor himself. Often it had occurred to me in my ponderings upon the subject, that had that altercation taken place in the public street, or at a private residence, it would not have terminated as it did. It was the circumstance of being alone in a solitary office, upstairs, of a building entirely unhallowed by humanizing domestic associations—an uncarpeted office, doubtless, of a dusty, haggard sort of appearance—this it must have been, which greatly helped to enhance the irritable desperation of the hapless Colt.

But when this old Adam of resentment rose in me and tempted me concerning Bartleby, I grappled him and threw him. How? Why, simply by recalling the divine injunction: "A new commandment give I unto you, that ye love one another." Yes, this it was that saved me. Aside from higher considerations, charity often operates as a vastly wise and prudent principle —a great safeguard to its possessor. Men have committed murder for jealousy's sake, and anger's sake, and hatred's sake, and selfishness' sake, and spiritual pride's sake; but no man that ever I heard of, ever committed a diabolical murder for sweet charity's sake. Mere self-interest, then, if no better motive can be enlisted, should, especially with high-tempered men, prompt all beings to charity and philanthropy. At any rate, upon the occasion in question, I strove to drown my exasperated feelings toward the scrivener by benevolently construing his conduct. Poor fellow, poor fellow! thought I, he doesn't mean anything; and besides, he has seen hard times, and ought to be indulged.

I endeavored also immediately to occupy myself, and at the same time to comfort my despondency. I tried to fancy that in the course of the morning, at such time as might prove agreeable to him, Bartleby, of his own free accord, would emerge from his hermitage, and take up some decided line of march in the direction of the door. But no. Half past twelve o'clock came; Turkey began to glow in the face, overturn his inkstand, and become generally obstreperous; Nippers abated down into quietude and courtesy; Ginger Nut munched his noon apple; and Bartleby remained standing at his window in one of his profoundest dead-wall reveries. Will it be credited? Ought I to acknowledge it? That afternoon I left the office without saying one further word to him.

Some days now passed, during which at leisure intervals I looked a little into "Edwards on the Will," and "Priestley on Necessity." Under the circumstances, those books induced a salutary feeling. Gradually I slid into the persuasion that these troubles of mine, touching the scrivener, had been all predestined from eternity, and Bartleby was billeted upon me for some mysterious purpose of an all-wise Providence, which it was not for a mere mortal like me to fathom. Yes, Bartleby, stay there behind your screen, thought I; I shall persecute you no more; you are harmless and noiseless as any of these old chairs; in short, I never feel so private as when I know you are here. At least I see it, I feel it; I penetrate to the predestinated purpose of my life. I am content. Others may have loftier parts to enact; but my mission in this world, Bartleby, is to furnish you with office room for such period as you may see fit to remain.

I believe that this wise and blessed frame of mind would have continued with me had it not been for the unsolicited and uncharitable remarks obtruded upon me by my professional friends who visited the rooms. But thus it often is, that the constant friction of illiberal minds wears out at last the best resolves of the more generous. Though to be sure, when I reflected upon it, it was not strange that people entering my office should be struck by the peculiar aspect of the unaccountable Bartleby, and so be tempted to throw out some sinister observations concerning him. Sometimes an attorney having business with me, and calling at my office, and finding no one but the scrivener there, would undertake to obtain some sort of precise information from him touching my whereabouts; but without heeding his idle talk, Bartleby would remain standing immovable in the middle of the room. So, after contemplating him in that position for a time, the attorney would depart, no wiser than he came.

Also, when a reference was going on, and the room full of lawyers and witnesses and business was driving fast, some deeply occupied legal gentleman present, seeing Bartleby wholly unemployed, would request him to run round to his (the legal gentleman's) office and fetch some papers for him. Thereupon, Bartleby would tranquilly decline, and yet remain idle as before. Then the lawyer would give a great stare, and turn to me. And what could I say? At last I was made aware that all through the circle of my professional acquaintance, a whisper of wonder was running round, having reference to the strange creature I kept at my office. This worried me very much. And as the idea came upon me of his possibly turning out a long-lived man, and keep occupying my chambers, and denying my authority; and perplexing my visitors; and scandalizing my professional reputation; and casting a general gloom over the premises; keeping soul and body together to the last upon his savings (for doubtless he spent but half a dime a day), and in the end perhaps outlive me, and claim possession of my office by right of his perpetual occupancy: as all these dark anticipations crowded upon me more and more, and my friends continually intruded their relentless remarks upon the apparition in my room, a great change was wrought in me. I resolved to gather all my faculties together, and forever rid me of this intolerable incubus.

Ere revolving any complicated project, however, adapted to this end, I first simply suggested to Bartleby the propriety of his permanent departure. In a calm and serious tone, I commended the idea to his careful and mature consideration. But having taken three days to meditate upon it, he apprised me that his original determination remained the same; in short, that he still preferred to abide with me.

What shall I do? I now said to myself, buttoning up my coat to the last button. What shall I do? what ought I to do? what does conscience say I *should* do with this man, or rather ghost? Rid myself of him, I must; go, he shall. But how? You will not thrust him, the poor, pale, passive mortal— you will not thrust such a helpless creature out of your door? you will not dishonor yourself by such cruelty? No, I will not, I cannot do that. Rather would I let him live and die here, and then mason up his remains in the wall. What then will you do? For all your coaxing, he will not budge. Bribes he leaves under your own paperweight on your table; in short, it is quite plain that he prefers to cling to you.

Then something severe, something unusual must be done. What! surely you will not have him collared by a constable, and commit his innocent pallor to the common jail? And, upon what ground could you procure such a thing to be done?—a vagrant, is he? What! he a vagrant, a wanderer, who refuses to budge? It is because he will *not* be a vagrant, then, that you seek to count him *as* a vagrant. That is too absurd. No visible means of support: there I have him. Wrong again: for indubitably he *does* support himself, and that is the only unanswerable proof that any man can show of his possessing the means so to do. No more then. Since he will not quit me, I must quit him. I will change my offices; I will move elsewhere; and give him fair notice, that if I find him on my new premises I will then proceed against him as a common trespasser.

Acting accordingly, next day I thus addressed him: "I find these chambers too far from the city hall; the air is unwholesome. In a word, I propose to remove my offices next week, and shall no longer require your services. I tell you this now, in order that you may seek another place."

He made no reply, and nothing more was said.

On the appointed day I engaged carts and men, proceeded to my chambers, and having but little furniture, everything was removed in a few hours. Throughout all, the scrivener remained standing behind the screen, which I directed to be removed the last thing. It was withdrawn; and being folded up like a huge folio, left him the motionless occupant of a naked room. I stood in the entry watching him a moment, while something from within me upbraided me.

I reentered, with my hand in my pocket—and—and my heart in my mouth.

"Goodbye, Bartleby; I am going—goodbye, and God some way bless you; and take that," slipping something in his hand. But it dropped upon the floor and then—strange to say—I tore myself from him whom I had so longed to be rid of.

Established in my new quarters, for a day or two I kept the door locked, and started at every footfall in the passages. When I returned to my rooms after any little absence, I would pause at the threshold for an instant, and attentively listen, ere applying my key. But these fears were needless. Bartleby never came nigh me.

I thought all was going well, when a perturbed looking stranger visited me, inquiring whether I was the person who had recently occupied rooms at No. —— Wall Street.

Full of forebodings, I replied that I was.

"Then sir," said the stranger, who proved a lawyer, "you are responsible for the man you left there. He refuses to do any copying, he refuses to do anything; and he says he prefers not to; and he refuses to quit the premises."

"I am very sorry, sir," said I, with assumed tranquillity, but an inward tremor, "but, really, the man you allude to is nothing to me—he is no relation or apprentice of mine, that you should hold me responsible for him."

"In mercy's name, who is he?"

"I certainly cannot inform you. I know nothing about him. Formerly I employed him as a copyist; but he has done nothing for me now for some time past."

"I shall settle him then—good morning, sir."

Several days passed, and I heard nothing more; and though I often felt a charitable prompting to call at the place and see poor Bartleby, yet a certain squeamishness of I know not what withheld me.

All is over with him, by this time, thought I at last, when through another week no further intelligence reached me. But coming to my room the day after, I found several persons waiting at my door in a high state of nervous excitement.

"That's the man—here he comes," cried the foremost one, whom I recognized as the lawyer who had previously called upon me alone.

"You must take him away, sir, at once," cried a portly person among them, advancing upon me, and whom I knew to be the landlord of No. —— Wall Street. "These gentlemen, my tenants, cannot stand it any longer; Mr. B——," pointing to the lawyer, "has turned him out of his room, and he now persists in haunting the building generally, sitting upon the banisters of the stairs by day, and sleeping in the entry by night. Everybody here is concerned; clients are leaving the offices; some fears are entertained of a mob; something you must do, and that without delay."

Aghast at this torrent, I fell back before it, and would fain have locked myself in my new quarters. In vain I persisted that Bartleby was nothing to me—no more than to anyone else there. In vain—I was the last person known to have anything to do with him, and they held me to the terrible account. Fearful then of being exposed in the papers (as one person present obscurely threatened) I considered the matter, and at length said, that if the lawyer would give me a confidential interview with the scrivener, in his (the lawyer's) own room, I would that afternoon strive my best to rid them of the nuisance they complained of.

Going upstairs to my old haunt, there was Bartleby silently sitting upon the banister at the landing.

"What are you doing here, Bartleby?" said I.

"Sitting upon the banister," he mildly replied.

I motioned him into the lawyer's room, who then left us.

"Bartleby," said I, "are you aware that you are the cause of great tribulation to me, by persisting in occupying the entry after being dismissed from the office?"

No answer.

"Now one of two things must take place. Either you must do something, or something must be done to you. Now what sort of business would you like to engage in? Would you like to reengage in copying for some one?"

"No; I would prefer not to make any change."

"Would you like a clerkship in a dry-goods store?"

"There is too much confinement about that. No, I would not like a clerkship; but I am not particular."

"Too much confinement," I cried, "why you keep yourself confined all the time!"

"I would prefer not to take a clerkship," he rejoined, as if to settle that little item at once.

"How would a bartender's business suit you? There is no trying of the eyesight in that."

"I would not like it at all; though, as I said before, I am not particular."

His unwonted wordiness inspirited me. I returned to the charge.

135

"Well then, would you like to travel through the country collecting bills for the merchants? That would improve your health."

"No, I would prefer to be doing something else."

"How then would going as a companion to Europe to entertain some young gentleman with your conversation—how would that suit you?"

"Not at all. It does not strike me that there is anything definite about that. I like to be stationary. But I am not particular."

"Stationary you shall be then," I cried, now losing all patience, and for the first time in all my exasperating connection with him fairly flying into a passion. "If you do not go away from these premises before night, I shall feel bound—indeed I *am* bound—to—to—to quit the premises myself!" I rather absurdly concluded, knowing not with what possible threat to try to frighten his immobility into compliance. Despairing of all further efforts, I was precipitately leaving him, when a final thought occurred to me—one which had not been wholly unindulged before.

"Bartleby," said I, in the kindest tone I could assume under such exciting circumstances, "will you go home with me now—not to my office, but my dwelling—and remain there till we can conclude upon some convenient arrangement for you at our leisure? Come, let us start now, right away."

"No: at present I would prefer not to make any change at all."

I answered nothing; but effectually dodging everyone by the suddenness and rapidity of my flight, rushed from the building, ran up Wall Street toward Broadway, and then jumping into the first omnibus was soon removed from pursuit. As soon as tranquillity returned I distinctly perceived that I had now done all that I possibly could, both in respect to the demands of the landlord and his tenants, and with regard to my own desire and sense of duty, to benefit Bartleby, and shield him from rude persecution. I now strove to be entirely carefree and quiescent; and my conscience justified me in the attempt; though indeed it was not so successful as I could have wished. So fearful was I of being again hunted out by the incensed landlord and his exasperated tenants, that, surrendering my business to Nippers, for a few days I drove about the upper part of the town and through the suburbs, in my rockaway; crossed over to Jersey City and Hoboken, and paid fugitive visits to Manhattanville and Astoria. In fact I almost lived in my rockaway for the time.

When again I entered my office, lo, a note from the landlord lay upon the desk. I opened it with trembling hands. It informed me that the writer had sent to the police, and had Bartleby removed to the Tombs as a vagrant. Moreover, since I knew more about him than anyone else, he wished me to appear at that place, and make a suitable statement of the facts. These tidings had a conflicting effect upon me. At first I was indignant; but at last almost approved. The landlord's energetic, summary disposition had led him to adopt a procedure which I do not think I would have decided upon myself; and yet as a last resort, under such peculiar circumstances, it seemed the only plan.

As I afterward learned, the poor scrivener, when told that he must be conducted to the Tombs, offered not the slightest obstacle, but in his own pale, unmoving way silently acquiesced.

Some of the compassionate and curious bystanders joined the party; and headed by one of the constables, arm-in-arm with Bartleby the silent procession filed its way through all the noise, and heat, and joy of the roaring thoroughfares at noon.

The same day I received the note I went to the Tombs, or, to speak more properly, the Halls of Justice. Seeking the right officer, I stated the purpose of my call, and was informed that the individual I described was indeed within. I then assured the functionary that Bartleby was a perfectly honest man, and greatly to be a compassionated (however unaccountable) eccentric. I narrated all I knew, and closed by suggesting the idea of letting him remain in as indulgent confinement as possible till something less harsh might be done—though indeed I hardly knew what. At all events, if nothing else could be decided upon, the almshouse must receive him. I then begged to have an interview.

Being under no disgraceful charge, and quite serene and harmless in all his ways, they had permitted him freely to wander about the prison, and especially in the enclosed grass-platted yards thereof. And so I found him there, standing all alone in the quietest of the yards, his face toward a high wall—while all around, from the narrow slits of the jail windows, I thought I saw peering out upon him the eyes of murderers and thieves.

"Bartleby!"

"I know you," he said, without looking round—"and I want nothing to say to you."

"It was not I that brought you here, Bartleby," said I, keenly pained at his implied suspicion. "And to you, this should not be so vile a place. Nothing reproachful attaches to you by being here. And see, it is not so sad a place as one might think. Look, there is the sky and here is the grass."

"I know where I am," he replied, but would say nothing more, and so I left him.

As I entered the corridor again a broad, meatlike man in an apron accosted me, and jerking his thumb over his shoulder said—"Is that your friend?"

"Yes."

"Does he want to starve? If he does, let him live on the prison fare, that's all."

"Who are you?" asked I, not knowing what to make of such an unofficially speaking person in such a place.

"I am the grub man. Such gentlemen as have friends here, hire me to provide them with something good to eat."

"Is this so?" said I, turning to the turnkey.

He said it was.

"Well then," said I, slipping some silver into the grub man's hands (for so they called him), "I want you to give particular attention to my friend there; let him have the best dinner you can get. And you must be as polite to him as possible."

"Introduce me, will you?" said the grub man, looking at me with an expression which seemed to say he was all impatience for an opportunity to give a specimen of his breeding.

Thinking it would prove of benefit to the scrivener, I acquiesced; and asking the grub man his name, went up with him to Bartleby.

"Bartleby, this is Mr. Cutlets; you will find him very useful to you."

"Your sarvant, sir, your sarvant," said the grub man, making a low salutation behind his apron. "Hope you find it pleasant here, sir;—spacious grounds—cool apartments, sir—hope you'll stay with us some time—try to make it agreeable. May Mrs. Cutlets and I have the pleasure of your company to dinner, sir, in Mrs. Cutlets' private room?"

"I prefer not to dine today," said Bartleby, turning away. "It would disagree with me; I am unused to dinners." So saying, he slowly moved to the other side of the enclosure and took up a position fronting the dead-wall.

"How's this?" said the grub man, addressing me with a stare of astonishment. "He's odd, ain't he?"

"I think he is a little deranged," said I, sadly.

"Deranged? deranged is it? Well now, upon my word, I thought that friend of yourn was a gentleman forger; they are always pale and genteel-like, them forgers. I can't help pity 'em—can't help it, sir. Did you know Monroe Edwards?" he added touchingly, and paused. Then, laying his hand pityingly on my shoulder, sighed, "he died of the consumption at Sing-Sing. So you weren't acquainted with Monroe?"

"No, I was never socially acquainted with any forgers. But I cannot stop longer. Look to my friend yonder. You will not lose by it. I will see you again."

Some few days after this, I again obtained admission to the Tombs, and went through the corridors in quest of Bartleby; but without finding him.

"I saw him coming from his cell not long ago," said a turnkey, "maybe he's gone to loiter in the yards."

So I went in that direction.

"Are you looking for the silent man?" said another turnkey passing me. "Yonder he lies—sleeping in the yard there. 'Tis not twenty minutes since I saw him lie down."

The yard was entirely quiet. It was not accessible to the common prisoners. The surrounding walls, of amazing thickness, kept off all sounds behind them. The Egyptian character of the masonry weighed upon me with its gloom. But a soft imprisoned turf grew underfoot. The heart of the eternal pyramids, it seemed, wherein by some strange magic, through the clefts grass seed, dropped by birds, had sprung.

Strangely huddled at the base of the wall—his knees drawn up, and lying on his side, his head touching the cold stones—I saw the wasted Bartleby. But nothing stirred. I paused; then went close up to him; stooped over, and saw that his dim eyes were open; otherwise he seemed profoundly sleeping. Something prompted me to touch him. I felt his hand, when a tingling shiver ran up my arm and down my spine to my feet.

The round face of the grub man peered upon me now. "His dinner is ready. Won't he dine today, either? Or does he live without dining?"

"Lives without dining," said I, and closed the eyes.

"Eh!—He's asleep, ain't he?"

"With kings and counselors," murmured I.

There would seem little need for proceeding further in this history. Imagination will readily supply the meager recital of poor Bartleby's interment. But ere parting with the reader, let me say, that if this little narrative has sufficiently interested him, to awaken curiosity as to who Bartleby was, and what manner of life he led prior to the present narrator's making his acquaintance, I can only reply, that in such curiosity I fully share—but am wholly unable to gratify it. Yet here I hardly know whether I should divulge one little item of rumor, which came to my ear a few months after the scrivener's decease. Upon what basis it rested, I could never ascertain; and hence, how true it is I cannot now tell. But inasmuch as this vague report has not been without a certain strange suggestive interest to me, however sad, it may prove the same with some others; and so I will briefly mention it. The report was this: that Bartleby had been a subordinate clerk in the dead letter office at Washington, from which he had been suddenly removed by a change in the administration. When I think over this rumor I cannot adequately express the emotions which seize me. Dead letters! does it not sound like dead men? Conceive a man by nature and misfortune prone to a pallid hopelessness: can any business seem more fitted to heighten it than that of continually handling these dead letters, and assorting them for the flames? For by the cartload they are annually burned. Sometimes from out the folded paper the pale clerk takes a ring—the finger it was meant for, perhaps, molders in the grave; a bank note sent in swiftest charity—he whom it would relieve, nor eats nor hungers any more; pardon for those who died despairing; hope for those who died unhoping; good tidings for those who died stifled by unrelieved calamities. On errands of life, these letters speed to death.

Ah Bartleby! Ah humanity!

Herman Melville

QUESTIONS

1. What does the narrator mean when he says of Bartleby that "no materials exist for a full and satisfactory biography of this man"? Why does he believe this is "an irreparable loss to literature"? (111)

2. Why does the narrator provide only the nicknames, "deemed expressive of their respective persons or characters," of his other employees— Turkey, Nippers, and Ginger Nut? (112) Why does he describe their habits in such detail?

3. When asked by the narrator to compare a copy, why does Bartleby say, "I would prefer not to"? (117)

4. What prevents the narrator from dismissing Bartleby?

5. When Bartleby refuses to go to the post office, why does he reply to the narrator's question, "You *will* not?," by answering, "I *prefer* not"? (121)

6. Why does the realization that Bartleby is living in his office cause the narrator to feel kinship with him, thinking they are both "sons of Adam"? (124)

7. What does the fact that the narrator begins "using this word *prefer* upon all sorts of not exactly suitable occasions" tell us about the narrator and his relationship to Bartleby? (126)

8. When Bartleby replies to the narrator's question of why he will no longer copy by asking, "Do you not see the reason for yourself?" why does the narrator assume that the reason is that Bartleby's vision has become impaired? (127)

9. Why is it that the narrator must tear himself "from him whom I had so longed to be rid of" when he leaves Bartleby for his new office? (134)

10. What is the significance of Bartleby being taken to jail as a vagrant after the narrator has reasoned that a vagrant is exactly what Bartleby is not?

11. Who or what is responsible for Bartleby's death?

12. What difference does it make to our understanding of Bartleby that he might have worked in the dead letter office? Why is the narrator so moved by this rumor?

13. What does the narrator wish to express by concluding the story with the exclamation, "Ah Bartleby! Ah humanity!"? (139)

14. By the end of the story, what does the narrator know about Bartleby?

15. Is Bartleby or the narrator the central figure in the story?

FOR FURTHER REFLECTION

1. Is it possible to fully know another person's motivation? Is it possible to fully know one's own?

2. To what extent is our behavior shaped by societal expectations?

3. In the absence of specific information about other people, why do we make assumptions about them?

4. When our actions ease our conscience, are we more often motivated by genuine sympathy for another or the need to maintain a certain self-image?

5. Does a capitalist system tend to enhance or diminish the qualities that make us most human?

CHRISTINA ROSSETTI

C hristina Rossetti (1830–1894) was the fourth and youngest child in a distinguished London family of writers and artists. Her father, the poet Gabriele Rossetti, had fled from Italy because of his associations with the revolutionary Carbonari, a group of freedom fighters seeking Neapolitan independence; once in London, he established himself as a professional tutor and then chair of Italian at King's College. Rossetti's mother, Frances Polidori, had been a governess and was the sister of the physician John Polidori, a member of the Byron-Shelley circle and author of the influential gothic novel, *The Vampyre*. Rossetti's siblings all went on to distinguished careers; most notably, her brother Gabriel Charles Dante became leader of the Victorian circle of avant-garde poets and painters known as the Pre-Raphaelite Brotherhood, which began to associate in 1848.

Rossetti, who had apparently discovered her gift for poetry before she was a teenager, was associated with the Brotherhood at its outset. At the age of seventeen, in the fall of 1848, she became engaged to one of the members of the Brotherhood, the artist James Collinson. During this time she began to publish a few poems in its short-lived magazine, *The Germ*, and posed as a model for some of the Brotherhood's painters. Rossetti broke off her relationship with Collinson in 1850 upon her discovery that he had converted to Roman Catholicism, and for the rest of her life, Rossetti's zealous Anglican faith would shape her vocational and artistic choices. Among her renunciations were theater, opera, and chess—the last activity one in which she discovered she was a fierce, and usually successful, competitor.

Rossetti lived at home with her parents throughout the 1850s, helping to take care of her father during the years of his declining health. But it is a distortion to think of her as going into a semireclusive state, like some kind of British version of Emily Dickinson. She volunteered for Florence Nightingale's nursing corps to Scutari, but was turned down on account of her youth; she briefly worked as a governess (though she claimed her bad health would make her unfit for the job on a permanent basis); and between 1860 and 1870 she volunteered as a social worker at the St. Mary Magdalene Home in Highgate, where she became an associate involved in helping prostitutes learn professions that would get them off the streets. During the decade of the 1860s, in which she published her first collections, *Goblin Market and Other Poems* (1862) and *The Prince's Progress and Other Poems* (1866), she also mingled at brother Gabriel's Tudor House with the London literati that frequently gathered there: among them Algernon Charles Swinburne, Robert Browning, and Lewis Carroll.

Rossetti would go on to publish four more books of poems, several collections of religious essays, and a collection of short stories and one of nursery rhymes. Yet *Goblin Market* remains her best-known work and one of the Victorian period's most important long poems. An early reviewer, writing in *The Spectator*, observed:

> *She handles her little marvel with that rare poetic discrimination which neither exhausts it of its simple wonders by pushing symbolism too far, nor keeps those wonders in the merely fabulous and capricious stage. In fact, she has produced a true children's poem, which is far more delightful to the mature than to children, though it would be delightful to all.*

CHRISTINA ROSSETTI

Goblin Market

Morning and evening
Maids heard the goblins cry:
"Come buy our orchard fruits,
Come buy, come buy:
Apples and quinces,   5
Lemons and oranges,
Plump unpecked cherries,
Melons and raspberries,
Bloom-down-cheeked peaches,
Swart-headed mulberries,   10
Wild free-born cranberries,
Crab apples, dewberries,
Pineapples, blackberries,
Apricots, strawberries;—
All ripe together   15
In summer weather,—
Morns that pass by,
Fair eyes that fly;
Come buy, come buy:
Our grapes fresh from the vine,   20
Pomegranates full and fine,
Dates and sharp bullaces,
Rare pears and greengages,
Damsons and bilberries,
Taste them and try: 25
Currants and gooseberries,
Bright-fire-like barberries,
Figs to fill your mouth,
Citrons from the South,

Sweet to tongue and sound to eye; 30
Come buy, come buy."
Evening by evening
Among the brookside rushes,
Laura bowed her head to hear,
Lizzie veiled her blushes: 35
Crouching close together
In the cooling weather,
With clasping arms and cautioning lips,
With tingling cheeks and fingertips.
"Lie close," Laura said, 40
Pricking up her golden head:
"We must not look at goblin men,
We must not buy their fruits:
Who knows upon what soil they fed
Their hungry thirsty roots?" 45
"Come buy," call the goblins
Hobbling down the glen.
"Oh," cried Lizzie, "Laura, Laura,
You should not peep at goblin men."
Lizzie covered up her eyes, 50
Covered close lest they should look;
Laura reared her glossy head,
And whispered like the restless brook:
"Look, Lizzie, look, Lizzie,
Down the glen tramp little men. 55
One hauls a basket,
One bears a plate,
One lugs a golden dish
Of many pounds' weight.
How fair the vine must grow 60
Whose grapes are so luscious;
How warm the wind must blow
Through those fruit bushes."
"No," said Lizzie: "No, no, no;
Their offers should not charm us, 65
Their evil gifts would harm us."
She thrust a dimpled finger
In each ear, shut eyes and ran:
Curious Laura chose to linger
Wondering at each merchant man. 70

One had a cat's face,
One whisked a tail,
One tramped at a rat's pace,
One crawled like a snail,
One like a wombat prowled obtuse and furry,   75
One like a ratel tumbled hurry skurry.
She heard a voice like voice of doves
Cooing all together:
They sounded kind and full of loves
In the pleasant weather.   80

Laura stretched her gleaming neck
Like a rush-imbedded swan,
Like a lily from the beck,
Like a moonlit poplar branch,
Like a vessel at the launch   85
When its last restraint is gone.

Backwards up the mossy glen
Turned and trooped the goblin men,
With their shrill repeated cry,
"Come buy, come buy."   90
When they reached where Laura was
They stood stock still upon the moss,
Leering at each other,
Brother with queer brother;
Signaling each other,   95
Brother with sly brother.
One set his basket down,
One reared his plate;
One began to weave a crown
Of tendrils, leaves, and rough nuts brown   100
(Men sell not such in any town);
One heaved the golden weight
Of dish and fruit to offer her:
"Come buy, come buy," was still their cry.
Laura stared but did not stir,   105
Longed but had no money.
The whisk-tailed merchant bade her taste
In tones as smooth as honey,
The cat-faced purr'd,

The rat-paced spoke a word   110
Of welcome, and the snail-paced even was heard;
One parrot-voiced and jolly
Cried "Pretty Goblin" still for "Pretty Polly";
One whistled like a bird.

But sweet-tooth Laura spoke in haste: 115
"Good Folk, I have no coin;
To take were to purloin:
I have no copper in my purse,
I have no silver either,
And all my gold is on the furze   120
That shakes in windy weather
Above the rusty heather."
"You have much gold upon your head."
They answered all together:
"Buy from us with a golden curl."   125
She clipped a precious golden lock,
She dropped a tear more rare than pearl,
Then sucked their fruit globes fair or red.
Sweeter than honey from the rock,
Stronger than man-rejoicing wine,   130
Clearer than water flowed that juice;
She never tasted such before,
How should it cloy with length of use?
She sucked and sucked and sucked the more
Fruits which that unknown orchard bore,   135
She sucked until her lips were sore;
Then flung the emptied rinds away
But gathered up one kernel stone,
And knew not was it night or day
As she turned home alone.   140

Lizzie met her at the gate
Full of wise upbraidings:
"Dear, you should not stay so late,
Twilight is not good for maidens;
Should not loiter in the glen   145
In the haunts of goblin men.
Do you not remember Jeanie,
How she met them in the moonlight,
Took their gifts both choice and many,

Ate their fruits and wore their flowers 150
Plucked from bowers
Where summer ripens at all hours?
But ever in the noonlight
She pined and pined away;
Sought them by night and day, 155
Found them no more, but dwindled and grew gray;
Then fell with the first snow,
While to this day no grass will grow
Where she lies low:
I planted daisies there a year ago 160
That never blow.
You should not loiter so."
"Nay, hush," said Laura:
"Nay, hush, my sister:
I ate and ate my fill, 165
Yet my mouth waters still:
Tomorrow night I will
Buy more"; and kissed her.
"Have done with sorrow;
I'll bring you plums tomorrow 170
Fresh on their mother twigs,
Cherries worth getting;
You cannot think what figs
My teeth have met in,
What melons icy-cold 175
Piled on a dish of gold
Too huge for me to hold,
What peaches with a velvet nap,
Pellucid grapes without one seed:
Odorous indeed must be the mead 180
Whereon they grow, and pure the wave they drink
With lilies at the brink,
And sugar-sweet their sap."

Golden head by golden head,
Like two pigeons in one nest 185
Folded in each other's wings,
They lay down in their curtained bed:
Like two blossoms on one stem,
Like two flakes of new-fallen snow,

Like two wands of ivory   190
Tipped with gold for awful kings.
Moon and stars gazed in at them,
Wind sang to them lullaby,
Lumbering owls forebore to fly,
Not a bat flapped to and fro   195
Round their nest:
Cheek to cheek and breast to breast
Locked together in one nest.

Early in the morning
When the first cock crowed his warning.   200
Neat like bees, as sweet and busy,
Laura rose with Lizzie:
Fetched in honey, milked the cows,
Aired and set to rights the house,
Kneaded cakes of whitest wheat,   205
Cakes for dainty mouths to eat,
Next churned butter, whipped up cream,
Fed their poultry, sat and sewed;
Talked as modest maidens should:
Lizzie with an open heart,   210
Laura in an absent dream,
One content, one sick in part;
One warbling for the mere bright day's delight,
One longing for the night.

At length slow evening came: 215
They went with pitchers to the reedy brook;
Lizzie most placid in her look,
Laura most like a leaping flame,
They drew the gurgling water from its deep.
Lizzie plucked purple and rich golden flags,   220
Then turning homeward said: "The sunset flushes
Those furthest loftiest crags;
Come, Laura, not another maiden lags.
No willful squirrel wags,
The beasts and birds are fast asleep."   225
But Laura loitered still among the rushes.
And said the bank was steep.

And said the hour was early still,
The dew not fallen, the wind not chill;
Listening ever, but not catching 230
The customary cry,
"Come buy, come buy,"
With its iterated jingle
Of sugar-baited words:
Not for all her watching 235
Once discerning even one goblin
Racing, whisking, tumbling, hobbling—
Let alone the herds
That used to tramp along the glen,
In groups or single, 240
Of brisk fruit-merchant men.
Till Lizzie urged, "O Laura, come;
I hear the fruit-call, but I dare not look:
You should not loiter longer at this brook:
Come with me home. 245
The stars rise, the moon bends her arc,
Each glowworm winks her spark,
Let us get home before the night grows dark:
For clouds may gather
Though this is summer weather, 250
Put out the lights and drench us through;
Then if we lost our way what should we do?"

Laura turned cold as stone
To find her sister heard that cry alone,
That goblin cry, 255
"Come buy our fruits, come buy."
Must she then buy no more such dainty fruit?
Must she no more such succous pasture find,
Gone deaf and blind?
Her tree of life dropped from the root: 260
She said not one word in her heart's sore ache:
But peering through the dimness, nought discerning,
Trudged home, her pitcher dripping all the way;
So crept to bed, and lay
Silent till Lizzie slept; 265
Then sat up in a passionate yearning.
And gnashed her teeth for balked desire, and wept
As if her heart would break.

Day after day, night after night,
Laura kept watch in vain   270
In sullen silence of exceeding pain.
She never caught again the goblin cry,
"Come buy, come buy";—
She never spied the goblin men
Hawking their fruits along the glen: 275
But when the noon waxed bright
Her hair grew thin and gray;
She dwindled, as the fair full moon doth turn
To swift decay and burn
Her fire away.   280

One day remembering her kernel stone
She set it by a wall that faced the south:
Dewed it with tears, hoped for a root,
Watched for a waxing shoot,
But there came none.   285
It never saw the sun,
It never felt the trickling moisture run:
While with sunk eyes and faded mouth
She dreamed of melons, as a traveler sees
False waves in desert drouth   290
With shade of leaf-crowned trees,
And burns the thirstier in the sandful breeze.

She no more swept the house,
Tended the fowls or cows,
Fetched honey, kneaded cakes of wheat,   295
Brought water from the brook:
But sat down listless in the chimneynook
And would not eat.

Tender Lizzie could not bear
To watch her sister's cankerous care,   300
Yet not to share.
She night and morning
Caught the goblins' cry:
"Come buy our orchard fruits,
Come buy, come buy":—   305
Beside the brook, along the glen,
She heard the tramp of goblin men,

The voice and stir
Poor Laura could not hear;
Longed to buy fruit to comfort her,   310
But feared to pay too dear.
She thought of Jeanie in her grave,
Who should have been a bride;
But who for joys brides hope to have
Fell sick and died   315
In her gay prime,
In earliest wintertime,
With the first glazing rime,
With the first snowfall of crisp wintertime.

Till Laura dwindling   320
Seemed knocking at Death's door.
Then Lizzie weighed no more
Better and worse;
But put a silver penny in her purse,
Kissed Laura, crossed the heath with clumps of furze   325
At twilight, halted by the brook:
And for the first time in her life
Began to listen and look.

Laughed every goblin
When they spied her peeping: 330
Came towards her hobbling,
Flying, running, leaping,
Puffing and blowing,
Chuckling, clapping, crowing,
Cluckling and gobbling,   335
Mopping and mowing,
Full of airs and graces,
Pulling wry faces,
Demure grimaces,
Catlike and ratlike,   340
Ratel- and wombatlike,
Snail-paced in a hurry,
Parrot-voiced and whistler,
Helter skelter, hurry skurry,
Chattering like magpies,   345
Fluttering like pigeons,

Gliding like fishes, —
Hugged her and kissed her:
Squeezed and caressed her:
Stretched up their dishes,   350
Panniers, and plates:
"Look at our apples
Russet and dun,
Bob at our cherries,
Bite at our peaches,   355
Citrons and dates,
Grapes for the asking,
Pears red with basking
Out in the sun,
Plums on their twigs;   360
Pluck them and suck them, —
Pomegranates, figs."

"Good folk," said Lizzie,
Mindful of Jeanie:
"Give me much and many":   365
Held out her apron,
Tossed them her penny
"Nay, take a seat with us,
Honor and eat with us,"
They answered grinning: 370
"Our feast is but beginning.
Night yet is early,
Warm and dew-pearly,
Wakeful and starry:
Such fruits as these   375
No man can carry;
Half their bloom would fly,
Half their dew would dry,
Half their flavor would pass by.
Sit down and feast with us.   380
Be welcome guest with us,
Cheer you and rest with us."—
"Thank you," said Lizzie: "But one waits
At home alone for me:
So without further parleying,   385
If you will not sell me any

Of your fruits though much and many,
Give me back my silver penny
I tossed you for a fee."—
They began to scratch their pates,   390
No longer wagging, purring,
But visibly demurring,
Grunting and snarling.
One called her proud,
Cross-grained, uncivil;   395
Their tones waxed loud,
Their looks were evil.
Lashing their tails
They trod and hustled her,
Elbowed and jostled her,   400
Clawed with their nails,
Barking, mewing, hissing, mocking,
Tore her gown and soiled her stocking,
Twitched her hair out by the roots,
Stamped upon her tender feet,   405
Held her hands and squeezed their fruits
Against her mouth to make her eat.

White and golden Lizzle stood,
Like a lily in a flood,—
Like a rock of blue-veined stone   410
Lashed by tides obstreperously,—
Like a beacon left alone
In a hoary roaring sea,
Sending up a golden fire,—
Like a fruit-crowned orange tree   415
White with blossoms honey-sweet
Sore beset by wasp and bee,—
Like a royal virgin town
Topped with gilded dome and spire
Close beleaguered by a fleet   420
Mad to tug her standard down.

One may lead a horse to water,
Twenty cannot make him drink.
Though the goblins cuffed and caught her,
Coaxed and fought her,   425

Bullied and besought her,
Scratched her, pinched her black as ink,
Kicked and knocked her,
Mauled and mocked her,
Lizzie uttered not a word;   430
Would not open lip from lip
Lest they should cram a mouthful in:
But laughed in heart to feel the drip
Of juice that syruped all her face,
And lodged in dimples of her chin,   435
And streaked her neck which quaked like curd.
At last the evil people,
Worn-out by her resistance,
Flung back her penny, kicked their fruit
Along whichever road they took,   440
Not leaving root or stone or shoot;
Some writhed into the ground,
Some dived into the brook
With ring and ripple,
Some scudded on the gale without a sound.   445
Some vanished in the distance.

In a smart, ache, tingle,
Lizzie went her way;
Knew not was it night or day;
Sprang up the bank, tore through the furze,   450
Threaded copse and dingle,
And heard her penny jingle
Bouncing in her purse,—
Its bounce was music to her ear.
She ran and ran   455
As if she feared some goblin man
Dogged her with gibe or curse
Or something worse:
But not one goblin skurried after,
Nor was she pricked by fear;   460
The kind heart made her windy-paced
That urged her home quite out of breath with haste
And inward laughter.

She cried, "Laura," up the garden,
"Did you miss me?   465
Come and kiss me.
Never mind my bruises,
Hug me, kiss me, suck my juices
Squeezed from goblin fruits for you,
Goblin pulp and goblin dew.   470
Eat me, drink me, love me;
Laura, make much of me;
For your sake I have braved the glen
And had to do with goblin merchant men."

Laura started from her chair,   475
Flung her arms up in the air,
Clutched her hair:
"Lizzie, Lizzie, have you tasted
For my sake the fruit forbidden?
Must your light like mine be hidden,   480
Your young life like mine be wasted,
Undone in mine undoing,
And ruined in my ruin,
Thirsty, cankered, goblin-ridden?"—
She clung about her sister,   485
Kissed and kissed and kissed her:
Tears once again
Refreshed her shrunken eyes,
Dropping like rain
After long sultry drouth;   490
Shaking with anguish, fear, and pain,
She kissed and kissed her with a hungry mouth.

Her lips began to scorch,
That juice was wormwood to her tongue,
She loathed the feast: 495
Writhing as one possessed she leaped and sung,
Rent all her robe, and wrung
Her hands in lamentable haste,
And beat her breast,
Her locks streamed like the torch   500
Borne by a racer at full speed,
Or like the mane of horses in their flight,

Or like an eagle when she stems the light
Straight toward the sun,
Or like a caged thing freed,   505
Or like a flying flag when armies run.

Swift fire spread through her veins, knocked at her heart,
Met the fire smoldering there
And overbore its lesser flame;
She gorged on bitterness without a name: 510
Ah fool, to choose such part
Of soul-consuming care!
Sense failed in the mortal strife:
Like the watchtower of a town
Which an earthquake shatters down,   515
Like a lightning-stricken mast,
Like a wind-uprooted tree
Spun about,
Like a foam-topped waterspout
Cast down headlong in the sea,   520
She fell at last;
Pleasure past and anguish past,
Is it death or is it life?

Life out of death.
That night long Lizzie watched by her,   525
Counted her pulse's flagging stir,
Felt for her breath,
Held water to her lips, and cooled her face
With tears and fanning leaves.
But when the first birds chirped about their eaves,   530
And early reapers plodded to the place
Of golden sheaves,
And dew-wet grass
Bowed in the morning winds so brisk to pass,
And new buds with new day   535
Opened of cuplike lilies on the stream,
Laura awoke as from a dream,
Laughed in the innocent old way,
Hugged Lizzie but not twice or thrice;
Her gleaming locks showed not one thread of gray,   540
Her breath was sweet as May,
And light danced in her eyes.

Days, weeks, months, years
Afterwards, when both were wives
With children of their own;   545
Their mother-hearts beset with fears,
Their lives bound up in tender lives:
Laura would call the little ones
And tell them of her early prime,
Those pleasant days long gone   550
Of not-returning time:
Would talk about the haunted glen,
The wicked quaint fruit-merchant men,
Their fruits like honey to the throat
But poison in the blood   555
(Men sell not such in any town):
Would tell them how her sister stood
In deadly peril to do her good,
And win the fiery antidote:
Then joining hands to little hands   560
Would bid them cling together,—
"For there is no friend like a sister
In calm or stormy weather;
To cheer one on the tedious way,
To fetch one if one goes astray,   565
To lift one if one totters down,
To strengthen whilst one stands."

QUESTIONS

1. Why does Lizzie refer to the goblin fruits as "evil gifts" if the fruits are for sale? (line 66)

2. Why does Lizzie run away and leave Laura alone?

3. Why are the merchant men given animal features and described as "brothers"? (line 94)

4. Why are we told twice that "Men sell not such in any town"? What is the significance of the parentheses in these lines? (lines 101, 556)

5. Why do the goblins want Laura to pay for the fruit with a lock of her golden hair, and why does she weep when she clips it to pay for the fruit?

6. Why does Laura take one kernel stone home with her?

7. If Laura ate her fill, then why does her mouth still water?

8. Why does Lizzie wake next morning with an open heart but Laura is "sick in part . . . longing for the night"? (lines 212–214)

9. Why is it Lizzie and not Laura who hears the goblins the second time? Why do the goblins laugh when they spy Lizzie "peeping"? (line 330)

10. How do we explain that Laura "wept/As if her heart would break," and "Her hair grew thin and gray"? (lines 267–268, 277)

11. Why does Lizzie decide to get more fruit for Laura if the fruit was the root of Laura's problem in the first place?

12. Is Laura dying because she ate the fruit or for lack of the fruit?

13. If Jeanie died after eating the goblins' fruit, then why does Laura want to buy fruit to restore Lizzie?

14. How do we explain that Lizzie "laughed in heart to feel the drip/Of juice that syruped all her face"? (lines 433–434) Why was she not afraid after being attacked by the goblins, but ran home with "inward laughter"? (line 463)

15. How is Lizzie able to resist the goblins while Jeanie and Laura succumbed?

16. Why does Lizzie call to Laura to "Eat me, drink me, love me;/... make much of me"? (lines 471–472)

17. Why does Laura kiss Lizzie with a "hungry mouth," then afterward loathe "the feast"? (lines 492, 495) What was the "bitterness without a name" that Laura "gorged on"? (line 510)

18. How is Laura able to return to "Life out of death"? (line 524)

19. How can the goblin men's fruits be "honey to the throat/But poison in the blood"? (554–555) And how can the same fruit also be the "antidote" to Laura's ailment? (line 559)

FOR FURTHER REFLECTION

1. Is it significant that the final stanza speaks of "wives," but not of husbands?

2. Is this poem effective as a cautionary tale?

3. If this poem is more than a cautionary tale, then what is it?

4. Are cautionary tales an effective way to teach children today about values?

5. Does Laura receive a moral education in this poem, or does she simply benefit from her sister Lizzie's wisdom?

MAX PLANCK

When Max Planck (1858–1947) began his study of physics in the late nineteenth century, a significant number of scientists believed that all the major principles necessary for explaining the physical world had already been formulated. By the end of Planck's life, the revolution in scientific thinking brought about by quantum theory had completely altered the way in which physics was practiced. This new theory had widespread influence far beyond science since it called into question some of the most fundamental assumptions of how we understand our place in the world. Planck was centrally important in bringing about these changes. At the same time, he has often been called a reluctant revolutionary, since the implications of quantum theory were contrary to his belief that the goal of science is to lead the way to insights of absolute certainty.

Planck was born in Kiel, Germany. For several generations his family had produced distinguished officials devoted to the service of church and state. Planck's own character strongly reflected this background and contributed to his outstanding ability in administering important research institutes at the University of Berlin and the Berlin Academy. He studied at the University of Berlin, where he was appointed professor of theoretical physics in 1889.

Planck's area of concentration was thermodynamics, the study of matter and energy with respect to the exchange of heat. According to the dominant Newtonian physics of that time, the future course of events is determined and predictable, based on exact measurement of the position and movement of objects. This worldview had come to dominate the philosophical outlook of many educated Westerners. As a result of his theoretical work on heat radiation, Planck found that the only explanation that made sense of experimental results required energy to be released in discrete packages, or quanta, rather than in a continuous gradation of magnitudes. Planck reported his findings in 1900 and, along with Albert Einstein, initiated quantum theory, one of the great streams of twentieth-century physics.

One of the well-established numerical constants of physics is named after Planck (and signified by the letter "h"). This extremely small number came to have central significance in setting the lower boundary of subatomic investigations. Planck understood that his theoretical work raised profound questions about the certainty of measurement and therefore the deterministic prediction of events. However, throughout his career he remained skeptical of indeterminacy in physics, maintaining that science should continue to seek simple, unifying laws rather than the probabilities characteristic of quantum theory.

Planck was a highly regarded teacher and received numerous honorary appointments and awards, including the Nobel Prize for physics in 1918. He continued to teach at the University of Berlin until his retirement in 1928, and in 1930 he was appointed president of the prestigious Kaiser Wilhelm Society for the Advancement of Science in Berlin. During the 1930s he directly confronted Adolf Hitler about the expulsion of Jews from academic positions in German universities. Unfortunately, his influence could not reverse the course of National Socialist policies, and the German scientific community was decimated by the emigration of some of its most eminent scientists, including Einstein. Planck chose to remain in Germany with his family, hoping to preserve some remnant of the intellectual greatness of German science. During World War II, he lost his personal property and his son was executed for taking part in a plot to assassinate Hitler. In 1948, the Kaiser Wilhelm Society was moved to Göttingen, where Planck had been living, and its name was changed to the Max Planck Society.

Physics and World Philosophy

The subject of this chapter is the connection between physics and the endeavor to attain a general philosophy of the world; and it may well be asked wherein this connection consists. Physics, it may be urged, is solely concerned with the objects and events of inanimate nature, while a general philosophy, if it is to be at all satisfactory, must embrace the whole of physical and intellectual life and must deal with questions of the soul, including the highest problems of ethics.

At first sight this objection may seem convincing. Yet it will not bear closer investigation. In the first place, inanimate nature is, after all, part of the world, so that any philosophy of the world claiming to be truly comprehensive must take notice of the laws of inanimate nature; and in the long run such a philosophy becomes untenable if it conflicts with inanimate nature. I need not here refer to the considerable number of religious dogmas to which physical science has dealt a fatal blow.

The influence of physics upon a general world philosophy is not, however, confined to such a negative or merely destructive activity; its contribution in a positive sense is of much greater importance. This is true with regard both to form and to content. It is common knowledge that the methods of physical science have proved so fruitful largely on account of their exactness and have on this account provided a model for not strictly scientific studies; while in regard to content it should be said that every science has its roots in life and that similarly physics can never be completely separated from its student; every student, after all, is a personality equipped with a set of intellectual and ethical properties. Hence the general philosophy of the student will always have some influence on his scientific work, while conversely the results of his studies cannot but exert some influence on his general philosophy. It will be the chief purpose of the present chapter to demonstrate this in detail with respect to physics.

I propose to begin with a general consideration. Any scientific treatment of a given material demands the introduction of a certain order into the material dealt with: the introduction of order and of comparison is essential if the available and steadily increasing matter is to be grasped; and the obtaining of such a grasp is essential if the problems are to be formulated and pursued. Order, however, demands classification; and to this extent any given science is faced by the problem of classifying the available material according to some principle. The question then arises, what is to be this principle? Its discovery is not only the first but, as ample experience proves, frequently the decisive step in the development of any given science.

It is important at this point to state that there is no one definite principle available a priori and enabling a classification suitable for every purpose to be made. This applies equally to every science. Hence it is impossible in this connection to assert that any science possesses a structure evolving from its own nature inevitably and apart from any arbitrary presupposition. It is important that this fact should be clearly grasped: it is of a fundamental significance because it demonstrates that it is essential, if there is to be any scientific knowledge, to determine the principle in accordance with which its studies are to be pursued. This determination cannot be made merely in accordance with practical considerations; questions of value also play their part.

Let us take a simple example from the most mature and exact of all sciences, mathematics. Mathematics deals with the magnitude of numbers. In order to obtain a survey of all numbers the obvious method would be to classify them by magnitude; in which case any two numbers are close to each other in proportion as the difference between them is small. Let us take two numbers which are practically equal in magnitude, one of them being the square root of 2 and the other 1.41421356237. The former figure is a few billionths greater than the latter and in every numerical calculation in physics or in astronomy the two numbers can be treated as completely identical. So soon, however, as numbers are classified in accordance with their origin and not in accordance with their magnitude a fundamental difference between the two numbers arises. The decimal fraction is a rational number and can be expressed by the ratio between two integers, while the square root is irrational and cannot be so expressed. If now it is asked whether these two numbers are closely related to each other or not, then any dispute on this question formulated in this manner would have no more meaning than a dispute between two persons facing each other and debating which side was right and which left.

I have taken this simple example because I am convinced that many scientific controversies, and among them many which aroused a maximum of bitterness, have ultimately been due to the fact that the two opponents were, without clearly stating it, employing different principles of classification in the arrangement of their arguments. Every kind of classification is inevitably vitiated by a certain element of caprice and hence of one-sidedness. The selection of the principle of classification is even more important in the natural sciences. As an example one might take botany. Some kind of nomenclature is essential and hence all plants must be divided according to species, genera, families, etc. But according as different principles of classification were selected, so different systems evolved. In the history of botany there have sometimes been sharp controversies between these systems, none of which can claim infallibility since each is affected by subjective bias. The natural system of plants now in general use, although superior to the earlier artificial systems, is not definitive nor clearly determined in every detail, but is subject to certain fluctuations corresponding to the different attitudes taken by leading investigators to the question of the most expedient principle of classification.

The necessity of introducing some classification and the caprice attaching to it is most striking and significant, however, in the nonscientific studies and especially in history. Whether history is classified vertically or horizontally, whether it is arranged according to political, ethnographic, linguistic, social, or economic principles, the necessity continually arises of making distinctions which are seen on close consideration to be fluid and inadequate for the simple reason that any kind of classification inevitably separates cognate subjects and sunders closely allied matters. Thus every science contains an element of caprice and hence of transitoriness in its very structure, a defect which cannot be eradicated because it is rooted in the nature of the case.

In turning to physics we are now faced by the task of classifying under various groups the events which we study. This much is a preliminary demand. Now all physical experiences are based upon our sense perceptions, and accordingly the first and obvious system of classification was in accordance with our senses. Physics was divided into mechanics, acoustics, optics, and heat. These were treated as distinct subjects. In course of time, however, it was seen that there was a close connection between these various subjects, and that it was much easier to establish exact physical laws if the senses are ignored and attention is concentrated on the events outside the senses—if, for example, the sound waves emanating from a sounding body are dealt with apart from the ear, and the rays of light emanating from a glowing body apart from the eye. This leads to a different classification of physics, certain parts of which are rearranged, while the organs of sense recede into the background. According to this principle the heat rays emanating from a hot stove ceased to be the province of heat and were assigned to optics, where they were dealt with as though entirely similar to light waves. Admittedly such a rearrangement, neglecting as it does the perceptions of the senses, contains an element of bias and arbitrariness. Goethe, who always insisted on the primacy of the senses, would have been horrified by such an arrangement; for Goethe always concentrated on the event in its totality, insisted on the superiority of the immediate sensation, and hence would never have agreed to a distinction between the organ of sight and the source of light.

If the eye were not of the nature of the sun
How could we see the light?

Yet it may be presumed that, had he lived a century later, Goethe would not have objected to the soothing light of an electric bulb on his desk, although its invention was made possible only by the particular physical theory which he had so vigorously opposed.

Neither Goethe nor his great adversary Newton could have suspected while alive that this successful theory when consistently developed was doomed to give way to the opposite one-sidedness. I do not wish to anticipate, however, and now revert to a description of the further development of physics.

Once the specific perceptions of the senses as fundamental concepts of physics had been eliminated from that science, it was a logical step to substitute suitable measuring instruments for the organs of sense. The eye gave way to the photographic film, the ear to the vibrating membrane, and the skin to the thermometer. The introduction of self-registering apparatus further eliminated subjective sources of error. The essential characteristic of this development, however, did not consist in the introduction of new measuring instruments of steadily growing sensitiveness and exactitude: the essential point was that the assumption that measurement gave immediate information about the nature of a physical event—whence it followed that the events were independent of the instruments used for measuring them— now became the foundation of the theory of physics. On this assumption a distinction must be made, whenever a physical measurement takes place, between the objective and actual event, which takes place completely independently, and the process of measuring, which is occasioned by the event and renders it perceptible. Physics deals with the actual events, and its object is to discover the laws which these events obey.

This method of interrogating nature has been justified in the past by the wealth of results obtained by classical physics; for classical physics followed the methods indicated by this view and the results applied in practical life to applied science and to kindred pursuits are familiar and visible to all. A detailed description is hence unnecessary.

Encouraged by this success physicists proceeded on the road which they had entered. They continued to apply the principle of *divide et impera*. After the actual events had been separated from the measuring instruments, bodies were divided up into molecules, molecules into atoms, and atoms into protons and electrons. Simultaneously space and time were divided into infinitely small intervals. Everywhere rigid laws were sought and found; as the process of subdivision went on, so the laws assumed simpler forms and there seemed to be no reason for not assuming that it might prove possible to reduce the laws of the physical macrocosm to the same spatial-temporal differential equations which are valid for the microcosm. These equations would then give for any given initial state of nature the recurring changes and hence by integration the states for all future time; a view of the physical events of the world as comprehensive as it was satisfactory by reason of its harmony.

The surprise was all the more striking and unpleasant when, at the beginning of the present century, the increasing delicacy and number of available methods of measurement showed, first in the field of heat radiation, later in that of light rays, and finally in that of electromechanics, that the classical theory as described above is faced by an insurmountable barrier. It may be best to give an example. In order to calculate the movement of an electron, classical physics must assume that its state is known, and this state embraces its position and its velocity. Now it was found that every method permitting of an exact measurement of the electron's position prohibits an exact measurement of its velocity: and it was further found that the inaccuracy of the latter measurement varies inversely with the accuracy of the former, and vice versa, the phenomenon being governed by a law which is accurately defined by the magnitude of Planck's constant. If the position of the electron is known exactly, its velocity is not known at all, and vice versa.

Clearly in these circumstances the differential equations of classical physics lose their fundamental importance; and for the time being the task of discovering in all their details the laws underlying the real physical processes must be regarded as insoluble. But of course it would be incorrect to infer that no such laws exist: the failure to discover a law will, on the contrary, have to be attributed to an inadequate formulation of the problem and a consequently incorrect posing of the question. The question now is wherein the mistake consists and how it can be removed.

It should be stressed first that it would be incorrect to speak of a breakdown of theoretical physics in the sense that everything achieved hitherto must be regarded as incorrect and must hence be rejected. The successes attained by classical physics are far too important to permit such drastic action. It is not the case that a new structure has to be erected, but that an old theory must be extended and elaborated, this being true especially with regard to microphysics; in the field of macrophysics, which deals with relatively large bodies and spaces of time, the classical theory will always retain its importance. Clearly then the mistake does not lie in the fundamentals of the theory, but in the fact that among the assumptions used for building it up there must be one to which the failure is due, the elimination of which would allow the theory to be further extended.

Let us consider the facts of reality. Theoretical physics is based on the assumption that there exist real events not depending upon our senses. This assumption must in all circumstances be maintained; and even physicists of positivist leanings make use of it. Even if this school maintains that the priority of the sense data is the sole foundation of physics, it is yet compelled, in order to escape an irrational solipsism, to assume that there are such things as individual deceptions of the senses and hallucinations; and these can be eliminated only on the assumption that physical observations can be reproduced at will. This, however, implies what is not evident a priori, namely, that the functional relations between sense data contain certain elements not depending upon the observer's personality nor upon the time and place of observation. It is precisely these elements which we describe as the real part of the physical event and of which we attempt to discover the laws.

We saw above that classical physics, besides assuming the existence of real events, has always further assumed the possibility of obtaining a complete grasp of the laws governing the real events, the method of obtaining this grasp being a progressive, spatial, and temporal subdivision in the direction of the infinitely small. More closely considered this assumption must be largely modified, since it leads, e.g., to the conclusion that the laws governing a real event can be completely understood if it is separated from the event by which it is measured. Now evidently the process of measuring can inform us about the real event only if there is some kind of causal connection between the two, and if there is such a connection, then the process of measuring will, in some degree, influence and disturb the event, with the consequence that the result of the measurement is falsified. This falsification and the consequent error will be great in proportion as the causal nexus between the real object and the measuring instrument is close and delicate; it will be possible to reduce it by relaxing the causal nexus or, to express it differently, by increasing the causal distance between the object and the measuring instrument. It is never possible to eliminate the interference altogether, since, if the causal distance is assumed to be infinitely great, i.e., if we completely sever the object from the measuring instrument, we learn nothing at all about the real event. Now the measuring of single atoms and electrons requires extremely delicate and sensitive methods and hence implies a close causal nexus; the exact determination of the position of an electron therefore implies a relatively powerful interference with its motion; and conversely the exact measurement of the velocity of an electron requires a relatively lengthy time. In the first case there is interference with the electron's velocity; in the second, its position in space becomes indefinite. This is the causal explanation of the inaccuracy described above.

Convincing as these considerations may appear, they do not reach the core of the problem. The fact that a physical event is interfered with by the measuring instrument is familiar in classical physics; and at first it is not apparent why increasing improvements in methods of measuring should not permit us ultimately to calculate in advance the amount of the interference when dealing with electrons. If, therefore, we wish to understand the failure of classical physics in the microcosm, we must carry our investigations somewhat deeper.

The study of this question was carried forward considerably by the establishment of quantum mechanics or wave mechanics, from whose equations observable atomic processes can be calculated in advance. If the rules are observed the results of such calculation agree exactly with experience. It is true that, unlike classical mechanics, quantum mechanics does not give the position of an individual electron at any given time; what it does is to state the probability that an electron will be at a given place at a given time; or alternatively, given a multitude of electrons, it states the number which in any given time will be at a given place.

This is a law of a purely statistical character. The fact that it has been confirmed by all measurements hitherto made, and the further fact that there is such a thing as the uncertainty relation, has induced certain physicists to conclude that statistical laws are the only valid foundations of every physical law, more particularly in the field of atomic physics; and to declare that any question about the causality of individual events is, physically, meaningless.

We here reach a point whose discussion is of particular importance, since it leads us to a fundamental question: what is the task and what are the achievements of physics? If we hold that the object of physics is to discover the laws governing the relation between the real events of nature, then causality becomes a part of physics, and its deliberate elimination must give rise to certain misgivings.

It should first be observed that the validity of statistical laws is entirely compatible with a strict causality. Classical physics contains numerous examples. Thus, we may explain the pressure of a gas on the wall of the containing vessel as due to the irregular impingement of numerous gas molecules flying about in all directions; but this explanation is compatible with the admission that the impingement of any one molecule upon another or upon the wall is governed by law and hence is completely determined causally. It may be objected that a strict causality can be regarded as definitely proved only if we are in a position to predict the entire course of the event; and it might be added that nobody can check the movement of any single molecule. To this we might reply that a rigorously exact prediction is never possible of any natural event, so that the validity of the law of causality can never be demonstrated by an immediate and exact experiment, since every measurement, however exact, inevitably involves certain errors of observation. Yet in spite of this the result of the measurement as well as individual errors of observation are attributed to definite causes. When we watch the waves breaking on the seashore, we have every right to feel convinced that the movement of every bubble is due to strict causal law, although we could never hope to follow its rise and fall, still less to calculate it in advance.

It is at this point that the uncertainty relation is brought forward. While classical physics was fashionable, it might be hoped that the inevitable errors of observation could be reduced beneath any given limit by an appropriate increase in the accuracy of measurements. This hope was destroyed by the discovery of Planck's constant, since the latter implies a fixed objective limitation of the exactitude which can be reached, within which limit there is no causality but only doubt and contingency.

We have already prepared a reply to this objection. The reason why the measurements of atomic physics are inexact need not necessarily be looked for in any failure of causality; it may equally well consist in the formulation of faulty concepts and hence of inappropriate questions.

It is precisely the reciprocal influence between the measurement and the real event which enabled us to understand the uncertainty relation at least to a certain degree. According to this view we can no more follow the movement of the individual electron than we can see a colored picture whose dimensions are smaller than the wavelength of its color.

It is true that we must reject as meaningless the hope that it might eventually prove possible indefinitely to reduce the inaccuracy of physical measurements by improving the instrument. Yet the existence of an objective limit like Planck's constant is a sure indication that a certain novel law is at work which has certainly nothing to do with statistics. Like Planck's constant, every other elementary constant, e.g., the charge or mass of an electron, is a definite real magnitude; and it seems wholly absurd to attribute a certain fundamental inexactitude to these universal constants, as those who deny causality would have to do if they wish to remain consistent.

The fact that there is a limit to the accuracy of the measurements in atomic physics becomes further intelligible if we consider that the instruments themselves consist of atoms and that the accuracy of any measuring instrument is limited by its own sensitiveness. A weighbridge cannot weigh to the nearest milligram.

Now what can we do if the best that we have is a weighbridge and there is no hope of obtaining anything more accurate? Would it not be better to give up hope of obtaining exact weights and to declare the pursuit of the milligram to be meaningless, rather than to pursue a task which cannot be solved by direct measurement? This argument underestimates the importance of theory: for theory takes us beyond direct measurement in a way which cannot be foretold a priori, and it does so by means of the so-called intellectual experiments which render us largely independent of the defects of the actual instruments.

It is wholly absurd to maintain that an intellectual experiment is important only in proportion as it can be checked by measurement; for if this were so, there could be no exact geometric proof. A line drawn on paper is not really a line but a more or less narrow strip, and a point a larger or smaller spot. Yet nobody doubts that geometric constructions yield a rigorous proof.

The intellectual experiment carries the mind of the investigator beyond the world and beyond actual measuring instruments and enables him to form hypotheses and to formulate questions which, when checked by actual experiment, enable him to perceive new laws even when these do not admit of direct measurement. An intellectual experiment is not tied down to any limits of accuracy, for thoughts are more subtle than atoms or electrons, nor is there any danger that the event which is measured can be influenced by the measuring instrument. An intellectual experiment requires one condition only for its success, and this is the admission of the validity of any non-self-contradictory law governing the relations between the events under observation. We cannot hope to find what is assumed not to be existent.

Admittedly an intellectual experiment is an abstraction; an abstraction, however, as essential to the experimenter and to the theorist as the abstract assumption that there is a real external world. Whenever we observe an event taking place in nature we must assume that something is happening independently of the observer, and conversely we must endeavor to eliminate as far as possible the defects of our senses and of our methods of measurement in order to grasp the details of the event with greater perfection. There is a kind of opposition between these two abstractions: while the real external world is the object, the ideal spirit which contemplates it is the subject. Neither can be logically demonstrated and hence no *reductio ad absurdum* is possible if their existence is denied. The history of physics bears witness, however, that they have played a decisive part throughout its development. The choicest and most original minds, men like Kepler, Newton, Leibniz, and Faraday, were inspired by the belief in the reality of the external world and in the rule of a higher reason in and beyond it.

It should never be forgotten that the most vital ideas in physics have this twofold origin. In the first instance the form which these ideas take is due to the peculiar imagination of the individual scientist: in course of time, however, they assume a more definite and independent form. It is true that there have always been in physics a number of erroneous ideas on which a quantity of labor was wasted: yet on the other hand, many problems which were at first rejected as meaningless by keen critics were eventually seen to possess the highest significance. Fifty years ago positivist physicists considered it meaningless to ask after the determination of the weight of a single atom—an illusory problem not admitting scientific treatment. Today the weight of an atom can be stated to within its ten-thousandth part, although our most delicate scales are no more fit to weigh it than a weighbridge is to determine milligrams. One should therefore beware of declaring meaningless a problem whose solution is not immediately apparent; there is no criterion for deciding a priori whether any given problem in physics has a meaning or not, a point frequently overlooked by the positivists. The only means of judging a problem correctly consists in examining the conclusions to which it leads. Now the assumption that there are rigid laws applicable to physics is of such fundamental importance that we should hesitate before we declare the question whether such laws are applicable to atomic physics to be a meaningless one. Our first endeavor, on the contrary, should be to trace out the problem of the applicability of laws in this field.

Our first step should be to ask why classical physics fails in the question of causality when the interference arising from the measuring instrument and the inadequate accuracy of the latter are both insufficient to explain this failure. Plainly we are forced to adopt the obvious but radical assumption that the elementary concepts of classical physics cease to be applicable in atomic physics.

Classical physics is based on the assumption that its laws are most clearly revealed in the infinitely small; for it assumes that the course of a physical event anywhere in the universe is completely determined by the state prevailing at this place and its immediate vicinity. Hence such physical magnitudes relating to the state of the physical event as position, velocity, intensity of the electric and magnetic field, etc., are of a purely local character, and the laws governing their relation can be completely expressed by spatial-temporal differential equations between these magnitudes. Clearly, however, this will not suffice for atomic physics, so that the above concepts must be made more complete or more universal. In which direction, however, is this to be done? Some indication may perhaps be found in the recognition, which is daily spreading wider, that the spatial-temporal differential equations do not suffice to exhaust the content of the events within a physical system and that the liminal conditions must also be taken into consideration. This applies even to wave mechanics. Now the field of the liminal conditions is always finite and its immediate interference in the causal nexus is a new manner of looking at causality and one hitherto foreign to classical physics.

The future will show whether progress is possible in this direction and how far it will lead. But whatever results it may ultimately reveal, it is certain that it will never enable us to grasp the real world in its totality any more than human intelligence will ever rise into the sphere of ideal spirit: these will always remain abstractions which by their very definition lie outside actuality. Nothing, however, forbids us to believe that we can progress steadily and without interruption to this unattainable goal; and it is precisely the task of science with its continual self-correction and self-improvement to work in this direction without cease once it has been recognized that it is a hopeful direction. This progress will be a real one and not an aimless zigzag, as is proved by the fact that each new stage reached enables us to survey all the previous stages, while those which remain to be covered are still obscure; just as a climber trying to reach higher altitudes looks down upon the distance he has covered in order to gain knowledge for the further ascent. A scientist is happy, not in resting on his attainments but in the steady acquisition of fresh knowledge.

I have so far confined myself to physics; but it may be felt that what has been said has a wider application. Natural science and the intellectual sciences cannot be rigorously separated. They form a single interconnected system, and if they are touched at any part the effects are felt through all the ramifications of the whole, the totality of which is forthwith set in motion. It would be absurd to assume that a fixed and certain law is predominant in physics unless the same were true also in biology and psychology.

We may perhaps here deal with free will. Our consciousness, which after all is the most immediate source of cognition, assures us that free will is supreme. Yet we are forced to ask whether human will is causally determined or not. Put in this way the question, as I have frequently tried to show, is a good example of the kind of problem which I have described as illusory, by which I mean that, taken literally, it has no exact meaning. In the present instance the apparent difficulty is due to an incomplete formulation of the question. The actual facts may be briefly stated as follows. From the standpoint of an ideal and all-comprehensive spirit, human will, like every material and spiritual event, is completely determined causally. Looked at subjectively, however, the will, insofar as it looks to the future, is not causally determined, because any cognition of the subject's will itself acts causally upon the will, so that any definitive cognition of a fixed causal nexus is out of the question. In other words, we might say that looked at from outside (objectively) the will is causally determined and that looked at from inside (subjectively) it is free. There is here no contradiction, any more than there was in the previous debate about the right- and left-hand side, and those who fail to agree to this overlook or forget the fact that the subject's will is never completely subordinate to its cognition and indeed always has the last word.

In principle, therefore, we are compelled to give up the attempt to determine in advance the motives guiding our actions on purely causal lines, i.e., by means of purely scientific cognition; in other words, there is no science and no intellect capable of answering the most important of all the questions facing us in our personal life, the question, that is, how we are to act.

It might thus be inferred that science ceases to play a part as soon as ethical problems arise. Yet such an inference would be wrong. We saw above that in dealing with the structure of any science, and in discussing its most suitable arrangement, a reciprocal interconnection between epistemological judgments and judgments of value was found to arise, and that no science can be wholly disentangled from the personality of the scientist. Modern physics has given us a clear indication pointing in the same direction. It has taught us that the nature of any system cannot be discovered by dividing it into its component parts and studying each part by itself, since such a method often implies the loss of important properties of the system. We must keep our attention fixed on the whole and on the interconnection between the parts.

The same is true of our intellectual life. It is impossible to make a clear cut between science, religion, and art. The whole is never equal simply to the sum of its various parts. And this is true also of mankind. It would be folly to attempt to obtain an understanding of mankind by studying a number of men however great; for each individual belongs to some community, to a family, a clan, or a nation—a community of which he must form a part, to which he must subordinate himself, and from which he cannot sever himself with impunity. For this reason every science, like every art and every religion, has grown up on a national foundation. It was the misfortune of the German people that this was forgotten for so many years.

It may be said that there is nothing new in this, and that it can be acknowledged without the aid of physics. This is true; and all that I wish to show is that the position of physics, far from being unique, leads us to the same results and the same views as every other science, however different may be the point from which it starts. The real strength of its position is, in fact, seen if our argument is further developed; for it is only then that its tendency can be most clearly seen, which is, to disregard its immediate origin and to expand in every direction like a healthily growing tree which tends to grow into the air and to stretch its branches in every direction, though at the same time it remains firmly rooted in the soil. If science is unable or unwilling to extend beyond the limits of the nation it is unworthy of the name of science; and in this connection physics enjoys an advantage over other branches of science. Nobody will dispute that the laws of nature are the same in every country; so that physics is not compelled to establish its international validity, unlike history where it has actually been asked whether an objective history can be an ideal to be aimed at. Ethics also is supranational, otherwise ethical relations could not exist between the members of different nations. Here again physics takes up a strong position. Scientifically it is based on the principle that it must contain no contradiction, which in terms of ethics implies honesty and truthfulness; and these qualities are valid for all civilized nations and for all time; so that this scientific principle may claim to rank among the first and most important of virtues. I do not think that I exaggerate in saying that an infraction of this ethical demand is discovered and repudiated more quickly and certainly in physics than in any other science.

It is rather shocking to notice the difference between such strictness and the thoughtless laxity with which similar faults are accepted in everyday life. I have not so much in mind the so-called conventional falsehoods which in practice are harmless and to a certain extent indispensable to daily intercourse: conventional falsehoods do not deceive precisely because they are conventional. The harm begins where there is an intention to deceive the other party and to convey to him a faulty impression. It is the duty of those who work in responsible positions to reform this matter ruthlessly as well as to set an example worth following.

Justice is inseparable from truthfulness: justice, after all, simply means the consistent application in practice of the ethical judgments which we pass on opinions and actions. The laws of nature remain fixed and unchanged whether applied to great or to small phenomena, and similarly the communal life of men requires equal rights for all, for great and small, for rich and poor. All is not well with the state if doubts arise about the certainty of the law, if rank and family are respected in the courts, if defenseless persons feel that they are no longer protected from the rapacity of powerful neighbors, and if the law is openly wrenched on grounds of so-called expediency. The populace has a keen sense of the security of the law, and nothing rendered Frederick the Great more popular than the legend of the miller of Sans Souci. Such principles made Germany and Prussia great; it is to be hoped that they will never be lost, and it is the duty of every patriot to work for their preservation and consolidation.

At the same time it must be understood that the goal at which we aim—a permanently satisfactory condition—can never be attained in its perfection. The best and maturist ethical principles must fail to take us to an ideal perfection: they can never do more than indicate the direction in which we can look for our ideal. If these facts are disregarded there is a danger that the seeker may despair altogether or may doubt the value of ethics, a state in which, especially if he is honest in his dealings with himself, he may easily end by attacking ethics. There are numerous examples of this among the philosophies of ethics. The case here is the same as in science: what is important is not to have a permanent possession, but to work unceasingly toward the ideal aim, to struggle daily and hourly toward a renewal of life, and despite every setback to strive toward improvement and perfection.

Yet in the end we may be tempted to ask whether such an unceasing though fundamentally hopeless struggle is not wholly unsatisfactory. It may be asked whether a philosophy has any value at all if its votaries are left without a single fixed point affording them a firm and immediate security in the continual perplexity and hurry of their existence.

Fortunately this question admits of an answer in the affirmative. There is a fixed point and a secure possession which even the least of us can call his own at all times; an inalienable treasure which guarantees to thinking and feeling men their highest happiness, since it assures their peace of mind, and thus has an eternal value. This possession is a pure mind and good will. These afford secure holding ground in the storms of life and they are the primary condition underlying any real satisfactory conduct, as equally they are the best safeguard against the tortures of remorse. They are the essential of every genuine science, and they are equally a sure standard by which to measure the ethical value of every individual.

> Those who are ever striving forward
> Them we can save.

QUESTIONS

1. What distinction is Planck making between the form and content of physics when he refers to its positive contribution to a general world philosophy?

2. What are the "questions of value" that Planck says play a part in determining principles of orderly classification in scientific treatments of the world? (166)

3. To what extent can science provide certain knowledge of the world if, as Planck claims, it "contains an element of caprice and hence of transitoriness in its very structure"? (167)

4. What advantage does Planck think is gained in the effort to establish exact physical laws by shifting attention from sense impressions to events outside the senses?

5. According to Planck, why does eliminating the central importance of sense impressions in physics lead to the assumption that measuring instruments can give "immediate information about the nature of a physical event"? (168)

6. Why did physicists seek rigid laws by dividing physical matter, space, and time into smaller and smaller components? Does Planck think that this procedure was successful?

7. How does uncertainty about simultaneously knowing the position and velocity of an electron lead Planck to question the assumptions of classical physics? Why does he insist the assumption that there are "real events not depending upon our senses" always be maintained? (169)

8. What does Planck mean by the "causal nexus" between the real object and the measuring instrument? (170)

9. Why does Planck reject the claim that statistical laws and the uncertainty relation make the causality of individual physical events meaningless?

10. How does an intellectual experiment, as Planck describes it, lead to new laws that do not permit direct measurement?

11. Why does Planck say that the most original minds in physics were

inspired by two opposing abstractions: "the belief in the reality of the external world and in the rule of a higher reason in and beyond it"? (173)

12. Why does Planck claim that the progressive understanding of the world provided by physics is real and not "an aimless zigzag"? (174)

13. How does Planck's argument about the objective and subjective aspects of human will lead him to the conclusion that there is no science capable of answering the question of how humans should act?

14. How does Planck think that the tendency of physics to extend beyond the limits of its national origins give it special status in helping to form a general philosophy of the world?

15. Is Planck claiming that the virtues of practicing genuine science are identical to the virtues of civic life?

FOR FURTHER REFLECTION

1. If Planck is correct in thinking that science is always connected to the personality and worldviews of its practitioners, should these connections be suppressed or maintained in order to make scientific progress?

2. How should one proceed, in science and in the civic realm, when new facts and circumstances call into question well-established laws?

3. If natural science forms a "single interconnected system" with other intellectual fields, as Planck claims, does this preclude or encourage the possibility of reducing everything to scientific explanations?

4. Is the virtue of truthfulness in science the same as truthfulness in everyday life? Is it necessary to understand art and religion in order to understand science?

5. What should we consider in order to decide whether or not to let the findings of science modify personal, religious, or political beliefs that we may hold?

J ohn M. Synge (1871–1909), a key figure in the Irish literary revival at the beginning of the twentieth century, was born into a wealthy landowning family in Newtown Villas, Rathfarnham, Ireland (today a suburb of Dublin). Protestant religion was a formative influence on the boy. The Synges counted five bishops and an archbishop among their number in the eighteenth century, and John's paternal grandfather was a member of the Brethren, later known as the Plymouth Brethren. John's maternal grandfather, the evangelical minister Dr. Traill, had made his reputation by ranting against Roman Catholics.

Synge's father died before his youngest son's first birthday, and young John was raised by two strong women: his mother Kathleen, and his grandmother, the widow of Dr. Traill. However, the rule of piety would change during John's teenage years. When he was fourteen, he read for the first time Charles Darwin on the theory of evolution, and that summer reading would have a profound effect. According to his autobiography, he renounced Christianity two or three years later, although he would remain perpetually curious about the various strains of mysticism swirling at the time through the ranks of the Irish intelligentsia.

Synge earned a degree in languages at Trinity College, Dublin, in 1892, where he had also distinguished himself as a musician. His study of music took him to Germany, France, and Italy for most of the 1890s. But it was his meeting with the poet William Butler Yeats in Paris in the winter of 1896 that put him on his career path. Yeats, who had been busy campaigning for Irish Home Rule, was also busy trying to start an Irish cultural revival. He sought to persuade young writers and artists to use Ireland for their material rather than fawning after Continental influences. Yeats wrote of his meeting with Synge: "He had wandered among people whose life is as picturesque as the Middle Ages, playing his fiddle to Italian sailors, and listening to stories in Bavarian woods, but life had cast no light into his writings. He had learned Irish years ago, but had begun to forget it, for the only language that interested him was that conventional language of modern poetry which has begun to make us all weary." Yeats told Synge to visit the Aran Islands on the west coast of Ireland, and to reconnect there with the common life and folklore of the people. Between 1899 and 1902 Synge followed Yeats's advice. He spent a part of each year amassing a wealth of stories, anecdotes, and details of everyday life in the villages up and down the Irish west coast.

The plays that grew out of this experience, including the tragedy *Riders to the Sea* (1904), made Synge a famous man. In the case of *The Playboy of the Western World*, first performed at the Abbey Theatre in Dublin in January 1907, notoriety was the key word. The Abbey Theatre enterprise had been launched by Yeats, Lady Gregory, and Synge with the ostensible purpose of reviving Irish cultural life. But the audience at the premiere performance recoiled at what they saw as Synge's insulting depiction of Irish peasantry. Rioting among the spectators broke out during the third act, according to Lady Gregory, when the term *shifts*—another word for undergarments—was uttered onstage. Yeats acknowledged Synge as a heroic and modern artistic voice whose audience was incapable of recognizing his genius.

Synge would finish the writing of one more play, *The Tinker's Wedding*, a drama so anticlerical that it has never, to this day, been performed at the Abbey Theatre. Synge succumbed to Hodgkin's disease in 1909, shortly before his thirty-eighth birthday.

The Playboy of the Western World

PREFACE

In writing *The Playboy of the Western World*, as in my other plays, I have used one or two words only that I have not heard among the country people of Ireland, or spoken in my own nursery before I could read the newspapers. A certain number of the phrases I employ I have heard also from herds and fishermen along the coast from Kerry to Mayo, or from beggar women and ballad singers nearer Dublin; and I am glad to acknowledge how much I owe to the folk imagination of these fine people. Anyone who has lived in real intimacy with the Irish peasantry will know that the wildest sayings and ideas in this play are tame indeed, compared with the fancies one may hear in any little hillside cabin in Geesala, or Carraroe, or Dingle Bay. All art is a collaboration; and there is little doubt that in the happy ages of literature, striking and beautiful phrases were as ready to the storyteller's or the playwright's hand, as the rich cloaks and dresses of his time. It is probable that when the Elizabethan dramatist took his ink horn and sat down to his work he used many phrases that he had just heard, as he sat at dinner, from his mother or his children. In Ireland, those of us who know the people have the same privilege. When I was writing *The Shadow of the Glen*, some years ago, I got more aid than any learning could have given me from a chink in the floor of the old Wicklow house where I was staying, that let me hear what was being said by the servant girls in the kitchen. This matter, I think, is of importance, for in countries where the imagination of the people, and the language they use, is rich and living, it is possible for a writer to be rich and copious in his words, and at the same time to give the reality, which is the root of all poetry, in a comprehensive and natural form. In the modern literature of towns, however, richness is found only in sonnets, or prose poems, or in one or two elaborate books that are far away from the profound and common interests of life. One has, on one side, Mallarmé and Huysmans producing this literature; and on the other, Ibsen and Zola dealing with the reality of life in joyless and pallid words. On the stage one must have reality, and one must have joy; and that is why the intellectual modern drama has failed, and people have grown sick of the false joy of the musical comedy, that has been given them in place of the rich joy found only in what is superb and wild in reality. In a good play every speech should be as fully flavoured as a nut or apple, and such speeches cannot be written by anyone who works among people who have shut their lips on poetry. In Ireland, for a few years more, we have a popular imagination that is fiery, and magnificent, and tender; so that those of us who wish to write start with a chance that is not given to writers in places where the springtime of the local life has been forgotten, and the harvest is a memory only, and the straw has been turned into bricks.

J. M. S.
January 21st, 1907.

PERSONS IN THE PLAY

CHRISTOPHER MAHON

OLD MAHON, *his father, a squatter*

MICHAEL JAMES FLAHERTY *(called* MICHAEL JAMES*), a publican*

MARGARET FLAHERTY *(called* PEGEEN MIKE*), his daughter*

SHAWN KEOGH, *her cousin, a young farmer*

WIDOW QUIN, *a woman of about thirty*

PHILLY CULLEN *and* JIMMY FARRELL, *small farmers*

SARA TANSEY, SUSAN BRADY, *and* HONOR BLAKE, *village girls*

A BELLMAN

SOME PEASANTS

*The action takes place near a village, on a wild coast of Mayo.
The first Act passes on an evening of autumn, the other two Acts
on the following day.*

ACT I

Country public house or shebeen, very rough and untidy. There is a sort of counter on the right with shelves, holding many bottles and jugs, just seen above it. Empty barrels stand near the counter. At back, a little to left of counter, there is a door into the open air, then, more to the left, there is a settle with shelves above it, with more jugs, and a table beneath a window. At the left there is a large open fireplace, with turf fire, and a small door into inner room. Pegeen, a wild-looking but fine girl, of about twenty, is writing at table. She is dressed in the usual peasant dress.

PEGEEN, *slowly as she writes.* Six yards of stuff for to make a yellow gown. A pair of lace boots with lengthy heels on them and brassy eyes. A hat is suited for a wedding day. A fine-tooth comb. To be sent with three barrels of porter in Jimmy Farrell's creel cart on the evening of the coming fair to Mister Michael James Flaherty. With the best compliments of this season. Margaret Flaherty.

SHAWN KEOGH, *a fat and fair young man, comes in as she signs, looks round awkwardly, when he sees she is alone.* Where's himself?

PEGEEN, *without looking at him.* He's coming. (*She directs letter.*) To Mister Sheamus Mulroy, Wine and Spirit Dealer, Castlebar.

SHAWN, *uneasily.* I didn't see him on the road.

PEGEEN. How would you see him (*licks stamp and puts it on letter*) and it dark night this half hour gone by?

SHAWN, *turning toward door again.* I stood awhile outside wondering would I have a right to pass on or to walk in and see you, Pegeen Mike (*comes to fire*), and I could hear the cows breathing and sighing in the stillness of the air, and not a step moving any place from this gate to the bridge.

PEGEEN, *putting letter in envelope.* It's above at the crossroads he is, meeting Philly Cullen and a couple more are going along with him to Kate Cassidy's wake.

SHAWN, *looking at her blankly.* And he's going that length in the dark night.

PEGEEN, *impatiently.* He is surely, and leaving me lonesome on the scruff of the hill. (*She gets up and puts envelope on dresser, then winds the clock.*) Isn't it long the nights are now, Shawn Keogh, to be leaving a poor girl with her own self counting the hours to the dawn of day?

SHAWN, *with awkward humour*. If it is, when we're wedded in a short while you'll have no call to complain, for I've little will to be walking off to wakes or weddings in the darkness of the night.

PEGEEN, *with rather scornful good-humour*. You're making mighty certain, Shaneen, that I'll wed you now.

SHAWN. Aren't we after making a good bargain, the way we're only waiting these days on Father Reilly's dispensation from the bishops, or the court of Rome.

PEGEEN, *looking at him teasingly, washing up at dresser*. It's a wonder, Shaneen, the Holy Father'd be taking notice of the likes of you; for if I was him I wouldn't bother with this place where you'll meet none but Red Linahan, has a squint in his eye, and Patcheen is lame in his heel, or the mad Mulrannies were driven from California and they lost in their wits. We're a queer lot these times to go troubling the Holy Father on his sacred seat.

SHAWN, *scandalized*. If we are, we're as good this place as another, maybe, and as good these times as we were for ever.

PEGEEN, *with scorn*. As good, is it? Where now will you meet the like of Daneen Sullivan knocked the eye from a peeler; or Marcus Quin, God rest him, got six months for maiming ewes, and he a great warrant to tell stories of holy Ireland till he'd have the old women shedding down tears about their feet. Where will you find the like of them, I'm saying?

SHAWN, *timidly*. If you don't, it's a good job, maybe; for (*with peculiar emphasis on the words*) Father Reilly has small conceit to have that kind walking around and talking to the girls.

PEGEEN, *impatiently, throwing water from basin out of the door*. Stop tormenting me with Father Reilly (*imitating his voice*) when I'm asking only what way I'll pass these twelve hours of dark, and not take my death with the fear. (*Looking out of door.*)

SHAWN, *timidly*. Would I fetch you the Widow Quin, maybe?

PEGEEN. Is it the like of that murderer? You'll not, surely.

SHAWN, *going to her, soothingly.* Then I'm thinking himself will stop along with you when he sees you taking on; for it'll be a long nighttime with great darkness, and I'm after feeling a kind of fellow above in the furzy ditch, groaning wicked like a maddening dog, the way it's good cause you have, maybe, to be fearing now.

PEGEEN, *turning on him sharply.* What's that? Is it a man you seen?

SHAWN, *retreating.* I couldn't see him at all; but I heard him groaning out, and breaking his heart. It should have been a young man from his words speaking.

PEGEEN, *going after him.* And you never went near to see was he hurted or what ailed him at all?

SHAWN. I did not, Pegeen Mike. It was a dark, lonesome place to be hearing the like of him.

PEGEEN. Well, you're a daring fellow, and if they find his corpse stretched above in the dews of dawn, what'll you say then to the peelers, or the justice of the peace?

SHAWN, *thunderstruck.* I wasn't thinking of that. For the love of God, Pegeen Mike, don't let on I was speaking of him. Don't tell your father and the men is coming above; for if they heard that story, they'd have great blabbing this night at the wake.

PEGEEN. I'll maybe tell them, and I'll maybe not.

SHAWN. They are coming at the door. Will you whisht, I'm saying?

PEGEEN. Whisht yourself.

She goes behind counter. Michael James, fat jovial publican, comes in followed by Philly Cullen, who is thin and mistrusting, and Jimmy Farrell, who is fat and amorous, about forty-five.

MEN, *together.* God bless you! The blessing of God on this place!

PEGEEN. God bless you kindly.

MICHAEL, *to men, who go to the counter.* Sit down now, and take your rest. (*Crosses to Shawn at the fire.*) And how is it you are, Shawn Keogh? Are you coming over the sands to Kate Cassidy's wake?

SHAWN. I am not, Michael James. I'm going home the shortcut to my bed.

PEGEEN, *speaking across the counter.* He's right, too, and have you no shame, Michael James, to be quitting off for the whole night, and leaving myself lonesome in the shop?

MICHAEL, *good-humouredly.* Isn't it the same whether I go for the whole night or a part only? and I'm thinking it's a queer daughter you are if you'd have me crossing backward through the Stooks of the Dead Women, with a drop taken.

PEGEEN. If I am a queer daughter, it's a queer father'd be leaving me lonesome these twelve hours of dark, and I piling the turf with the dogs barking, and the calves mooing, and my own teeth rattling with the fear.

JIMMY, *flatteringly.* What is there to hurt you, and you a fine, hardy girl would knock the head of any two men in the place?

PEGEEN, *working herself up.* Isn't there the harvest boys with their tongues red for drink, and the ten tinkers is camped in the east glen, and the thousand militia—bad cess to them!—walking idle through the land. There's lots surely to hurt me, and I won't stop alone in it, let himself do what he will.

MICHAEL. If you're that afeard, let Shawn Keogh stop along with you. It's the will of God, I'm thinking, himself should be seeing to you now.

They all turn on Shawn.

SHAWN, *in horrified confusion.* I would and welcome, Michael James, but I'm afeard of Father Reilly; and what at all would the Holy Father and the cardinals of Rome be saying if they heard I did the like of that?

MICHAEL, *with contempt.* God help you! Can't you sit in by the hearth with the light lit and herself, beyond in the room? You'll do that surely, for I've heard tell there's a queer fellow above, going mad or getting his death, maybe, in the gripe of the ditch, so she'd be safer this night with a person here.

SHAWN, *with plaintive despair*. I'm afeard of Father Reilly, I'm saying.
Let you not be tempting me, and we near married itself.

PHILLY, *with cold contempt*. Lock him in the west room. He'll stay then and
have no sin to be telling to the priest.

MICHAEL, *to Shawn, getting between him and the door*. Go up now.

SHAWN, *at the top of his voice*. Don't stop me, Michael James. Let me out of
the door, I'm saying, for the love of the Almighty God. Let me out
(*trying to dodge past him*). Let me out of it, and may God grant you his
indulgence in the hour of need.

MICHAEL, *loudly*. Stop your noising, and sit down by the hearth.

Gives him a push and goes to counter laughing.

SHAWN, *turning back, wringing his hands*. Oh, Father Reilly and the saints
of God, where will I hide myself today? Oh, St. Joseph and St. Patrick
and St. Brigid and St. James, have mercy on me now!

Shawn turns round, sees door clear, and makes a rush for it.

MICHAEL, *catching him by the coattail*. You'd be going, is it?

SHAWN, *screaming*. Leave me go, Michael James, leave me go, you old
pagan, leave me go, or I'll get the curse of the priests on you, and
of the scarlet-coated bishops of the courts of Rome.

*With a sudden movement he pulls himself out of his coat, and disappears out of
the door, leaving his coat in Michael's hands.*

MICHAEL, *turning round, and holding up coat*. Well, there's the coat of a
Christian man. Oh, there's sainted glory this day in the lonesome
west; and by the will of God I've got you a decent man, Pegeen, you'll
have no call to be spying after if you've a score of young girls, maybe,
weeding in your fields.

PEGEEN, *taking up the defence of her property*. What right have you to be
making game of a poor fellow for minding the priest, when it's your
own the fault is, not paying a penny potboy to stand along with me
and give me courage in the doing of my work?

She snaps the coat away from him, and goes behind counter with it.

MICHAEL, *taken aback*. Where would I get a potboy? Would you have me send the bellman screaming in the streets of Castlebar?

SHAWN, *opening the door a chink and putting in his head, in a small voice*. Michael James!

MICHAEL, *imitating him*. What ails you?

SHAWN. The queer dying fellow's beyond looking over the ditch. He's come up, I'm thinking, stealing your hens. (*Looks over his shoulder.*) God help me, he's following me now (*he runs into room*), and if he's heard what I said, he'll be having my life, and I going home lonesome in the darkness of the night.

For a perceptible moment they watch the door with curiosity. Someone coughs outside. Then Christy Mahon, a slight young man, comes in very tired and frightened and dirty.

CHRISTY, *in a small voice*. God save all here!

MEN. God save you kindly!

CHRISTY, *going to the counter*. I'd trouble you for a glass of porter, woman of the house. (*He puts down coin.*)

PEGEEN, *serving him*. You're one of the tinkers, young fellow, is beyond camped in the glen?

CHRISTY. I am not; but I'm destroyed walking.

MICHAEL, *patronizingly*. Let you come up then to the fire. You're looking famished with the cold.

CHRISTY. God reward you! (*He takes up his glass and goes a little way across to the left, then stops and looks about him.*) Is it often the polis do be coming into this place, master of the house?

MICHAEL. If you'd come in better hours, you'd have seen "Licensed for the Sale of Beer and Spirits, to be Consumed on the Premises," written in white letters above the door, and what would the polis want spying on me, and not a decent house within four miles, the way every living Christian is a bona fide, saving one widow alone?

CHRISTY, *with relief.* It's a safe house, so.

He goes over to the fire, sighing and moaning. Then he sits down, putting his glass beside him, and begins gnawing a turnip, too miserable to feel the others staring at him with curiosity.

MICHAEL, *going after him.* Is it yourself is fearing the polis? You're wanting, maybe?

CHRISTY. There's many wanting.

MICHAEL. Many, surely, with the broken harvest and the ended wars. (*He picks up some stockings, etc., that are near the fire, and carries them away furtively.*) It should be larceny, I'm thinking?

CHRISTY, *dolefully.* I had it in my mind it was a different word and a bigger.

PEGEEN. There's a queer lad. Were you never slapped in school, young fellow, that you don't know the name of your deed?

CHRISTY, *bashfully.* I'm slow at learning, a middling scholar only.

MICHAEL. If you're a dunce itself, you'd have a right to know that larceny's robbing and stealing. Is it for the like of that you're wanting?

CHRISTY, *with a flash of family pride.* And I the son of a strong farmer (*with a sudden qualm*), God rest his soul, could have bought up the whole of your old house awhile since, from the butt of his tail-pocket, and not have missed the weight of it gone.

MICHAEL, *impressed.* If it's not stealing, it's maybe something big.

CHRISTY, *flattered.* Aye; it's maybe something big.

JIMMY. He's a wicked-looking young fellow. Maybe he followed after a young woman on a lonesome night.

CHRISTY, *shocked.* Oh, the saints forbid, mister; I was all times a decent lad.

PHILLY, *turning on Jimmy.* You're a silly man, Jimmy Farrell. He said his father was a farmer awhile since, and there's himself now in a poor state. Maybe the land was grabbed from him, and he did what any decent man would do.

MICHAEL, *to Christy, mysteriously.* Was it bailiffs?

CHRISTY. The divil a one.

MICHAEL. Agents?

CHRISTY. The divil a one.

MICHAEL. Landlords?

CHRISTY, *peevishly.* Ah, not at all, I'm saying. You'd see the like of them stories on any little paper of a Munster town. But I'm not calling to mind any person, gentle, simple, judge or jury, did the like of me.

They all draw nearer with delighted curiosity.

PHILLY. Well, that lad's a puzzle-the-world.

JIMMY. He'd beat Dan Davies' circus, or the holy missioners making sermons on the villainy of man. Try him again, Philly.

PHILLY. Did you strike golden guineas out of solder, young fellow, or shilling coins itself?

CHRISTY. I did not, mister, not sixpence nor a farthing coin.

JIMMY. Did you marry three wives maybe? I'm told there's a sprinkling have done that among the holy Luthers of the preaching north.

CHRISTY, *shyly.* I never married with one, let alone with a couple or three.

PHILLY. Maybe he went fighting for the Boers, the like of the man beyond, was judged to be hanged, quartered, and drawn. Were you off east, young fellow, fighting bloody wars for Kruger and the freedom of the Boers?

CHRISTY. I never left my own parish till Tuesday was a week.

PEGEEN, *coming from counter.* He's done nothing, so. (*To Christy.*) If you didn't commit murder or a bad, nasty thing ; or false coining, or robbery, or butchery, or the like of them, there isn't anything that would be worth your troubling for to run from now. You did nothing at all.

CHRISTY, *his feelings hurt*. That's an unkindly thing to be saying to a poor orphaned traveler, has a prison behind him, and hanging before, and hell's gap gaping below.

PEGEEN, *with a sign to the men to be quiet*. You're only saying it. You did nothing at all. A soft lad the like of you wouldn't slit the windpipe of a screeching sow.

CHRISTY, *offended*. You're not speaking the truth.

PEGEEN, *in mock rage*. Not speaking the truth, is it? Would you have me knock the head of you with the butt of the broom?

CHRISTY, *twisting round on her with a sharp cry of horror*. Don't strike me. I killed my poor father, Tuesday was a week, for doing the like of that.

PEGEEN, *with blank amazement*. Is it killed your father?

CHRISTY, *subsiding*. With the help of God I did, surely, and that the Holy Immaculate Mother may intercede for his soul.

PHILLY, *retreating with Jimmy*. There's a daring fellow.

JIMMY. Oh, glory be to God!

MICHAEL, *with great respect*. That was a hanging crime, mister honey. You should have had good reason for doing the like of that.

CHRISTY, *in a very reasonable tone*. He was a dirty man, God forgive him, and he getting old and crusty, the way I couldn't put up with him at all.

PEGEEN. And you shot him dead?

CHRISTY, *shaking his head*. I never used weapons. I've no license, and I'm a law-fearing man.

MICHAEL. It was with a hilted knife maybe? I'm told, in the big world, it's bloody knives they use.

CHRISTY, *loudly, scandalized*. Do you take me for a slaughter boy?

PEGEEN. You never hanged him, the way Jimmy Farrell hanged his dog from the license, and had it screeching and wriggling three hours at the butt of a string, and himself swearing it was a dead dog, and the peelers swearing it had life?

CHRISTY. I did not, then. I just riz the loy and let fall the edge of it on the ridge of his skull, and he went down at my feet like an empty sack, and never let a grunt or groan from him at all.

MICHAEL, *making a sign to Pegeen to fill Christy's glass.* And what way weren't you hanged, mister? Did you bury him then?

CHRISTY, *considering.* Aye. I buried him then. Wasn't I digging spuds in the field?

MICHAEL. And the peelers never followed after you the eleven days that you're out?

CHRISTY, *shaking his head.* Never a one of them, and I walking forward facing hog, dog, or divil on the highway of the road.

PHILLY, *nodding wisely.* It's only with a common weekday kind of a murderer them lads would be trusting their carcase, and that man should be a great terror when his temper's roused.

MICHAEL. He should then. (*To Christy.*) And where was it, mister honey, that you did the deed?

CHRISTY, *looking at him with suspicion.* Oh, a distant place, master of the house, a windy corner of high, distant hills.

PHILLY, *nodding with approval.* He's a close man, and he's right, surely.

PEGEEN. That'd be a lad with the sense of Solomon to have for a potboy, Michael James, if it's the truth you're seeking one at all.

PHILLY. The peelers is fearing him, and if you'd that lad in the house there isn't one of them would come smelling around if the dogs itself were lapping poteen from the dung pit of the yard.

JIMMY. Bravery's a treasure in a lonesome place, and a lad would kill his father, I'm thinking, would face a foxy divil with a pitchpike on the flags of hell.

PEGEEN. It's the truth they're saying, and if I'd that lad in the house, I wouldn't be fearing the looséd kharki cutthroats, or the walking dead.

CHRISTY, *swelling with surprise and triumph*. Well, glory be to God!

MICHAEL, *with deference*. Would you think well to stop here and be potboy, mister honey, if we gave you good wages, and didn't destroy you with the weight of work.

SHAWN, *coming forward uneasily*. That'd be a queer kind to bring into a decent, quiet household with the like of Pegeen Mike.

PEGEEN, *very sharply*. Will you whisht? Who's speaking to you?

SHAWN, *retreating*. A bloody-handed murderer the like of . . .

PEGEEN, *snapping at him*. Whisht, I am saying; we'll take no fooling from your like at all. (*To Christy with a honeyed voice.*) And you, young fellow, you'd have a right to stop, I'm thinking, for we'd do our all and utmost to content your needs.

CHRISTY, *overcome with wonder*. And I'd be safe this place from the searching law?

MICHAEL. You would, surely. If they're not fearing you, itself, the peelers in this place is decent, drouthy, poor fellows, wouldn't touch a cur dog and not giving warning in the dead of night.

PEGEEN, *very kindly and persuasively*. Let you stop a short while anyhow. Aren't you destroyed walking with your feet in bleeding blisters, and your whole skin needing washing like a Wicklow sheep.

CHRISTY, *looking round with satisfaction*. It's a nice room, and if it's not humbugging me you are, I'm thinking that I'll surely stay.

JIMMY, *jumps up*. Now, by the grace of God, herself will be safe this night, with a man killed his father holding danger from the door, and let you come on, Michael James, or they'll have the best stuff drunk at the wake.

MICHAEL, *going to the door with men*. And begging your pardon, mister, what name will we call you, for we'd like to know?

CHRISTY. Christopher Mahon.

MICHAEL. Well, God bless you, Christy, and a good rest till we meet again when the sun'll be rising to the noon of day.

CHRISTY. God bless you all.

MEN. God bless you.

They go out, except Shawn, who lingers at door.

SHAWN, *to Pegeen*. Are you wanting me to stop along with you and keep you from harm?

PEGEEN, *gruffly*. Didn't you say you were fearing Father Reilly?

SHAWN. There'd be no harm staying now, I'm thinking, and himself in it too.

PEGEEN. You wouldn't stay when there was need for you, and let you step off nimble this time when there's none.

SHAWN. Didn't I say it was Father Reilly. . . .

PEGEEN. Go on, then, to Father Reilly (*in a jeering tone*), and let him put you in the holy brotherhoods, and leave that lad to me.

SHAWN. If I meet the Widow Quin . . .

PEGEEN. Go on, I'm saying, and don't be waking this place with your noise. (*She hustles him out and bolts door*.) That lad would wear the spirits from the saints of peace. (*Bustles about, then takes off her apron and pins it up in the window as a blind, Christy watching her timidly. Then she comes to him and speaks with bland good-humour*.) Let you stretch out now by the fire, young fellow. You should be destroyed travelling.

CHRISTY, *shyly again, drawing off his boots*. I'm tired surely, walking wild eleven days, and waking fearful in the night.

He holds up one of his feet, feeling his blisters, and looking at them with compassion.

PEGEEN, *standing beside him, watching him with delight*. You should have had great people in your family, I'm thinking, with the little small feet you have, and you with a kind of quality name, the like of what you'd find on the great powers and potentates of France and Spain.

CHRISTY, *with pride*. We were great, surely, with wide and windy acres of rich Munster land.

PEGEEN. Wasn't I telling you, and you a fine, handsome young fellow with a noble brow?

CHRISTY, *with a flash of delighted surprise*. Is it me?

PEGEEN. Aye. Did you never hear that from the young girls where you come from in the west or south?

CHRISTY, *with venom*. I did not, then. Oh, they're bloody liars in the naked parish where I grew a man.

PEGEEN. If they are itself, you've heard it these days, I'm thinking, and you walking the world telling out your story to young girls or old.

CHRISTY. I've told my story no place till this night, Pegeen Mike, and it's foolish I was here, maybe, to be talking free; but you're decent people, I'm thinking, and yourself a kindly woman, the way I wasn't fearing you at all.

PEGEEN, *filling a sack with straw*. You've said the like of that, maybe, in every cot and cabin where you've met a young girl on your way.

CHRISTY, *going over to her, gradually raising his voice*. I've said it nowhere till this night, I'm telling you; for I've seen none the like of you the eleven long days I am walking the world, looking over a low ditch or a high ditch on my north or south, into stony, scattered fields, or scribes of bog, where you'd see young, limber girls, and fine, prancing women making laughter with the men.

PEGEEN. If you weren't destroyed travelling, you'd have as much talk and streeleen, I'm thinking, as Owen Roe O'Sullivan or the poets of the Dingle Bay; and I've heard all times it's the poets are your like—fine, fiery fellows with great rages when their temper's roused.

CHRISTY, *drawing a little nearer to her*. You've a power of rings, God bless you, and would there be any offence if I was asking are you single now?

PEGEEN. What would I want wedding so young?

CHRISTY, *with relief*. We're alike so.

PEGEEN, *she puts sack on settle and beats it up.* I never killed my father. I'd be afeard to do that, except I was the like of yourself with blind rages tearing me within, for I'm thinking you should have had great tussling when the end was come.

CHRISTY, *expanding with delight at the first confidential talk he has ever had with a woman.* We had not then. It was a hard woman was come over the hill; and if he was always a crusty kind, when he'd a hard woman setting him on not the divil himself or his four fathers could put up with him at all.

PEGEEN, *with curiosity.* And isn't it a great wonder that one wasn't fearing you?

CHRISTY, *very confidentially.* Up to the day I killed my father, there wasn't a person in Ireland knew the kind I was, and I there drinking, waking, eating, sleeping, a quiet, simple poor fellow with no man giving me heed.

PEGEEN, *getting a quilt out of cupboard and putting it on the sack.* It was the girls were giving you heed, maybe, and I'm thinking it's most conceit you'd have to be gaming with their like.

CHRISTY, *shaking his head, with simplicity.* Not the girls itself, and I won't tell you a lie. There wasn't anyone heeding me in that place saving only the dumb beasts of the field.

He sits down at fire.

PEGEEN, *with disappointment.* And I thinking you should have been living the like of a king of Norway or the eastern world.

She comes and sits beside him after placing bread and mug of milk on the table.

CHRISTY, *laughing piteously.* The like of a king, is it? And I after toiling, moiling, digging, dodging from the dawn till dusk; with never a sight of joy or sport saving only when I'd be abroad in the dark night poaching rabbits on hills, for I was a divil to poach, God forgive me (very naively), and I near got six months for going with a dung fork and stabbing a fish.

PEGEEN. And it's that you'd call sport, is it, to be abroad in the darkness with yourself alone.

CHRISTY. I did, God help me, and there I'd be as happy as the sunshine of St. Martin's Day, watching the light passing the north or the patches of fog, till I'd hear a rabbit starting to screech and I'd go running in the furze. Then, when I'd my full share, I'd come walking down where you'd see the ducks and geese stretched sleeping on the highway of the road, and before I'd pass the dunghill, I'd hear himself snoring out—a loud, lonesome snore he'd be making all times, the while he was sleeping; and he a man'd be raging all times, the while he was waking, like a gaudy officer you'd hear cursing and damning and swearing oaths.

PEGEEN. Providence and Mercy, spare us all!

CHRISTY. It's that you'd say surely if you seen him and he after drinking for weeks, rising up in the red dawn, or before it maybe, and going out into the yard as naked as an ash tree in the moon of May, and shying clods against the visage of the stars till he'd put the fear of death into the banbhs and the screeching sows.

PEGEEN. I'd be well-nigh afeard of that lad myself, I'm thinking. And there was no one in it but the two of you alone?

CHRISTY. The divil a one, though he'd sons and daughters walking all great states and territories of the world, and not a one of them, to this day, but would say their seven curses on him, and they rousing up to let a cough or sneeze, maybe, in the deadness of the night.

PEGEEN, *nodding her head*. Well, you should have been a queer lot. I never cursed my father the like of that, though I'm twenty and more years of age.

CHRISTY. Then you'd have cursed mine, I'm telling you, and he a man never gave peace to any, saving when he'd get two months or three, or be locked in the asylums for battering peelers or assaulting men, (*with depression*) the way it was a bitter life he led me till I did up a Tuesday and halve his skull.

PEGEEN, *putting her hand on his shoulder*. Well, you'll have peace in this place, Christy Mahon, and none to trouble you, and it's near time a fine lad like you should have your good share of the earth.

CHRISTY. It's time surely, and I a seemly fellow with great strength in me and bravery of . . .

Someone knocks.

CHRISTY, *clinging to Pegeen*. Oh, glory! it's late for knocking, and this last while I'm in terror of the peelers, and the walking dead. (*Knocking again.*)

PEGEEN. Who's there?

VOICE, *outside*. Me.

PEGEEN. Who's me?

VOICE. The Widow Quin.

PEGEEN, *jumping up and giving him the bread and milk*. Go on now with your supper, and let on to be sleepy, for if she found you were such a warrant to talk, she'd be stringing gabble till the dawn of day.

He takes bread and sits shyly with his back to the door.

PEGEEN, *opening door, with temper*. What ails you, or what is it you're wanting at this hour of the night?

WIDOW QUIN, *coming in a step and peering at Christy*. I'm after meeting Shawn Keogh and Father Reilly below, who told me of your curiosity man, and they fearing by this time he was maybe roaring, romping on your hands with drink.

PEGEEN, *pointing to Christy*. Look now is he roaring, and he stretched out drowsy with his supper and his mug of milk. Walk down and tell that to Father Reilly and to Shaneen Keogh.

WIDOW QUIN, *Coming forward*. I'll not see them again, for I've their word to lead that lad forward for to lodge with me.

PEGEEN, *in blank amazement*. This night is it?

WIDOW QUIN, *going over*. This night. "It isn't fitting," says the priesteen, "to have his likeness lodging with an orphaned girl." (*To Christy.*) God save you, mister!

CHRISTY, *shyly*. God save you kindly!

WIDOW QUIN, *looking at him with half-amused curiosity*. Well, aren't you a little smiling fellow? It should have been great and bitter torments did rouse your spirits to a deed of blood.

CHRISTY, *doubtfully*. It should, maybe.

WIDOW QUIN. It's more than "maybe" I'm saying and it'd soften my heart to see you sitting so simple with your cup and cake, and you fitter to be saying your catechism than slaying your da.

PEGEEN, *at counter, washing glasses*. There's talking when any'd see he's fit to be holding his head high with the wonders of the world. Walk on from this, for I'll not have him tormented, and he destroyed travelling since Tuesday was a week.

WIDOW QUIN, *peaceably*. We'll be walking surely when his supper's done, and you'll find we're great company, young fellow, when it's of the like of you and me you'd hear the penny poets singing in an August fair.

CHRISTY, *innocently*. Did you kill your father?

PEGEEN, *contemptuously*. She did not. She hit himself with a worn pick, and the rusted poison did corrode his blood the way he never overed it, and died after. That was a sneaky kind of murder did win small glory with the boys itself. (*She crosses to Christy's left.*)

WIDOW QUIN, *with good-humour*. If it didn't, maybe all knows a widow woman has buried her children and destroyed her man is a wiser comrade for a young lad than a girl, the like of you, who'd go helter-skeltering after any man would let you a wink upon the road.

PEGEEN, *breaking out into wild rage*. And you'll say that, Widow Quin, and you gasping with the rage you had racing the hill beyond to look on his face.

WIDOW QUIN, *laughing derisively*. Me, is it? Well, Father Reilly has cuteness to divide you now. (*She pulls Christy up.*) There's great temptation in a man did slay his da, and we'd best be going, young fellow; so rise up and come with me.

PEGEEN, *seizing his arm*. He'll not stir. He's potboy in this place, and I'll not have him stolen off and kidnapped while himself's abroad.

WIDOW QUIN. It'd be a crazy potboy'd lodge him in the shebeen where he works by day, so you'd have a right to come on, young fellow, till you see my little houseen, a perch off on the rising hill.

PEGEEN. Wait till morning, Christy Mahon. Wait till you lay eyes on her leaky thatch is growing more pasture for her buck goat than her square of fields, and she without a tramp itself to keep in order her place at all.

WIDOW QUIN. When you see me contriving in my little gardens, Christy Mahon, you'll swear the Lord God formed me to be living lone, and that there isn't my match in Mayo for thatching, or mowing, or shearing a sheep.

PEGEEN, *with noisy scorn.* It's true the Lord formed you to contrive indeed. Doesn't the world know you reared a black ram at your own breast, so that the Lord Bishop of Connaught felt the elements of a Christian, and he eating it after a kidney stew? Doesn't the world know you've been seen shaving the foxy skipper from France for a threepenny bit and a sop of grass tobacco would wring the liver from a mountain goat you'd meet leaping the hills?

WIDOW QUIN, *with amusement.* Do you hear her now, young fellow? Do you hear the way she'll be rating at your own self when a week is by?

PEGEEN, *to Christy.* Don't heed her. Tell her to go on into her pigsty and not plague us here.

WIDOW QUIN. I'm going; but he'll come with me.

PEGEEN, *shaking him.* Are you dumb, young fellow?

CHRISTY, *timidly to Widow Quin.* God increase you; but I'm potboy in this place, and it's here I liefer stay.

PEGEEN, *triumphantly.* Now you have heard him, and go on from this.

WIDOW QUIN, *looking round the room.* It's lonesome this hour crossing the hill, and if he won't come along with me, I'd have a right maybe to stop this night with yourselves. Let me stretch out on the settle, Pegeen Mike; and himself can lie by the hearth.

PEGEEN, *short and fiercely.* Faith, I won't. Quit off or I will send you now.

WIDOW QUIN, *gathering her shawl up.* Well, it's a terror to be aged a score. (*To Christy.*) God bless you now, young fellow, and let you be wary, or there's right torment will await you here if you go romancing with her like, and she waiting only, as they bade me say, on a sheepskin parchment to be wed with Shawn Keogh of Killakeen.

CHRISTY, *going to Pegeen as she bolts door.* What's that she's after saying?

PEGEEN. Lies and blather, you've no call to mind. Well, isn't Shawn Keogh an impudent fellow to send up spying on me? Wait till I lay hands on him. Let him wait, I'm saying.

CHRISTY. And you're not wedding him at all?

PEGEEN. I wouldn't wed him if a bishop came walking for to join us here.

CHRISTY. That God in glory may be thanked for that.

PEGEEN. There's your bed now. I've put a quilt upon you I'm after quilting awhile since with my own two hands, and you'd best stretch out now for your sleep, and may God give you a good rest till I call you in the morning when the cocks will crow.

CHRISTY, *as she goes to inner room.* May God and Mary and St. Patrick bless you and reward you for your kindly talk. (*She shuts the door behind her. He settles his bed slowly, feeling the quilt with immense satisfaction.*) Well, it's a clean bed and soft with it, and it's great luck and company I've won me in the end of time—two fine women fighting for the likes of me—till I'm thinking this night wasn't I a foolish fellow not to kill my father in the years gone by.

ACT II

Scene as before. Brilliant morning light. Christy, looking bright and cheerful, is cleaning a girl's boots.

CHRISTY, *to himself, counting jugs on dresser.* Half a hundred beyond. Ten there. A score that's above. Eighty jugs. Six cups and a broken one. Two plates. A power of glasses. Bottles, a schoolmaster'd be hard set to count, and enough in them, I'm thinking, to drunken all the wealth and wisdom of the County Clare. (*He puts down the boot carefully.*) There's her boots now, nice and decent for her evening use, and isn't it grand brushes she has? (*He puts them down and goes by degrees to the looking glass.*) Well, this'd be a fine place to be my whole life talking out with swearing Christians, in place of my old dogs and cat; and I stalking around, smoking my pipe and drinking my fill, and never a day's work but drawing a cork an odd time, or wiping a glass, or rinsing out a shiny tumbler for a decent man. (*He takes the looking glass from the wall and puts it on the back of a chair; then sits down in front of it and begins washing his face.*) Didn't I know rightly I was handsome, though it was the divil's own mirror we had beyond, would twist a squint across an angel's brow; and I'll be growing fine from this day, the way I'll have a soft lovely skin on me and won't be the like of the clumsy young fellows do be ploughing all times in the earth and dung. (*He starts.*) Is she coming again? (*He looks out.*) Stranger girls. God help me, where'll I hide myself away and my long neck naked to the world? (*He looks out.*) I'd best go to the room maybe till I'm dressed again.

He gathers up his coat and the looking glass, and runs into the inner room. The door is pushed open, and Susan Brady looks in, and knocks on door.

SUSAN. There's nobody in it. (*Knocks again.*)

NELLY, *pushing her in and following her, with Honor Blake and Sara Tansey.* It'd be early for them both to be out walking the hill.

SUSAN. I'm thinking Shawn Keogh was making game of us, and there's no such man in it at all.

HONOR, *pointing to straw and quilt.* Look at that. He's been sleeping there in the night. Well, it'll be a hard case if he's gone off now, the way we'll never set our eyes on a man killed his father, and we after rising early and destroying ourselves running fast on the hill.

NELLY. Are you thinking them's his boots?

SARA, *taking them up.* If they are, there should be his father's track on them. Did you never read in the papers the way murdered men do bleed and drip?

SUSAN. Is that blood there, Sara Tansey?

SARA, *smelling it.* That's bog water, I'm thinking; but it's his own they are, surely, for I never seen the like of them for whitey mud, and red mud, and turf on them, and the fine sands of the sea. That man's been walking, I'm telling you.

She goes down right, putting on one of his boots.

SUSAN, *going to window.* Maybe he's stolen off to Belmullet with the boots of Michael James, and you'd have a right so to follow after him, Sara Tansey, and you the one yoked the ass cart and drove ten miles to set your eyes on the man bit the yellow lady's nostril on the northern shore. (*She looks out.*)

SARA, *running to window, with one boot on.* Don't be talking, and we fooled today. (*Putting on the other boot.*) There's a pair do fit me well, and I'll be keeping them for walking to the priest, when you'd be ashamed this place, going up winter and summer with nothing worthwhile to confess at all.

HONOR, *who has been listening at door.* Whisht! there's someone inside the room. (*She pushes door a chink open.*) It's a man.

Sara kicks off boots and puts them where they were. They all stand in a line looking through chink.

SARA. I'll call him. Mister! Mister! (*He puts in his head.*) Is Pegeen within?

CHRISTY, *coming in as meek as a mouse, with the looking glass held behind his back.* She's above on the cnuceen, seeking the nanny goats, the way she'd have a sup of goats' milk for to colour my tea.

SARA. And asking your pardon, is it you's the man killed his father?

CHRISTY, *sidling toward the nail where the glass was hanging.* I am, God help me!

SARA, *taking eggs she has brought*. Then my thousand welcomes to you, and I've run up with a brace of duck's eggs for your food today. Pegeen's ducks is no use, but these are the real rich sort. Hold out your hand and you'll see it's no lie I'm telling you.

CHRISTY, *coming forward shyly, and holding out his left hand*. They're a great and weighty size.

SUSAN. And I run up with a pat of butter, for it'd be a poor thing to have you eating your spuds dry, and you after running a great way since you did destroy your da.

CHRISTY. Thank you kindly.

HONOR. And I brought you a little cut of cake, for you should have a thin stomach on you, and you that length walking the world.

NELLY. And I brought you a little laying pullet—boiled and all she is—was crushed at the fall of night by the curate's car. Feel the fat of that breast, mister.

CHRISTY. It's bursting, surely.

He feels it with the back of his hand, in which he holds the presents.

SARA. Will you pinch it? Is your right hand too sacred for to use at all? (*She slips round behind him.*) It's a glass he has. Well, I never seen to this day a man with a looking glass to his back. Them that kills their fathers is a vain lot surely. (*Girls giggle.*)

CHRISTY, *smiling innocently and piling presents on glass*. I'm very thankful to you all today. . . .

WIDOW QUIN, *coming in quickly, at door*. Sara Tansey, Susan Brady, Honor Blake! What in glory has you here at this hour of day?

GIRLS, *giggling*. That's the man killed his father.

WIDOW QUIN, *coming to them*. I know well it's the man; and I'm after putting him down in the sports below for racing, leaping, pitching, and the Lord knows what.

SARA, *exuberantly*. That's right, Widow Quin. I'll bet my dowry that he'll lick the world.

WIDOW QUIN. If you will, you'd have a right to have him fresh and nourished in place of nursing a feast. (*Taking presents.*) Are you fasting or fed, young fellow?

CHRISTY. Fasting, if you please.

WIDOW QUIN, *loudly*. Well, you're the lot. Stir up now and give him his breakfast. (*To Christy.*) Come here to me (*she puts him on bench beside her while the girls make tea and get his breakfast*), and let you tell us your story before Pegeen will come, in place of grinning your ears off like the moon of May.

CHRISTY, *beginning to be pleased*. It's a long story; you'd be destroyed listening.

WIDOW QUIN. Don't be letting on to be shy, a fine, gamey, treacherous lad the like of you. Was it in your house beyond you cracked his skull?

CHRISTY, *shy but flattered*. It was not. We were digging spuds in his cold, sloping, stony, divil's patch of a field.

WIDOW QUIN. And you went asking money of him, or making talk of getting a wife would drive him from his farm?

CHRISTY. I did not, then; but there I was, digging and digging, and "You squinting idiot," says he, "let you walk down now and tell the priest you'll wed the Widow Casey in a score of days."

WIDOW QUIN. And what kind was she?

CHRISTY, *with horror*. A walking terror from beyond the hills, and she two score and five years, and two hundredweights and five pounds in the weighing scales, with a limping leg on her, and a blinded eye, and she a woman of noted misbehaviour with the old and young.

GIRLS, *clustering round him, serving him*. Glory be!

WIDOW QUIN. And what did he want driving you to wed with her? (*She takes a bit of the chicken.*)

CHRISTY, *eating with growing satisfaction*. He was letting on I was wanting a protector from the harshness of the world, and he without a thought the whole while but how he'd have her hut to live in and her gold to drink.

WIDOW QUIN. There's maybe worse than a dry hearth and a widow woman and your glass at night. So you hit him then?

CHRISTY, *getting almost excited*. I did not. "I won't wed her," says I, "when all knows she did suckle me for six weeks when I came into the world, and she a hag this day with a tongue on her has the crows and seabirds scattered, the way they wouldn't cast a shadow on her garden with the dread of her curse."

WIDOW QUIN, *teasingly*. That one should be right company.

SARA, *eagerly*. Don't mind her. Did you kill him then?

CHRISTY. "She's too good for the like of you," says he, "and go on now or I'll flatten you out like a crawling beast has passed under a dray." "You will not if I can help it," says I. "Go on," says he, "or I'll have the divil making garters of your limbs tonight." "You will not if I can help it," says I.

He sits up brandishing his mug.

SARA. You were right surely.

CHRISTY, *impressively*. With that the sun came out between the cloud and the hill, and it shining green in my face. "God have mercy on your soul," says he, lifting a scythe. "Or on your own," says I, raising the loy.

SUSAN. That's a grand story.

HONOR. He tells it lovely.

CHRISTY, *flattered and confident, waving bone*. He gave a drive with the scythe, and I gave a lep to the east. Then I turned around with my back to the north, and I hit a blow on the ridge of his skull, laid him stretched out, and he split to the knob of his gullet.

He raises the chicken bone to his Adam's apple.

GIRLS, *together*. Well, you're a marvel! Oh, God bless you! You're the lad, surely!

SUSAN. I'm thinking the Lord God sent him this road to make a second husband to the Widow Quin, and she with a great yearning to be wedded, though all dread her here. Lift him on her knee, Sara Tansey.

WIDOW QUIN. Don't tease him.

SARA, *going over to dresser and counter very quickly, and getting two glasses and porter*. You're heroes, surely, and let you drink a supeen with your arms linked like the outlandish lovers in the sailor's song. (*She links their arms and gives them the glasses.*) There now. Drink a health to the wonders of the western world, the pirates, preachers, poteen makers, with the jobbing jockies; parching peelers, and the juries fill their stomachs selling judgments of the English law.

Brandishing the bottle.

WIDOW QUIN. That's a right toast, Sara Tansey. Now, Christy.

They drink with their arms linked, he drinking with his left hand, she with her right. As they are drinking, Pegeen Mike comes in with a milk can and stands aghast. They all spring away from Christy. He goes down left. Widow Quin remains seated.

PEGEEN, *angrily, to Sara*. What is it you're wanting?

SARA, *twisting her apron*. An ounce of tobacco.

PEGEEN. Have you tuppence?

SARA. I've forgotten my purse.

PEGEEN. Then you'd best be getting it and not be fooling us here. (*To the Widow Quin, with more elaborate scorn.*) And what is it you're wanting, Widow Quin?

WIDOW QUIN, *insolently*. A penn'orth of starch.

PEGEEN, *breaking out*. And you without a white shift or a shirt in your whole family since the drying of the flood. I've no starch for the like of you, and let you walk on now to Killamuck.

WIDOW QUIN, *turning to Christy, as she goes out with the girls.* Well, you're mighty huffy this day, Pegeen Mike, and you, young fellow, let you not forget the sports and racing when the noon is by.

They go out.

PEGEEN, *imperiously.* Fling out that rubbish and put them cups away. (*Christy tidies away in great haste.*) Shove in the bench by the wall. (*He does so.*) And hang that glass on the nail. What disturbed it at all?

CHRISTY, *very meekly.* I was making myself decent only, and this is a fine country for young lovely girls.

PEGEEN, *sharply.* Whisht your talking of girls.

Goes to counter on right.

CHRISTY. Wouldn't any wish to be decent in a place . . .

PEGEEN. Whisht, I'm saying.

CHRISTY, *looks at her face for a moment with great misgivings, then as a last effort takes up a loy, and goes toward her, with feigned assurance.* It was with a loy the like of that I killed my father.

PEGEEN, *still sharply.* You've told me that story six times since the dawn of day.

CHRISTY, *reproachfully.* It's a queer thing you wouldn't care to be hearing it and them girls after walking four miles to be listening to me now.

PEGEEN, *turning round astonished.* Four miles!

CHRISTY, *apologetically.* Didn't himself say there were only bona fides living in the place?

PEGEEN. It's bona fides by the road they are, but that lot came over the river lepping the stones. It's not three perches when you go like that, and I was down this morning looking on the papers the post boy does have in his bag. (*With meaning and emphasis.*) For there was great news this day, Christopher Mahon. (*She goes into room on left.*)

CHRISTY, *suspiciously.* Is it news of my murder?

PEGEEN, *inside.* Murder, indeed!

CHRISTY, *loudly.* A murdered da?

PEGEEN, *coming in again and crossing right.* There was not, but a story filled half a page of the hanging of a man. Ah, that should be a fearful end, young fellow, and it worst of all for a man destroyed his da; for the like of him would get small mercies, and when it's dead he is they'd put him in a narrow grave, with cheap sacking wrapping him round, and pour down quicklime on his head, the way you'd see a woman pouring any frishfrash from a cup.

CHRISTY, *very miserably.* Oh, God help me! Are you thinking I'm safe? You were saying at the fall of night I was shut of jeopardy and I here with yourselves.

PEGEEN, *severely.* You'll be shut of jeopardy no place if you go talking with a pack of wild girls the like of them do be walking abroad with the peelers, talking whispers at the fall of night.

CHRISTY, *with terror.* And you're thinking they'd tell?

PEGEEN, *with mock sympathy.* Who knows, God help you?

CHRISTY, *loudly.* What joy would they have to bring hanging to the likes of me?

PEGEEN. It's queer joys they have, and who knows the thing they'd do, if it'd make the green stones cry itself to think of you swaying and swiggling at the butt of a rope, and you with a fine, stout neck, God bless you! the way you'd be a half an hour, in great anguish, getting your death.

CHRISTY, *getting his boots and putting them on.* If there's that terror of them, it'd be best, maybe, I went on wandering like Esau or Cain and Abel on the sides of Neifin or the Erris plain.

PEGEEN, *beginning to play with him.* It would, maybe, for I've heard the circuit judges this place is a heartless crew.

CHRISTY, *bitterly.* It's more than judges this place is a heartless crew. (*Looking up at her.*) And isn't it a poor thing to be starting again, and I a lonesome fellow will be looking out on women and girls the way the needy fallen spirits do be looking on the Lord?

PEGEEN. What call have you to be that lonesome when there's poor girls walking Mayo in their thousands now?

CHRISTY, *grimly*. It's well you know what call I have. It's well you know it's a lonesome thing to be passing small towns with the lights shining sideways when the night is down, or going in strange places with a dog noising before you and a dog noising behind, or drawn to the cities where you'd hear a voice kissing and talking deep love in every shadow of the ditch, and you passing on with an empty, hungry stomach failing from your heart.

PEGEEN. I'm thinking you're an odd man, Christy Mahon. The oddest walking fellow I ever set my eyes on to this hour today.

CHRISTY. What would any be but odd men and they living lonesome in the world?

PEGEEN. I'm not odd, and I'm my whole life with my father only.

CHRISTY, *with infinite admiration*. How would a lovely, handsome woman the like of you be lonesome when all men should be thronging around to hear the sweetness of your voice, and the little infant children should be pestering your steps, I'm thinking, and you walking the roads.

PEGEEN. I'm hard set to know what way a coaxing fellow the like of yourself should be lonesome either.

CHRISTY. Coaxing.

PEGEEN. Would you have me think a man never talked with the girls would have the words you've spoken today? It's only letting on you are to be lonesome, the way you'd get around me now.

CHRISTY. I wish to God I was letting on; but I was lonesome all times, and born lonesome, I'm thinking, as the moon of dawn. (*Going to door.*)

PEGEEN, *puzzled by his talk*. Well, it's a story I'm not understanding at all why you'd be worse than another, Christy Mahon, and you a fine lad with the great savagery to destroy your da.

CHRISTY. It's little I'm understanding myself, saving only that my heart's scalded this day, and I going off stretching out the earth between us, the way I'll not be waking near you another dawn of the year till the two of us do arise to hope or judgment with the saints of God, and now I'd best be going with my wattle in my hand, for hanging is a poor thing (*turning to go*), and it's little welcome only is left me in this house today.

PEGEEN, *sharply*. Christy. (*He turns round.*) Come here to me. (*He goes toward her.*) Lay down that switch and throw some sods on the fire. You're potboy in this place, and I'll not have you mitch off from us now.

CHRISTY. You were saying I'd be hanged if I stay.

PEGEEN, *quite kindly at last*. I'm after going down and reading the fearful crimes of Ireland for two weeks or three, and there wasn't a word of your murder. (*Getting up and going over to the counter.*) They've likely not found the body. You're safe so with ourselves.

CHRISTY, *astonished, slowly*. It's making game of me you were (*following her with fearful joy*), and I can stay so, working at your side, and I not lonesome from this mortal day.

PEGEEN. What's to hinder you staying, except the widow woman or the young girls would inveigle you off?

CHRISTY, *with rapture*. And I'll have your words from this day filling my ears, and that look is come upon you meeting my two eyes, and I watching you loafing around in the warm sun, or rinsing your ankles when the night is come.

PEGEEN, *kindly, but a little embarrassed*. I'm thinking you'll be a loyal young lad to have working around, and if you vexed me awhile since with your leaguing with the girls, I wouldn't give a thraneen for a lad hadn't a mighty spirit in him and a gamey heart.

Shawn Keogh runs in carrying a cleeve on his back, followed by the Widow Quin.

SHAWN, *to Pegeen*. I was passing below, and I seen your mountainy sheep eating cabbages in Jimmy's field. Run up or they'll be bursting, surely.

PEGEEN. Oh, God mend them!

She puts a shawl over her head and runs out.

CHRISTY, *looking from one to the other. Still in high spirits.* I'd best go to her aid maybe. I'm handy with ewes.

WIDOW QUIN, *closing the door.* She can do that much, and there is Shaneen has long speeches for to tell you now.

She sits down with an amused smile.

SHAWN, *taking something from his pocket and offering it to Christy.* Do you see that, mister?

CHRISTY, *looking at it.* The half of a ticket to the Western States!

SHAWN, *trembling with anxiety.* I'll give it to you and my new hat (*pulling it out of hamper*); and my breeches with the double seat (*pulling it out*); and my new coat is woven from the blackest shearings for three miles around (*giving him the coat*); I'll give you the whole of them, and my blessing, and the blessing of Father Reilly itself, maybe, if you'll quit from this and leave us in the peace we had till last night at the fall of dark.

CHRISTY, *with a new arrogance.* And for what is it you're wanting to get shut of me?

SHAWN, *looking to the Widow for help.* I'm a poor scholar with middling faculties to coin a lie, so I'll tell you the truth, Christy Mahon. I'm wedding with Pegeen beyond, and I don't think well of having a clever, fearless man the like of you dwelling in her house.

CHRISTY, *almost pugnaciously.* And you'd be using bribery for to banish me?

SHAWN, *in an imploring voice.* Let you not take it badly, mister honey; isn't beyond the best place for you, where you'll have golden chains and shiny coats and you riding upon hunters with the ladies of the land.

He makes an eager sign to the Widow Quin to come to help him.

WIDOW QUIN, *coming over.* It's true for him, and you'd best quit off and not have that poor girl setting her mind on you, for there's Shaneen thinks she wouldn't suit you, though all is saying that she'll wed you now.

Christy beams with delight.

SHAWN, *in terrified earnest.* She wouldn't suit you, and she with the divil's own temper the way you'd be strangling one another in a score of days. (*He makes the movement of strangling with his hands.*) It's the like of me only that she's fit for; a quiet simple fellow wouldn't raise a hand upon her if she scratched itself.

WIDOW QUIN, *putting Shawn's hat on Christy.* Fit them clothes on you anyhow, young fellow, and he'd maybe loan them to you for the sports. (*Pushing him toward inner door.*) Fit them on and you can give your answer when you have them tried.

CHRISTY, *beaming, delighted with the clothes.* I will then. I'd like herself to see me in them tweeds and hat.

He goes into room and shuts the door.

SHAWN, *in great anxiety.* He'd like herself to see them. He'll not leave us, Widow Quin. He's a score of divils in him the way it's well-nigh certain he will wed Pegeen.

WIDOW QUIN, *jeeringly.* It's true all girls are fond of courage and do hate the like of you.

SHAWN, *walking about in desperation.* Oh, Widow Quin, what'll I be doing now? I'd inform again him, but he'd burst from Kilmainham and he'd be sure and certain to destroy me. If I wasn't so God-fearing, I'd near have courage to come behind him and run a pike into his side. Oh, it's a hard to be an orphan and not to have your father that you're used to, and you'd easy kill and make yourself a hero in the sight of all. (*Coming up to her.*) Oh, Widow Quin, will you find me some contrivance when I've promised you a ewe?

WIDOW QUIN. A ewe's a small thing, but what would you give me if I did wed him and did save you so?

SHAWN, *with astonishment.* You?

WIDOW QUIN. Aye. Would you give me the red cow you have and the mountainy ram, and the right of way across your rye path, and a load of dung at Michaelmas, and turbary upon the western hill?

SHAWN, *radiant with hope.* I would, surely, and I'd give you the wedding ring I have, and the loan of a new suit, the way you'd have him decent on the wedding day. I'd give you two kids for your dinner, and a gallon of poteen, and I'd call the piper on the long car to your wedding from Crossmolina or from Ballina. I'd give you . . .

WIDOW QUIN. That'll do, so, and let you whisht, for he's coming now again.

Christy comes in very natty in the new clothes. Widow Quin goes to him admiringly.

WIDOW QUIN. If you seen yourself now, I'm thinking you'd be too proud to speak to us at all, and it'd be a pity surely to have your like sailing from Mayo to the western world.

CHRISTY, *as proud as a peacock.* I'm not going. If this is a poor place itself, I'll make myself contented to be lodging here.

Widow Quin makes a sign to Shawn to leave them.

SHAWN. Well, I'm going measuring the racecourse while the tide is low, so I'll leave you the garments and my blessing for the sports today. God bless you! (*He wriggles out.*)

WIDOW QUIN, *admiring Christy.* Well, you're mighty spruce, young fellow. Sit down now while you're quiet till you talk with me.

CHRISTY, *swaggering.* I'm going abroad on the hillside for to seek Pegeen.

WIDOW QUIN. You'll have time and plenty for to seek Pegeen, and you heard me saying at the fall of night the two of us should be great company.

CHRISTY. From this out I'll have no want of company when all sorts is bringing me their food and clothing (*he swaggers to the door, tightening his belt*), the way they'd set their eyes upon a gallant orphan cleft his father with one blow to the breeches belt. (*He opens door, then staggers back*) Saints of glory! Holy angels from the throne of light!

WIDOW QUIN, *going over.* What ails you?

CHRISTY. It's the walking spirit of my murdered da!

WIDOW QUIN, *looking out.* Is it that tramper?

CHRISTY, *wildly.* Where'll I hide my poor body from that ghost of hell?

The door is pushed open, and old Mahon appears on threshold. Christy darts in behind door.

WIDOW QUIN, *in great amusement.* God save you, my poor man.

MAHON, *gruffly.* Did you see a young lad passing this way in the early morning or the fall of night?

WIDOW QUIN. You're a queer kind to walk in not saluting at all.

MAHON. Did you see the young lad?

WIDOW QUIN, *stiffly.* What kind was he?

MAHON. An ugly young streeler with a murderous gob on him, and a little switch in his hand. I met a tramper seen him coming this way at the fall of night.

WIDOW QUIN. There's harvest hundreds do be passing these days for the Sligo boat. For what is it you're wanting him, my poor man?

MAHON. I want to destroy him for breaking the head on me with the clout of a loy. (*He takes off a big hat, and shows his head in a mass of bandages and plaster, with some pride.*) It was he did that, and amn't I a great wonder to think I've traced him ten days with that rent in my crown.

WIDOW QUIN, *taking his head in both hands and examining it with extreme delight.* That was a great blow. And who hit you? A robber maybe?

MAHON. It was my own son hit me, and he the divil a robber, or anything else, but a dirty, stuttering lout.

WIDOW QUIN, *letting go his skull and wiping her hands in her apron.* You'd best be wary of a mortified scalp, I think they call it, lepping around with that wound in the splendour of the sun. It was a bad blow, surely, and you should have vexed him fearful to make him strike that gash in his da.

MAHON. Is it me?

WIDOW QUIN, *amusing herself.* Aye. And isn't it a great shame when the old and hardened do torment the young.

MAHON, *raging*. Torment him is it? And I after holding out with the patience of a martyred saint till there's nothing but destruction on, and I'm driven out in my old age with none to aid me.

WIDOW QUIN, *greatly amused*. It's a sacred wonder the way that wickedness will spoil a man.

MAHON. My wickedness, is it? Amn't I after saying it is himself has me destroyed, and he a liar on walls, a talker of folly, a man you'd see stretched the half of the day in the brown ferns with his belly to the sun.

WIDOW QUIN. Not working at all?

MAHON. The divil a work, or if he did itself, you'd see him raising up a haystack like the stalk of a rush, or driving our last cow till he broke her leg at the hip, and when he wasn't at that he'd be fooling over little birds he had—finches and felts—or making mugs at his own self in the bit of a glass we had hung on the wall.

WIDOW QUIN, *looking at Christy*. What way was he so foolish? It was running wild after the girls maybe?

MAHON, *with a shout of derision*. Running wild, is it? If he seen a red petticoat coming swinging over the hill, he'd be off to hide in the sticks, and you'd see him shooting out his sheep's eyes between the little twigs and the leaves, and his two ears rising like a hare looking, out through a gap. Girls, indeed!

WIDOW QUIN. It was drink maybe?

MAHON. And he a poor fellow would get drunk on the smell of a pint. He'd a queer rotten stomach, I'm telling you, and when I gave him three pulls from my pipe awhile since, he was taken with contortions till I had to send him in the ass cart to the females' nurse.

WIDOW QUIN, *clasping her hands*. Well, I never, till this day, heard tell of a man the like of that!

MAHON. I'd take a mighty oath you didn't, surely, and wasn't he the laughing joke of every female woman where four baronies meet, the way the girls would stop their weeding if they seen him coming the road to let a roar at him, and call him the looney of Mahon's.

WIDOW QUIN. I'd give the world and all to see the like of him. What kind was he?

MAHON. A small, low fellow.

WIDOW QUIN. And dark?

MAHON. Dark and dirty.

WIDOW QUIN, *considering*. I'm thinking I seen him.

MAHON, *eagerly*. An ugly young blackguard.

WIDOW QUIN. A hideous, fearful villain, and the spit of you.

MAHON. What way is he fled?

WIDOW QUIN. Gone over the hills to catch a coasting steamer to the north or south.

MAHON. Could I pull up on him now?

WIDOW QUIN. If you'll cross the sands below where the tide is out, you'll be in it as soon as himself, for he had to go round ten miles by the top of the bay. (*She points to the door.*) Strike down by the head beyond and then follow on the roadway to the north and east. (*Mahon goes abruptly.*)

WIDOW QUIN, *shouting after him*. Let you give him a good vengeance when you come up with him, but don't put yourself in the power of the law, for it'd be a poor thing to see a judge in his black cap reading out his sentence on a civil warrior the like of you. (*She swings the door to and looks at Christy, who is cowering in terror, for a moment, then she bursts into a laugh.*) Well, you're the walking Playboy of the Western World, and that's the poor man you had divided to his breeches belt.

CHRISTY, *looking out; then, to her*. What'll Pegeen say when she hears that story? What'll she be saying to me now?

WIDOW QUIN. She'll knock the head of you, I'm thinking, and drive you from the door. God help her to be taking you for a wonder, and you a little schemer making up a story you destroyed your da.

CHRISTY, *turning to the door, nearly speechless with rage, half to himself.* To be letting on he was dead, and coming back to his life, and following after me like an old weasel tracing a rat, and coming in here laying desolation between my own self and the fine women of Ireland, and he a kind of carcase that you'd fling upon the sea. . . .

WIDOW QUIN, *more soberly.* There's talking for a man's one only son.

CHRISTY, *breaking out.* His one son, is it? May I meet him with one tooth and it aching, and one eye to be seeing seven and seventy divils in the twists of the road, and one old timber leg on him to limp into the scalding grave. (*Looking out.*) There he is now crossing the strands, and that the Lord God would send a high wave to wash him from the world.

WIDOW QUIN, *scandalized.* Have you no shame? (*Putting her hand on his shoulder and turning him round.*) What ails you? Near crying, is it?

CHRISTY, *in despair and grief.* Amn't I after seeing the love-light of the star of knowledge shining from her brow, and hearing words would put you thinking on the holy Brigid speaking to the infant saints, and now she'll be turning again, and speaking hard words to me, like an old woman with a spavindy ass she'd have, urging on a hill.

WIDOW QUIN. There's poetry talk for a girl you'd see itching and scratching, and she with a stale stink of poteen on her from selling in the shop.

CHRISTY, *impatiently.* It's her like is fitted to be handling merchandise in the heavens above, and what'll I be doing now, I ask you, and I a kind of wonder was jilted by the heavens when a day was by.

There is a distant noise of girls' voices. Widow Quin looks from window and comes to him, hurriedly.

WIDOW QUIN. You'll be doing like myself, I'm thinking, when I did destroy my man, for I'm above many's the day, odd times in great spirits, abroad in the sunshine, darning a stocking or stitching a shift; and odd times again looking out on the schooners, hookers, trawlers is sailing the sea, and I thinking on the gallant hairy fellows are drifting beyond, and myself long years living alone.

CHRISTY, *interested.* You're like me, so.

WIDOW QUIN. I am your like, and it's for that I'm taking a fancy to you, and I with my little houseen above where there'd be myself to tend you, and none to ask were you a murderer or what at all.

CHRISTY. And what would I be doing if I left Pegeen?

WIDOW QUIN. I've nice jobs you could be doing—gathering shells to make a whitewash for our hut within, building up a little goose house, or stretching a new skin on an old curragh I have; and if my hut is far from all sides, it's there you'll meet the wisest old men, I tell you, at the corner of my wheel, and it's there yourself and me will have great times whispering and hugging. . . .

VOICES, *outside, calling far away.* Christy! Christy Mahon! Christy!

CHRISTY. Is it Pegeen Mike?

WIDOW QUIN. It's the young girls, I'm thinking coming to bring you to the sports below, and what is it you'll have me to tell them now?

CHRISTY. Aid me for to win Pegeen. It's herself only that I'm seeking now. (*Widow Quin gets up and goes to window.*) Aid me for to win her, and I'll be asking God to stretch a hand to you in the hour of death, and lead you short cuts through the Meadows of Ease, and up the floor of heaven to the footstool of the Virgin's Son.

WIDOW QUIN. There's praying!

VOICES, *nearer.* Christy! Christy Mahon!

CHRISTY, *with agitation.* They're coming. Will you swear to aid and save me, for the love of Christ?

WIDOW QUIN, *looks at him for a moment.* If I aid you, will you swear to give me a right of way I want, and a mountainy ram, and a load of dung at Michaelmas, the time that you'll be master here?

CHRISTY. I will, by the elements and stars of night.

WIDOW QUIN. Then we'll not say a word of the old fellow, the way Pegeen won't know your story till the end of time.

CHRISTY. And if he chances to return again?

WIDOW QUIN. We'll swear he's a maniac and not your da. I could take an oath I seen him raving on the sands today. (*Girls run in.*)

SUSAN. Come on to the sports below. Pegeen says you're to come.

SARA TANSEY. The lepping's beginning, and we've a jockey's suit to fit upon you for the mule race on the sands below.

HONOR. Come on, will you?

CHRISTY. I will then if Pegeen's beyond.

SARA. She's in the boreen making game of Shaneen Keogh.

CHRISTY. Then I'll be going to her now.

He runs out, followed by the girls.

WIDOW QUIN. Well, if the worst comes in the end of all, it'll be great game to see there's none to pity him but a widow woman, the like of me, has buried her children and destroyed her man.

She goes out.

ACT III

Scene as before. Later in the day. Jimmy comes in, slightly drunk.

JIMMY, *calls.* Pegeen! (*Crosses to inner door.*) Pegeen Mike! (*Comes back again into the room.*) Pegeen! (*Philly comes in in the same state. To Philly.*) Did you see herself?

PHILLY. I did not; but I sent Shawn Keogh with the ass cart for to bear him home. (*Trying cupboards, which are locked.*) Well, isn't he a nasty man to get into such staggers at a morning wake; and isn't herself the divil's daughter for locking, and she so fussy after that young gaffer, you might take your death with drouth and none to heed you?

JIMMY. It's little wonder she'd be fussy, and he after bringing bankrupt ruin on the roulette man, and the trick-o'-the-loop man, and breaking the nose of the cockshot man, and winning all in the sports below, racing, lepping, dancing, and the Lord knows what! He's right luck, I'm telling you.

PHILLY. If he has, he'll be rightly hobbled yet, and he not able to say ten words without making a brag of the way he killed his father, and the great blow he hit with the loy.

JIMMY. A man can't hang by his own informing, and his father should be rotten by now.

Old Mahon passes window slowly.

PHILLY. Supposing a man's digging spuds in that field with a long spade, and supposing he flings up the two halves of that skull, what'll be said then in the papers and the courts of law?

JIMMY. They'd say it was an old Dane, maybe, was drowned in the flood. (*Old Mahon comes in and sits down near door listening.*) Did you never hear tell of the skulls they have in the city of Dublin, ranged out like blue jugs in a cabin of Connaught?

PHILLY. And you believe that?

JIMMY, *pugnaciously.* Didn't a lad see them and he after coming, from harvesting in the Liverpool boat? "They have them there," says he, "making a show of the great people there was one time walking the world. White skulls and black skulls and yellow skulls, and some with full teeth, and some haven't only but one."

PHILLY. It was no lie, maybe, for when I was a young lad there was a graveyard beyond the house with the remnants of a man who had thighs as long as your arm. He was a horrid man, I'm telling you, and there was many a fine Sunday I'd put him together for fun, and he with shiny bones, you wouldn't meet the like of these days in the cities of the world.

MAHON, *getting up.* You wouldn't, is it? Lay your eyes on that skull, and tell me where and when there was another the like of it, is splintered only from the blow of a loy.

PHILLY. Glory be to God! And who hit you at all?

MAHON, *triumphantly.* It was my own son hit me. Would you believe that?

JIMMY. Well, there's wonders hidden in the heart of man!

PHILLY, *suspiciously.* And what way was it done?

MAHON, *wandering about the room.* I'm after walking hundreds and long scores of miles, winning clean beds and the fill of my belly four times in the day, and I doing nothing but telling stories of that naked truth. (*He comes to them a little aggressively.*) Give me a supeen and I'll tell you now.

Widow Quin comes in and stands aghast behind him. He is facing Jimmy and Philly, who are on the left.

JIMMY. Ask herself beyond. She's the stuff hidden in her shawl.

WIDOW QUIN, *coming to Mahon quickly.* You here, is it? You didn't go far at all?

MAHON. I seen the coasting steamer passing and I got a drouth upon me and a cramping leg, so I said, "The divil go along with him," and turned again. (*Looking under her shawl.*) And let you give me a supeen, for I'm destroyed travelling since Tuesday was a week.

WIDOW QUIN, *getting a glass, in a cajoling tone.* Sit down then by the fire and take your ease for a space. You've a right to be destroyed indeed, with your walking, and fighting, and facing the sun (*giving him poteen from a stone jar she has brought in*). There now is a drink for you, and may it be to your happiness and length of life.

MAHON, *taking glass greedily, and sitting down by fire.* God increase you!

WIDOW QUIN, *taking men to the right stealthily.* Do you know what? That man's raving from his wound today, for I met him awhile since telling a rambling tale of a tinker had him destroyed. Then he heard of Christy's deed, and he up and says it was his son had cracked his skull. Oh, isn't madness a fright, for he'll go killing someone yet, and he thinking it's the man has struck him so?

JIMMY, *entirely convinced.* It's a fright surely. I knew a party was kicked in the head by a red mare, and he went killing horses a great while, till he eat the insides of a clock and died after.

PHILLY, *with suspicion.* Did he see Christy?

WIDOW QUIN. He didn't. (*With a warning gesture.*) Let you not be putting him in mind of him, or you'll be likely summoned if there's murder done. (*Looking round at Mahon.*) Whisht! He's listening. Wait now till you hear me taking him easy and unravelling all. (*She goes to Mahon.*) And what way are you feeling, mister? Are you in contentment now?

MAHON, *slightly emotional from his drink.* I'm poorly only, for it's a hard story the way I'm left today, when it was I did tend him from his hour of birth, and he a dunce never reached his second book, the way he'd come from school, many's the day, with his legs lamed under him, and he blackened with his beatings like a tinker's ass. It's a hard story, I'm saying, the way some do have their next and nighest raising up a hand of murder on them, and some is lonesome getting their death with lamentation in the dead of night.

WIDOW QUIN, *not knowing what to say.* To hear you talking so quiet, who'd know you were the same fellow we seen pass today

MAHON. I'm the same surely. The wrack and ruin of threescore years; and it's a terror to live that length, I tell you, and to have your sons going to the dogs against you, and you wore out scolding them, and skelping them, and God knows what.

PHILLY, *to Jimmy*. He's not raving. (*To Widow Quin*.) Will you ask him what kind was his son?

WIDOW QUIN, *to Mahon, with a peculiar look*. Was your son that hit you a lad of one year and a score maybe, a great hand at racing and lepping and licking the world?

MAHON, *turning on her with a roar of rage*. Didn't you hear me say he was the fool of men, the way from this out he'll know the orphan's lot, with old and young making game of him, and they swearing, raging, kicking at him like a mangy cur.

A great burst of cheering outside, some way off.

MAHON, *putting his hands to his ears*. What in the name of God do they want roaring below?

WIDOW QUIN, *with the shade of a smile*. They're cheering a young lad, the champion Playboy of the Western World. (*More cheering*.)

MAHON, *going to window*. It'd split my heart to hear them, and I with pulses in my brainpan for a week gone by. Is it racing they are?

JIMMY, *looking from door*. It is, then. They are mounting him for the mule race will be run upon the sands. That's the playboy on the winkered mule.

MAHON, *puzzled*. That lad, is it? If you said it was a fool he was, I'd have laid a mighty oath he was the likeness of my wandering son. (*Uneasily, putting his hand to his head*.) Faith, I'm thinking I'll go walking for to view the race.

WIDOW QUIN, *stopping him, sharply*. You will not. You'd best take the road to Belmullet, and not be dilly-dallying in this place where there isn't a spot you could sleep.

PHILLY, *coming forward*. Don't mind her. Mount there on the bench and you'll have a view of the whole. They're hurrying before the tide will rise, and it'd be near over if you went down the pathway through the crags below.

MAHON, *mounts on bench, Widow Quin beside him.* That's a right view again the edge of the sea. They're coming now from the point. He's leading. Who is he at all?

WIDOW QUIN. He's the champion of the world, I tell you, and there isn't a hap'orth isn't falling lucky to his hands today.

PHILLY, *looking out, interested in the race.* Look at that. They're pressing him now.

JIMMY. He'll win it yet.

PHILLY. Take your time, Jimmy Farrell. It's too soon to say.

WIDOW QUIN, *shouting.* Watch him taking the gate. There's riding.

JIMMY, *cheering.* More power to the young lad!

MAHON. He's passing the third.

JIMMY. He'll lick them yet.

WIDOW QUIN. He'd lick them if he was running races with a score itself.

MAHON. Look at the mule he has, kicking the stars.

WIDOW QUIN. There was a lep! (*Catching hold of Mahon in her excitement.*) He's fallen! He's mounted again! Faith, he's passing them all!

JIMMY. Look at him skelping her!

PHILLY. And the mountain girls hooshing him on!

JIMMY. It's the last turn! The post's cleared for them now!

MAHON. Look at the narrow place. He'll be into the bogs! (*With a yell.*) Good rider! He's through it again!

JIMMY. He's neck and neck!

MAHON. Good boy to him! Flames, but he's in!

Great cheering, in which all join.

MAHON, *with hesitation.* What's that? They're raising him up. They're coming this way. (*With a roar of rage and astonishment.*) It's Christy, by the stars of God! I'd know his way of spitting and he astride the moon.

He jumps down and makes a run for the door, but Widow Quin catches him and pulls him back.

WIDOW QUIN. Stay quiet, will you? That's not your son. (*To Jimmy.*) Stop him, or you'll get a month for the abetting of manslaughter and be fined as well.

JIMMY. I'll hold him.

MAHON, *struggling.* Let me out! Let me out, the lot of you, till I have my vengeance on his head today.

WIDOW QUIN, *shaking him vehemently.* That's not your son. That's a man is going to make a marriage with the daughter of this house, a place with fine trade, with a licence, and with poteen too.

MAHON, *amazed.* That man marrying a decent and a moneyed girl! Is it mad yous are? Is it in a crazy-house for females that I'm landed now?

WIDOW QUIN. It's mad yourself is with the blow upon your head. That lad is the wonder of the western world.

MAHON. I seen it's my son.

WIDOW QUIN. You seen that you're mad. (*Cheering outside.*) Do you hear them cheering him in the zigzags of the road? Aren't you after saying that your son's a fool, and how would they be cheering a true idiot born?

MAHON, *getting distressed.* It's maybe out of reason that that man's himself. (*Cheering again.*) There's none surely will go cheering him. Oh, I'm raving with a madness that would fright the world! (*He sits down with his hand to his head.*) There was one time I seen ten scarlet divils letting on they'd cork my spirit in a gallon can; and one time I seen rats as big as badgers sucking the lifeblood from the butt of my lug; but I never till this day confused that dribbling idiot with a likely man. I'm destroyed surely.

WIDOW QUIN. And who'd wonder when it's your brainpan that is gaping now?

MAHON. Then the blight of the sacred drouth upon myself and him, for I never went mad to this day, and I not three weeks with the Limerick girls drinking myself silly and parlatic from the dusk to dawn. (*To Widow Quin, suddenly.*) Is my visage astray?

WIDOW QUIN. It is, then. You're a sniggering maniac, a child could see.

MAHON, *getting up more cheerfully.* Then I'd best be going to the union beyond, and there'll be a welcome before me, I tell you (*with great pride*), and I a terrible and fearful case, the way that there I was one time, screeching in a straightened waistcoat, with seven doctors writing out my sayings in a printed book. Would you believe that?

WIDOW QUIN. If you're a wonder itself, you'd best be hasty, for them lads caught a maniac one time and pelted the poor creature till he ran out, raving and foaming, and was drowned in the sea.

MAHON, *with philosophy.* It's true mankind is the divil when your head's astray. Let me out now and I'll slip down the boreen, and not see them so.

WIDOW QUIN, *showing him out.* That's it. Run to the right, and not one will see.

He runs off.

PHILLY, *wisely.* You're at some gaming, Widow Quin; but I'll walk after him and give him his dinner and a time to rest, and I'll see then if he's raving or as sane as you.

WIDOW QUIN, *annoyed.* If you go near that lad, let you be wary of your head, I'm saying. Didn't you hear him telling he was crazed at times?

PHILLY. I heard him telling a power; and I'm thinking we'll have right sport before night will fall.

He goes out.

JIMMY. Well, Philly's a conceited and foolish man. How could that madman have his senses and his brainpan slit? I'll go after them and see him turn on Philly now.

He goes; Widow Quin hides poteen behind counter. Then hubbub outside.

VOICES. There you are! Good jumper! Grand lepper! Darlint boy! He's
the racer! Bear him on, will you!

*Christy comes in, in jockey's dress, with Pegeen Mike, Sara, and other girls
and men.*

PEGEEN, *to crowd.* Go on now and don't destroy him and he drenching with
sweat. Go along, I'm saying, and have your tug of warring till he's
dried his skin.

CROWD. Here's his prizes! A bagpipes! A fiddle was played by a poet in the
years gone by! A flat and three-thorned blackthorn would lick the
scholars out of Dublin town!

CHRISTY, *taking prizes from the men.* Thank you kindly, the lot of you. But
you'd say it was little only I did this day if you'd seen me awhile since
striking my one single blow.

TOWN CRIER, *outside ringing a bell.* Take notice, last event of this day!
Tug of warring on the green below! Come on, the lot of you! Great
achievements for all Mayo men!

PEGEEN. Go on and leave him for to rest and dry. Go on, I tell you,
for he'll do no more.

She hustles crowd out; Widow Quin following them.

MEN, *going.* Come on, then. Good luck for the while!

PEGEEN, *radiantly, wiping his face with her shawl.* Well, you're the lad, and
you'll have great times from this out when you could win that wealth
of prizes, and you sweating in the heat of noon!

CHRISTY, *looking at her with delight.* I'll have great times if I win the
crowning prize I'm seeking now, and that's your promise that you'll
wed me in a fortnight, when our banns is called.

PEGEEN, *backing away from him.* You've right daring to go ask me that,
when all knows you'll be starting to some girl in your own townland,
when your father's rotten in four months, or five.

CHRISTY, *indignantly.* Starting from you, is it? (*He follows her.*) I will not, then, and when the airs is warming, in four months or five, it's then yourself and me should be pacing Neifin in the dews of night, the times sweet smells do be rising, and you'd see a little, shiny new moon, maybe, sinking on the hills.

PEGEEN, *looking at him playfully.* And it's that kind of a poacher's love you'd make, Christy Mahon, on the sides of Neifin, when the night is down?

CHRISTY. It's little you'll think if my love's a poacher's, or an earl's itself, when you'll feel my two hands stretched around you, and I squeezing kisses on your puckered lips, till I'd feel a kind of pity for the Lord God is all ages sitting lonesome in his golden chair.

PEGEEN. That'll be right fun, Christy Mahon, and any girl would walk her heart out before she'd meet a young man was your like for eloquence, or talk at all.

CHRISTY, *encouraged.* Let you wait, to hear me talking, till we're astray in Erris, when Good Friday's by, drinking a sup from a well, and making mighty kisses with our wetted mouths, or gaming in a gap of sunshine, with yourself stretched back unto your necklace, in the flowers of the earth.

PEGEEN, *in a low voice, moved by his tone.* I'd be nice so, is it?

CHRISTY, *with rapture.* If the mitred bishops seen you that time, they'd be the like of the holy prophets, I'm thinking, do be straining the bars of Paradise to lay eyes on the Lady Helen of Troy, and she abroad, pacing back and forward, with a nosegay in her golden shawl.

PEGEEN, *with real tenderness.* And what is it I have, Christy Mahon, to make me fitting entertainment for the like of you, that has such poet's talking, and such bravery of heart.

CHRISTY, *in a low voice.* Isn't there the light of seven heavens in your heart alone, the way you'll be an angel's lamp to me from this out, and I abroad in the darkness, spearing salmons in the Owen or the Carrowmore?

PEGEEN. If I was your wife I'd be along with you those nights, Christy Mahon, the way you'd see I was a great hand at coaxing bailiffs, or coining funny nicknames for the stars of night.

CHRISTY. You, is it? Taking your death in the hailstones, or in the fogs of dawn.

PEGEEN. Yourself and me would shelter easy in a narrow bush; (*with a qualm of dread*) but we're only talking, maybe, for this would be a poor, thatched place to hold a fine lad is the like of you.

CHRISTY, *putting his arm round her.* If I wasn't a good Christian, it's on my naked knees I'd be saying my prayers and paters to every jackstraw you have roofing your head, and every stony pebble is paving the laneway to your door.

PEGEEN, *radiantly.* If that's the truth I'll be burning candles from this out to the miracles of God that have brought you from the south today, and I with my gowns bought ready, the way that I can wed you, and not wait at all.

CHRISTY. It's miracles, and that's the truth. Me there toiling a long while, and walking a long while, not knowing at all I was drawing all times nearer to this holy day.

PEGEEN. And myself, a girl, was tempted often to go sailing the seas till I'd marry a Jew-man, with ten kegs of gold, and I not knowing at all there was the like of you drawing nearer, like the stars of God.

CHRISTY. And to think I'm long years hearing women talking that talk, to all bloody fools, and this the first time I've heard the like of your voice talking sweetly for my own delight.

PEGEEN. And to think it's me is talking sweetly, Christy Mahon, and I the fright of seven townlands for my biting tongue. Well, the heart's a wonder; and, I'm thinking, there won't be our like in Mayo, for gallant lovers, from this hour today. (*Drunken singing is heard outside.*) There's my father coming from the wake, and when he's had his sleep we'll tell him, for he's peaceful then.

They separate.

MICHAEL, *singing outside.*

The jailer and the turnkey
They quickly ran us down,

And brought us back as prisoners
Once more to Cavan town.

He comes in supported by Shawn.

There we lay bewailing
All in a prison bound. . . .

He sees Christy. Goes and shakes him drunkenly by the hand, while Pegeen and Shawn talk on the left.

MICHAEL, *to Christy.* The blessing of God and the holy angels on your head, young fellow. I hear tell you're after winning all in the sports below; and wasn't it a shame I didn't bear you along with me to Kate Cassidy's wake, a fine, stout lad, the like of you, for you'd never see the match of it for flows of drink, the way when we sunk her bones at noonday in her narrow grave, there were five men, aye, and six men, stretched out retching speechless on the holy stones.

CHRISTY, *uneasily, watching Pegeen.* Is that the truth?

MICHAEL. It is, then; and aren't you a louty schemer to go burying your poor father unbeknownst when you'd a right to throw him on the crupper of a Kerry mule and drive him westward, like holy Joseph in the days gone by, the way we could have given him a decent burial, and not have him rotting beyond, and not a Christian drinking a smart drop to the glory of his soul?

CHRISTY, *gruffly.* It's well enough he's lying, for the likes of him.

MICHAEL, *slapping him on the back.* Well, aren't you a hardened slayer? It'll be a poor thing for the household man where you go sniffing for a female wife; and (*pointing to Shawn*) look beyond at that shy and decent Christian I have chosen for my daughter's hand, and I after getting the gilded dispensation this day for to wed them now.

CHRISTY. And you'll be wedding them this day, is it?

MICHAEL, *drawing himself up.* Aye. Are you thinking, if I'm drunk itself, I'd leave my daughter living single with a little frisky rascal is the like of you?

PEGEEN, *breaking away from Shawn.* Is it the truth the dispensation's come?

MICHAEL, *triumphantly.* Father Reilly's after reading it in gallous Latin, and "It's come in the nick of time," says he; "so I'll wed them in a hurry, dreading that young gaffer who'd capsize the stars."

PEGEEN, *fiercely.* He's missed his nick of time, for it's that lad, Christy Mahon, that I'm wedding now.

MICHAEL, *loudly, with horror.* You'd be making him a son to me, and he wet and crusted with his father's blood?

PEGEEN. Aye. Wouldn't it be a bitter thing for a girl to go marrying the like of Shaneen, and he a middling kind of a scarecrow, with no savagery or fine words in him at all?

MICHAEL, *gasping and sinking on a chair.* Oh, aren't you a heathen daughter to go shaking the fat of my heart, and I swamped and drownded with the weight of drink? Would you have them turning on me the way that I'd be roaring to the dawn of day with the wind upon my heart? Have you not a word to aid me, Shaneen? Are you not jealous at all?

SHAWN, *in great misery.* I'd be afeard to be jealous of a man did slay his da?

PEGEEN. Well, it'd be a poor thing to go marrying your like. I'm seeing there's a world of peril for an orphan girl, and isn't it a great blessing I didn't wed you before himself came walking from the west or south?

SHAWN. It's a queer story you'd go picking a dirty tramp up from the highways of the world.

PEGEEN, *playfully.* And you think you're a likely beau to go straying along with, the shiny Sundays of the opening year, when it's sooner on a bullock's liver you'd put a poor girl thinking than on the lily or the rose?

SHAWN. And have you no mind of my weight of passion, and the holy dispensation, and the drift of heifers I'm giving, and the golden ring?

PEGEEN. I'm thinking you're too fine for the like of me, Shawn Keogh of Killakeen, and let you go off till you'd find a radiant lady with droves of bullocks on the plains of Meath, and herself bedizened in the diamond jeweleries of Pharaoh's ma. That'd be your match, Shaneen. So God save you now! (*She retreats behind Christy.*)

SHAWN. Won't you hear me telling you . . . ?

CHRISTY, *with ferocity*. Take yourself from this, young fellow, or I'll maybe add a murder to my deeds today.

MICHAEL, *springing up with a shriek*. Murder is it? Is it mad yous are? Would you go making murder in this place, and it piled with poteen for our drink tonight? Go on to the foreshore if it's fighting you want, where the rising tide will wash all traces from the memory of man.

Pushing Shawn toward Christy.

SHAWN, *shaking himself free, and getting behind Michael*. I'll not fight him, Michael James. I'd liefer live a bachelor, simmering in passions to the end of time, than face a lepping savage the like of him has descended from the Lord knows where. Strike him yourself, Michael James, or you'll lose my drift of heifers and my blue bull from Sneem.

MICHAEL. Is it me fight him, when it's father-slaying he's bred to now? (*Pushing Shawn.*) Go on, you fool, and fight him now.

SHAWN, *coming forward a little*. Will I strike him with my hand?

MICHAEL. Take the loy is on your western side.

SHAWN. I'd be afeard of the gallows if I struck with that.

CHRISTY, *taking up the loy*. Then I'll make you face the gallows or quit off from this. (*Shawn flies out of the door.*)

CHRISTY. Well, fine weather be after him (*going to Michael, coaxingly*), and I'm thinking you wouldn't wish to have that quaking blackguard in your house at all. Let you give us your blessing and hear her swear her faith to me, for I'm mounted on the spring tide of the stars of luck, the way it'll be good for any to have me in the house.

PEGEEN, *at the other side of Michael*. Bless us now, for I swear to God I'll wed him, and I'll not renege.

MICHAEL, *standing up in the centre, holding on to both of them*. It's the will of God, I'm thinking, that all should win an easy or a cruel end, and it's the will of God that all should rear up lengthy families for the nurture of the earth. What's a single man, I ask you, eating a bit in one house and drinking a sup in another, and he with no place of his own, like an old braying jackass strayed upon the rocks? (*To Christy.*) It's many would be in dread to bring your like into their house for to end them, maybe, with a sudden end; but I'm a decent man of Ireland, and I liefer face the grave untimely and I seeing a score of grandsons growing up little gallant swearers by the name of God, than go peopling my bedside with puny weeds the like of what you'd breed, I'm thinking, out of Shaneen Keogh. (*He joins their hands.*) A daring fellow is the jewel of the world, and a man did split his father's middle with a single clout should have the bravery of ten, so may God and Mary and St. Patrick bless you, and increase you from this mortal day.

CHRISTY *and* PEGEEN. Amen, O Lord!

Hubbub outside. Old Mahon rushes in, followed by all the crowd and Widow Quin. He makes a rush at Christy, knocks him down, and begins to beat him.

PEGEEN, *dragging back his arm.* Stop that, will you? Who are you at all?

MAHON. His father, God forgive me!

PEGEEN, *drawing back.* Is it rose from the dead?

MAHON. Do you think I look so easy quenched with the tap of a loy? (*Beats Christy again.*)

PEGEEN, *glaring at Christy.* And it's lies you told, letting on you had him slitted, and you nothing at all.

CHRISTY, *catching Mahon's stick.* He's not my father. He's a raving maniac would scare the world. (*Pointing to Widow Quin.*) Herself knows it is true.

CROWD. You're fooling Pegeen! The Widow Quin seen him this day, and you likely knew! You're a liar!

CHRISTY, *dumbfounded.* It's himself was a liar, lying stretched out with an open head on him, letting on he was dead.

MAHON. Weren't you off racing the hills before I got my breath with the start I had seeing you turn on me at all?

PEGEEN. And to think of the coaxing glory we had given him, and he after doing nothing but hitting a soft blow and chasing northward in a sweat of fear. Quit off from this.

CHRISTY, *piteously.* You've seen my doings this day, and let you save me from the old man; for why would you be in such a scorch of haste to spur me to destruction now?

PEGEEN. It's there your treachery is spurring me, till I'm hard set to think you're the one I'm after lacing in my heartstrings half an hour gone by. (*To Mahon.*) Take him on from this, for I think bad the world should see me raging for a Munster liar, and the fool of men.

MAHON. Rise up now to retribution, and come on with me.

CROWD, *jeeringly.* There's the playboy! There's the lad thought he'd rule the roost in Mayo! Slate him now, mister.

CHRISTY, *getting up in shy terror.* What is it drives you to torment me here, when I'd asked the thunders of the might of God to blast me if I ever did hurt to any saving only that one single blow.

MAHON, *loudly.* If you didn't, you're a poor good-for-nothing, and isn't it by the like of you the sins of the whole world are committed?

CHRISTY, *raising his hands.* In the name of the Almighty God. . . .

MAHON. Leave troubling the Lord God. Would you have him sending down droughts, and fevers, and the old hen and the cholera morbus?

CHRISTY, *to Widow Quin.* Will you come between us and protect me now?

WIDOW QUIN. I've tried a lot, God help me, and my share is done.

CHRISTY, *looking round in desperation.* And I must go back into my torment is it, or run off like a vagabond straying through the unions with the dusts of August making mud stains in the gullet of my throat; or the winds of March blowing on me till I'd take an oath I felt them making whistles of my ribs within?

SARA. Ask Pegeen to aid you. Her like does often change.

CHRISTY. I will not, then, for there's torment in the splendour of her like, and she a girl any moon of midnight would take pride to meet, facing southward on the heaths of Keel. But what did I want crawling forward to scorch my understanding at her flaming brow?

PEGEEN, *to Mahon, vehemently, fearing she will break into tears.* Take him on from this or I'll set the young lads to destroy him here.

MAHON, *going to him, shaking his stick.* Come on now if you wouldn't have the company to see you skelped.

PEGEEN, *half laughing through her tears.* That's it, now the world will see him pandied, and he an ugly liar was playing off the hero, and the fright of men.

CHRISTY, *to Mahon, very sharply.* Leave me go!

CROWD. That's it. Now, Christy. If them two set fighting, it will lick the world.

MAHON, *making a grab at Christy.* Come here to me.

CHRISTY, *more threateningly.* Leave me go, I'm saying.

MAHON. I will, maybe, when your legs is limping, and your back is blue.

CROWD. Keep it up, the two of you. I'll back the old one. Now the playboy.

CHRISTY, *in low and intense voice.* Shut your yelling, for if you're after making a mighty man of me this day by the power of a lie, you're setting me now to think if it's a poor thing to be lonesome, it's worse, maybe, go mixing with the fools of earth.

Mahon makes a movement toward him.

CHRISTY, *almost shouting.* Keep off . . . lest I do show a blow unto the lot of you would set the guardian angels winking in the clouds above.

He swings round with a sudden rapid movement and picks up a loy.

CROWD, *half-frightened, half-amused.* He's going mad! Mind yourselves! Run from the idiot!

CHRISTY. If I am an idiot, I'm after hearing my voice this day saying words would raise the topknot on a poet in a merchant's town. I've won your racing, and your lepping, and . . .

MAHON. Shut your gullet and come on with me.

CHRISTY. I'm going, but I'll stretch you first.

He runs at old Mahon with the loy, chases him out of the door, followed by crowd and Widow Quin. There is a great noise outside, then a yell, and dead silence for a moment. Christy comes in, half-dazed, and goes to the fire.

WIDOW QUIN, *coming in hurriedly, and going to him.* They're turning again you. Come on, or you'll be hanged, indeed.

CHRISTY. I'm thinking, from this out, Pegeen'll be giving me praises, the same as in the hours gone by.

WIDOW QUIN, *impatiently.* Come by the backdoor. I'd think bad to have you stifled on the gallows tree.

CHRISTY, *indignantly.* I will not, then. What good'd be my lifetime if I left Pegeen?

WIDOW QUIN. Come on, and you'll be no worse than you were last night; and you with a double murder this time to be telling to the girls.

CHRISTY. I'll not leave Pegeen Mike.

WIDOW QUIN, *impatiently.* Isn't there the match of her in every parish public, from Binghamstown unto the plain of Meath? Come on, I tell you, and I'll find you finer sweethearts at each waning moon.

CHRISTY. It's Pegeen I'm seeking only, and what'd I care if you brought me a drift of chosen females, standing in their shifts itself, maybe, from this place to the eastern world?

SARA, *runs in, pulling off one of her petticoats.* They're going to hang him. (*Holding out petticoat and shawl.*) Fit these upon him, and let him run off to the east.

WIDOW QUIN. He's raving now; but we'll fit them on him, and I'll take him in the ferry to the Achill boat.

CHRISTY, *struggling feebly.* Leave me go, will you? when I'm thinking of my luck today, for she will wed me surely, and I a proven hero in the end of all.

They try to fasten petticoat round him.

WIDOW QUIN. Take his left hand, and we'll pull him now. Come on, young fellow.

CHRISTY, *suddenly starting up.* You'll be taking me from her? You're jealous is it, of her wedding me? Go on from this.

He snatches up a stool, and threatens them with it.

WIDOW QUIN, *going.* It's in the madhouse they should put him, not in jail, at all. We'll go by the backdoor to call the doctor, and we'll save him so.

She goes out, with Sara, through inner room. Men crowd in the doorway. Christy sits down again by the fire.

MICHAEL, *in a terrified whisper.* Is the old lad killed surely?

PHILLY. I'm after feeling the last gasps quitting his heart.

They peer in at Christy.

MICHAEL, *with a rope.* Look at the way he is. Twist a hangman's knot on it, and slip it over his head, while he's not minding at all.

PHILLY. Let you take it, Shaneen. You're the soberest of all that's here.

SHAWN. Is it me to go near him, and he the wickedest and worst with me? Let you take it, Pegeen Mike.

PEGEEN. Come on, so.

She goes forward with the others, and they drop the double hitch over his head.

CHRISTY. What ails you?

SHAWN, *triumphantly, as they pull the rope tight on his arms.* Come on to the peelers, till they stretch you now.

CHRISTY. Me?

MICHAEL. If we took pity on you the Lord God would, maybe, bring us ruin from the law today, so you'd best come easy, for hanging is an easy and a speedy end.

CHRISTY. I'll not stir. (*To Pegeen.*) And what is it you'll say to me, and I after doing it this time in the face of all?

PEGEEN. I'll say, a strange man is a marvel, with his mighty talk; but what's a squabble in your backyard, and the blow of a loy, have taught me that there's a great gap between a gallous story and a dirty deed. (*To men.*) Take him from this, or the lot of us will be likely put on trial for his deed today.

CHRISTY, *with horror in his voice.* And it's yourself will send me off, to have a horny-fingered hangman hitching his bloody slipknots at the butt of my ear.

MEN, *pulling rope.* Come on, will you?

He is pulled down on the floor.

CHRISTY, *twisting his legs round the table.* Cut the rope, Pegeen, and I'll quit the lot of you, and live from this out, like the madmen of Keel, eating muck and green weeds on the faces of the cliffs.

PEGEEN. And leave us to hang, is it, for a saucy liar, the like of you? (*To men.*) Take him on, out from this.

SHAWN. Pull a twist on his neck, and squeeze him so.

PHILLY. Twist yourself. Sure he cannot hurt you, if you keep your distance from his teeth alone.

SHAWN. I'm afeard of him. (*To Pegeen.*) Lift a lighted sod, will you, and scorch his leg.

PEGEEN, *blowing the fire with a bellows.* Leave go now, young fellow, or I'll scorch your shins.

CHRISTY. You're blowing for to torture me. (*His voice rising and growing stronger.*) That's your kind, is it? Then let the lot of you be wary, for, if I've to face the gallows, I'll have a gay march down, I tell you, and shed the blood of some of you before I die.

SHAWN, *in terror.* Keep a good hold, Philly. Be wary, for the love of God. For I'm thinking he would liefest wreak his pains on me.

CHRISTY, *almost gaily.* If I do lay my hands on you, it's the way you'll be at the fall of night, hanging as a scarecrow for the fowls of hell. Ah, you'll have a gallous jaunt, I'm saying, coaching out through Limbo with my father's ghost.

SHAWN, *to Pegeen.* Make haste, will you? Oh, isn't he a holy terror, and isn't it true for Father Reilly, that all drink's a curse that has the lot of you so shaky and uncertain now?

CHRISTY. If I can wring a neck among you, I'll have a royal judgment looking on the trembling jury in the courts of law. And won't there be crying out in Mayo the day I'm stretched upon the rope, with ladies in their silks and satins sniveling in their lacy kerchiefs, and they rhyming songs and ballads on the terror of my fate?

He squirms round on the floor and bites Shawn's leg.

SHAWN, *shrieking.* My leg's bit on me. He's the like of a mad dog, I'm thinking, the way that I will surely die.

CHRISTY, *delighted with himself.* You will, then, the way you can shake out hell's flags of welcome for my coming in two weeks or three, for I'm thinking Satan hasn't many have killed their da in Kerry, and in Mayo, too.

Old Mahon comes in behind on all fours and looks on unnoticed.

MEN, *to Pegeen.* Bring the sod, will you?

PEGEEN, *coming over.* God help him so! (*Burns his leg.*)

CHRISTY, *kicking and screaming.* Oh, glory be to God!

He kicks loose from the table, and they all drag him toward the door.

JIMMY, *seeing old Mahon.* Will you look what's come in?

They all drop Christy and run left.

CHRISTY, *scrambling on his knees face to face with old Mahon.* Are you coming
   to be killed a third time, or what ails you now?

MAHON. For what is it they have you tied?

CHRISTY. They're taking me to the peelers to have me hanged for
   slaying you.

MICHAEL, *apologetically.* It is the will of God that all should guard their
   little cabins from the treachery of law, and what would my daughter
   be doing if I was ruined or was hanged itself?

MAHON, *grimly, loosening Christy.* It's little I care if you put a bag on her
   back, and went picking cockles till the hour of death; but my son and
   myself will be going our own way, and we'll have great times from
   this out telling stories of the villainy of Mayo, and the fools is here.
   (*To Christy, who is freed.*) Come on now.

CHRISTY. Go with you, is it? I will, then, like a gallant captain with his
   heathen slave. Go on now and I'll see you from this day stewing
   my oatmeal and washing my spuds, for I'm master of all fights from
   now. (*Pushing Mahon.*) Go on, I'm saying.

MAHON. Is it me?

CHRISTY. Not a word out of you. Go on from this.

MAHON, *walking out and looking back at Christy over his shoulder.* Glory be to
   God! (*With a broad smile.*) I am crazy again. (*Goes.*)

CHRISTY. Ten thousand blessings upon all that's here, for you've turned me
   a likely gaffer in the end of all, the way I'll go romancing through a
   romping lifetime from this hour to the dawning of the judgment day.

He goes out.

MICHAEL. By the will of God, we'll have peace now for our drinks. Will
   you draw the porter, Pegeen?

SHAWN, *going up to her.* It's a miracle Father Reilly can wed us in the end of all, and we'll have none to trouble us when his vicious bite is healed.

PEGEEN, *hitting him a box on the ear.* Quit my sight. (*Putting her shawl over her head and breaking out into wild lamentations.*) Oh, my grief, I've lost him surely. I've lost the only Playboy of the Western World.

John M. Synge

QUESTIONS

1. Why do the villagers show admiration for Christy after he reveals that he killed his father? Why do the people of Mayo treat Christy as a hero?

2. Why does Pegeen offer Christy a safe haven and a job after hearing his account of how he murdered his father?

3. Why, according to Widow Quin, is there a "great temptation in a man did slay his da"? (202) Why is Widow Quin attracted to Christy?

4. How do we explain that it is Widow Quin who remains loyal to Christy throughout the play?

5. Why do we see Widow Quin negotiate first with Shawn and then with Christy? Is the Widow Quin out for herself, or is she sincere in her concern for Christy?

6. In what way does Widow Quin think she and Christy are alike?

7. The villagers think Christy a brave and clever hero; Mahon thinks him a lying, cowardly, woman-fearing dunce. What view are we to take?

8. Are we to think Christy has transformed himself into a hero by the end of the play?

9. If, according to his father, Christy has been a loser in his hometown, how can he win all the athletic games in Mayo?

10. Pegeen asks, "And what is it I have, Christy Mahon, to make me fitting entertainment for the like of you." (232) Why is Christy attracted to Pegeen?

11. Why would Michael James want Christy to know in vivid detail about the vomiting drunkenness at Kate Cassidy's wake?

12. Why do we see the villagers quickly turn on Christy when his father appears?

13. What does Mahon mean when he says to Christy, "and isn't it by the like of you the sins of the whole world are committed"? (238)

14. What is the motivation of the women, according to the stage direction, when "They try to fasten petticoat round [Christy]"? (241)

15. Why do Christy and Mahon appear to reconcile at the end of the play? Why do we see them leave together?

16. Why does Mahon declare, "Glory be to God! I am crazy again," as he leaves with Christy? (244)

17. Why does Christy leave giving the villagers "ten thousand blessings"? (244)

18. After turning violently against Christy, why does Pegeen break into wild lamentations as he departs?

FOR FURTHER REFLECTION

1. Does this play achieve the goal stated by Synge in the preface to explore "the profound and common interests of life"?

2. Do you agree with Synge's decision to call this play a "comedy"?

3. How do we explain the burst of poetic language in Christy's dialogue with Pegeen, perhaps the most audibly rich passage in the entire play? Why is Christy so suddenly poetic during this scene?

FRIEDRICH HAYEK

Friedrich August von Hayek (1899–1992), one of the most influential economists of the twentieth century and a prime mover of libertarian political thought, was born to a family in Vienna, Austria, that possessed wealth, education, and social connections. His mother, Felicitas, came from well-to-do landowning gentry; his father, August, a medical doctor, was a passionate researcher in botany and lectured part-time at the University of Vienna. Friedrich, the oldest of the couple's three sons, was a precocious and voracious reader who also enjoyed assisting with his father's botany collections and learning to ski, sail, and mountain climb. However, he showed little desire for academic achievement. At the age of fourteen, after failing Latin, Greek, and mathematics, he was forced to repeat a grade.

During his military service in World War I, Hayek decided to study economics, and after Austria's defeat in 1918 he returned to the University of Vienna. There he entertained a brief and mild flirtation with Marxism but eventually found the free-market philosophy of Carl Menger and the critique of socialism by another mentor, Ludwig von Mises, more compelling. He took degrees in law and political science and then studied economics at New York University. Returning to Austria, he wrote his early major publications on interest rates, government monetary policy, and business cycles. In 1931, he left Austria for the London School of Economics, where he taught for eighteen years and wrote the book that made him famous. *The Road to Serfdom* (1944) made the case for less, rather than more, government involvement in the marketplace; according to Hayek, central planning of economic affairs is an incursion on individual liberty bearing deleterious and sometimes disastrous consequences. In making this argument, Hayek established himself as a rival to John Maynard Keynes at Cambridge. Hayek became a part of the University of Chicago's Committee on Social Thought in 1950, taught there for twelve years, and then finished out his teaching career at the University of Freiburg, in Germany, and afterward at the University of Salzburg, in Austria.

In 1974, Hayek was awarded the Nobel Prize for Economics. For many observers, the events of the 1980s—which included the adoption of free-market principles by the Reagan and Thatcher administrations as well as the implosion of the Soviet communist bloc in 1989—seemed to vindicate the prescience of Hayek's theory, which, when he began advocating it in the early 1930s, seemed far out of the mainstream.

Hayek's powerfully argued views on economics must be understood as organically connected to his view of individual liberty, making him as much a political theorist as an economist. In his view, economic and political activity cannot be disentangled, and so it is no surprise that Hayek refused to practice economics in the narrow sense. Indeed, Hayek's paramount concern is to think clearly about how individual freedoms can be furthered within the confines of the political and economic laws that govern the social order.

FRIEDRICH HAYEK

Planning and Democracy

The statesman who should attempt to direct private people in what manner they ought to employ their capitals, would not only load himself with a most unnecessary attention, but assume an authority which could safely be trusted to no council and senate whatever, and which would nowhere be so dangerous as in the hands of a man who had folly and presumption enough to fancy himself fit to exercise it. —ADAM SMITH

The common features of all collectivist systems may be described, in a phrase ever dear to socialists of all schools, as the deliberate organization of the labors of society for a definite social goal. That our present society lacks such "conscious" direction toward a single aim, that its activities are guided by the whims and fancies of irresponsible individuals, has always been one of the main complaints of its socialist critics.

In many ways this puts the basic issue very clearly. And it directs us at once to the point where the conflict arises between individual freedom and collectivism. The various kinds of collectivism—communism, fascism, etc.—differ among themselves in the nature of the goal toward which they want to direct the efforts of society. But they all differ from liberalism and individualism in wanting to organize the whole of society and all its resources for this unitary end and in refusing to recognize autonomous spheres in which the ends of the individuals are supreme. In short, they are totalitarian in the true sense of this new word that we have adopted to describe the unexpected but nevertheless inseparable manifestations of what in theory we call collectivism.

The "social goal," or "common purpose," for which society is to be organized is usually vaguely described as the "common good," the "general welfare," or the "general interest." It does not need much reflection to see that these terms have no sufficiently definite meaning to determine a particular course of action. The welfare and the happiness of millions cannot be measured on a single scale of less and more. The welfare of a people, like the happiness of a man, depends on a great many things that can be provided in an infinite variety of combinations. It cannot be adequately expressed as a single end, but only as a hierarchy of ends, a comprehensive scale of values in which every need of every person is given its place. To direct all our activities according to a single plan presupposes that every one of our needs is given its rank in an order of values that must be complete enough to make it possible to decide among all the different courses from which the planner has to choose. It presupposes, in short, the existence of a complete ethical code in which all the different human values are allotted their due place.

The conception of a complete ethical code is unfamiliar, and it requires some effort of imagination to see what it involves. We are not in the habit of thinking of moral codes as more or less complete. The fact that we are constantly choosing between different values without a social code prescribing how we ought to choose does not surprise us and does not suggest to us that our moral code is incomplete. In our society there is neither occasion nor reason why people should develop common views about what should be done in such situations. But where all the means to be used are the property of society and are to be used in the name of society according to a unitary plan, a "social" view about what ought to be done must guide all decisions. In such a world we should soon find that our moral code is full of gaps.

We are not concerned here with the question whether it would be desirable to have such a complete ethical code. It may merely be pointed out that up to the present the growth of civilization has been accompanied by a steady diminution of the sphere in which individual actions are bound by fixed rules. The rules of which our common moral code consists have progressively become fewer and more general in character. From the primitive man, who was bound by an elaborate ritual in almost every one of his daily activities, who was limited by innumerable taboos, and who could scarcely conceive of doing things in a way different from his fellows, morals have more and more tended to become merely limits circumscribing the sphere within which the individual could behave as he liked. The adoption of a common ethical code comprehensive enough to determine a unitary economic plan would mean a complete reversal of this tendency.

The essential point for us is that no such complete ethical code exists. The attempt to direct all economic activity according to a single plan would raise innumerable questions to which the answer could be provided only by a moral rule, but to which existing morals have no answer and where there exists no agreed view on what ought to be done. People will have either no definite views or conflicting views on such questions, because in the free society in which we have lived there has been no occasion to think about them and still less to form common opinions about them.

Not only do we not possess such an all-inclusive scale of values: it would be impossible for any mind to comprehend the infinite variety of different needs of different people who compete for the available resources and to attach a definite weight to each. For our problem it is of minor importance whether the ends for which any person cares comprehend only his own individual needs, or whether they include the needs of his closer or even those of his more distant fellows—that is, whether he is egoistic or altruistic in the ordinary senses of these words. The point that is so important is the basic fact that it is impossible for any man to survey more than a limited field, to be aware of the urgency of more than a limited number of needs. Whether his interests center on his own physical needs, or whether he takes a warm interest in the welfare of every human being he knows, the ends about which he can be concerned will always be only an infinitesimal fraction of the needs of all men.

This is the fundamental fact on which the whole philosophy of individualism is based. It does not assume, as is often asserted, that man is egoistic or selfish or ought to be. It merely starts from the indisputable fact that the limits of our powers of imagination make it impossible to include in our scale of values more than a sector of the needs of the whole society, and that, since, strictly speaking, scales of value can exist only in individual minds, nothing but partial scales of values exist—scales that are inevitably different from and often inconsistent with each other. From this the individualist concludes that the individuals should be allowed, within defined limits, to follow their own values and preferences rather than somebody else's; that within these spheres the individual's system of ends should be supreme and not subject to any dictation by others. It is this recognition of the individual as the ultimate judge of his ends, the belief that as far as possible his own views ought to govern his actions, that forms the essence of the individualist position.

This view does not, of course, exclude the recognition of social ends, or rather of a coincidence of individual ends that makes it advisable for men to combine for their pursuit. But it limits such common action to the instances where individual views coincide; what are called "social ends" are for it merely identical ends of many individuals—or ends to the achievement of which individuals are willing to contribute in return for the assistance they receive in the satisfaction of their own desires. Common action is thus limited to the fields where people agree on common ends. Very frequently these common ends will not be ultimate ends to the individuals but means that different persons can use for different purposes. In fact, people are most likely to agree on common action where the common end is not an ultimate end to them but a means capable of serving a great variety of purposes.

When individuals combine in a joint effort to realize ends they have in common, the organizations, like the state, that they form for this purpose are given their own system of ends and their own means. But any organization thus formed remains one "person" among others—in the case of the state much more powerful than any of the others, it is true—yet still with its separate and limited sphere in which alone its ends are supreme. The limits of this sphere are determined by the extent to which the individuals agree on particular ends; and the probability that they will agree on a particular course of action necessarily decreases as the scope of such action extends. There are certain functions of the state on the exercise of which there will be practical unanimity among its citizens; there will be others on which there will be agreement of a substantial majority; and so on, until we come to fields where, although each individual might wish the state to act in some way, there will be almost as many views about what the government should do as there are different people.

We can rely on voluntary agreement to guide the action of the state only so long as it is confined to spheres where agreement exists. But not only when the state undertakes direct control in fields where there is no such agreement is it bound to suppress individual freedom. We unfortunately cannot indefinitely extend the sphere of common action and still leave the individual free in his own sphere. Once the communal sector, in which the state controls all the means, exceeds a certain proportion of the whole, the effects of its actions dominate the whole system. Although the state controls directly the use of only a large part of the available resources, the effects of its decisions on the remaining part of the economic system become so great that indirectly it controls almost everything. Where, as was, for example, true in Germany as early as 1928, the central and local authorities directly control the use of more than half the national income (according to an official German estimate then, 53 percent), they control indirectly almost the whole economic life of the nation. There is, then, scarcely an individual end that is not dependent for its achievement on the action of the state, and the "social scale of values" that guides the state's action must embrace practically all individual ends.

It is not difficult to see what must be the consequences when democracy embarks upon a course of planning that in its execution requires more agreement than in fact exists. The people may have agreed on adopting a system of directed economy because they have been convinced that it will produce great prosperity. In the discussions leading to the decision, the goal of planning will have been described by some such term as "common welfare," which only conceals the absence of real agreement on the ends of planning. Agreement will in fact exist only on the mechanism to be used. But it is a mechanism that can be used only for a common end; and the question of the precise goal toward which all activity is to be directed will arise as soon as the executive power has to translate the demand for a single plan into a particular plan. Then it will appear that the agreement on the desirability of planning is not supported by agreement on the ends the plan is to serve. The effect of the people's agreeing that there must be central planning without agreeing on the ends will be rather as if a group of people were to commit themselves to take a journey together without agreeing where they want to go: with the result that they may all have to make a journey that most of them do not want at all. That planning creates a situation in which it is necessary for us to agree on a much larger number of topics than we have been used to, and that in a planned system we cannot confine collective action to the tasks on which we can agree but are forced to produce agreement on everything in order that any action can be taken at all, is one of the features that contributes more than most to determining the character of a planned system.

It may be the unanimously expressed will of the people that its parliament should prepare a comprehensive economic plan, yet neither the people nor its representatives need therefore be able to agree on any particular plan. The inability of democratic assemblies to carry out what seems to be a clear mandate of the people will inevitably cause dissatisfaction with democratic institutions. Parliaments come to be regarded as ineffective "talking shops," unable or incompetent to carry out the tasks for which they have been chosen. The conviction grows that if efficient planning is to be done, the direction must be "taken out of politics" and placed in the hands of experts—permanent officials or independent autonomous bodies.

The difficulty is well known to socialists. It will soon be half a century since the Webbs began to complain of "the increased incapacity of the House of Commons to cope with its work."[1] More recently, Professor Laski has elaborated the argument:

> It is common ground that the present parliamentary machine is quite
> unsuited to pass rapidly a great body of complicated legislation. The
> National Government, indeed, has in substance admitted this by
> implementing its economy and tariff measures not by detailed debate
> in the House of Commons but by a wholesale system of delegated
> legislation. A Labour Government would, I presume, build upon the
> amplitude of this precedent. It would confine the House of Commons
> to the two functions it can properly perform: the ventilation of
> grievances and the discussion of general principles of its measures. Its
> Bills would take the form of general formulae conferring wide powers
> on the appropriate government departments; and those powers would
> be exercised by Order in Council which could, if desired, be attacked
> in the House by means of a vote of no confidence. The necessity and
> value of delegated legislation has recently been strongly reaffirmed by
> the Donoughmore Committee; and its extension is inevitable if the
> process of socialisation is not to be wrecked by the normal methods of
> obstruction which existing parliamentary procedure sanctions.

---

1. Sidney and Beatrice Webb, *Industrial Democracy* (1897), 800n.

And to make it quite clear that a socialist government must not allow itself to be too much fettered by democratic procedure, Professor Laski at the end of the same article raised the question "whether in a period of transition to socialism, a Labour Government can risk the overthrow of its measures as a result of the next general election"—and left it significantly unanswered. [2]

It is important clearly to see the causes of this admitted ineffectiveness of parliaments when it comes to a detailed administration of the economic affairs of a nation. The fault is neither with the individual representatives nor with parliamentary institutions as such but with the contradictions inherent in the task with which they are charged. They are not asked to act where they can agree, but to produce agreement on everything—the whole direction of the resources of the nation. For such a task the system of majority decision is, however, not suited. Majorities will be found where it is a choice between limited alternatives; but it is a superstition to believe that there must be a majority view on everything. There is no reason why there should be a majority in favor of any one of the different possible courses of positive action if their number is legion. Every member of the legislative assembly might prefer some particular plan for the direction of economic activity to no plan, yet no one plan may appear preferable to a majority to no plan at all.

Nor can a coherent plan be achieved by breaking it up into parts and voting on particular issues. A democratic assembly voting and amending a comprehensive economic plan clause by clause, as it deliberates on an ordinary bill, makes nonsense. An economic plan, to deserve the name, must have a unitary conception. Even if a parliament could, proceeding step by step, agree on some scheme, it would certainly in the end satisfy nobody. A complex whole in which all the parts must be most carefully adjusted to each other cannot be achieved through a compromise between conflicting views. To draw up an economic plan in this fashion is even less possible than, for example, successfully to plan a military campaign by democratic procedure. As in strategy it would become inevitable to delegate the task to the experts.

---

2. H. J. Laski, "Labour and the Constitution," *New Statesman and Nation*, no. 81, n.s. (September 10, 1932): 277. In a book (*Democracy in Crisis* [1933], particularly p. 87) in which Professor Laski later elaborated these ideas, his determination that parliamentary democracy must not be allowed to form an obstacle to the realization of socialism is even more plainly expressed: not only would a socialist government "take vast powers and legislate under them by ordinance and decree" and "suspend the classic formulae of normal opposition" but the "continuance of parliamentary government would depend on its [i.e., the Labour government's] possession of guarantees from the Conservative Party that its work of transformation would not be disrupted by repeal in the event of its defeat at the polls"!

As Professor Laski invokes the authority of the Donoughmore Committee, it may be worth recalling that Professor Laski was a member of that committee and presumably one of the authors of its report.

Yet the difference is that while the general who is put in charge of a campaign is given a single end to which, for the duration of the campaign, all the means under his control have to be exclusively devoted, there can be no such single goal given to the economic planner, and no similar limitation of the means imposed upon him. The general has not got to balance different independent aims against each other; there is for him only one supreme goal. But the ends of an economic plan, or of any part of it, cannot be defined apart from the particular plan. It is the essence of the economic problem that the making of an economic plan involves the choice between conflicting or competing ends—different needs of different people. But which ends do so conflict, which will have to be sacrificed if we want to achieve certain others, in short, which are the alternatives between which we must choose, can only be known to those who know all the facts; and only they, the experts, are in a position to decide which of the different ends are to be given preference. It is inevitable that they should impose their scale of preferences on the community for which they plan.

This is not always clearly recognized, and delegation is usually justified by the technical character of the task. But this does not mean that only the technical detail is delegated, or even that the inability of parliaments to understand the technical detail is the root of the difficulty.[3] Alterations in the structure of civil law are no less technical and no more difficult to appreciate in all their implications; yet nobody has yet seriously suggested that legislation there should be delegated to a body of experts. The fact is that in these fields legislation does not go beyond general rules on which true majority agreement can be achieved, while in the direction of economic activity the interests to be reconciled are so divergent that no true agreement is likely to be reached in a democratic assembly.

---

3. It is instructive in this connection briefly to refer to the government document in which in recent years these problems have been discussed. As long as thirteen years ago, that is, before England finally abandoned economic liberalism, the process of delegating legislative powers had already been carried to a point where it was felt necessary to appoint a committee to investigate "what safeguards are desirable or necessary to secure the sovereignty of Law." In its report the Donoughmore Committee (*Report of the [Lord Chancellor's] Committee in Ministers' Powers*, Cmd. 4060 [1932]) showed that even at that date Parliament had resorted "to the practice of wholesale and indiscriminate delegation" but regarded this (it was before we had really glanced into the totalitarian abyss!) as an inevitable and relatively innocuous development. And it is probably true that delegation as such need not be a danger to freedom. The interesting point is why delegation had become necessary on such a scale. First place among the causes enumerated in the report is given to the fact that "Parliament nowadays passes so many laws every year" and that "much of the detail is so technical as to be unsuitable for Parliamentary discussion." But if this were all, there would be no reason why the detail should not be worked out *before* rather than after Parliament passes a law. What is probably in many cases a much more important reason why, "If Parliament were not willing to delegate law-making power, Parliament would be unable to pass the kind and quantity of legislation which public opinion requires," is innocently revealed in the little sentence that "many of the laws affect people's lives so closely that elasticity is essential"! What does this mean if not conferment of arbitrary power—power limited by no fixed principles and that in the opinion of Parliament cannot be limited by definite and unambiguous rules?

It should be recognized, however, that it is not the delegation of lawmaking power as such that is so objectionable. To oppose delegation as such is to oppose a symptom instead of the cause and, as it may be a necessary result of other causes, to weaken the case. So long as the power that is delegated is merely the power to make general rules, there may be very good reasons why such rules should be laid down by local rather than by the central authority. The objectionable feature is that delegation is so often resorted to because the matter in hand cannot be regulated by general rules but only by the exercise of discretion in the decision of particular cases. In these instances delegation means that some authority is given power to make with the force of law what to all intents and purposes are arbitrary decisions (usually described as "judging the case on its merits").

The delegation of particular technical tasks to separate bodies, while a regular feature, is yet only the first step in the process whereby a democracy that embarks on planning progressively relinquishes its powers. The expedient of delegation cannot really remove the causes that make all the advocates of comprehensive planning so impatient with the impotence of democracy. The delegation of particular powers to separate agencies creates a new obstacle to the achievement of a single coordinated plan. Even if, by this expedient, a democracy should succeed in planning every sector of economic activity, it would still have to face the problem of integrating these separate plans into a unitary whole. Many separate plans do not make a planned whole—in fact, as the planners ought to be the first to admit, they may be worse than no plan. But the democratic legislature will long hesitate to relinquish the decisions on really vital issues, and so long as it does so it makes it impossible for anyone else to provide the comprehensive plan. Yet agreement that planning is necessary, together with the inability of democratic assemblies to produce a plan, will evoke stronger and stronger demands that the government or some single individual should be given powers to act on their own responsibility. The belief is becoming more and more widespread that if things are to get done, the responsible authorities must be freed from the fetters of democratic procedure.

The cry for an economic dictator is a characteristic stage in the movement toward planning. It is now several years since one of the most acute of foreign students of England, the late Élie Halévy, suggested that "if you take a composite photograph of Lord Eustace Percy, Sir Oswald Mosley, and Sir Stafford Cripps, I think you would find this common feature—you would find them all agreeing to say: 'We are living in economic chaos and we cannot get out of it except under some kind of dictatorial leadership.'"[4] The number of influential public men whose inclusion would not materially alter the features of the "composite photograph" has since grown considerably.

---

4. "Socialism and the Problems of Democratic Parliamentarism," *International Affairs*, XIII, 501.

In Germany, even before Hitler came into power, the movement had already progressed much further. It is important to remember that for some time before 1933, Germany had reached a stage in which it had, in effect, to be governed dictatorially. Nobody could then doubt that for the time being democracy had broken down and that sincere democrats like Brüning were no more able to govern democratically than Schleicher or von Papen. Hitler did not have to destroy democracy; he merely took advantage of the decay of democracy and at the critical moment obtained the support of many to whom, though they detested Hitler, he yet seemed the only man strong enough to get things done.

The argument by which the planners usually try to reconcile us with this development is that so long as democracy retains ultimate control, the essentials of democracy are not affected. Thus Karl Mannheim writes:

"The only [sic] way in which a planned society differs from that of the nineteenth century is that more and more spheres of social life, and ultimately each and all of them, are subjected to state control. But if a few controls can be held in check by parliamentary sovereignty, so can many . . . In a democratic state sovereignty can be boundlessly strengthened by plenary powers without renouncing democratic control." [5]

This belief overlooks a vital distinction. Parliament can, of course, control the execution of tasks where it can give definite directions, where it has first agreed on the aim and merely delegates the working out of the detail. The situation is entirely different when the reason for the delegation is that there is no real agreement on the ends, when the body charged with the planning has to choose between ends of whose conflict parliament is not even aware, and when the most that can be done is to present to it a plan that has to be accepted or rejected as a whole. There may and probably will be criticism; but as no majority can agree on an alternative plan, and the parts objected to can almost always be represented as essential parts of the whole, it will remain quite ineffective. Parliamentary discussion may be retained as a useful safety valve and even more as a convenient medium through which the official answers to complaints are disseminated. It may even prevent some flagrant abuses and successfully insist on particular shortcomings being remedied. But it cannot direct. It will at best be reduced to choosing the persons who are to have practically absolute power. The whole system will tend toward that plebiscitarian dictatorship in which the head of the government is from time to time confirmed in his position by popular vote, but where he has all the powers at his command to make certain that the vote will go in the direction he desires.

---

5. *Man and Society in an Age of Reconstruction* (1940), 340.

It is the price of democracy that the possibilities of conscious control are restricted to the fields where true agreement exists and that in some fields things must be left to chance. But in a society that for its functioning depends on central planning, this control cannot be made dependent on a majority's being able to agree; it will often be necessary that the will of a small minority be imposed upon the people, because this minority will be the largest group able to agree among themselves on the question at issue. Democratic government has worked successfully where, and so long as, the functions of government were, by a widely accepted creed, restricted to fields where agreement among a majority could be achieved by free discussion; and it is the great merit of the liberal creed that it reduced the range of subjects on which agreement was necessary to one on which it was likely to exist in a society of free men. It is now often said that democracy will not tolerate "capitalism." If "capitalism" means here a competitive system based on free disposal over private property, it is far more important to realize that only within this system is democracy possible. When it becomes dominated by a collectivist creed, democracy will inevitably destroy itself.

We have no intention, however, of making a fetish of democracy. It may well be true that our generation talks and thinks too much of democracy and too little of the values that it serves. It cannot be said of democracy, as Lord Acton truly said of liberty, that it "is not a means to a higher political end. It is itself the highest political end. It is not for the sake of a good public administration that it is required, but for the security in the pursuit of the highest objects of civil society, and of private life." Democracy is essentially a means, a utilitarian device for safeguarding internal peace and individual freedom. As such it is by no means infallible or certain. Nor must we forget that there has often been much more cultural and spiritual freedom under an autocratic rule than under some democracies—and it is at least conceivable that under the government of a very homogeneous and doctrinaire majority democratic government might be as oppressive as the worst dictatorship. Our point, however, is not that dictatorship must inevitably extirpate freedom, but rather that planning leads to dictatorship because dictatorship is the most effective instrument of coercion and the enforcement of ideals and, as such, essential if central planning on a large scale is to be possible. The clash between planning and democracy arises simply from the fact that the latter is an obstacle to the suppression of freedom that the direction of economic activity requires. But insofar as democracy ceases to be a guaranty of individual freedom, it may well persist in some form under a totalitarian regime. A true "dictatorship of the proletariat," even if democratic in form, if it undertook centrally to direct the economic system, would probably destroy personal freedom as completely as any autocracy has ever done.

The fashionable concentration on democracy as the main value threatened is not without danger. It is largely responsible for the misleading and unfounded belief that so long as the ultimate source of power is the will of the majority, the power cannot be arbitrary. The false assurance that many people derive from this belief is an important cause of the general unawareness of the dangers that we face. There is no justification for the belief that so long as power is conferred by democratic procedure, it cannot be arbitrary; the contrast suggested by this statement is altogether false: it is not the source but the limitation of power that prevents it from being arbitrary. Democratic control *may* prevent power from becoming arbitrary, but it does not do so by its mere existence. If democracy resolves on a task that necessarily involves the use of power that cannot be guided by fixed rules, it must become arbitrary power.

QUESTIONS

1. Why does Hayek prefer society to be guided by the "whims and fancies" of individualists rather than by "deliberate organization"? (251)

2. According to Hayek, how do governments recognize the autonomous spheres in which the ends of the individuals are supreme?

3. Does Hayek believe in any notion of the "common good" or "general welfare"? (251)

4. Why does Hayek believe that it is a sign of civilization's "growth" that "the rules of which our common moral code consists have progressively become fewer and more general in character"? (252)

5. According to Hayek, how does the individual know what the "defined limits" are with regard to ethics? (253) Who sets these limits, according to Hayek, and what are these limits?

6. Why does Hayek think that a democratic assembly is appropriate for making civil law but inappropriate for directing economic activity?

7. According to Hayek, what are some of the "fields where agreement among a majority could be achieved by free discussion"? (259)

8. According to Hayek, why is democracy possible only when it embraces "a competitive system based on free disposal over private property"? (256, 259)

9. If Hayek so vocally defends "democratic procedure," then why does he say, "We have no intention, however, of making a fetish of democracy"? (256, 259)

FOR FURTHER REFLECTION

1. Are there any needs common to all persons at all times? If so, what might they be?

2. What values does Hayek exhibit when he says, "The fact that we are constantly choosing between different values without a social code prescribing how we ought to choose does not . . . suggest to us that our moral code is incomplete. In our society there is neither occasion nor reason why people should develop common views about what should be done in such situations"?

3. Is it true that we talk and think too much of democracy and too little of the values that democracy serves?

4. Does the guarantee of individual freedom require any sort of planning?

JOHN RAWLS

John Rawls (1921–2002) was one of the preeminent political philosophers in American history. Born in Baltimore into a relatively privileged home, he graduated from Princeton University in 1943 with a degree in philosophy. After serving in the U.S. Army in the Pacific during World War II, he returned to Princeton, where he received his doctorate in 1950. He then embarked on a teaching career at several major universities, spending the greater part of his working life as a professor at Harvard.

In his youth, Rawls lived through the Great Depression, and his later political theories appear to reflect a strong belief that Franklin D. Roosevelt's New Deal economic policies had rightly cushioned the impact of the Depression on the most vulnerable members of American society. Another experience that seems to have guided his mature work was his witnessing firsthand, while stationed in occupied Japan, the calamitous aftermath of the failure of an authoritarian, hierarchical state—including the effects of the nuclear bombing of Hiroshima. He also saw the start of a vast practical experiment when American military authorities created an entirely new political culture for the conquered nation.

Carrying these perspectives into his academic writing, Rawls asked, What are the natures of justice, morality, and ethics? He inquired how and whether their meanings change according to time and locality and tried to answer these questions, with a goal of defining the "just society," by adapting the social contract theories of Rousseau, Hegel, and Kant to fit an egalitarian, democratic context. Rawls concluded that while a democratic state cannot—and should not—attempt to settle coercively all the differing interests, opinions, and desires of its individual citizens, a just society must nevertheless actively embrace all of these citizens with the guarantee of a minimum of legal rights. Those rights would include a living standard adequate to sustain life, basic dignity, and basic protections, along with reasonably certain lifelong access to equal opportunity of employment, income, and social mobility.

Much of Rawls's work endeavors to codify political relationships that are suitable for the ideals of a democracy, devising principles that define a just society and hypothetical mechanisms for attaining them. Chief among these principles are the liberty principle and the difference principle, both of which are elaborated in his masterwork, *A Theory of Justice* (1971), and the paper excerpted here, "Distributive Justice" (1967). As its title implies, this paper deals with how a society can fairly distribute rights, resources, and responsibilities to its members.

Rawls's academic career and intellectual maturation paralleled both the development of the United States into a superpower and the growth of the domestic civil rights movement. His work celebrates America's egalitarian traditions and experience, but far from being an expression of simplistic national chauvinism, it provides a practical gift to humanity: a theoretical template for a political culture that could be used anywhere to create stable, law-guided regimes that would function on behalf of all their citizens.

JOHN RAWLS
Distributive Justice

W e may think of a human society as a more or less self-sufficient association regulated by a common conception of justice and aimed at advancing the good of its members. As a cooperative venture for mutual advantage, it is characterized by a conflict as well as an identity of interests. There is an identity of interests, since social cooperation makes possible a better life for all than any would have if everyone were to try to live by his own efforts; yet at the same time men are not indifferent to how the greater benefits produced by their joint labors are distributed, for in order to further their own aims each prefers a larger to a lesser share. A conception of justice is a set of principles for choosing between the social arrangements that determine this division and for underwriting a consensus about the proper distributive shares.

Now at first sight the most rational conception of justice would seem to be utilitarian. For consider: each man in realizing his own good can certainly balance his own losses against his own gains. We can impose a sacrifice on ourselves now for the sake of a greater advantage later. A man quite properly acts, as long as others are not affected, to achieve his own greatest good, to advance his ends as far as possible. Now, why should not a society act on precisely the same principle? Why is not that which is rational in the case of one man right in the case of a group of men? Surely the simplest and most direct conception of the right, and so of justice, is that of maximizing the good. This assumes a prior understanding of what is good, but we can think of the good as already given by the interests of rational individuals. Thus just as the principle of individual choice is to achieve one's greatest good, to advance so far as possible one's own system of rational desires, so the principle of social choice is to realize the greatest good (similarly defined) summed over all the members of society. We arrive at the principle of utility in a natural way: by this principle a society is rightly ordered, and hence just, when its institutions are arranged so as to realize the greatest sum of satisfactions.

The striking feature of the principle of utility is that it does not matter, except indirectly, how this sum of satisfactions is distributed among individuals, any more than it matters, except indirectly, how one man distributes his satisfactions over time. Since certain ways of distributing things affect the total sum of satisfactions, this fact must be taken into account in arranging social institutions; but according to this principle the explanation of commonsense precepts of justice and their seemingly stringent character is that they are those rules that experience shows must be strictly respected and departed from only under exceptional circumstances if the sum of advantages is to be maximized. The precepts of justice are derivative from the one end of attaining the greatest net balance of satisfactions. There is no reason in principle why the greater gains of some should not compensate for the lesser losses of others; or why the violation of the liberty of a few might not be made right by a greater good shared by many. It simply happens, at least under most conditions, that the greatest sum of advantages is not generally achieved in this way. From the standpoint of utility the strictness of commonsense notions of justice has a certain usefulness, but as a philosophical doctrine it is irrational.

If, then, we believe that as a matter of principle each member of society has an inviolability founded on justice that even the welfare of everyone else cannot override, and that a loss of freedom for some is not made right by a greater sum of satisfactions enjoyed by many, we shall have to look for another account of the principles of justice. The principle of utility is incapable of explaining the fact that in a just society the liberties of equal citizenship are taken for granted, and the rights secured by justice are not subject to political bargaining nor to the calculus of social interests. Now, the most natural alternative to the principle of utility is its traditional rival, the theory of the social contract. The aim of the contract doctrine is precisely to account for the strictness of justice by supposing that its principles arise from an agreement among free and independent persons in an original position of equality and hence reflect the integrity and equal sovereignty of the rational persons who are the contractees. Instead of supposing that a conception of right, and so a conception of justice, is simply an extension of the principle of choice for one man to society as a whole, the contract doctrine assumes that the rational individuals who belong to society must choose together, in one joint act, what is to count among them as just and unjust. They are to decide among themselves once and for all what is to be their conception of justice. This decision is thought of as being made in a suitably defined initial situation, one of the significant features of which is that no one knows his position in society, nor even his place in the distribution of natural talents and abilities. The principles of justice to which all are forever bound are chosen in the absence of this sort of specific information. A veil of ignorance prevents anyone from being advantaged or disadvantaged by the contingencies of social class and fortune; and hence the bargaining problems that arise in everyday life from the possession of this knowledge do not affect the choice of principles. On the contract doctrine, then, the theory of justice, and indeed ethics itself, is part of the general theory of rational choice, a fact perfectly clear in its Kantian formulation.

Once justice is thought of as arising from an original agreement of this kind, it is evident that the principle of utility is problematic. For why should rational individuals who have a system of ends they wish to advance agree to a violation of their liberty for the sake of a greater balance of satisfaction enjoyed by others? It seems more plausible to suppose that, when situated in an original position of equal right, they would insist upon institutions that returned compensating advantages for any sacrifices required. A rational man would not accept an institution merely because it maximized the sum of advantages irrespective of its effect on his own interests. It appears, then, that the principle of utility would be rejected as a principle of justice, although we shall not try to argue this important question here. Rather, our aim is to give a brief sketch of the conception of distributive shares implicit in the principles of justice that, it seems, would be chosen in the original position. The philosophical appeal of utilitarianism is that it seems to offer a single principle on the basis of which a consistent and complete conception of right can be developed. The problem is to work out a contractarian alternative in such a way that it has comparable if not all the same virtues.

In our discussion we shall make no attempt to derive the two principles of justice that we shall examine; that is, we shall not try to show that they would be chosen in the original position. It must suffice that it is plausible that they would be, at least in preference to the standard forms of traditional theories. Instead we shall be mainly concerned with three questions: first, how to interpret these principles so that they define a consistent and complete conception of justice; second, whether it is possible to arrange the institutions of a constitutional democracy so that these principles are satisfied, at least approximately; and third, whether the conception of distributive shares that they define is compatible with commonsense notions of justice. The significance of these principles is that they allow for the strictness of the claims of justice; and if they can be understood so as to yield a consistent and complete conception, the contractarian alternative would seem all the more attractive.

The two principles of justice that we shall discuss may be formulated as follows: first, each person engaged in an institution or affected by it has an equal right to the most extensive liberty compatible with a like liberty for all; and second, inequalities as defined by the institutional structure or fostered by it are arbitrary unless it is reasonable to expect that they will work out to everyone's advantage and provided that the positions and offices to which they attach or from which they may be gained are open to all. These principles regulate the distributive aspects of institutions by controlling the assignment of rights and duties throughout the whole social structure, beginning with the adoption of a political constitution in accordance with which they are then to be applied to legislation. It is upon a correct choice of a basic structure of society, its fundamental system of rights and duties, that the justice of distributive shares depends.

The two principles of justice apply in the first instance to this basic structure, that is, to the main institutions of the social system and their arrangement, how they are combined together. Thus this structure includes the political constitution and the principal economic and social institutions that together define a person's liberties and rights and affect his life prospects, what he may expect to be and how well he may expect to fare. The intuitive idea here is that those born into the social system at different positions, say in different social classes, have varying life prospects determined, in part, by the system of political liberties and personal rights and by the economic and social opportunities that are made available to these positions. In this way the basic structure of society favors certain men over others, and these are the basic inequalities, the ones that affect their whole life prospects. It is inequalities of this kind, presumably inevitable in any society, with which the two principles of justice are primarily designed to deal.

Now the second principle holds that an inequality is allowed only if there is reason to believe that the institution with the inequality, or permitting it, will work out for the advantage of every person engaged in it. In the case of the basic structure this means that all inequalities that affect life prospects, say the inequalities of income and wealth that exist between social classes, must be to the advantage of everyone. Since the principle applies to institutions, we interpret this to mean that inequalities must be to the advantage of the representative man for each relevant social position; they should improve each such man's expectation. Here we assume that it is possible to attach to each position an expectation, and that this expectation is a function of the whole institutional structure: it can be raised and lowered by reassigning rights and duties throughout the system. Thus the expectation of any position depends upon the expectations of the others, and these in turn depend upon the pattern of rights and duties established by the basic structure. But it is not clear what is meant by saying that inequalities must be to the advantage of every representative man, and hence our first question. . . .

⁓ᴥ⁓

. . . [An] interpretation that is immediately suggested is to choose some social position by reference to which the pattern of expectations as a whole is to be judged, and then to maximize with respect to the expectations of this representative man consistent with the demands of equal liberty and equality of opportunity. Now, the one obvious candidate is the representative man of those who are least favored by the system of institutional inequalities. Thus we arrive at the following idea: the basic structure of the social system affects the life prospects of typical individuals according to their initial places in society, say the various income classes into which they are born, or depending upon certain natural attributes, as when institutions make discriminations between men and women or allow certain advantages to be gained by those with greater natural abilities. The fundamental problem of distributive justice concerns the differences in life prospects that come about in this way. We interpret the second principle to hold that these differences are just if and only if the greater expectations of the more advantaged, when playing a part in the working of the whole social system, improve the expectations of the least advantaged. The basic structure is just throughout when the advantages of the more fortunate promote the well-being of the least fortunate, that is, when a decrease in their advantages would make the least fortunate even worse off than they are. The basic structure is perfectly just when the prospects of the least fortunate are as great as they can be.

In interpreting the second principle (or rather the first part of it which we may, for obvious reasons, refer to as the difference principle), we assume that the first principle requires a basic equal liberty for all, and that the resulting political system, when circumstances permit, is that of a constitutional democracy in some form. There must be liberty of the person and political equality as well as liberty of conscience and freedom of thought. There is one class of equal citizens that defines a common status for all. We also assume that there is equality of opportunity and a fair competition for the available positions on the basis of reasonable qualification. Now, given this background, the differences to be justified are the various economic and social inequalities in the basic structure that must inevitably arise in such a scheme. These are the inequalities in the distribution of income and wealth and the distinctions in social prestige and status that attach to the various positions and classes. The difference principle says that these inequalities are just if and only if they are part of a larger system in which they work out to the advantage of the most unfortunate representative man. The just distributive shares determined by the basic structure are those specified by this constrained maximum principle.

Thus, consider the chief problem of distributive justice, that concerning the distribution of wealth as it affects the life prospects of those starting out in the various income groups. These income classes define the relevant representative men from which the social system is to be judged. Now, a son of a member of the entrepreneurial class (in a capitalist society) has a better prospect than that of the son of an unskilled laborer. This will be true, it seems, even when the social injustices that presently exist are removed and the two men are of equal talent and ability; the inequality cannot be done away with as long as something like the family is maintained, What, then, can justify this inequality in life prospects? According to the second principle it is justified only if it is to the advantage of the representative man who is worst off, in this case the representative unskilled laborer. The inequality is permissible because lowering it would, let's suppose, make the workingman even worse off than he is. Presumably, given the principle of open offices (the second part of the second principle), the greater expectations allowed to entrepreneurs has the effect in the longer run of raising the life prospects of the laboring class. The inequality in expectation provides an incentive so that the economy is more efficient, industrial advance proceeds at a quicker pace, and so on, the end result of which is that greater material and other benefits are distributed throughout the system. Of course, all of this is familiar, and whether true or not in particular cases, it is the sort of thing that must be argued if the inequality in income and wealth is to be acceptable by the difference principle.

We should now verify that this interpretation of the second principle gives a natural sense in which everyone may be said to be made better off. Let us suppose that inequalities are chain connected; that is, if an inequality raises the expectations of the lowest position, it raises the expectations of all positions in between. For example, if the greater expectations of the representative entrepreneur raises that of the unskilled laborer, it also raises that of the semiskilled. Let us further assume that inequalities are close-knit; that is, it is impossible to raise (or lower) the expectation of any representative man without raising (or lowering) the expectations of every other representative man and, in particular, without affecting one way or the other that of the least fortunate. There is no loose-jointedness, so to speak, in the way in which expectations depend upon one another. Now, with these assumptions, everyone does benefit from an inequality that satisfies the difference principle, and the second principle as we have formulated it reads correctly. For the representative man who is better off in any pairwise comparison gains by being allowed to have his advantage, and the man who is worse off benefits from the contribution that all inequalities make to each position below. Of course, chain connection and close-knitness may not obtain; but in this case those who are better off should not have a veto over the advantages available for the least advantaged. The stricter interpretation of the difference principle should be followed, and all inequalities should be arranged for the advantage of the most unfortunate even if some inequalities are not to the advantage of those in middle positions. Should these conditions fail, then, the second principle would have to be stated in another way.

It may be observed that the difference principle represents, in effect, an original agreement to share in the benefits of the distribution of natural talents and abilities, whatever this distribution turns out to be, in order to alleviate as far as possible the arbitrary handicaps resulting from our initial starting places in society. Those who have been favored by nature, whoever they are, may gain from their good fortune only on terms that improve the well-being of those who have lost out. The naturally advantaged are not to gain simply because they are more gifted, but only to cover the costs of training and cultivating their endowments and for putting them to use in a way that improves the position of the less fortunate. We are led to the difference principle if we wish to arrange the basic social structure so that no one gains (or loses) from his luck in the natural lottery of talent and ability, or from his initial place in society, without giving (or receiving) compensating advantages in return. (The parties in the original position are not said to be attracted by this idea and so agree to it; rather, given the symmetries of their situation, and particularly their lack of knowledge, and so on, they will find it to their interest to agree to a principle that can be understood in this way.) And we should note also that when the difference principle is perfectly satisfied, the basic structure is optimal by the efficiency principle. There is no way to make anyone better off without making someone else worse off, namely, the least fortunate representative man. Thus the two principles of justice define distributive shares in a way compatible with efficiency, at least as long as we move on this highly abstract level. If we want to say (as we do, although it cannot be argued here) that the demands of justice have an absolute weight with respect to efficiency, this claim may seem less paradoxical when it is kept in mind that perfectly just institutions are also efficient.

Our second question is whether it is possible to arrange the institutions of a constitutional democracy so that the two principles of justice are satisfied, at least approximately. We shall try to show that this can be done provided the government regulates a free economy in a certain way. More fully, if law and government act effectively to keep markets competitive, resources fully employed, and property and wealth widely distributed over time, and to maintain the appropriate social minimum, then if there is equality of opportunity underwritten by education for all, the resulting distribution will be just. Of course, all of these arrangements and policies are familiar. The only novelty in the following remarks, if there is any novelty at all, is that this framework of institutions can be made to satisfy the difference principle. To argue this, we must sketch the relations of these institutions and how they work together.

First of all, we assume that the basic social structure is controlled by a just constitution that secures the various liberties of equal citizenship. Thus the legal order is administered in accordance with the principle of legality, and liberty of conscience and freedom of thought are taken for granted. The political process is conducted, so far as possible, as a just procedure for choosing between governments and for enacting just legislation. From the standpoint of distributive justice, it is also essential that there be equality of opportunity in several senses. Thus, we suppose that in addition to maintaining the usual social overhead capital, government provides for equal educational opportunities for all either by subsidizing private schools or by operating a public school system. It also enforces and underwrites equality of opportunity in commercial ventures and in the free choice of occupation. This result is achieved by policing business behavior and by preventing the establishment of barriers and restriction to the desirable positions and markets. Lastly, there is a guarantee of a social minimum that the government meets by family allowances and special payments in times of unemployment, or by a negative income tax.

In maintaining this system of institutions the government may be thought of as divided into four branches. Each branch is represented by various agencies (or activities thereof) charged with preserving certain social and economic conditions. These branches do not necessarily overlap with the usual organization of government but should be understood as purely conceptual. Thus the allocation branch is to keep the economy feasibly competitive, that is, to prevent the formation of unreasonable market power. Markets are competitive in this sense when they cannot be made more so consistent with the requirements of efficiency and the acceptance of the facts of consumer preferences and geography. The allocation branch is also charged with identifying and correcting, say by suitable taxes and subsidies wherever possible, the more obvious departures from efficiency caused by the failure of prices to measure accurately social benefits and costs. The stabilization branch strives to maintain reasonably full employment so that there is no waste through failure to use resources and the free choice of occupation and the deployment of finance is supported by strong effective demand. These two branches together are to preserve the efficiency of the market economy generally.

The social minimum is established through the operations of the transfer branch . . . since this is a crucial matter; but for the moment, a few general remarks will suffice. The main idea is that the workings of the transfer branch take into account the precept of need and assign it an appropriate weight with respect to the other commonsense precepts of justice. A market economy ignores the claims of need altogether. Hence there is a division of labor between the parts of the social system as different institutions answer to different commonsense precepts. Competitive markets (properly supplemented by government operations) handle the problem of the efficient allocation of labor and resources and set a weight to the conventional precepts associated with wages and earnings (the precepts of each according to his work and experience, or responsibility and the hazards of the job, and so on), whereas the transfer branch guarantees a certain level of well-being and meets the claims of need. Thus it is obvious that the justice of distributive shares depends upon the whole social system and how it distributes total income, wages plus transfers. There is with reason strong objection to the competitive determination of total income, since this would leave out of account the claims of need and of a decent standard of life. From the standpoint of the original position it is clearly rational to insure oneself against these contingencies. But now, if the appropriate minimum is provided by transfers, it may be perfectly fair that the other part of total income is competitively determined. Moreover, this way of dealing with the claims of need is doubtless more efficient, at least from a theoretical point of view, than trying to regulate prices by minimum wage standards and so on. It is preferable to handle these claims by a separate branch that supports a social minimum. Henceforth, in considering whether the second principle of justice is satisfied, the answer turns on whether the total income, that is, wages plus transfers, of the least advantaged is such as to maximize their long-term expectations consistent with the demands of liberty.

Finally, the distribution branch is to preserve an approximately just distribution of income and wealth over time by affecting the background conditions of the market from period to period. Two aspects of this branch may be distinguished. First of all, it operates a system of inheritance and gift taxes. The aim of these levies is not to raise revenue, but gradually and continually to correct the distribution of wealth and to prevent the concentrations of power to the detriment of liberty and equality of opportunity. It is perfectly true, as some have said, that unequal inheritance of wealth is no more inherently unjust than unequal inheritance of intelligence; as far as possible the inequalities founded on either should satisfy the difference principle. Thus, the inheritance of greater wealth is just as long as it is to the advantage of the worst off and consistent with liberty, including equality of opportunity. Now by the latter we do not mean, of course, the equality of expectations between classes, since differences in life prospects arising from the basic structure are inevitable, and it is precisely the aim of the second principle to say when these differences are just. Instead, equality of opportunity is a certain set of institutions that ensures equally good education and chances of culture for all and that keeps open the competition for positions on the basis of qualities reasonably related to performance, and so on. It is these institutions that are put in jeopardy when inequalities and concentrations of wealth reach a certain limit; and the taxes imposed by the distribution branch are to prevent this limit from being exceeded. Naturally enough, where this limit lies is a matter for political judgment guided by theory, practical experience, and plain hunch; on this question the theory of justice has nothing to say.

The second part of the distribution branch is a scheme of taxation for raising revenue to cover the costs of public goods, to make transfer payments, and the like. This scheme belongs to the distribution branch, since the burden of taxation must be justly shared. Although we cannot examine the legal and economic complications involved, there are several points in favor of proportional expenditure taxes as part of an ideally just arrangement. For one thing, they are preferable to income taxes at the level of commonsense precepts of justice, since they impose a levy according to how much a man takes out of the common store of goods and not according to how much he contributes (assuming that income is fairly earned in return for productive efforts). On the other hand, proportional taxes treat everyone in a clearly defined uniform way (again assuming that income is fairly earned), and hence it is preferable to use progressive rates only when they are necessary to preserve the justice of the system as a whole, that is, to prevent large fortunes hazardous to liberty and equality of opportunity, and the like. If proportional expenditure taxes should also prove more efficient, say because they interfere less with incentives, or whatever, this would make the case for them decisive provided a feasible scheme could be worked out. Yet these are questions of political judgment that are not our concern; and, in any case, a proportional expenditure tax is part of an idealized scheme that we are describing. It does not follow that even steeply progressive income taxes, given the injustice of existing systems, do not improve justice and efficiency, all things considered. In practice we must usually choose between unjust arrangements, and then it is a matter of finding the lesser injustice.

Whatever form the distribution branch assumes, the argument for it is to be based on justice: we must hold that once it is accepted, the social system as a whole—the competitive economy surrounded by a just constitutional and legal framework—can be made to satisfy the principles of justice with the smallest loss in efficiency. The long-term expectations of the least advantaged are raised to the highest level consistent with the demands of equal liberty. In discussing the choice of a distribution scheme we have made no reference to the traditional criteria of taxation according to ability to pay or benefits received; nor have we mentioned any of the variants of the sacrifice principle. These standards are subordinate to the two principles of justice; once the problem is seen as that of designing a whole social system, they assume the status of secondary precepts with no more independent force than the precepts of common sense in regard to wages. To suppose otherwise is not to take a sufficiently comprehensive point of view. In setting up a just distribution branch these precepts may or may not have a place, depending upon the demands of the two principles of justice when applied to the entire system. . . .

˜ᴗᴢᴗ˜

. . . To establish just distributive shares, a just total system of institutions must be set up and impartially administered. Given a just constitution and the smooth working of the four branches of government, and so on, there exists a procedure such that the actual distribution of wealth, whatever it turns out to be, is just. It will have come about as a consequence of a just system of institutions satisfying the principles to which everyone would agree and against which no one can complain. The situation is one of pure procedural justice, since there is no independent criterion by which the outcome can be judged. Nor can we say that a particular distribution of wealth is just because it is one that could have resulted from just institutions although it has not, as this would be to allow too much. Clearly there are many distributions that may be reached by just institutions, and this is true whether we count patterns of distributions among social classes or whether we count distributions of particular goods and services among particular individuals. There are indefinitely many outcomes, and what makes one of these just is that it has been achieved by actually carrying out a just scheme of cooperation as it is publicly understood. It is the result that has arisen when everyone receives that to which he is entitled given his and others' actions guided by their legitimate expectations and their obligations to one another. We can no more arrive at a just distribution of wealth except by working together within the framework of a just system of institutions than we can win or lose fairly without actually betting.

This account of distributive shares is simply an elaboration of the familiar idea that economic rewards will be just once a perfectly competitive price system is organized as a fair game. But in order to do this we have to begin with the choice of a social system as a whole, for the basic structure of the entire arrangement must be just. The economy must be surrounded with the appropriate framework of institutions, since even a perfectly efficient price system has no tendency to determine just distributive shares when left to itself. Not only must economic activity be regulated by a just constitution and controlled by the four branches of government, but a just saving function must be adopted to estimate the provision to be made for future generations. Thus, we cannot, in general, consider only piecewise reforms, for unless all of these fundamental questions are properly handled, there is no assurance that the resulting distributive shares will be just; while if the correct initial choices of institutions are made, the matter of distributive justice may be left to take care of itself. Within the framework of a just system men may be permitted to form associations and groupings as they please so long as they respect the like liberty of others. With social ingenuity it should be possible to invent many different kinds of economic and social activities appealing to a wide variety of tastes and talents; and as long as the justice of the basic structure of the whole is not affected, men may be allowed, in accordance with the principle of free association, to enter into and to take part in whatever activities they wish. The resulting distribution will be just, whatever it happens to be. The system of institutions that we have described is, let's suppose, the basic structure of a well-ordered society. This system exhibits the content of the two principles of justice by showing how they may be perfectly satisfied; and it defines a social ideal by reference to which political judgment among second bests, and the long-range direction of reform, may be guided.

We may conclude by considering the third question: whether this conception of distributive shares is compatible with commonsense notions of justice. In elaborating the contract doctrine we have been led to what seems to be a rather special, even eccentric, conception, the peculiarities of which center in the difference principle. Clear statements of it seem to be rare, and it differs rather widely from traditional utilitarian and intuitionist notions. But this question is not an easy one to answer, for philosophical conceptions of justice, including the one we have just put forward, and our commonsense convictions are not very precise. Moreover, a comparison is made difficult by our tendency in practice to adopt combinations of principles and precepts the consequences of which depend essentially upon how they are weighted; but the weighting may be undefined and allowed to vary with circumstances, and thus relies on the intuitive judgments that we are trying to systematize.

Consider the following conception of right: social justice depends positively on two things, the equality of distribution (understood as equality in levels of well-being) and total welfare (understood as the sum of utilities taken over all individuals). On this view one social system is better than another without ambiguity if it is better on both counts, that is, if the expectations it defines are both less unequal and sum to a larger total. Another conception of right can be obtained by substituting the principle of a social minimum for the principle of equality; and thus an arrangement of institutions is preferable to another without ambiguity if the expectations sum to a larger total and it provides for a higher minimum. The idea here is to maximize the sum of expectations subject to the constraint that no one be allowed to fall below some recognized standard of life. In these conceptions the principles of equality and of a social minimum represent the demands of justice, and the principle of total welfare that of efficiency. The principle of utility assumes the role of the principle of efficiency, the force of which is limited by a principle of justice.

Now in practice, combinations of principles of this kind are not without value. There is no question but that they identify plausible standards by reference to which policies may be appraised, and given the appropriate background of institutions, they may give correct conclusions. Consider the first conception: a person guided by it may frequently decide rightly. For example, he would be in favor of equality of opportunity, for it seems evident that having more equal chances for all both improves efficiency and decreases inequality. The real question arises, however, when an institution is approved by one principle but not by the other. In this case everything depends on how the principles are weighted, but how is this to be done? The combination of principles yields no answer to this question, and the judgment must be left to intuition. For every arrangement combining a particular total welfare with a particular degree of inequality one simply has to decide, without the guidance from principle, how much of an increase (or decrease) in total welfare, say, compensates for a given decrease (or increase) in equality.

Anyone using the two principles of justice, however, would also appear to be striking a balance between equality and total welfare. How do we know, then, that a person who claims to adopt a combination of principles does not, in fact, rely on the two principles of justice in weighing them, not consciously certainly, but in the sense that the weights he gives to equality and total welfare are those that he would give to them if he applied the two principles of justice? We need not say, of course, that those who in practice refer to a combination of principles, or whatever, rely on the contract doctrine, but only that until their conception of right is completely specified the question is still open. The leeway provided by the determination of weights leaves the matter unsettled.

Moreover, the same sort of situation arises with other practical standards. It is widely agreed, for example, that the distribution of income should depend upon the claims of entitlement, such as training and experience, responsibility and contribution, and so on, weighed against the claims of need and security. But how are these commonsense precepts to be balanced? Again, it is generally accepted that the ends of economic policy are competitive efficiency, full employment, an appropriate rate of growth, a decent social minimum, and a more equal distribution of income. In a modern democratic state these aims are to be advanced in ways consistent with equal liberty and equality of opportunity. There is no argument with these objectives; they would be recognized by anyone who accepted the two principles of justice. But different political views balance these ends differently, and how are we to choose between them? The fact is that we agree to little when we acknowledge precepts and ends of this kind; it must be recognized that a fairly detailed weighting is implicit in any complete conception of justice. Often we content ourselves with enumerating commonsense precepts and objectives of policy adding that on particular questions we must strike a balance between them, having studied the relevant facts. While this is sound practical advice, it does not express a conception of justice. Whereas on the contract doctrine all combinations of principle, precepts, and objectives of policy are given a weight in maximizing the expectations of the lowest income class consistent with making the required saving and maintaining the system of equal liberty and equality of opportunity.

Thus despite the fact that the contract doctrine seems at first to be a somewhat special conception, particularly in its treatment of inequalities, it may still express the principles of justice that stand in the background and control the weights expressed in our everyday judgments. Whether this is indeed the case can be decided only by developing the consequences of the two principles in more detail and noting if any discrepancies turn up. Possibly there will be no conflicts; certainly we hope there are none with the fixed points of our considered judgments. The main question perhaps is whether one is prepared to accept the further definition of one's conception of right that the two principles represent. For, as we have seen, common sense presumably leaves the matter of weights undecided. The two principles may not so much oppose ordinary ideas as provide a relatively precise principle where common sense has little to say.

Finally, it is a political convention in a democratic society to appeal to the common good. No political party would admit to pressing for legislation to the disadvantage of any recognized social interest. But how, from a philosophical point of view, is this convention to be understood? Surely it is something more than the principle of efficiency, and we cannot assume that government always affects everyone's interests equally. Yet since we cannot maximize with respect to more than one point of view, it is natural, given the ethos of a democratic society, to single out that of the least advantaged and maximize their long-term prospects consistent with the liberties of equal citizenship. Moreover, it does seem that the policies that we most confidently think to be just do at least contribute positively to the well-being of this class, and hence that these policies are just throughout. Thus the difference principle is a reasonable extension of the political convention of a democracy once we face up to the necessity of choosing a complete conception of justice.

QUESTIONS

1. What does Rawls mean by the "principle of utility"? (267)

2. Why does Rawls think that the "strictness of commonsense notions of justice" are irrational as a philosophical doctrine? (268)

3. How would the "original position" and the "veil of ignorance" operate in Rawls's conception of a "just" society? (268)

4. How might Rawls's highly abstract theories of creating a just society be implemented in practice?

5. What is the difference Rawls refers to in the "difference principle"? (271)

6. What is the distinction between "chain connected" and "close-knit" inequalities? (272)

7. What type of transfer is Rawls referring to with the term *transfer branch*?

8. How could it be to the advantage of the worst-off citizens for more privileged citizens to inherit greater wealth, as Rawls says it can?

9. What does Rawls mean by a "feasible scheme" for proportional tax? (276)

10. What "loss in efficiency" does Rawls assume is inherent in setting up a just system of government? (276)

11. How can Rawls be confident that if social groupings and activities are allowed to develop within the context of a just system, the resulting distribution must be just, "whatever it happens to be"? (278)

12. What is it that Rawls feels one cannot "maximize" with respect to more than one point of view? (280)

FOR FURTHER REFLECTION

1. How does Rawls suggest that a society's choices to obtain its greatest good may be different from those of an individual?

2. Does Rawls see a just government as having practical advantages as well as ethical ones?

3. Can you identify any specific factor Rawls feels could thwart true distributive justice in the absence of just formative institutions?

4. How could the greater expectations of entrepreneurs raise the life prospects of the laboring class?

5. Is "just," for Rawls, the same as "fair"?

FRANK O'CONNOR

Frank O'Connor (1903–1966), the pseudonym for Michael O'Donovan, was born in the slums of Cork City, Ireland. He grew up learning to fear and dislike his father, "Big" Mick O'Donovan, a soldier and alcoholic who played the bass drum in a couple of military bands and was frequently unemployed. O'Connor's mother, Minnie, worked as a maid and tried to shield her only child from his father's drunken rages. Young O'Connor found that reading offered him something of an escape and spent hours in his attic bedroom reading everything from Shakespeare to comics.

He underperformed at school, often absent from class because of chronic headaches. But Minnie wanted her son to attend the best school in Ireland, so in 1913 she begged the Christian Brothers at North Monastery, a prestigious preparatory school, to admit him. The Brothers shortly determined that O'Connor was not university material and transferred him to the technical school, where his general lack of coordination in shop and science classes made him something of a menace to himself and his classmates. In 1916, the Christian Brothers asked him to leave the school.

In April that same year the bloody events of the Easter Rebellion gripped the country. The failed bid of Irish nationalists to seize control of Dublin was followed by the British army's execution of fifteen rebel leaders by firing squad, and this further inflamed Irish nationalism and rage against the British occupation. O'Connor's family did not go untouched. Minnie smuggled guns in her shopping bags for the Irish Republican Army. O'Connor, who had been captivated by the story of how rebel leader Patrick Pearse wrote a poem for his mother the night before his execution, now spent hours on end in the Carnegie Library, hungry to continue his education. By the time he was sixteen, O'Connor was teaching for the Gaelic League, giving Irish lessons in the countryside, and also volunteering his services to the IRA. At the age of seventeen, he published his first poem, in the *Sunday Independent*.

O'Connor became increasingly enmeshed in the country's politics, which took a more complicated and bitter turn in 1922 after the republicans objected to the terms of the new Irish Free State, which had left the new nation with only twenty-six of Ireland's thirty-two counties under full Irish control. Civil war broke out. In the first direct military action of his career, O'Connor was taken prisoner and sent to Gormanstown Internment Camp for a year, where he met other future Irish luminaries. There, ironically, he was able to further his education through the prison's program of lectures, concerts, and ample library resources.

In 1924, O'Connor attained a public library post. He used the pseudonym Frank O'Connor for the first time in 1925, in a translation of an old Irish poem appearing in the *Irish Statesman*. He became friends with George Russell—better known as A. E., William Butler Yeats, and other literati. In 1931, O'Connor sold his short story "Guests of the Nation" to *Atlantic Monthly* magazine, and a volume of stories carrying the title of the story was published in the same year to considerable acclaim. During his distinguished career, O'Connor would publish upward of 150 stories; direct the Abbey Theatre, in Dublin; and serve as broadcaster for the Ministry of Information in London during World War II. Forty-five of O'Connor's stories were published in the *New Yorker* between 1945 and 1961, and in the 1950s he was a visiting professor at Northwestern University, Harvard, and the University of Chicago. In 1961, he moved back to Ireland, where he died in 1966.

FRANK O'CONNOR

Guests of the Nation

1

A t dusk the big Englishman Belcher would shift his long legs out of
the ashes and ask, "Well, chums, what about it?" and Noble or me
would say, "As you please, chum" (for we had picked up some of their
curious expressions), and the little Englishman 'Awkins would light the
lamp and produce the cards. Sometimes Jeremiah Donovan would come up
of an evening and supervise the play, and grow excited over 'Awkins's cards
(which he always played badly), and shout at him as if he was one of our own,
"Ach, you divil you, why didn't you play the tray?" But, ordinarily, Jeremiah
was a sober and contented poor devil like the big Englishman Belcher and
was looked up to at all only because he was a fair hand at documents, though
slow enough at these, I vow. He wore a small cloth hat and big gaiters over
his long pants, and seldom did I perceive his hands outside the pockets of
that pants. He reddened when you talked to him, tilting from toe to heel
and back and looking down all the while at his big farmer's feet. His uncommon
broad accent was a great source of jest to me, I being from the town, as you
may recognise.

I couldn't at the time see the point of me and Noble being with Belcher
and 'Awkins at all, for it was and is my fixed belief you could have planted
that pair in any untended spot from this to Claregalway and they'd have stayed
put and flourished like a native weed. I never seen in my short experience two
men that took to the country as they did.

They were handed on to us by the Second Battalion to keep when the
search for them became too hot, and Noble and myself, being young, took
charge with a natural feeling of responsibility. But little 'Awkins made us
look like right fools when he displayed he knew the countryside as well as
we did and something more. "You're the bloke they calls Bonaparte," he
said to me. "Well, Bonaparte, Mary Brigid Ho'Connell was arskin abaout
you and said 'ow you'd a pair of socks belonging to 'er young brother." For
it seemed, as they explained it, that the Second used to have little evenings

of their own, and some of the girls of the neighbourhood would turn in, and, seeing they were such decent fellows, our lads couldn't well ignore the two Englishmen, but invited them in and were hail-fellow-well-met with them. 'Awkins told me he learned to dance "The Walls of Limerick" and "The Siege of Ennis" and "The Waves of Tory" in a night or two, though naturally he could not return the compliment, because our lads at that time did not dance foreign dances on principle.

So whatever privileges and favours Belcher and 'Awkins had with the Second they duly took with us, and after the first evening we gave up all pretence of keeping a close eye on their behaviour. Not that they could have got far, for they had a notable accent and wore khaki tunics and overcoats with civilian pants and boots. But it's my belief that they never had an idea of escaping and were quite contented with their lot.

Now, it was a treat to see how Belcher got off with the old woman of the house we were staying in. She was a great warrant to scold, and crotchety even with us, but before ever she had a chance of giving our guests, as I may call them, a lick of her tongue, Belcher had made her his friend for life. She was breaking sticks at the time, and Belcher, who hadn't been in the house for more than ten minute, jumped up out of his seat and went across to her.

"Allow me, madam." he says, smiling his queer little smile; "please allow me," and takes the hatchet from her hand. She was struck too parlatic to speak, and ever after Belcher would be at her heels, carrying a bucket, or basket, or load of turf, as the case might be. As Noble wittily remarked, he got into looking before she leapt, and hot water or any little thing she wanted, Belcher would have it ready before her. For such a huge man (and though I am five foot ten myself I had to look up to him) he had an uncommon shortness—or should I say lack—of speech. It took us some time to get used to him walking in and out like a ghost, without a syllable out of him. Especially because 'Awkins talked enough for a platoon, it was strange to hear big Belcher with his toes in the ashes come out with a solitary "Excuse me, chum," or "That's right, chum." His one and only abiding passion was cards, and I will say for him that he was a good card player. He could have fleeced me and Noble many a time; only if we lost to him. 'Awkins lost to us, and 'Awkins played with the money Belcher gave him.

'Awkins lost to us because he talked too much, and I think now we lost to Belcher for the same reason. 'Awkins and Noble would spit at one another about religion into the early hours of the morning, the little Englishman as you could see worrying the soul out of young Noble (whose brother was a priest) with a string of questions that would puzzle a cardinal. And to make it worse, even in treating of these holy subjects, 'Awkins had a deplorable tongue; I never in all my career struck across a man who could mix such a variety of cursing and bad language into the simplest topic. Oh, a terrible man was little 'Awkins, and a fright to argue! He never did a stroke of work, and when he had no one else to talk to he fixed his claws into the old woman.

I am glad to say that in her he met his match, for one day when he tried to get her to complain profanely of the drought, she gave him a great comedown by blaming the drought upon Jupiter Pluvius (a deity neither 'Awkins nor I had ever heard of, though Noble said among the pagans he was held to have something to do with the rain). And another day the same 'Awkins was swearing at the capitalists for starting the German war, when the old dame laid down her iron, puckered up her little crab's mouth, and said: "Mr. 'Awkins, you can say what you please about the war, thinking to deceive me because I'm an ignorant old woman, but I know well what started the war. It was that Italian count that stole the heathen divinity out of the temple in Japan, for believe me, Mr. 'Awkins, nothing but sorrow and want follows them that disturbs the hidden powers!" Oh, a queer old dame, as you remark!

2

So one evening we had our tea together, and 'Awkins lit the lamp and we all sat in to cards. Jeremiah Donovan came in, too, and sat down and watched us for a while. Though he was a shy man and didn't speak much, it was easy to see he had no great love for the two Englishmen, and I was surprised it hadn't struck me so clearly before. Well, like that in the story, a terrible dispute blew up late in the evening between 'Awkins and Noble, about capitalists and priests and love of your own country.

"The capitalists," says 'Awkins with an angry gulp, "the capitalists pays the priests to tell you abaout the next world, so's you waon't notice what they do in this!"

"Nonsense, man," says Noble, losing his temper. "Before ever a capitalist was thought of people believed in the next world."

'Awkins stood up as if he was preaching a sermon. "Oh, they did, did they?" he says with a sneer. "They believed all the things you believe, that's what you mean? And you believe that God created Hadam, and Hadam created Shem, and Shem created Jehoshophat. You believe all the silly hold fairy tale about Heve and Heden and the happle. Well, listen to me, chum. If you're entitled to 'old to a silly belief like that, I'm entitled to 'old to my own silly belief—which is that the fust thing your God created was a bleedin' capitalist, with mirality and Rolls-Royce complete. Am I right, chum?" he says then to Belcher.

"You're right, chum," says Belcher, with his queer smile, and gets up from the table to stretch his long legs into the fire and stroke his moustache. So, seeing that Jeremiah Donovan was going, and there was no knowing when the conversation about religion would be over, I took my hat and went out with him. We strolled down towards the village together, and then he suddenly stopped, and blushing and mumbling and shifting, as his way was, from toe to heel, he said I ought to be behind keeping guard on the prisoners. And I, having it put to me so suddenly, asked him what the hell he wanted a guard on the prisoners at all for, and said that so far as Noble and me were concerned we had talked it over and would rather be out with a column. "What use is that pair to us?" I asked him.

He looked at me for a spell and said, "I thought you knew we were keeping them as hostages." "Hostages—?" says I, not quite understanding. "The enemy," he says in his heavy way, "have prisoners belong' to us, and now they talk of shooting them. If they shoot our prisoners, we'll shoot theirs, and serve them right." "Shoot them?" said I, the possiblity just beginning to dawn on me. "Shoot them, exactly," said he. "Now," said I, "wasn't it very unforeseen of you not to tell me and Noble that?" "How so?" he asks. "Seeing that we were acting as guards upon them, of course." "And hadn't you reason enough to guess that much?" "We had not, Jeremiah Donovan, we had not. How were we to know when the men were on our hands so long?" "And what difference does it make? The enemy have our prisoners as long or longer, haven't they?" "It makes a great difference," said I. "How so?" said he sharply; but I couldn't tell him the difference it made, for I was struck too silly to speak. "And when may we expect to be released from this anyway?" said I. "You may expect it tonight," says he. "Or tomorrow or the next day at latest. So if it's hanging around here that worries you, you'll be free soon enough."

I cannot explain it even now, how sad I felt, but I went back to the cottage a miserable man. When I arrived the discussion was still on, 'Awkins holding forth to all and sundry that there was no next world at all and Noble answering in his best canonical style that there was. But I saw 'Awkins was after having the best of it. "Do you know what, chum?" he was saying, with his saucy smile. "I think you're jest as big a bleedin' hunbeliever as I am. You say you believe in the next world, and you know jest as much abaout the next world as I do, which is sweet damn-all. What's 'eaven? You dunno. Where's 'eaven? You dunno. Who's in 'eaven? You dunno. You know sweet damn-all! I arsk you again, do they wear wings?"

"Very well then," says Noble. "They do; is that enough for you? They do wear wings." "Where do they get them, then? Who makes them? 'Ave they a fact'ry for wings? 'Ave they a sort of store where you 'ands in your chit and tikes your bleedin' wings? Answer me that."

"Oh, you're an impossible man to argue with," says Noble. "Now, listen to me—." And the pair of them went off again.

It was long after midnight when we locked up the Englishmen and went to bed ourselves. As I blew out the candle I told Noble what Jeremiah Donovan had told me. Noble took it very quietly. After we had been in bed about an hour he asked me did I think we ought to tell the Englishmen. I having thought of the same thing myself (among many others) said no, because it was more than likely the English wouldn't shoot our men, and anyhow it wasn't to be supposed the brigade who were always up and down with the Second Battalion and knew the Englishmen well would be likely to want them bumped off. "I think so," says Noble. "It would be sort of cruelty to put the wind up them now." "It was very unforeseen of Jeremiah Donovan anyhow," says I, and by Noble's silence I realised he took my meaning.

So I lay there half the night, and thought and thought, and picturing myself and young Noble trying to prevent the brigade from shooting 'Awkins and Belcher sent a cold sweat out through me. Because there were men on the brigade you daren't let nor hinder without a gun in your hand, and at any rate, in those days disunion between brothers seemed to me an awful crime. I knew better after.

It was next morning we found it so hard to face Belcher and 'Awkins with a smile. We went about the house all day scarcely saying a word. Belcher didn't mind us much; he was stretched into the ashes as usual with his usual look of waiting in quietness for something unforeseen to happen, but little 'Awkins gave us a bad time with his audacious gibing and questioning. He was disgusted at Noble's not answering him back. "Why can't you tike your beating like a man, chum?" he says. "You with your Hadam and Heve! I'm a communist—or an anarchist. An anarchist, that's what I am." And for hours after he went round the house, mumbling when the fit took him, "Hadam and Heve! Hadam and Heve!"

3

I don't know clearly how we got over that day, but get over it we did, and a great relief it was when the tea things were cleared away and Belcher said in his peaceable manner, "Well, chums, what about it?" So we all sat round the table and 'Awkins produced the cards, and at that moment I heard Jeremiah Donovan's footsteps up the path, and a dark presentiment crossed my mind. I rose quietly from the table and laid my hand on him before he reached the door. "What do you want?" I asked him. "I want those two soldier friends of yours," he says reddening. "Is that the way it is, Jeremiah Donovan?" I ask. "That's the way. There were four of our lads went west this morning, one of them a boy of sixteen." "That's bad, Jeremiah," says I.

At that moment Noble came out, and we walked down the path together talking in whispers. Feeney, the local intelligence officer, was standing by the gate. "What are you going to do about it?" I asked Jeremiah Donovan. "I want you and Noble to bring them out: you can tell them they're being shifted again; that'll be the quietest way." "Leave me out of that," says Noble suddenly. Jeremiah Donovan looked at him hard for a minute or two. "All right so," he said peaceably. "You and Feeney collect a few tools from the shed and dig a hole by the far end of the bog. Bonaparte and I'll be after you in about twenty minutes. But whatever else you do, don't let anyone see you with the tools. No one must know but the four of ourselves."

We saw Feeney and Noble go round to the houseen, where the tools were kept, and sidle in. Everything, if I can so express myself, was tottering before my eyes, and I left Jeremiah Donovan to do the explaining as best he could, while I took a seat and said nothing. He told them they were to go back to the Second. 'Awkins let a mouthful of curses out of him at that, and it was plain that Belcher, though he said nothing, was duly perturbed. The old woman was for having them stay in spite of us, and she did not shut her mouth until Jeremiah Donovan lost his temper and said some nasty things to her. Within the house by this time it was pitch-dark, but no one thought of lighting the lamp, and in the darkness the two Englishmen fetched their khaki topcoats and said goodbye to the woman of the house. "Just as a man mikes a 'ome of a bleedin' place," mumbles 'Awkins shaking her by the hand, "some bastard at headquarters thinks you're too cushy and shunts you off." Belcher shakes her hand very hearty. "A thousand thanks, madam," he says, "a thousand thanks for everything . . ." as though he'd made it all up.

We go round to the back of the house and down towards the fatal bog. Then Jeremiah Donovan comes out with what is in his mind. "There were four of our lads shot by your fellows this morning, so now you're to be bumped off." "Cut that stuff out," says 'Awkins, flaring up. "It's bad enough to be mucked about such as we are without you plying at soldiers." "It's true," says Jeremiah Donovan. "I'm sorry, 'Awkins, but 'tis true," and comes out with the usual rigmarole about doing our duty and obeying our superiors. "Cut it out," says 'Awkins irritably. "Cut it out!"

Then, when Donovan sees he is not being believed he turns to me. "Ask Bonaparte here," he says. "I don't need to arsk Bonaparte. Me and Bonaparte are chums." "Isn't it true, Bonaparte?" says Jeremiah Donovan solemnly to me. "It is," I say sadly, "it is." 'Awkins stops. "Now, for Christ's sike . . ." "I mean it, chum," I say. "You daon't saound as if you mean it. You knaow well you don't mean it." "Well, if he don't I do," says Jeremiah Donovan. "Why the 'ell sh'd you want to shoot me, Jeremiah Donovan?" "Why the hell should your people take out four prisoners and shoot them in cold blood upon a barrack square?" I perceive Jeremiah Donovan is trying to encourage himself with hot words.

Anyway, he took little 'Awkins by the arm and dragged him on, but it was impossible to make him understand that we were in earnest. From which you will perceive how difficult it was for me, as I kept feeling my Smith and Wesson and thinking what I would do if they happened to put up a fight or run for it, and wishing in my heart they would. I knew if only they ran I would never fire on them. "Was Noble in this?" 'Awkins wanted to know, and we said yes. He laughed. But why should Noble want to shoot him? What had he done to us? Weren't we chums (the word lingers painfully in my memory)? Weren't we? Didn't we understand him and didn't he understand us? Did either of us imagine for an instant that he'd shoot us for all the so-and-so brigadiers in the so-and-so British army? By this time I began to perceive in the dusk the desolate edges of the bog that was to be their last earthly bed, and so great a sadness overtook my mind I could not answer him. We walked along the edge of it in the darkness, and every now and then 'Awkins would call a halt and begin again, just as if he was wound up, about us being chums, and I was in despair that nothing but the cold and open grave made ready for his presence would convince him that we meant it all. But all the same, if you can understand, I didn't want him to be bumped off.

4

At last we saw the unsteady glint of a lantern in the distance and made towards it. Noble was carrying it, and Feeney stood somewhere in the darkness behind, and somehow the picture of the two of them so silent in the boglands was like the pain of death in my heart. Belcher, on recognising Noble, said, " 'Allo, chum," in his usual peaceable way, but 'Awkins flew at the poor boy immediately, and the dispute began all over again, only that Noble hadn't a word to say for himself and stood there with the swaying lantern between his gaitered legs.

It was Jeremiah Donovan who did the answering. 'Awkins asked for the twentieth time (for it seemed to haunt his mind) if anybody thought he'd shoot Noble. "You would," says Jeremiah Donovan shortly. "I wouldn't, damn you!" "You would if you knew you'd be shot for not doing it." "I wouldn't, not if I was to be shot twenty times over; he's my chum. And Belcher wouldn't—isn't that right, Belcher?" "That's right, chum," says Belcher peaceably. "Damned if I would. Anyway, who says Noble'd be shot if I wasn't bumped off? What d'you think I'd do if I was in Noble's place and we were out in the middle of a blasted bog?" "What would you do?" "I'd go with him wherever he was going. I'd share my last bob with him and stick by 'im through thick and thin."

"We've had enough of this," says Jeremiah Donovan, cocking his revolver. "Is there any message you want to send before I fire?" "No, there isn't, but . . ." "Do you want to say your prayers?" 'Awkins came out with a cold-blooded remark that shocked even me and turned on Noble again. "Listen to me, Noble," he said. "You and me are chums. You won't come over to my side, so I'll come over to your side. Is that fair? Just you give me a rifle and I'll go with you wherever you want."

Nobody answered him.

"Do you understand?" he said. "I'm through with it all. I'm a deserter or anything else you like, but from this on I'm one of you. Does that prove to you that I mean what I say?" Noble raised his head, but as Donovan began to speak he lowered it again without answering. "For the last time, have you any messages to send?" says Donovan in a cold excited voice.

"Ah, shut up, you, Donovan; you don't understand me, but these fellows do. They're my chums; they stand by me and I stand by them. We're not the capitalist tools you seem to think us."

I alone of the crowd saw Donovan raise his Webley to the back of 'Awkins's neck, and as he did so I shut my eyes and tried to say a prayer. 'Awkins had begun to say something else when Donovan let fly, and as I opened my eyes at the bang, I saw him stagger at the knees and lie out flat at Noble's feet, slowly, and as quiet as a child, with the lantern light falling sadly upon on his lean legs and bright farmer's boots. We all stood very still for a while watching him settle out in the last agony.

Then Belcher quietly takes out a handkerchief and begins to tie it about his own eyes (for in our excitement we had forgotten to offer the same for 'Awkins), and, seeing it is not big enough, turns and asks for a loan of mine. I give it to him, and as he knots the two together he points with his foot at 'Awkins. "'E's not quite dead," he says. "Better give 'im another." Sure enough 'Awkins's left knee as we see it under the lantern is rising again. I bend down and put my gun to his ear; then, recollecting myself and the company of Belcher, I stand up again with a few hasty words. Belcher understands what is in my mind. "Give 'im 'is first," he says. "I don't mind. Poor bastard, we dunno what's 'appening to 'im now." As by this time I am beyond all feeling, I kneel down again and skilfully give 'Awkins the last shot so as to put him forever out of pain.

Belcher, who is fumbling a bit awkwardly with the handkerchiefs, comes out with a laugh when he hears the shot. It is the first time I have heard him laugh, and it sends a shiver down my spine, coming as it does so inappropriately upon the tragic death of his old friend. "Poor blighter," he says quietly. "And last night he was so curious abaout it all. It's very queer, chums, I always think. Naow, 'e knows as much abaout it as they'll ever let 'im know, and last night 'e was all in the dark."

Donovan helps him to tie the handkerchiefs about his eyes. "Thanks, chum," he says. Donovan asks him if there are any messages he would like to send. "Naow, chum," he says, "none for me. If any of you likes to write to 'Awkins's mother, you'll find a letter from 'er in 'is pocket. But my missus left me eight years ago. Went away with another fellow and took the kid with her. I likes the feelin' of a 'ome, (as you may 'ave noticed), but I couldn't start again after that."

We stand around like fools now that he can no longer see us. Donovan looks at Noble, and Noble shakes his head. Then Donovan raises his Webley again, and just at that moment Belcher laughs his queer nervous laugh again. He must think we are talking of him; anyway, Donovan lowers his gun. "'Scuse me, chums," says Belcher. "I feel I'm talking the 'ell of a lot . . . and so silly . . . abaout me being so 'andy abaout a 'ouse. But this thing come on me so sudden. You'll forgive me, I'm sure." "You don't want to say a prayer?" asks Jeremiah Donovan. "No, chum," he replies, "I don't think that'd 'elp. I'm ready if you want to get it over." "You understand," says Jeremiah Donovan, "it's not so much our doing. It's our duty, so to speak." Belcher's head is raised like a real blind man's, so that you can only see his nose and chin in the lamplight. "I never could make out what duty was myself," he said. "but I think you're all good lads, if that's what you mean. I'm not complaining." Noble, with a look of desperation, signals to Donovan, and in a flash Donovan raises his gun and fires. The big man goes over like a sack of meal, and this time there is no need of a second shot.

I don't remember much about the burying but that it was worse than all the rest, because we had to carry the warm corpses a few yards before we sunk them in the windy bog. It was all mad lonely, with only a bit of lantern between ourselves and the pitch-blackness, and birds hooting and screeching all round, disturbed by the guns. Noble had to search 'Awkins first to get the letter from his mother. Then, having smoothed all signs of the grave away, Noble and I collected our tools, and said goodbye to the others, and went back along the desolate edge of the treacherous bog without a word. We put the tools in the houseen and went into the house. The kitchen was pitch-black and cold, just as we left it, and the old woman was sitting over the hearth telling her beads. We walked past her into the room, and Noble struck a match to light the lamp. Just then she rose quietly and came to the doorway, being not at all so bold or crabbed as usual.

"What did ye do with them?" she says in a sort of whisper, and Noble took such a mortal start the match quenched in his trembling hand. "What's that?" he asks without turning round. "I heard ye," she said. "What did you hear?" asks Noble, but sure he wouldn't deceive a child the way he said it. "I heard ye. Do ye think I wasn't listening to ye putting the things back in the houseen?" Noble struck another match, and this time the lamp lit for him. "Was that what ye did with them?" she said, and Noble said nothing—after all, what could he say?

So then, by God, she fell on her two knees by the door and began telling her beads, and after a minute or two Noble went on his knees by the fireplace, so I pushed my way out past her and stood at the door, watching the stars and listening to the damned shrieking of the birds. It is so strange what you feel at such moments, and not to be written afterwards. Noble says he felt he seen everything ten times as big, perceiving nothing around him but the little patch of black bog with the two Englishmen stiffening into it; but with me it was the other way, as though the patch of bog where the Englishmen were was a thousand miles away from me, and even Noble mumbling just behind me and the old woman and the birds and the bloody stars were all far away, and I was somehow very small and very lonely. And anything that ever happened me after I never felt the same about again.

QUESTIONS

1. Why does the old woman refer to "Jupiter Pluvius" and the "heathen divinity out of the temple in Japan"? (287)

2. What is the old woman referring to when she speaks of "the hidden powers"? (287)

3. What is the purpose of Hawkins's and Noble's argument comparing theism and Marxism? Does the story ultimately indicate a clear winner to these disputes?

4. Is Bonaparte's unawareness that the Englishmen are not just prisoners but hostages (whose lives are in jeopardy) the result of Donovan deliberately withholding this information, or of an unintended misunderstanding?

5. Why do Donovan and Bonaparte disagree on whether the length of time the prisoners have been held in custody makes any difference?

6. When Donovan says, that it will "serve them right" about shooting the hostages in retaliation if the British execute Irishmen, does "them" refer to the government in London (an abstraction) or the individuals, Hawkins and Belcher? (288)

7. Given Bonaparte's familiarity with the prisoners and his strong objection to killing them, why doesn't he help them, or at least warn them?

8. Bonaparte says that "in those days disunion between brothers seemed to me an awful crime. I knew better after." (289) What does he mean by that last sentence?

9. Why does Donovan insist on keeping the execution secret, if it is done in retaliation for the execution of Irish prisoners by the British?

10. Why does Donovan provide such detail to Hawkins in his rhetorical question, "Why the hell should your people take out four prisoners and shoot them in cold blood upon a barrack square?" (290)

11. Is Hawkins telling the truth when he says he would never shoot Noble?

12. When Hawkins offers to join the Irish side, is it just a ploy to stay alive, or does he actually see his "friendship" with his Irish guards as more important than loyalty to his native England?

13. Is Belcher heroic to forgive his executioners, or is he deluded in considering them his "chums" who are just doing what they are obliged to do?

14. Would Noble and Bonaparte have felt the same degree of regret if the old woman had not stayed up waiting for them or asked where they had been?

FOR FURTHER REFLECTION

1. Does the title "Guests of the Nation" suggest any particular interpretation of this piece?

2. Does Donovan accurately describe his situation when he says that "it's not so much our doing. It's our duty, so to speak"?

3. Has Bonaparte changed his political convictions as a result of this experience, or has he simply learned to feel regret and horror about it?

4. By the rules of warfare, were Donovan and his Irish compatriots justified in killing Belcher and Hawkins?

5. What ways do people find to dissociate their consciences from responsibility for reprehensible acts in which they have become involved? Are any of these ways legitimate?

6. What might be the fundamental difference between Bonaparte and both Noble and the old woman that causes him to react so differently to the deaths of the English hostages?

Winner of the 1991 Nobel Prize in Literature, Nadine Gordimer (1923–) was born in Springs, a small mining town near Johannesburg, South Africa. She began writing as a child and published her first short story when she was fifteen. The library was a place of refuge for a white, English-speaking girl in a predominantly black country, and a Jewish student at a Catholic convent school. The stories of New Zealand writer Katherine Mansfield showed her that it was possible to write about a world that was familiar to her: "I realized here was somebody who was writing about this other world, whose seasons at least I shared. Then I understood it was possible to be a writer even if you didn't live in England." She has also cited D. H. Lawrence, Henry James, and Ernest Hemingway as influences. Gordimer published her first book, *Face to Face,* a collection of short stories, in 1949, and her first novel, *The Lying Days,* in 1953. Her later short-story collections include *Livingstone's Companions* (1971), *A Soldier's Embrace* (1980), and *Something Out There* (1984). Among her most highly regarded novels are *The Conservationist* (1974; winner of the Booker Prize), *Burger's Daughter* (1979), *July's People* (1981), *A Sport of Nature* (1987), and *None to Accompany Me* (1994). Gordimer's nonfiction collections include *The Essential Gesture: Writing, Politics, and Places* (1988), *Writing and Being* (1995), and *Living in Hope and History: Notes from Our Century* (1999).

Gordimer has been very protective of her private life, but she was a vocal critic of apartheid, the legally enforced system of racial discrimination in South Africa, especially after the arrest of a close friend in 1960. She befriended Nelson Mandela and joined the African National Congress before it was legal to do so, and she regularly gave speeches and took part in demonstrations. Gordimer has written that the writer's subject is "the consciousness of his own era." Indeed, though her books can stand as a kind of history of South Africa's human rights nightmare during the latter half of the twentieth century, their concerns are nonetheless universal. The intersection of public and private life is a recurring theme. Her work bears witness to the outrageous injustices of apartheid, but it also depicts the subtlest effects on relationships of the social and political environment—whatever its specific features may be. Reading Gordimer, we see that what we initially think of as our own pure perceptions of others are in fact often shaped by the beliefs and prejudices we cannot help bringing to any encounter.

Published in *Six Feet of the Country* (1956), "Which New Era Would That Be?" brings together Jake, a relatively affluent, middle-aged, mixed-race man, and Jennifer, a young, white, liberal activist woman. As soon as he meets Jennifer, Jake identifies her as belonging to a type he knows well and has no use for—a white woman who presumes to share his emotional reactions to apartheid's laws. This situation enables Gordimer to explore the difficulties inherent in acting on behalf of people whose suffering you cannot possibly experience in the same way as they do. More broadly, the story raises questions about how we relate to one another. Since we are all, ultimately, confined to our own thoughts and feelings, on what basis can community, not to mention intimacy, be established? The literal meaning of *apartheid*, an English word derived from Afrikaans, is "apartness." In "Which New Era Would That Be?" Gordimer invites us to look at the full range of forces that sustain the distance between her characters.

Which New Era
Would That Be?

J ake Alexander, a big, fat coloured man, half Scottish, half African, was
shaking a large pan of frying bacon on the gas stove in the back room
of his Johannesburg printing shop when he became aware that someone
was knocking on the door at the front of the shop. The sizzling fat and the
voices of the five men in the back room with him almost blocked sounds
from without, and the knocking was of the steady kind that might have
been going on for quite a few minutes. He lifted the pan off the flame with
one hand and with the other made an impatient silencing gesture, directed
at the bacon as well as the voices. Interpreting the movement as one of caution,
the men hurriedly picked up the tumblers and cups in which they had been
taking their end-of-the-day brandy at their ease, and tossed the last of it
down. Little yellow Klaas, whose hair was like ginger-coloured wire wool,
stacked the cups and glasses swiftly and hid them behind the dirty curtain
that covered a row of shelves.

"Who's that?" yelled Jake, wiping his greasy hands down his pants.

There was a sharp and playful tattoo, followed by an English voice:
"Me—Alister. For heaven's sake, Jake!"

The fat man put the pan back on the flame and tramped through the
dark shop, past the idle presses, to the door, and flung it open. "Mr. Halford"
he said. "Well, good to see you. Come in, man. In the back there, you can't
hear a thing." A young Englishman with gentle eyes, a stern mouth, and
flat, colourless hair which grew in an untidy, confused spiral from a double
crown stepped back to allow a young woman to enter ahead of him. Before
he could introduce her, she held out her hand to Jake, smiling, and shook
his firmly. "Good evening. Jennifer Tetzel," she said.

"Jennifer, this is Jake Alexander," the young man managed to get in,
over her shoulder.

The two had entered the building from the street through an archway
lettered NEW ERA BUILDING. "Which new era would that be?" the young
woman had wondered aloud, brightly, while they were waiting in the dim
hallway for the door to be opened, and Alister Halford had not known

whether the reference was to the discovery of deep-level gold mining that had saved Johannesburg from the ephemeral fate of a mining camp in the nineties, or to the optimism after the settlement of labour troubles in the twenties, or to the recovery after the world went off the gold standard in the thirties—really, one had no idea of the age of these buildings in this rundown end of the town. Now, coming in out of the deserted hallway gloom, which smelled of dust and rotting wood—the smell of waiting—they were met by the live, cold tang of ink and the homely, lazy odour of bacon fat—the smell of acceptance. There was not much light in the deserted workshop. The host blundered to the wall and switched on a bright naked bulb, up in the ceiling. The three stood blinking at one another for a moment: a coloured man with the fat of the man-of-the-world upon him, grossly dressed—not out of poverty but obviously because he liked it that way—in a rayon sports shirt that gaped and showed two hairy stomach rolls hiding his navel in a lipless grin, the pants of a good suit misbuttoned and held up round the waist by a tie instead of a belt, and a pair of expensive sports shoes, worn without socks; a young Englishman in a worn greenish tweed suit with a neo-Edwardian cut to the waistcoat that labelled it a leftover from undergraduate days; a handsome white woman who, as the light fell upon her, was immediately recognizable to Jake Alexander.

He had never met her before, but he knew the type well—had seen it over and over again at meetings of the Congress of Democrats, and other organizations where progressive whites met progressive blacks. These were the white women who, Jake knew, persisted in regarding themselves as your equal. That was even worse, he thought, than the parsons who persisted in regarding *you* as *their* equal. The parsons had had ten years at school and seven years at a university and theological school; you had carried sacks of vegetables from the market to white people's cars from the time you were eight years old until you were apprenticed to a printer, and your first woman, like your mother, had been a servant, whom you had visited in a backyard room, and your first gulp of whisky, like many of your other pleasures, had been stolen while a white man was not looking. Yet the good parson insisted that your picture of life was exactly the same as his own: *you* felt as *he* did. But these women—oh, Christ!—these women felt as *you* did. They were sure of it. They thought they understood the humiliation of the black man walking the streets only by the permission of a pass written out by a white person, and the guilt and swagger of the coloured man light-faced enough to slink, fugitive from his own skin, into the preserves—the cinemas, bars, libraries—marked Europeans Only. Yes, breathless with stout sensitivity, they insisted on walking the whole teeter-totter of the colour line. There was no escaping their understanding. They even insisted on feeling the resentment *you* must feel at their identifying themselves with your feelings . . .

Here was the black hair of a determined woman (last year they wore it pulled tightly back into an oddly perched knot; this year it was cropped and curly as a lap dog's); the round, bony brow unpowdered in order to show off the tan; the red mouth; the unrouged cheeks; the big, lively, handsome eyes, dramatically painted, that would look into yours with such intelligent, eager honesty—eager to mirror what Jake Alexander, a big, fat coloured man interested in women, money, brandy, and boxing, was feeling. Who the hell wants a woman to look at you honestly, anyway? What has all this to do with a *woman*—with what men and women have for each other in their eyes? She was wearing a wide black skirt, a white cotton blouse baring a good deal of her breasts, and earrings that seemed to have been made by a blacksmith out of bits of scrap iron. On her feet she had sandals whose narrow thongs wound between her toes, and the nails of the toes were painted plum colour. By contrast, her hands were neglected-looking—sallow, unmanicured—and on one thin finger there swivelled a huge gold seal ring. She was good-looking, he supposed with disgust.

He stood there, fat, greasy, and grinning at the two visitors so lingeringly that his grin looked insolent. Finally he asked, "What brings you this end of town, Mr. Halford? Sightseeing with the lady?"

The young Englishman gave Jake's arm a squeeze, where the short sleeve of the rayon shirt ended. "Just thought I'd look you up, Jake," he said, jolly.

"Come on in, come on in," said Jake on a rising note, shambling ahead of them into the company of the back room. "Here, what about a chair for the lady?" He swept a pile of handbills from the seat of a kitchen chair onto the dusty concrete floor, picked up the chair, and planked it down again in the middle of the group of men, who had risen awkwardly at the visitors' entrance. "You know Maxie Ndube? And Temba?" Jake said, nodding at two of the men who surrounded him.

Alister Halford murmured with polite warmth his recognition of Maxie, a small, dainty-faced African in neat, businessman's dress, then said inquiringly and hesitantly to Temba, "Have we? When?"

Temba was a coloured man—a mixture of the bloods of black slaves and white masters, blended long ago, in the days when the Cape of Good Hope was a port of refreshment for the Dutch East India Company. He was tall and pale, with a large Adam's apple, enormous black eyes, and the look of a musician in a jazz band; you could picture a trumpet lifted to the ceiling in those long yellow hands, that curved spine hunched forward to shield a low note. "In Durban last year, Mr. Halford, you remember?" he said eagerly. "I'm sure we met—or perhaps I only saw you there."

"Oh, at the Congress? Of course I remember you!" Halford apologized. "You were in a delegation from the Cape?"

"Miss—?" Jake Alexander waved a hand between the young woman, Maxie, and Temba.

"Jennifer. Jennifer Tetzel," she said again clearly, thrusting out her hand. There was a confused moment when both men reached for it at once and then hesitated, each giving way to the other. Finally the hand shaking was accomplished, and the young woman seated herself confidently on the chair.

Jake continued, offhand, "Oh, and of course Billy Boy"—Alister signalled briefly to a black man with sad, bloodshot eyes who stood awkwardly, back a few steps, against some rolls of paper—"and Klaas and Albert." Klaas and Albert had in their mixed blood some strain of the Bushman, which gave them a batrachian yellowness and toughness, like one of those toads that (prehistoric as the Bushman is) are mythically believed to have survived into modern times (hardly more fantastically than the Bushman himself has survived) by spending centuries shut up in an air bubble in a rock. Like Billy Boy, Klaas and Albert had backed away, and, as if abasement against the rolls of paper, the wall, or the window were a greeting in itself, the two little coloured men and the big African only stared back at the masculine nods of Alister and the bright smile of the young woman.

"You up from the Cape for anything special now?" Alister said to Temba as he made a place for himself on a corner of a table that was littered with photographic blocks, bits of type, poster proofs, a bottle of souring milk, a bow tie, a pair of red braces, and a number of empty Coca-Cola bottles.

"I've been living in Durban for a year. Just got the chance of a lift to Jo'burg," said the gangling Temba.

Jake had set himself up easily, leaning against the front of the stove and facing Miss Jennifer Tetzel on her chair. He jerked his head towards Temba and said, "Real banana boy." Young white men brought up in the strong Anglo-Saxon tradition of the province of Natal are often referred to, and refer to themselves, as "banana boys," even though fewer and fewer of them have any connection with the dwindling number of vast banana estates that once made their owners rich. Jake's broad face, where the bright-pink cheeks of a Highland complexion—inherited, along with his name, from his Scottish father—showed oddly through his coarse beige skin, creased up in appreciation of his own joke. And Temba threw back his head and laughed, his Adam's apple bobbing, at the idea of himself as a cricket-playing white public-school boy.

"There's nothing like Cape Town, is there?" said the young woman to him, her head charmingly on one side, as if this conviction were something she and he shared.

"Miss Tetzel's up here to look us over. She's from Cape Town," Alister explained.

She turned to Temba with her beauty, her strong provocativeness, full on, as it were. "So we're neighbours?"

Jake rolled one foot comfortably over the other, and a spluttering laugh pursed out the pink inner membrane of his lips.

"Where did you live?" she went on, to Temba.

"Cape Flats," he said. Cape Flats is a desolate coloured slum in the bush outside Cape Town.

"Me, too," said the girl, casually.

Temba said politely, "You're kidding," and then looked down uncomfortably at his hands, as if they had been guilty of some clumsy movement. He had not meant to sound so familiar; the words were not the right ones.

"I've been there nearly ten months," she said.

"Well, some people've got queer tastes," Jake remarked, laughing, to no one in particular, as if she were not there.

"How's that?" Temba was asking her shyly, respectfully.

She mentioned the name of a social rehabilitation scheme that was in operation in the slum. "I'm assistant director of the thing at the moment. It's connected with the sort of work I do at the university, you see, so they've given me fifteen months' leave from my usual job."

Maxie noticed with amusement the way she used the word *job*, as if she were a plumber's mate; he and his educated African friends—journalists and schoolteachers—were careful to talk only of their "professions." "Good works," he said, smiling quietly.

She planted her feet comfortably before her, wriggling on the hard chair, and said to Temba with mannish frankness, "It's a ghastly place. How in God's name did you survive living there? I don't think I can last out more than another few months, and I've always got my flat in Cape Town to escape to on Sundays, and so on."

While Temba smiled, turning his protruding eyes aside slowly, Jake looked straight at her and said, "Then why do you, lady, why *do* you?"

"Oh, I don't know. Because I don't see why anyone else—any one of the people who live there—should have to, I suppose." She laughed before anyone else could at the feebleness, the philanthropic uselessness of what she was saying. "Guilt, what have you . . ."

Maxie shrugged, as if at the mention of some expensive illness he had never been able to afford and whose symptoms he could not imagine.

There was a moment of silence; the two coloured men and the big black man standing back against the wall watched anxiously, as if some sort of signal might be expected, possibly from Jake Alexander, their boss, the man who, like themselves, was not white, yet who owned his own business and had a car and money and strange friends—sometimes even white people, such as these. The three of them were dressed in the ill-matched castoff clothing that all humble workpeople who are not white wear in Johannesburg, and they had not lost the ability of rural people to stare, unembarrassed and unembarrassing.

Jake winked at Alister; it was one of his mannerisms—a bookie's wink, a stage comedian's wink. "Well, how's it going, boy, how's it going?" he said. His turn of phrase was barroom bonhomie; with luck, he *could* get into a bar, too. With a hat to cover his hair and his coat collar well up, and only a bit of greasy pink cheek showing, he had slipped into the bars of the shabbier Johannesburg hotels with Alister many times and got away with it. Alister, on the other hand, had got away with the same sort of thing narrowly several times, too, when he had accompanied Jake to a shebeen in a coloured location, where it was illegal for a white man to be, as well as illegal for anyone at all to have a drink; twice Alister had escaped a raid by jumping out of a window. Alister had been in South Africa only eighteen months, as correspondent for a newspaper in England, and because he was only two or three years away from undergraduate escapades such incidents seemed to give him a kind of nostalgic pleasure; he found them funny. Jake, for his part, had decided long ago (with the great help of the money he had made) that he would take the whole business of the colour bar as humorous. The combination of these two attitudes, stemming from such immeasurably different circumstances, had the effect of making their friendship less self-conscious than is usual between a white man and a coloured one.

"They tell me it's going to be a good thing on Saturday night?" said Alister, in the tone of questioning someone in the know. He was referring to a boxing match between two coloured heavyweights, one of whom was a protégé of Jake.

Jake grinned deprecatingly, like a fond mother. "Well, Pikkie's a good boy," he said. "I tell you, it'll be something to see." He danced about a little on his clumsy toes in pantomime of the way a boxer nimbles himself and collapsed against the stove, his belly shaking with laughter at his breathlessness.

"Too much smoking, too many brandies, Jake," said Alister.

"With me, it's too many women, boy."

"We were just congratulating Jake," said Maxie in his soft, precise voice, the indulgent, tongue-in-cheek tone of the protégé who is superior to his patron, for Maxie was one of Jake's boys, too—of a different kind. Though Jake had decided that for him being on the wrong side of a colour bar was ludicrous, he was as indulgent to those who took it seriously and politically, the way Maxie did, as he was to any up-and-coming youngster who, say, showed talent in the ring or wanted to go to America and become a singer. They could all make themselves free of Jake's pocket, and his printing shop, and his room in the lower end of the town, where the building had fallen below the standard of white people but was far superior to the kind of thing most coloureds and blacks were accustomed to.

"Congratulations on what?" the young white woman asked. She had a way of looking up around her, questioningly, from face to face, that came of long familiarity with being the centre of attention at parties.

"Yes, you can shake my hand, boy," said Jake to Alister. "I didn't see it, but these fellows tell me that my divorce went through. It's in the papers today."

"Is that so? But from what I hear, you won't be a free man long," Alister said teasingly.

Jake giggled, and pressed at one gold-filled tooth with a strong fingernail. "You heard about the little parcel I'm expecting from Zululand?" he asked.

"Zululand?" said Alister. "I thought your Lila came from Stellenbosch." Maxie and Temba laughed.

"Lila? *What* Lila?" said Jake with exaggerated innocence.

"You're behind the times," said Maxie to Alister.

"You know I like them—well, sort of round," said Jake. "Don't care for the thin kind, in the long run."

"But Lila had red hair!" Alister goaded him. He remembered the incongruously dyed, straightened hair on a fine coloured girl whose nostrils dilated in the manner of certain fleshy water-plants seeking prey.

Jennifer Tetzel got up and turned the gas off on the stove, behind Jake. "That bacon'll be like charred string," she said.

Jake did not move—merely looked at her lazily. "This is not the way to talk with a lady around." He grinned, unapologetic.

She smiled at him and sat down, shaking her earrings. "Oh, I'm divorced myself. Are we keeping you people from your supper? Do go ahead and eat. Don't bother about us."

Jake turned around, gave the shrunken rashers a mild shake and put the pan aside. "Hell, no," he said. "Anytime. But"—turning to Alister—"won't you have something to eat?" He looked about, helpless and unconcerned, as if to indicate an absence of plates and a general careless lack of equipment such as white women would be accustomed to use when they ate. Alister said quickly, no, he had promised to take Jennifer to Moorjee's.

Of course, Jake should have known; a woman like that would *want* to be taken to eat at an Indian place in Vrededorp, even though she was white, and free to eat at the best hotel in town. He felt suddenly, after all, the old gulf opening between himself and Alister: what did *they* see in such women—bristling, sharp, all-seeing, knowing women who talked like men, who wanted to show all the time that, apart from sex, they were exactly the same as men? He looked at Jennifer and her clothes and thought of the way a white woman could look: one of those big, soft, European women with curly yellow hair, with very high-heeled shoes that made them shake softly when they walked, with a strong scent, like hot flowers, coming up, it seemed, from their jutting breasts under the lace and pink and blue and all the other pretty things they wore—women with nothing resistant about them except, buried in white, boneless fingers, those red, pointed nails that scratched faintly at your palms.

"You should have been along with me at lunch today," said Maxie to no one in particular. Or perhaps the soft voice, a vocal tiptoe, was aimed at Alister, who was familiar with Maxie's work as an organizer of African trade unions. The group in the room gave him their attention (Temba with the little encouraging grunt of one who has already heard the story), but Maxie paused a moment, smiling ruefully at what he was about to tell. Then he said, "You know George Elson?" Alister nodded. The man was a white lawyer who had been arrested twice for his participation in anti-colour-bar movements.

"Oh, George? I've worked with George often in Cape Town," put in Jennifer.

"Well," continued Maxie, "George Elson and I went out to one of the industrial towns on the East Rand. We were interviewing the bosses, you see, not the men, and at the beginning it was all right, though once or twice the girls in the offices thought I was George's driver—'Your boy can wait outside.'" He laughed, showing small, perfect teeth; everything about him was finely made—his straight-fingered dark hands, the curved African nostrils of his small nose, his little ears, which grew close to the sides of his delicate head. The others were silent, but the young woman laughed, too.

"We even got tea in one place," Maxie went on. "One of the girls came in with two cups and a tin mug. But old George took the mug."

Jennifer Tetzel laughed again, knowingly.

"Then, just about lunchtime, we came to this place I wanted to tell you about. Nice chap, the manager. Never blinked an eye at me; called me mister. And after we'd talked, he said to George, 'Why not come home with me for lunch?' So of course George said, 'Thanks, but I'm with my friend here.' 'Oh, that's OK,' said the chap. 'Bring him along.' Well, we go along to this house, and the chap disappears into the kitchen, and then he comes back and we sit in the lounge and have a beer, and then the servant comes along and says lunch is ready. Just as we're walking into the dining room, the chap takes me by the arm and says, 'I've had *your* lunch laid on a table on the stoep. You'll find it's all perfectly clean and nice, just what we're having ourselves.'"

"Fantastic," murmured Alister.

Maxie smiled and shrugged, looking around at them all. "It's true."

"After he'd asked you, and he'd sat having a drink with you?" Jennifer said closely, biting in her lower lip, as if this were a problem to be solved psychologically.

"Of course," said Maxie.

Jake was shaking with laughter, like some obscene silenus. There was no sound out of him, but saliva gleamed on his lips, and his belly, at the level of Jennifer Tetzel's eyes, was convulsed.

Temba said soberly, in the tone of one whose goodwill makes it difficult for him to believe in the unease of his situation, "I certainly find it worse here than at the Cape. I can't remember, y'know, about buses. I keep getting put off European buses."

Maxie pointed to Jake's heaving belly. "Oh, I'll tell you a better one than that," he said. "Something that happened in the office one day. Now, the trouble with me is, apparently, I don't talk like a native." This time everyone laughed, except Maxie himself, who, with the instinct of a good raconteur, kept a polite, modest, straight face.

"You know, that's true," interrupted the young white woman. "You have none of the usual softening of the vowels of most Africans. And you haven't got an Afrikaans accent, as some Africans have, even if they get rid of the African thing."

"Anyway, I'd had to phone a certain firm several times," Maxie went on, "and I'd got to know the voice of the girl at the other end, and she'd got to know mine. As a matter of fact, she must have liked the sound of me, because she was getting very friendly. We fooled about a bit, exchanged first names, like a couple of kids—hers was Peggy—and she said, eventually, 'Aren't you ever going to come to the office yourself?'" Maxie paused a moment, and his tongue flicked at the side of his mouth in a brief, nervous gesture. When he spoke again, his voice was flat, like the voice of a man who is telling a joke and suddenly thinks that perhaps it is not such a good one after all. "So I told her I'd be in next day, about four. I walked in, sure enough, just as I said I would. She was a pretty girl, blonde, you know, with very tidy hair—I guessed she'd just combed it to be ready for me. She looked up and said, 'Yes?' holding out her hand for the messenger's book or parcel she thought I'd brought. I took her hand and shook it and said, 'Well, here I am, on time—I'm Maxie, Maxie Ndube.'"

"What'd she do?" asked Temba eagerly.

The interruption seemed to restore Maxie's confidence in his story. He shrugged gaily. "She almost dropped my hand, and then she pumped it like a mad thing, and her neck and ears went so red I thought she'd burn up. Honestly, her ears were absolutely shining. She tried to pretend she'd known all along, but I could see she was terrified someone would come from the inner office and see her shaking hands with a native. So I took pity on her and went away. Didn't even stay for my appointment with her boss. When I went back to keep the postponed appointment the next week, we pretended we'd never met."

Temba was slapping his knee. "God, I'd have loved to see her face!" he said.

Jake wiped away a tear from his fat cheek—his eyes were light blue and produced tears easily when he laughed—and said, "That'll teach you not to talk swanky, man. Why can't you talk like the rest of us?"

"Oh, I'll watch out on the 'missus' and 'baas' stuff in future," said Maxie.

Jennifer Tetzel cut into their laughter with her cool, practical voice. "Poor little girl, she probably liked you awfully, Maxie, and was really disappointed. You mustn't be too harsh on her. It's hard to be punished for not being black."

The moment was one of astonishment rather than irritation. Even Jake, who had been sure that there could be no possible situation between white and black he could not find amusing, only looked quickly from the young woman to Maxie, in a hiatus between anger, which he had given up long ago, and laughter, which suddenly failed him. On his face was admiration more than anything else—sheer, grudging admiration. This one was the best yet. This one was the coolest ever.

"Is it?" said Maxie to Jennifer, pulling in the corners of his mouth and regarding her from under slightly raised eyebrows. Jake watched. Oh, she'd have a hard time with Maxie. Maxie wouldn't give up his suffering-tempered blackness so easily. You hadn't much hope of knowing what Maxie was feeling at any given moment, because Maxie not only never let you know but made you guess wrong. But this one was the best yet.

She looked back at Maxie, opening her eyes very wide, twisting her sandalled foot on the swivel of its ankle, smiling. "Really, I assure you it is."

Maxie bowed to her politely, giving way with a falling gesture of his hand.

Alister had slid from his perch on the crowded table, and now, prodding Jake playfully in the paunch, he said, "We have to get along."

Jake scratched his ear and said again, "Sure you won't have something to eat?"

Alister shook his head. "We had hoped you'd offer us a drink, but—"

Jake wheezed with laughter but this time was sincerely concerned. "Well, to tell you the truth, when we heard the knocking, we just swallowed the last of the bottle off, in case it was someone it shouldn't be. I haven't a drop in the place till tomorrow. Sorry, chappie. Must apologize to you, lady, but we black men've got to drink in secret. If we'd've known it was you two . . ."

Maxie and Temba had risen. The two wizened coloured men, Klaas and Albert, and the sombre black Billy Boy shuffled helplessly, hanging about.

Alister said, "Next time, Jake, next time. We'll give you fair warning and you can lay it on."

Jennifer shook hands with Temba and Maxie, called, "Goodbye! Goodbye!" to the others, as if they were somehow out of earshot in that small room. From the door, she suddenly said to Maxie, "I feel I must tell you. About that other story—your first one, about the lunch. I don't believe it. I'm sorry, but I honestly don't. It's too illogical to hold water."

It was the final self-immolation by honest understanding. There was absolutely no limit to which that understanding would not go. Even if she could not believe Maxie, she must keep her determined good faith with him by confessing her disbelief. She would go to the length of calling him a liar to show by frankness how much she respected him—to insinuate, perhaps, that she was *with him*, even in the need to invent something about a white man that she, because she herself was white, could not believe. It was her last bid for Maxie.

The small, perfectly made man crossed his arms and smiled, watching her go. Maxie had no price.

Jake saw his guests out of the shop and switched off the light after he had closed the door behind them. As he walked back through the dark, where his presses smelled metallic and cool, he heard, for a few moments, the clear voice of the white woman and the low, noncommittal English murmur of Alister, his friend, as they went out through the archway into the street.

He blinked a little as he came back to the light and the faces that confronted him in the back room. Klaas had taken the dirty glasses from behind the curtain and was holding them one by one under the tap in the sink. Billy Boy and Albert had come closer out of the shadows and were leaning their elbows on a roll of paper. Temba was sitting on the table, swinging his foot. Maxie had not moved, and stood just as he had, with his arms folded. No one spoke.

Jake began to whistle softly through the spaces between his front teeth, and he picked up the pan of bacon, looked at the twisted curls of meat, jellied now in cold white fat, and put it down again absently. He stood a moment, heavily, regarding them all, but no one responded. His eye encountered the chair that he had cleared for Jennifer Tetzel to sit on. Suddenly he kicked it, hard, so that it went flying onto its side. Then, rubbing his big hands together and bursting into loud whistling to accompany an impromptu series of dance steps, he said, "Now, boys!" and as they stirred, he planked the pan down on the ring and turned the gas up till it roared beneath it.

QUESTIONS

1. About women like Jennifer, Jake thinks there is "no escaping their understanding." (300) Does he escape Jennifer's understanding?

2. Why does the narrator emphasize Jake's fatness?

3. Is Jake's reaction to Jennifer more the result of his attitude toward women or his attitude toward whites?

4. What is meant by the narrator's question, paraphrasing Jake's thinking, "What has all this to do with a *woman*—with what men and women have for each other in their eyes"? (301)

5. When Jake concludes that Jennifer is good-looking, why does he feel disgust?

6. Why does Jake refer to Temba as a "real banana boy"? (302)

7. Why does Jennifer laugh at "the feebleness, the philanthropic uselessness" of the reason she offers for living in Cape Flats? (303) Are we meant to agree with this characterization?

8. Why does Jake think of someone like Maxie, who takes the color bar "seriously and politically," as he would think of any "up-and-coming youngster who, say, showed talent in the ring or wanted to go to America and become a singer"? (304)

9. What do Jake's thoughts about "the way a white woman could look" tell us about him? (305)

10. What distinguishes Jennifer's and Jake's responses to Maxie's story about the man who invited Maxie and George to lunch?

11. Why does Maxie suddenly lose confidence in his story about the girl on the telephone who thinks he is white?

12. When Jennifer says it's "hard to be punished for not being black," why does Jake respond with "sheer, grudging admiration" instead of laughter? In what sense does he think Jennifer is "the best yet"? (308)

13. Why does Maxie bow to Jennifer politely when she assures him it is hard to be punished for not being black?

14. When Alister says he wished Jake had offered them a drink, why is Jake "sincerely concerned"? (308)

15. Why does Jake kick the chair Jennifer had been using?

16. By the end of the story, are we meant to think that Jake's assessment upon first meeting Jennifer was fair?

FOR FURTHER REFLECTION

1. Is opposition to an injustice you have not suffered as legitimate as opposition to one you have?

2. How might humor be useful in the face of injustice?

3. Is it possible to avoid making assumptions about individuals based on the traits they appear to share with other people?

4. Can you recall an instance in which you did not appreciate another person's effort to understand something you experienced? Why were you not appreciative?

5. Is political oppression an inevitable feature of human society, or do you think a future entirely without oppression anywhere in the world is possible?

R aymond Carver (1938 –1988) was born in Oregon and grew up in Yakima, Washington, a town east of the Cascade Mountains. His father was employed in the local sawmill; his mother worked in retail and waited tables. Carver married his sixteen-year-old sweetheart, Maryann Burke, when he was nineteen, and the couple had two children by the time he was twenty. After leaving his job at the sawmill, Carver proceeded to take day classes at the local community college and worked a series of night jobs: delivery boy, gas station attendant, janitor.

In 1958, Carver moved with his family to Paradise, California, and enrolled at Chico State College, where he took creative-writing courses with John Gardner, who was for Carver an important mentor and influence. Carver's first published short story, "The Furious Seasons," appeared in the student literary magazine, *Selection*, in 1961. Two years later he graduated from Humboldt State and was admitted to the Iowa Writers' Workshop, where he was able to stay only one year due to financial hardship. Back in Sacramento in 1964, Carver continued to write and work odd jobs—as a hotel desk clerk, as a stock boy, and then, for three years, as a custodian at Mercy Hospital.

"Will You Please Be Quiet, Please?" was included in *The Best American Short Stories 1967*. In that same year, Carver's father died, at the age of fifty-three, from acute alcoholism, and Carver's own drinking, already a problem, accelerated. As he described it in one interview, "I more or less gave up, threw in the towel, and took to full-time drinking as a serious pursuit." He also declared bankruptcy and took his first white-collar job, as a science textbook editor at Science Research Associates, in Palo Alto.

He was fired by the publisher three years later, but in spite of the pressures of family, poverty, and drink, by the early 1970s Carver had established himself as a talented young short-story writer and poet, earning several literary awards and getting teaching appointments at the Iowa Writers' Workshop and campuses on the West Coast. His worsening alcohol abuse forced him to quit teaching at Santa Barbara, and he went through a second bankruptcy. During this stage he lived in a chronic state of extremes: bouts of binge drinking that nearly killed him, and excruciating periods of drying out at rehabilitation centers. In 1977, he joined Alcoholics Anonymous, giving up drinking for good. His marriage also ended, and for the last ten years of his life, he lived with the poet Tess Gallagher. Carver's books during this final decade cemented his reputation: *Will You Please Be Quiet, Please* (1976) was nominated for a National Book Award; the title story of *What We Talk About When We Talk About Love* (1981) was included in the Pushcart Prize anthology; *Cathedral* (1983) was nominated for both a National Book Critics Circle Award and a Pulitzer Prize; and *Where Water Comes Together with Other Water* (1985) won *Poetry* magazine's Levinson Prize. In 1987, Carver discovered that he had lung cancer, and he died the next year.

If during the early part of his career Carver was often identified with the "minimalist" or "dirty realist" schools of American fiction, by the time of his death Carver was frequently compared to masters of the short story including Chekhov and Cheever. In an interview during the last year of his life, Carver observed that certain critics accused him of "painting too dark a picture of American life, of not putting a happy face on America." Critic Morris Dickstein has likened Carver's stories to the pared-down human figures and interiors seen in Edward Hopper's paintings, and novelist Robert Stone has called Carver "the best American short-story writer since Hemingway."

What We Talk About When We Talk About Love

M y friend Mel McGinnis was talking. Mel McGinnis is a cardiologist, and sometimes that gives him the right.

The four of us were sitting around his kitchen table drinking gin. Sunlight filled the kitchen from the big window behind the sink. There were Mel and me and his second wife, Teresa—Terri, we called her—and my wife, Laura. We lived in Albuquerque then. But we were all from somewhere else.

There was an ice bucket on the table. The gin and the tonic water kept going around, and we somehow got on the subject of love. Mel thought real love was nothing less than spiritual love. He said he'd spent five years in a seminary before quitting to go to medical school. He said he still looked back on those years in the seminary as the most important years in his life.

Terri said the man she lived with before she lived with Mel loved her so much he tried to kill her. Then Terri said, "He beat me up one night. He dragged me around the living room by my ankles. He kept saying, 'I love you, I love you, you bitch.' He went on dragging me around the living room. My head kept knocking on things." Terri looked around the table. "What do you do with love like that?"

She was a bone-thin woman with a pretty face, dark eyes, and brown hair that hung down her back. She liked necklaces made of turquoise, and long pendant earrings.

"My God, don't be silly. That's not love, and you know it," Mel said. "I don't know what you'd call it, but I sure know you wouldn't call it love."

"Say what you want to, but I know it was," Terri said. "It may sound crazy to you, but it's true just the same. People are different, Mel. Sure, sometimes he may have acted crazy. Okay. But he loved me. In his own way maybe, but he loved me. There was love there, Mel. Don't say there wasn't."

Mel let out his breath. He held his glass and turned to Laura and me. "The man threatened to kill me," Mel said. He finished his drink and reached for the gin bottle. "Terri's a romantic. Terri's of the kick-me-so-I'll-know-you-love-me school. Terri, hon, don't look that way." Mel reached across the table and touched Terri's cheek with his fingers. He grinned at her.

"Now he wants to make up," Terri said.

"Make up what?" Mel said. "What is there to make up? I know what I know. That's all."

"How'd we get started on this subject, anyway?" Terri said. She raised her glass and drank from it. "Mel always has love on his mind," she said. "Don't you, honey?" She smiled, and I thought that was the last of it.

"I just wouldn't call Ed's behavior love. That's all I'm saying, honey," Mel said. "What about you guys?" Mel said to Laura and me. "Does that sound like love to you?"

"I'm the wrong person to ask," I said. "I didn't even know the man. I've only heard his name mentioned in passing. I wouldn't know. You'd have to know the particulars. But I think what you're saying is that love is an absolute."

Mel said, "The kind of love I'm talking about is. The kind of love I'm talking about, you don't try to kill people."

Laura said, "I don't know anything about Ed, or anything about the situation. But who can judge anyone else's situation?"

I touched the back of Laura's hand. She gave me a quick smile. I picked up Laura's hand. It was warm, the nails polished, perfectly manicured. I encircled the broad wrist with my fingers, and I held her.

"When I left, he drank rat poison," Terri said. She clasped her arms with her hands. "They took him to the hospital in Santa Fe. That's where we lived then, about ten miles out. They saved his life. But his gums went crazy from it. I mean, they pulled away from his teeth. After that, his teeth stood out like fangs. My God," Terri said. She waited a minute, then let go of her arms and picked up her glass.

"What people won't do!" Laura said.

"He's out of the action now," Mel said. "He's dead."

Mel handed me the saucer of limes. I took a section, squeezed it over my drink, and stirred the ice cubes with my finger.

"It gets worse," Terri said. "He shot himself in the mouth. But he bungled that too. Poor Ed," she said. Terri shook her head.

"Poor Ed nothing," Mel said. "He was dangerous."

Mel was forty-five years old. He was tall and rangy with curly soft hair. His face and arms were brown from the tennis he played. When he was sober, his gestures, all his movements, were precise, very careful.

"He did love me though, Mel. Grant me that," Terri said. "That's all I'm asking. He didn't love me the way you love me. I'm not saying that. But he loved me. You can grant me that, can't you?"

"What do you mean, he bungled it?" I said.

Laura leaned forward with her glass. She put her elbows on the table and held her glass in both hands. She glanced from Mel to Terri and waited

316

with a look of bewilderment on her open face, as if amazed that such things happened to people you were friendly with.

"How'd he bungle it when he killed himself?" I said.

"I'll tell you what happened," Mel said. "He took this twenty-two pistol he'd bought to threaten Terri and me with. Oh, I'm serious, the man was always threatening. You should have seen the way we lived in those days. Like fugitives. I even bought a gun myself. Can you believe it? A guy like me? But I did. I bought one for self-defense and carried it in the glove compartment. Sometimes I'd have to leave the apartment in the middle of the night. To go to the hospital, you know? Terri and I weren't married then, and my first wife had the house and kids, the dog, everything, and Terri and I were living in this apartment here. Sometimes, as I say, I'd get a call in the middle of the night and have to go in to the hospital at two or three in the morning. It'd be dark out there in the parking lot, and I'd break into a sweat before I could even get to my car. I never knew if he was going to come up out of the shrubbery or from behind a car and start shooting. I mean, the man was crazy. He was capable of wiring a bomb, anything. He used to call my service at all hours and say he needed to talk to the doctor, and when I'd return the call, he'd say, 'Son of a bitch, your days are numbered.' Little things like that. It was scary, I'm telling you."

"I still feel sorry for him," Terri said.

"It sounds like a nightmare," Laura said. "But what exactly happened after he shot himself?"

Laura is a legal secretary. We'd met in a professional capacity. Before we knew it, it was a courtship. She's thirty-five, three years younger than I am. In addition to being in love, we like each other and enjoy one another's company. She's easy to be with.

"What happened?" Laura said.

Mel said, "He shot himself in the mouth in his room. Someone heard the shot and told the manager. They came in with a passkey, saw what had happened, and called an ambulance. I happened to be there when they brought him in, alive but past recall. The man lived for three days. His head swelled up to twice the size of a normal head. I'd never seen anything like it, and I hope I never do again. Terri wanted to go in and sit with him when she found out about it. We had a fight over it. I didn't think she should see him like that. I didn't think she should see him, and I still don't. "

"Who won the fight?" Laura said.

"I was in the room with him when he died," Terri said. "He never came up out of it. But I sat with him. He didn't have anyone else."

"He was dangerous," Mel said. "If you call that love, you can have it."

"It was love," Terri said. "Sure, it's abnormal in most people's eyes. But he was willing to die for it. He did die for it."

317

"I sure as hell wouldn't call it love," Mel said. "I mean, no one knows what he did it for. I've seen a lot of suicides, and I couldn't say anyone ever knew what they did it for."

Mel put his hands behind his neck and tilted his chair back. "I'm not interested in that kind of love," he said. "If that's love, you can have it."

Terri said, "We were afraid. Mel even made a will out and wrote to his brother in California who used to be a Green Beret. Mel told him who to look for if something happened to him."

Terri drank from her glass. She said, "But Mel's right—we lived like fugitives. We were afraid. Mel was, weren't you, honey? I even called the police at one point, but they were no help. They said they couldn't do anything until Ed actually did something. Isn't that a laugh?" Terri said.

She poured the last of the gin into her glass and waggled the bottle. Mel got up from the table and went to the cupboard. He took down another bottle.

"Well, Nick and I know what love is," Laura said. "For us, I mean," Laura said. She bumped my knee with her knee. "You're supposed to say something now," Laura said, and turned her smile on me.

For an answer, I took Laura's hand and raised it to my lips. I made a big production out of kissing her hand. Everyone was amused.

"We're lucky," I said.

"You guys," Terri said. "Stop that now. You're making me sick. You're still on the honeymoon, for God's sake. You're still gaga, for crying out loud. Just wait. How long have you been together now? How long has it been? A year? Longer than a year?"

"Going on a year and a half," Laura said, flushed and smiling.

"Oh, now," Terri said. "Wait awhile."

She held her drink and gazed at Laura.

"I'm only kidding," Terri said.

Mel opened the gin and went around the table with the bottle.

"Here, you guys," he said. "Let's have a toast. I want to propose a toast. A toast to love. To true love," Mel said.

We touched glasses.

"To love," we said.

Outside in the backyard, one of the dogs began to bark. The leaves of the aspen that leaned past the window ticked against the glass. The afternoon sun was like a presence in this room, the spacious light of ease and generosity. We could have been anywhere, somewhere enchanted. We raised our glasses again and grinned at each other like children who had agreed on something forbidden.

"I'll tell you what real love is," Mel said. "I mean, I'll give you a good example. And then you can draw your own conclusions." He poured more gin into his glass. He added an ice cube and a sliver of lime. We waited and sipped our drinks. Laura and I touched knees again. I put a hand on her warm thigh and left it there.

"What do any of us really know about love?" Mel said. "It seems to me we're just beginners at love. We say we love each other and we do, I don't doubt it. I love Terri and Terri loves me, and you guys love each other too. You know the kind of love I'm talking about now. Physical love, that impulse that drives you to someone special, as well as love of the other person's being, his or her essence, as it were. Carnal love and, well, call it sentimental love, the day-to-day caring about the other person. But sometimes I have a hard time accounting for the fact that I must have loved my first wife too. But I did, I know I did. So I suppose I am like Terri in that regard. Terri and Ed." He thought about it and then he went on. "There was a time when I thought I loved my first wife more than life itself. But now I hate her guts. I do. How do you explain that? What happened to that love? What happened to it is what I'd like to know. I wish someone could tell me. Then there's Ed. Okay, we're back to Ed. He loves Terri so much he tries to kill her, and he winds up killing himself." Mel stopped talking and swallowed from his glass. "You guys have been together eighteen months and you love each other. It shows all over you. You glow with it. But you both loved other people before you met each other. You've both been married before, just like us. And you probably loved other people before that too, even. Terri and I have been together five years, been married for four. And the terrible thing, the terrible thing is, but the good thing too, the saving grace, you might say, is that if something happened to one of us—excuse me for saying this—but if something happened to one of us tomorrow, I think the other one, the other person, would grieve for a while, you know, but then the surviving party would go out and love again, have someone else soon enough. All this, all of this love we're talking about, it would just be a memory. Maybe not even a memory. Am I wrong? Am I way off base? Because I want you to set me straight if you think I'm wrong. I want to know. I mean, I don't know anything, and I'm the first one to admit it."

"Mel, for God's sake," Terri said. She reached out and took hold of his wrist. "Are you getting drunk? Honey? Are you drunk?"

"Honey, I'm just talking," Mel said. "All right? I don't have to be drunk to say what I think. I mean, we're all just talking, right?" Mel said. He fixed his eyes on her.

"Sweetie, I'm not criticizing," Terri said.

She picked up her glass.

"I'm not on call today," Mel said. "Let me remind you of that. I am not on call," he said.

319

"Mel, we love you," Laura said.

Mel looked at Laura. He looked at her as if he could not place her, as if she was not the woman she was.

"Love you too, Laura," Mel said. "And you, Nick, love you too. You know something?" Mel said. "You guys are our pals," Mel said.

He picked up his glass.

Mel said, "I was going to tell you about something. I mean, I was going to prove a point. You see, this happened a few months ago, but it's still going on right now, and it ought to make us feel ashamed when we talk like we know what we're talking about when we talk about love."

"Come on now," Terri said. "Don't talk like you're drunk if you're not drunk."

"Just shut up for once in your life," Mel said very quietly. "Will you do me a favor and do that for a minute? So as I was saying, there's this old couple who had this car wreck out on the interstate. A kid hit them and they were all torn to shit and nobody was giving them much chance to pull through."

Terri looked at us and then back at Mel. She seemed anxious, or maybe that's too strong a word.

Mel was handing the bottle around the table.

"I was on call that night," Mel said. "It was May or maybe it was June. Terri and I had just sat down to dinner when the hospital called. There'd been this thing out on the interstate. Drunk kid, teenager, plowed his dad's pickup into this camper with this old couple in it. They were up in their midseventies, that couple. The kid—eighteen, nineteen, something—he was DOA. Taken the steering wheel through his sternum. The old couple, they were alive, you understand. I mean, just barely. But they had everything. Multiple fractures, internal injuries, hemorrhaging, contusions, lacerations, the works, and they each of them had themselves concussions. They were in a bad way, believe me. And, of course, their age was two strikes against them. I'd say she was worse off than he was. Ruptured spleen along with everything else. Both kneecaps broken. But they'd been wearing their seat belts and, God knows, that's what saved them for the time being."

"Folks, this is an advertisement for the National Safety Council," Terri said. "This is your spokesman, Dr. Melvin R. McGinnis, talking." Terri laughed. "Mel," she said, "sometimes you're just too much. But I love you, hon," she said.

"Honey, I love you," Mel said.

He leaned across the table. Terri met him halfway. They kissed.

"Terri's right," Mel said as he settled himself again. "Get those seat belts on. But seriously, they were in some shape, those oldsters. By the time I got down there, the kid was dead, as I said. He was off in a corner, laid out on a gurney. I took one look at the old couple and told the ER nurse to get me a neurologist and an orthopedic man and a couple of surgeons down there right away."

He drank from his glass. "I'll try to keep this short," he said. "So we took the two of them up to the OR and worked like fuck on them most of the night. They had these incredible reserves, those two. You see that once in a while. So we did everything that could be done, and toward morning we're giving them a fifty-fifty chance, maybe less than that for her. So here they are, still alive the next morning. So, okay, we move them into the ICU, which is where they both kept plugging away at it for two weeks, hitting it better and better on all the scopes. So we transfer them out to their own room."

Mel stopped talking. "Here," he said, "let's drink this cheapo gin the hell up. Then we're going to dinner, right? Terri and I know a new place. That's where we'll go, to this new place we know about. But we're not going until we finish up this cut-rate, lousy gin."

Terri said, "We haven't actually eaten there yet. But it looks good. From the outside, you know."

"I like food," Mel said. "If I had it to do all over again, I'd be a chef, you know? Right, Terri?" Mel said.

He laughed. He fingered the ice in his glass.

"Terri knows," he said. "Terri can tell you. But let me say this. If I could come back again in a different life, a different time and all, you know what? I'd like to come back as a knight. You were pretty safe wearing all that armor. It was all right being a knight until gunpowder and muskets and pistols came along."

"Mel would like to ride a horse and carry a lance," Terri said.

"Carry a woman's scarf with you everywhere," Laura said.

"Or just a woman," Mel said.

"Shame on you," Laura said.

Terri said, "Suppose you came back as a serf. The serfs didn't have it so good in those days," Terri said.

"The serfs never had it good," Mel said. "But I guess even the knights were vessels to someone. Isn't that the way it worked? But then everyone is always a vessel to someone. Isn't that right, Terri? But what I liked about knights, besides their ladies, was that they had that suit of armor, you know, and they couldn't get hurt very easy. No cars in those days, you know? No drunk teenagers to tear into your ass."

"Vassals," Terri said.

"What?" Mel said.

"Vassals," Terri said. "They were called vassals, not vessels."

"Vassals, vessels," Mel said, "what the fuck's the difference? You knew

Raymond Carver

what I meant anyway. All right," Mel said. "So I'm not educated. I learned my stuff. I'm a heart surgeon, sure, but I'm just a mechanic. I go in and I fuck around and I fix things. Shit," Mel said.

"Modesty doesn't become you," Terri said.

"He's just a humble sawbones," I said. "But sometimes they suffocated in all that armor, Mel. They'd even have heart attacks if it got too hot and they were too tired and worn-out. I read somewhere that they'd fall off their horses and not be able to get up because they were too tired to stand with all that armor on them. They got trampled by their own horses sometimes."

"That's terrible," Mel said. "That's a terrible thing, Nicky. I guess they'd just lay there and wait until somebody came along and made a shish kebab out of them."

"Some other vessel," Terri said.

"That's right," Mel said. "Some vassal would come along and spear the bastard in the name of love. Or whatever the fuck it was they fought over in those days."

"Same things we fight over these days," Terri said.

Laura said, "Nothing's changed."

The color was still high in Laura's cheeks. Her eyes were bright. She brought her glass to her lips.

Mel poured himself another drink. He looked at the label closely, as if studying a long row of numbers. Then he slowly put the bottle down on the table and slowly reached for the tonic water.

"What about the old couple?" Laura said. "You didn't finish that story you started."

Laura was having a hard time lighting her cigarette. Her matches kept going out.

The sunshine inside the room was different now, changing, getting thinner. But the leaves outside the window were still shimmering, and I stared at the pattern they made on the panes and on the Formica counter. They weren't the same patterns, of course.

"What about the old couple?" I said.

"Older but wiser," Terri said.

Mel stared at her.

Terri said, "Go on with your story, hon. I was only kidding. Then what happened?"

"Terri, sometimes," Mel said.

"Please, Mel," Terri said. "Don't always be so serious, sweetie. Can't you take a joke?"

"Where's the joke?" Mel said.

He held his glass and gazed steadily at his wife.

"What happened?" Laura said.

Mel fastened his eyes on Laura. He said, "Laura, if I didn't have Terri and if I didn't love her so much, and if Nick wasn't my best friend, I'd fall in love with you. I'd carry you off, honey," he said.

"Tell your story," Terri said. "Then we'll go to that new place, okay?"

"Okay," Mel said. "Where was I?" he said. He stared at the table and then he began again.

"I dropped in to see each of them every day, sometimes twice a day if I was up doing other calls anyway. Casts and bandages, head to foot, the both of them. You know, you've seen it in the movies. That's just the way they looked, just like in the movies. Little eye-holes and nose-holes and mouth-holes. And she had to have her legs slung up on top of it. Well, the husband was very depressed for the longest while. Even after he found out that his wife was going to pull through, he was still very depressed. Not about the accident, though. I mean, the accident was one thing, but it wasn't everything. I'd get up to his mouth-hole, you know, and he'd say, no, it wasn't the accident exactly, but it was because he couldn't see her through his eyeholes. He said that was what was making him feel so bad. Can you imagine? I'm telling you, the man's heart was breaking because he couldn't turn his goddamn head and *see* his goddamn wife."

Mel looked around the table and shook his head at what he was going to say.

"I mean, it was killing the old fart just because he couldn't *look* at the fucking woman."

We all looked at Mel.

"Do you see what I'm saying?" he said.

Maybe we were a little drunk by then. I know it was hard keeping things in focus. The light was draining out of the room, going back through the window where it had come from. Yet nobody made a move to get up from the table to turn on the overhead light.

"Listen," Mel said. "Let's finish this fucking gin. There's about enough left here for one shooter all around. Then let's go eat. Let's go to the new place."

"He's depressed," Terri said. "Mel, why don't you take a pill?"

Mel shook his head. "I've taken everything there is."

"We all need a pill now and then," I said.

"Some people are born needing them," Terri said.

She was using her finger to rub at something on the table. Then she stopped rubbing.

"I think I want to call my kids," Mel said. "Is that all right with everybody? I'll call my kids," he said.

Terri said, "What if Marjorie answers the phone? You guys, you've heard us on the subject of Marjorie? Honey, you know you don't want to talk to Marjorie. It'll make you feel even worse."

"I don't want to talk to Marjorie," Mel said. "But I want to talk to my kids."

"There isn't a day goes by that Mel doesn't say he wishes she'd get married again. Or else die," Terri said. "For one thing," Terri said, "she's bankrupting us. Mel says it's just to spite him that she won't get married again. She has a boyfriend who lives with her and the kids, so Mel is supporting the boyfriend too."

"She's allergic to bees," Mel said. "If I'm not praying she'll get married again, I'm praying she'll get herself stung to death by a swarm of fucking bees. "

"Shame on you," Laura said.

"Bzzzzzzz," Mel said, turning his fingers into bees and buzzing them at Terri's throat. Then he let his hands drop all the way to his sides.

"She's vicious," Mel said. "Sometimes I think I'll go up there dressed like a beekeeper. You know, that hat that's like a helmet with the plate that comes down over your face, the big gloves, and the padded coat? I'll knock on the door and let loose a hive of bees in the house. But first I'd make sure the kids were out, of course."

He crossed one leg over the other. It seemed to take him a lot of time to do it. Then he put both feet on the floor and leaned forward, elbows on the table, his chin cupped in his hands.

"Maybe I won't call the kids, after all. Maybe it isn't such a hot idea. Maybe we'll just go eat. How does that sound?"

"Sounds fine to me," I said. "Eat or not eat. Or keep drinking. I could head right on out into the sunset."

"What does that mean, honey?" Laura said.

"It just means what I said," I said. "It means I could just keep going. That's all it means."

"I could eat something myself," Laura said. "I don't think I've ever been so hungry in my life. Is there something to nibble on?"

"I'll put out some cheese and crackers," Terri said.

But Terri just sat there. She did not get up to get anything.

Mel turned his glass over. He spilled it out on the table.

"Gin's gone," Mel said.

Terri said, "Now what?"

I could hear my heart beating. I could hear everyone's heart. I could hear the human noise we sat there making, not one of us moving, not even when the room went dark.

QUESTIONS

1. Why is it so important for Terri to believe that Ed had loved her?

2. Why is Mel so insistent that Ed did *not* love Terri?

3. Are we meant to doubt whether Mel and Terri love each other?

4. When Terri says, "People are different," does she mean that love also has different definitions? (315)

5. Why, after toasting love, do Mel, Terri, Laura, and Nick feel "like children who had agreed on something forbidden"? (318)

6. Why does Mel say he wants the other three to set him straight if he's wrong about love?

7. Why does Terri seem anxious (or something like it) when Mel begins his story about the old couple injured in a car accident?

8. Why does Mel tell the others he wants to come back as a knight?

9. Is Terri mocking either Mel or his story when she says, "Older but wiser"? (322)

10. Why is Mel so moved by the fact that the injured old man's heart was breaking because he couldn't see his wife?

11. Why does Terri ask Mel whether he wants to take a pill?

12. Near the end of the story, what does it mean that Nick could head right out into the sunset—that he "could just keep going"? (324)

13. What difference does it make that these people are talking about love while getting drunk?

14. Why does the story end with the two couples sitting in the dark without moving while Nick is hearing "the human noise we sat there making"? (324)

FOR FURTHER REFLECTION

1. Do we agree more with Mel that love is an "absolute" or with Laura, who argues that you can't judge someone else's situation?

2. What is "true love" between two persons? (Who do you know who's had it? What did they have?)

3. Can someone love another person and still physically abuse him or her?

4. Why does intense love sometimes turn into intense hate?

5. Why do some relationships break down, while others thrive for a lifetime?

6. Which of these four characters has the best understanding of the meaning of love?

DISCUSSION GUIDES FOR

Frankenstein
by Mary Shelley

Eichmann in Jerusalem
by Hannah Arendt

Mary Shelley (1797–1851) was born in London, the daughter of two well-known writers and radical political thinkers. Her mother, the feminist Mary Wollstonecraft, died eleven days after Shelley was born. Shelley grew up worshiping her father, William Godwin (to whom *Frankenstein* is dedicated). Emotionally distant, he nonetheless oversaw her education and held high expectations for her intellectual development and literary ambition. It was through her father that Mary met the Romantic poet Percy Bysshe Shelley, then a young married man who admired Godwin's work and frequently visited their home. Mary was sixteen and Percy was still married (and his wife pregnant) when they eloped to the Continent to escape Godwin's wrath, taking with them Claire Clairmont, Mary's stepsister.

Much of Mary Shelley's life was marked by tumult and tragedy, giving her ample material for the themes of abandonment and loss that pervade *Frankenstein.* A daughter was born prematurely when Mary was seventeen and died a few days later. In the summer of 1816, Mary, Percy, and Claire were neighbors with the poet Lord Byron in Switzerland, when Byron proposed that for entertainment the assembled company, which included Byron's personal physician, each write "a ghost story." Mary began to write *Frankenstein.* That same year, her half-sister, Fanny Imlay, committed suicide. A few weeks later, Percy's wife, Harriet, drowned. And in December, Mary and Percy were married in London. They had three more children, only one of whom survived childhood, before Percy Shelley drowned at sea in 1822.

During her lifetime, Mary Shelley wrote several novels, including *Frankenstein* (1818) and *The Last Man* (1826). She collected Percy Shelley's posthumous poetry and wrote biographical essays as well as numerous articles and stories for magazines. She died in London, at age 53.

ABOUT
FRANKENSTEIN

Mary Shelley's *Frankenstein* begat another monster—the frequently cartooned, green-skinned Frankenstein of popular culture, who roams the streets on Halloween in the company of mummies and skeletons. In the novel, the monster is nameless, and Victor Frankenstein is the creature's creator, an earnestly romantic, idealistic, and well-educated young gentleman whose studies in "natural philosophy" (38) and chemistry evolve from "a fervent longing to penetrate the secrets of nature" (39). However, it is a tribute to the power of Shelley's work that it has spawned a parody, no matter how skewed, much as Frankenstein's creation parodies the divine creation of Adam.

There is some logic, too, in the popular tendency to conflate the monster and his creator under the name of "Frankenstein." As the novel progresses, Frankenstein and his monster vie for the role of protagonist. We are predisposed to identify with Frankenstein, whose character is admired by his virtuous friends and family and even by the ship captain who rescues him, deranged by his quest for vengeance, from the ice floe. He is a human being, after all. However, despite his philanthropic ambition to "banish disease from the human frame and render man invulnerable to any but a violent death" (40), Frankenstein becomes enmeshed in a loathsome pursuit that causes him to destroy his own health and shun his "fellow-creatures as if . . . guilty of a crime" (55). His irresponsibility causes the death of those he loves most, and he falls under the control of his own creation.

The monster exhibits a similar kind of duality, arousing sympathy as well as horror in all who hear his tale. He demands our compassion to the extent that we recognize ourselves in his existential loneliness. Rejected by his creator and utterly alone, he learns what he can of human nature from eavesdropping on a family of cottage dwellers, and he educates himself by reading a few carefully selected titles that have fortuitously fallen across his path, among them *Paradise Lost.* "Who was I? What was I? Whence did I come?" (125), he asks himself. Like Milton's Satan, who almost inadvertently becomes the compelling protagonist of *Paradise Lost,* the monster has much to recommend him.

Despite his criminal acts, the monster's self-consciousness and his ability to educate himself raise the question of what it means to be human. It is difficult to think of the monster as anything less than human in his plea for understanding from Frankenstein: "Believe me, Frankenstein: I was benevolent; my soul glowed with love and humanity; but am I not alone, miserably alone? You, my creator, abhor me; what hope can I gather from your fellow-creatures, who owe me nothing? they spurn and hate me" (97). When his anonymous acts of kindness toward the cottage dwellers are repaid with baseless hatred, we have to wonder whether it is the world he inhabits, as opposed to something innate, that causes him to commit atrocities. Nonetheless, he retains a conscience and an intense longing for another kind of existence.

By their own accounts, both Frankenstein and the monster begin with benevolent intentions and become murderers. The monster may seem more sympathetic because he is by nature an outsider, whereas Frankenstein deliberately removes himself from human society. When Frankenstein first becomes engrossed in his efforts to create life, collecting materials from the dissecting room and slaughterhouse, he breaks his ties with friends and family, becoming increasingly isolated. His father reprimands him for this, prompting Frankenstein to ask himself what his single-minded quest for knowledge has cost him and whether or not it is morally justifiable. Looking back, he concludes that, contrary to his belief at the time, it is not: "if no man allowed any pursuit whatsoever to interfere with the tranquillity of his domestic affections, Greece had not been enslaved; Caesar would have spared his country; America would have been discovered more gradually; and the empires of Mexico and Peru had not been destroyed" (54). Passages such as this one suggest the possibility that Shelley is writing about the potentially disastrous consequences of not only human ambition but also a specific kind of masculine ambition. The point of view here may be that of a nineteenth-century woman offering a feminist critique of history.

Far more than the simple ghost story a teenaged Shelley set out to write, *Frankenstein* borrows elements of Gothic horror, anticipates science fiction, and asks enduring questions about human nature and the relationship between God and man. Modern man *is* the monster, estranged from his creator—sometimes believing his own origins to be meaningless and accidental—and full of rage at the conditions of his existence. Modern man is also Frankenstein, likewise estranged from his creator—usurping the powers of God and irresponsibly tinkering with nature, full of benign purpose and malignant results. *Frankenstein* is both a criticism of humanity, especially of the human notions of technical progress, science, and enlightenment, and a deeply humanistic work full of sympathy for the human condition.

Note: All page references are from the Penguin edition of *Frankenstein* (2003).

QUESTIONS

1. Is Robert Walton's ambition similar to Frankenstein's, as Frankenstein believes?

2. Why is the fifteen-year-old Frankenstein so impressed with the oak tree destroyed by lightning in a thunderstorm?

3. Why does Frankenstein become obsessed with creating life?

4. Why is Frankenstein filled with disgust, calling the monster "my enemy," as soon as he has created him? (60)

5. What does the monster think his creator owes him?

6. Why does Frankenstein agree to create a bride for the monster, then procrastinate and finally break his promise?

7. Why can't Frankenstein tell anyone—even his father or Elizabeth—why he blames himself for the deaths of William, Justine, and Henry Clerval?

8. Why doesn't Frankenstein realize that the monster's pledge, "I shall be with you on your wedding-night," threatens Elizabeth as well as himself? (163)

9. Why does Frankenstein find new purpose in life when he decides to seek revenge on the monster "until he or I shall perish in mortal conflict"? (196)

10. Why are Frankenstein and his monster both ultimately miserable, bereft of human companionship, and obsessed with revenge? Are they in the same situation at the end of the novel?

11. Why doesn't Walton kill the monster when he has the chance?

FOR FURTHER REFLECTION

1. Was it wrong for Frankenstein to inquire into the origins of life?

2. What makes the creature a monster rather than a human being?

3. Is the monster, who can be persuasive, always telling the truth?

B orn in Hanover, Germany, eminent political philosopher Hannah Arendt (1906–1975) grew up in Königsberg (once part of East Prussia and later renamed Kaliningrad as part of the Soviet Union). From an early age, Arendt proved herself a gifted student. She began her university studies in the cosmopolitan Weimar era, was deeply influenced by philosophers Martin Heidegger and Karl Jaspers, and received her Ph.D. from the University of Heidelberg in 1928.

Before the Nazis came to power, Arendt was a political activist and worked with German Zionists to publicize Nazi persecution of Jews. In 1933, she fled to Paris, where she married the philosophy professor Heinrich Blücher, and they managed to emigrate to the United States in 1941. In New York City, Arendt continued to work for Jewish causes and was chief editor at Schocken Books. Her monumental work *The Origins of Totalitarianism* was published in 1951, and numerous other books of political philosophy followed, including *The Human Condition* and the controversial *Eichmann in Jerusalem*. Arendt taught at many universities, including Princeton, the University of Chicago, and the New School for Social Research.

ABOUT
EICHMANN IN JERUSALEM

Even before its publication as a book in 1963, Hannah Arendt's *Eichmann in Jerusalem: A Report on the Banality of Evil* (which originally appeared as a series of articles in *The New Yorker*) generated much controversy. Critics attributed to her coverage of the Adolf Eichmann trial a host of purposes other than simple reporting, such as exposing the role of the Jewish leadership in the Holocaust and raising larger questions about German guilt and the nature of totalitarianism. Arendt was prompted to clarify her intentions in a postscript to the book, claiming in its final sentence, "The present report deals with nothing but the extent to which the court in Jerusalem succeeded in fulfilling the demands of justice" (298). Evaluating the court's success, however, proves to be a more complex endeavor than this statement implies.

Adolf Eichmann, the Nazi lieutenant colonel responsible for transporting countless Jews to concentration camps and, in most cases, to their deaths, escaped Germany after World War II and made his way to Argentina, where he lived under a false name until 1960. That year, intelligence operatives from the young nation of Israel kidnapped Eichmann and brought him to Jerusalem to face charges of crimes against the Jewish people, crimes against humanity, and membership in three of the four organizations that the Nuremberg Trials had classified as "criminal." The facts of Eichmann's case had been established before the trial and were never in dispute. However, genocide was a new kind of crime; that the Israeli court did not recognize it as such is, in Arendt's view, "at the root of all the failures and shortcomings" (267) of the trial. Arendt writes, "Justice demands that the accused be prosecuted, defended, and judged, and that all the other questions of seemingly greater import . . . be left in abeyance" (5). Much of Arendt's book illustrates that the larger issues were not set aside during the Eichmann trial, showing how the case "was built on what the Jews had suffered, not on what Eichmann had done" (6).

Eichmann told the court that he saw himself as a friend of the Jews, helping them leave a culture for which they were unsuited and move on to better lives elsewhere. He considered himself an ally of Zionists, whom he thought shared his idealism. Arendt believes him—at least, she believes that this was how he saw himself. Despite all the efforts of the prosecution, Arendt writes, "everybody could see that this man was not a monster, but it was difficult indeed not to suspect that he was a clown" (54). The transcript of Eichmann's examination by Israeli police while awaiting trial prompts her to observe that the horrible can be not only ludicrous but outright funny (48). She dwells on his shallow intellect, his clichéd speech (which she interprets as a means of consoling himself), his infinite capacity for self-deception, and his profound detachment from reality.

Arendt portrays Eichmann as a "joiner," a conformist, describing him as "a leaf in the whirlwind of time" (32). It is this aspect of his character, according to her, rather than any deeply held convictions shared with the Nazi Party or a rabid hatred of Jews, that accounts for his actions during the war. Apart from determining Eichmann's motivation is the question that, as Arendt observes, must be asked of any criminal defendant: was he aware that his actions were in fact criminal? The prosecution had to assume that he was, as "all 'normal persons'" would be (26). But Arendt asserts that, "under the conditions of the Third Reich only 'exceptions' could be expected to react 'normally'" (26–27). With considerable insight and detail, Arendt explains how Germany's leaders went about creating these conditions, to the point that "conscience as such had apparently got lost in Germany." There were individuals who resisted, she notes, but "their voices were never heard" (103).

In Arendt's view, the real circumstances of Eichmann's actions never came fully to light during the trial. This is why, in part, the trial obscures what for Arendt is "the lesson that this long course in human wickedness had taught us—the lesson of the fearsome, word-and-thought-defying *banality of evil* (252). Eichmann claimed that as his job shifted from forcing Jews from their homes to arranging for them to be killed, he was troubled by the new policy but felt duty-bound to obey his superiors. In fact, he said that not following orders was the only thing that would have given him a bad conscience. As far as Arendt can determine, only once did Eichmann act in a way that could perhaps be construed as resistance, when he decided to send a transport of Jews and Gypsies to the ghetto of Lódz instead of to Russian territory, where they would have been immediately shot. But, Arendt writes, "his conscience functioned in the expected way" (95) only for about four weeks.

Arendt does not address directly the question of what Eichmann might have done had his conscience continued functioning "normally." Yet in documenting the results of Nazi efforts to rid other countries of Jews, she concludes that "under conditions of terror most people will comply but *some people will not,* just as the lesson of the countries to which the Final Solution was proposed is that 'it could happen' in most places but *it did not happen everywhere.* Humanly speaking, no more is required, and no more can be reasonably asked, for this planet to remain a place fit for human habitation" (233). We could take this as evidence that the only hope of preventing future catastrophes must lie in a morality that is inherent in human nature. On the other hand, Arendt considers Eichmann "terribly and terrifyingly normal" (276). *Eichmann in Jerusalem* leaves us wondering not only if justice was achieved in Eichmann's case but also whether the lessons Arendt believes the trial has taught will make a difference in the future.

Note: All page references are from the Penguin edition of *Eichmann in Jerusalem* (1994).

QUESTIONS

1. What does Arendt mean by "the banality of evil"? (252)

2. Why does Eichmann cooperate so fully with the Israelis, to the point of volunteering to hang himself?

3. Why does the defense often fail to present evidence that would have helped Eichmann's case?

4. According to Arendt, how "normal" is Eichmann?

5. Is the fact that Eichmann turns out not to be a "monster" a good or a bad thing in terms of its implications for the future?

6. How could Eichmann have seen himself as a friend of the Jews?

7. In Arendt's words, Eichmann's definition of an "idealist" is someone who is "prepared to sacrifice for his idea everything and, especially, everybody." (42) According to this definition, is Eichmann an idealist?

8. The judgment in Eichmann's trial states that "the degree of responsibility increases as we draw further away from the man who uses the fatal instrument with his own hands." (247) In what sense could this be true?

9. Why does Arendt consider Eichmann's "almost total inability ever to look at anything from the other fellow's point of view" a decisive flaw? (47–48)

10. What does Arendt mean when she writes, "like most true stories, [it] is incomplete"? (111)

FOR FURTHER REFLECTION

1. Does *Eichmann in Jerusalem* help to explain why the Holocaust happened?

2. In terms of responsibility, where should the line be drawn between acts committed by individuals and "acts of state"?

3. Can we ever know with certainty an individual's motivation for doing something?

4. Do you agree with Arendt that "in politics obedience and support are the same"?

CONNECTING THEMES

This anthology can be read sequentially or thematically; there are any number of general topics or themes, and it is likely that perceptive readers will see some of these interconnections between the fifteen different readings as well as the two longer works for which there are discussion guides. In some instances, the authors represented in *Great Conversations 2* were familiar with the works of the others—both as predecessors and contemporaries— and their writings seem to respond to one another directly, sometimes echoing, sometimes responding to a similar subject in a slightly different way or disagreeing entirely.

Here are some different possibilities for considering these readings in groups or clusters organized around topic and theme. In certain instances, teachers or group leaders may want to consider a pair of readings on a particular theme; the lists that follow, neither exhaustive nor definitive, can be plundered selectively to good effect. What is important is that readers of *Great Conversations 2* enter into the dialogue with these authors, as contemporary participants.

I. Economic Life

Melville

Hayek

Rawls

II. Faith and Belief

Donne

Descartes

Dostoevsky

O'Connor

III. Irrationality

Samson

Gogol

Dostoevsky

Poe

Melville

Rossetti

Synge

Carver

Shelley

IV. Knowing the Self

Samson

Donne

Descartes

Gogol

Poe

Melville

O'Connor

Carver

Shelley

V. Political Justice

Hayek

Rawls

Gordimer

Arendt

VI. Power and Coercion

Samson

Dostoevsky

Melville

O'Connor

Carver

Shelley

Arendt

VII. The Search for Truth

Descartes

Planck

Shelley

VIII. Sex and Love

Samson

Donne

Poe

Rossetti

Synge

Carver

ACKNOWLEDGMENTS

All possible care has been taken to trace ownership and secure permission for each selection in this anthology. The Great Books Foundation wishes to thank the following authors, publishers, and representatives for permission to reprint copyrighted material:

The Story of Samson (JUDGES 13–16), from THE NEW OXFORD ANNOTATED BIBLE. Copyright 1989 by the Division of Christian Education of the National Council of the Churches of Christ in the USA. Reprinted by permission. All rights reserved.

Meditation One and *Meditation Two*, from MEDITATIONS ON FIRST PHILOSOPHY IN WHICH THE EXISTENCE OF GOD AND THE DISTINCTION OF THE SOUL FROM THE BODY ARE DEMONSTRATED, by René Descartes. Translated from the Latin by Donald A. Cress. Copyright 1993 (Third Edition) by Hackett Publishing Company, Inc. Reprinted by permission.

The Nose, from DIARY OF A MADMAN AND OTHER STORIES, by Nikolai Gogol, translated by Andrew R. MacAndrew. Copyright 1960, renewed 1988 by Andrew R. MacAndrew. Reprinted by permission of Dutton Signet, a division of Penguin Group (USA) Inc.

The Grand Inquisitor, from THE BROTHERS KARAMAZOV, by Fyodor Dostoevsky. Translated and annotated by Richard Pevear and Larissa Volokhonsky. Copyright 1990 by Richard Pevear and Larissa Volokhonsky. Reprinted by permission of Farrar, Straus & Giroux.

Bartleby the Scrivener, from THE PIAZZA TALES AND OTHER PROSE PIECES, 1839–1860, Volume 9, by Herman Melville. Copyright 1987 by the Northwestern University Press. Reprinted by permission.

Planning and Democracy, from THE ROAD TO SERFDOM, by F. A. Hayek. Introduction by Milton Friedman. Copyright 1944, renewed 1974, 1994 by the University of Chicago. All rights reserved. Published 1994. Reprinted by permission of the University of Chicago Press.

Distributive Justice, originally published in PHILOSOPHY, POLITICS, AND SOCIETY, by John Rawls. Edited by Peter Laslett and W. G. Runciman (Oxford: Blackwell, 1967). Reprinted by permission of Blackwell Publishing.

Guests of the Nation, from FRANK O'CONNOR: COLLECTED STORIES, by Frank O'Connor. Copyright 1981 by Harriet O'Donovan Sheehy, Executrix of the Estate of Frank O'Connor. Reprinted by permission of Alfred A. Knopf, a division of Random House, Inc.

Which New Era Would That Be?, from SIX FEET OF THE COUNTRY AND OTHER STORIES, by Nadine Gordimer. Copyright 1956, renewed 1984, by Nadine Gordimer. Reprinted by permission of Russell & Volkening as agents for the author.

What We Talk About When We Talk About Love, from WHAT WE TALK ABOUT WHEN WE TALK ABOUT LOVE, by Raymond Carver. Copyright 1980, 1981 by Raymond Carver. Reprinted by permission of Alfred A. Knopf, Inc.